# WHITHER GOVERNANCE
# REFLECTIONS OF AN ASSAM CIVILIAN

# WHITHER GOVERNANCE
## Reflections of an Assam Civilian

K. SREEDHAR RAO

*Published by*
SOUTH ASIA FOUNDATION

*Distributed by*
CONCEPT PUBLISHING COMPANY, NEW DELHI-110059

ISBN 81-88287-00-8 (H.B.)

First Published 2002



*Published by*

Shilpi Sahay
Executive Secretary

**South Asia Foundation**
Second Floor, 80B Shahpur Jat
New Delhi - 110049

*Printed & Distributed by*
**Concept Publishing Company**
A/15-16, Commercial Block, Mohan Garden,
NEW DELHI - 110059

*Phones:* 5648039, 5649024
*Fax :* 091-11-5648053
*E-Mail:* publishing@conceptpub.com

TO MY MOTHER
SMT SEETHA BAI

who was such a great source of strength at the most difficult of times and whose whole life was devoted to serving others most selflessly in the true *Gita* spirit.

# CONTENTS

# FOREWORD

Though a good part of my service life has been spent outside my parent cadre, Assam, the state has been my first love, having spent some twenty five years there, and many of my pleasantest memories relate to my early days in that state. The years that I had spent in the Brahmaputra valley districts and in Shillong which was then the capital of Assam had exposed me to the unique and rich culture of this whole area, while impressing upon me the serious problems one had to deal with in administering the state having such bewildering complexities.

It is because of my intimate relationship with Assam and my deep and continuing interest in issues relating to internal security that I value this contribution of Shri Sreedhar Rao whom I have known from around 1965 onwards and with whom I have shared quite a few anxious moments while dealing with the 'foreigners agitation' during 1979–80. I share with him the anxieties he has expressed about the current situation in Assam as indeed about the entire North Eastern region. I often wonder as to what really needs to be done to bring about peace and prosperity in the area. It is clear that there can be no prosperity if there is no peace, and insurgency and instability, being basically destructive, have proved to be perfect recipes for disaster, even if for argument's sake one admits that there are indeed some very legitimate reasons for dissatisfaction and unrest in the region. Insurgencies have never resulted in the final resolution of any problem wherever they have occurred in the world and, as Gandhiji had so eloquently pointed out, violence breeds only more violence leading to intensification of animosities. It needs to be stressed that extreme demands can only invite extreme reactions. As Shri Rao has emphasized there is a great deal of merit in looking at compromise solutions, which can largely take care of the causes of dissatisfaction, and then on proceed to tackle the basic problems of the, society, namely poverty, unemployment and lack of tangible economic and social progress. Such basic issues can seldom be attended to effectively so long as there is unrest.

The central theme that the author has projected is the immediate need to arrest the precipitous decline in the standards of governance, that this country has experienced over the years. While, no doubt, many others have bemoaned this decline, the author focuses very pointedly on the causes for the decline and the impact that such a phenomenon has had on the internal security situation in the country and in particular the northeast and with regard to the management of the country's external borders. The particularly sharp decline in the standards of policing that has taken place with the once powerful and effective police station / thana system going into virtual oblivion, having been thoroughly politicised has been rightly highlighted.

The chapters on Assam bring out in eminently readable style, the particular character of the administration in the state and the serious complications one has to face in dealing with a highly fragmented social structure, undergoing unprecedented stresses and strains, while being plagued by divisive tendencies. The problems, however, are in no way insurmountable and can be overcome, if the basic issue of providing good governance and an effective and responsive administration is urgently and adequately addressed.

Shri Rao's experiences have been of a rich variety. His account on Sikkim's extraordinary and unique culture and ethos is highly educative and encourages one to believe that the qualities found among the Sikkimese can be very profitably adopted by others in this country. Sikkim does indeed prove the point being stressed in this book that peace and prosperity are indivisible, are intimately linked and combined with good governance progress can indeed be rapid.

I have no doubt that Shri Rao's experiences and his reflections will be of considerable interest to all those concerned with the management of the country's security both internal and external, and those in the services. I commend this work as a valuable contribution to the literature on the governance of our nation.

New Delhi
October 2001

K.P.S. Gill

# PREFACE

The idea of the modern Indian state has for long confounded a large number of Cassandras, posing as political theorists, who are still convinced that the country will sooner or later unravel. Few, if any, democratic experiments have had to tackle the kind of economic, political, religious, cultural and social diversity that defines India. And yet India survives, noisily, chaotically, unsystematically, but without either forsaking democracy or forcibly homogenising its diversity. To be sure, the Indian state has had to respond to a "million mutinies", to use the writer V.S. Naipaul's description, and a number of sub-national challenges that have threatened to periodically disintegrate this colossus. But despite these myriad problems, India has entered the 21st century more confident of its identity, than most states did after centuries of trial and error. What makes India tick? And how has it been able to cope with contradictions that routinely question its survival?

There are no easy answers, but it is clear that there is a unique Indian way of conflict management that combines a mix of constitutionalism, embedded in democracy and federalism, and force. The steel frame of the Indian bureaucracy, which has often been rather uncharitably - derided as a colonial institution, has played a vital role in the governance of the country and in ensuring that India has not fallen into anarchy. As an academic, who opted out of career in the civil service, I have-over the years- learnt to appreciate and even admire the role played by institutions like the Indian Administrative Service (IAS). It is, therefore, with great pleasure that I can recommend Shri K. Sreedhar Rao's book *Whither Governance Reflections of An Assam* [illegible] accounts by one of the country's responsibilities included an enviable variety of jobs, but it was particularly in dealing with sensitive issues of internal security, especially in the Northeast, that Shri Rao proved his mettle. At a time when India is still plagued with many for the problems that Shri Rao sought to manage, his book is essential reading for all those interested in the future of the country.

New Delhi
January, 2002

Amitabh Mattoo

# INTRODUCTION

Not many of the officers who have served in the North-East of India have deemed it proper to put down their experiences in writing. An effort of this nature by officers with first hand knowledge of the area would have eminently served the cause of understanding of this turbulent region by the people in general and, particularly by those who have an interest in the governance of these remoter, strategically significant areas. The North-East even today represents to the average Indian, lands that are too distant too complicated, violent and possibly ungovernable, faced with insuperable problems which nobody seems to be serious about solving. That the North-East is a part of the country with unsurpassed natural beauty, with a rich unique cultural heritage and abundant natural resources, inhabited by a people who are basically gentle and decent, who given the right policies can progress as fast as the rest of the country, is known only in a few quarters. That there are very deep cultural linkages built up over centuries between the North-East and the rest of India, that Manipur represents the eastern most extension of the great Indian-Hindu civilization, within the political boundaries of India, that Islam has left its mark on the area (there is even a one fourth Mecca in a place called HAJO in Assam) are all facts which are seldom highlighted.

N.K. Rustomji, no doubt, has written about this area in his 'Enchanted Frontiers', having served as an ICS officer in this region, but his work does not deal with the social and economic issues, which have bedeviled the area leading to the current separatist and insurgent activities. K.M.L. Chabra, an IAS officer of the Tamil Nadu cadre, who in the Home Ministry had dealt with Assam, has covered some of the issues. I believe B.P. Singh has also made a significant contribution to knowledge of the area.

To my mind working in the North-East is an experience beyond compare where you have to face extraordinary challenges calling for the fullest utilization of all faculties on a continuous basis. Those who serve in other states have no doubt their own crop of problems but they can legitimately be classified as 'normal' problems, whereas in the North-East the 'unexpected' seems to be almost always round the corner, and to face such eventualities you have to innovate and experiment without the usual bureaucratic 'precedents' to fall back upon. Even at a young age one had to rely solely on one's own judgement and right or wrong you had to take decisions on the spot, with there being so little scope or time to refer the matter to your superiors. The buck definitely stopped on top of your table and indeed on top of your head.

I have had the privilege of serving in Assam, Meghalaya and Sikkim, not to mention my fairly long stints in the ministry of Commerce, Defence, the Cabinet Secretariat and the Ministry of Welfare in the Government of India. Very few officers in the country would have gone through the kind of experiences I have had to encounter during my career spanning the period from 1963 to 1999. Examples of these are the Bangladesh liberation War of 1971 when I was Deputy Commissioner in Cacher of Assam, a communally sensitive border district, the prolonged the agitation, as it turned out to be, by the All Assam Students' Union (AASU) called the 'Anti Foreigner Agitation' and the insurgency situation involving the United Liberation Front of Assam and the Bodo Security Force. My tenure in Sikkim as Development Commissioner and Chief Secretary exposed me to a unique civilization and an exemplary way of life, once again vastly adding to the richness and quality of memorable experiences.

My intention in writing this book is to add to the knowledge relating to these farflung areas based on my personal experiences and to analyze the causes for the current situation in these parts. I have had the opportunity of dealing with these issues while holding various offices in the area as also during my tenure in the Cabinet Secretariat, witnessing the steady growth of fissiparous tendencies and the equally steady decline in the willingness as well as the ability of the state to tackle the problems, leading to the present situation where there is visible all round disillusionment with the institutions of state and little or no hope for peace or prosperity for the region in the near future. It is my conviction, however, that given adequate imagination and determination the problems of the area can be successfully tackled and the region enabled to contribute its mite towards nation building as much as any other part of the country. It will be my endeavour to discuss, in good measure, the possibilities in this regard.

The other major concern is the decline in efficiency of institutions of governance in this country the rusting of the legendary steel frame as it were, and the consequent tendency towards the emergence of alternative mechanisms outside the pale of the Constitution, which have taken root primarily because they seem to offer a speedier, if not more effective, system for the people to resort to. An enquiry as to why such a phenomenon has taken place is, to my mind, a worthwhile exercise. Further, the serious adverse consequences for the nation's internal and external security caused by this decline, especially at a time when the nature of such threats and causes thereof are undergoing significant changes, need to be carefully assessed. The vast changes that are sweeping the world in terms of globalisation, opening up of markets, increased trade and financial flows and the new challenges that these developments pose, increasing the necessity of strengthening institutional mechanisms, also need to be adequately reflected upon.

This book is an attempt to draw pointed attention to all these concerns.

# ACKNOWLEDGEMENTS

This book would not have been written but for the constant prodding of my wife Saraswati Rao, who having seen first hand all my travails felt strongly that what I have been through must be recorded. She convinced me that today's civil servants will greatly benefit by lessons drawn from my experiences and improve their outlook and attitudes towards their tasks. To her I owe a deep debt of gratitude for not only having stood by me throughout my journey in the civil service but having given me the confidence to put down my memories on paper and corrected me whenever my recollections were not entirely accurate.

My daughter-in-law Vandana and son Vivek acted as the liaison team in Delhi keeping in close touch with the publishers and ensuring that the inevitable glitches in the process of bringing out a book are all smoothened out. To them goes the credit of seeing to it that all I have written comes out in print.

My greatest debt is no doubt reserved for Rahul Barua, the Secretary General of the South Asia Foundation, who took upon himself the entire responsibility of getting the work edited and published. But for his single minded devotion 'my reflections' may have never seen the light of the day. Rahul has been a very patient and tolerant guiding spirit behind this endeavour, who inspired me to believe that whatever I have had to say in the book will be of considerable value and interest to many in the academia and in the bureaucracy who concern themselves with the problems of governance of our complex polity and the peace and security of the people of this country. To him my very special gratitude.

Also to Harriet David of the South Asia Foundation who so painstakingly carried out the proof corrections.

# 1

# ENTERING THE CIVIL SERVICE

Franklin Delano Roosevelt is quoted as having stated that there is no calling nobler than public service. I do consider myself fortunate to have been a public servant for well over thirty five years and having served in some of the more difficult parts of the country and during periods which cannot but be described as turbulent. The nobility of the calling I had opted for has been repeatedly underlined all through my service life.

The idea of entering the civil service occurred to me while still in school at Ooty in the Niligiris of Tamilnadu where the collectorate was not far from the house where I lived, and was the biggest building in the town. We had no idea of what went on inside that august looking building, as at that time we were only interested in the big open space in front of the collector's office, which we used as a football field. Football was the ruling passion throughout my school days and every available minute was utilised to kick a ball whatever its size or shape. Before the start of the school in the morning, during the lunch interval and of course after school hours until darkness our minds were almost exclusively focused upon the football. Those who represented the school in the various football tournaments were great heroes in our eyes.

The District Collector came into our world during prize distribution ceremonies, the Independence Day, the Republic Day, etc. I still recall Lobo Prabhu, an ICS officer of great repute, who spoke to us in English (half understood by most of us, as our medium of instruction was Tamil) telling us as to how glad he was to be among us students, especially since he normally dealt with criminals most of his time. I suppose he was referring to his work as the District Magistrate, maintaining law and order in what was then a very peaceful district.

Ooty was a wonderful place to spend one's childhood, with a very salubrious climate, plenty of open spaces and botanical gardens coming to full bloom during the spring. This period attracted wealthy tourists and in the late forties and early 1950s a whole lot of rajas and maharajas, the most notable of whom was the Maharaja of Mysore who, by his sheer size, could make his presence felt. He was known as His Highness the Roller of Mysore. We were fascinated by what appeared to us his innumerable Rolls Royce cars, a new one appearing almost every other day. One learnt later that the Maharaja was a very accomplished soul, a Sanskrit scholar of distinction and an enlightened ruler who did a great deal for education in his kingdom including women's education, and for the diversification of the state's economy. He, it appears, had a substantial number of shares in the Rolls Royce company and hence the large number of Rolls cars that he owned.

Having watched the Collector in action in Ooty, mainly on ceremonial occasions, the thought did germinate that the job appeared to be a jolly good one and an effort could be made to see if I could obtain a job of this nature. Two of my three sisters were married two government officers, one in the Post and Telegraphs Department and the other in the Railways. They and my father, who was a lawyer specializing in civil cases (he refused to take up criminal cases as he could not bear the thought of sending a human being to jail), greatly encouraged me in this thought. Ironically in my early days in the IAS, I have sent quite a few criminals to jail, and even conducted committal proceedings with respect to alleged murderers.

I was definitely an above average student in my school standing first quite often, though the school itself did not command much of a reputation. It was not an elitist school run by the local municipal board, and the standard of instruction was pretty low, though some of the teachers were truly devoted. Not surprisingly, the results in the final examinations were invariably poor and in my particular batch, I was the only one from that school to have obtained the BA degree without failing in any of the examinations. All others had fallen by the wayside and only three or four finally became graduates.

One great influence during my formative years was the very well stocked library next to my house. It was housed in a beautiful building with spacious grounds very English in character and ambience, and a reading room with very large windows—easily fifteen or twenty feet in height—through which plenty of sunlight poured in. There were very comfortable chairs and sofas, and such an extraordinary variety of magazines that I found it a rewarding and pleasurable experience to spend hours browsing through all the wealth of material. The experience greatly contributed to vastly improving my command over the English language and I gained fascinating insights into all that was happening around the world at that time. World War II had just ended and I have recollections of the great ideological confrontation between the USSR and the Western powers that was just beginning. It was at that time I happened to read an article on Hitler's invasion of Poland with photographs of the German generals and their Polish counterparts. Since then military history has fascinated me and I have read a great deal about Nazi Germany and the war. During my service career, I have had occasion to travel to Germany quite a few times. I have visited many German cities—Berlin, Frankfurt, Kiel, Lubeck, Hamburg, Hannover, Essen, Bockum. Friedreckshafen, Shrobenhousen; many of the Germans with whom I had to deal with were impressed by the extent of my knowledge about their country and its history. I was anxious to see the Fuehrer bunker where Adolf Hitler had spent his last days, but it had been deliberately obliterated. There is just a flattened open space under which the bunker once existed. The 'Berghof' Hitler's mountain retreat in the Bavarian Alps has also been similarly destroyed. I was told that all this was done with a view to avoiding these, becoming places of pilgrimage.

In spite of the poor reputation of my school, I was able to get admission into Loyola College, Madras, a very prestigious institution. My marks in the final examinations possibly did the trick. Loyola was a very fine institution with a formidable reputation for academic excellence and very strict discipline. Slaves of Loyola as contrasted to the princes and princesses of the Presidency College of Madras was the appellation given to us. Loyola was also considered for very justifiable reasons as a breeding ground for civil servants and any one who had done well in Loyola in BA (Hons) Economics, etc., had a very good chance of getting into the services. Statistics during the fifties and sixties if the twentieth century does support such a belief. A number of very distinguished civil servants of post-independent India had gone through the portals of this revered institution. Loyola is also the alma mater of one of India's most respected President R. Venkataraman, with whom I had the privilege of working in the Ministry of Defence.

The standard of instruction at Loyola was quite high though I would not rate it as outstanding. All my college years were spent in Loyola from pre-University to Masters, I studied only in one college. Indeed, I have studied in only one school and have held only one job namely the IAS. I may add that I have one wife and one son.

The outstanding feature of education at Loyola was the inculcation of a set of exemplary values. I am not sure if the Economics we were taught was comparable to that in other institutions even within the country but the greatest asset acquired at Loyola is self-discipline. From day one, we learnt the value of punctuality, the need to be conscious of our responsibilities, the need to value our time as well that of others, the need to appreciate and be sensitive to the feelings and needs of others, and honour the given word. These values, I have no hesitation in saying, have stood me in very good stead throughout my entire career.

The other attractive features of the college were the great library and the fine sports facilities. My fascination with books and the library, since my school days because of the proximity of the Niligiris Library to my house in Ooty, was greatly enhanced during the period I spent in Loyola. Also, with eleven tennis courts and examples like Ramanathan Krishnan, who was a few years senior in the college, I acquired a taste for tennis, a game I was able play with passable competence till almost the last days in my service life. Debating was another skill I acquired during this period and at the postgraduate level I was considered an accomplished speaker, winning quite a few laurels for the college.

A feature of Loyola, common perhaps with other such institutions, was the active discrimination against noncatholics. Fine teachers such as Anantharama Seshan or Ganapathy who really knew the subject they were expected to teach and equally importantly knew the art of creating an interest in the subject among the students and imparting knowledge in a manner that was intelligible to even some of the weaker students, could not aspire to become heads of department, leave alone become the Principal of the college, whereas those comparatively less erudite, less talented, with far less gray matter, and junior in age were imposed as heads of departments only on the basis of their religious persuasion. Little wonder that such specimens commanded no respect from many of us. This system continues and is, I suppose, one of the manifestations of our secular ethos.

Nevertheless, I owe a deep debt of gratitude to this fine institution for having equipped my mind with the ability to face a variety of challenges and instilling in me a very high degree of self confidence.

Our existence in Loyola can, to a very large extent, be described as monastic and even cloistered. Our attention was almost exclusively focused on three things—the lecture hall, the library and the tennis court. Of course, considerable 'mugging' was expected and regular periodic tests kept us constantly on the alert and prepared us very well for the final assault at the university level. The female of the species were not entertained as students and it was on the rare occasion of inter-collegiate debates that one did get a glimpse of them, most of whom appeared to be timid and diffident and only rarely did any of them win any prizes in spite of their being an unwritten weightage in their favour.

It was at the post-graduate level when inter collegiate classes were held at the Madras University campus twice a week, that female students participated in regular classes, becoming objects of curiosity, but even here there was segregation of a rigorous order. The infrequent contacts and conversations were confined to asking for a book or paper one had prepared and presented. All this has changed and even in conservative Madras, interaction among sexes is far more extensive, not confined only academic matters.

A notable figure in these inter-collegiate lectures was Professor Shanmugasundaram, who was reader at that time. Quite a colourful personality with a very Marxian-looking beard and remarkable scholarship. His method of teaching was also quite unique in that he would come prepared with written lectures which he read fairly slowly, and we were expected to take down every word of wisdom that flowed from his lips. Not everyone managed to write down all that he said, but those like me who did achieve this fairly difficult feat, I dare say did benefit a great deal. More useful than the lectures were the seminars, he used to conduct where he encouraged us to prepare and present papers and defend our ideas against a fairly savage attack led by him.

It was the practice at that time for our lecturers to give us certificates at the end of the course, with fulsome praise on our performance which came in handy while hunting for a job. In the certificate Prof Sundaram gave me, he was quite generous in complimenting me for my diligence, scholarship and industry and quite significantly he also stated that I had in me 'the makings of a good administrator'. What particular act of mine led him to this conclusion I cannot say but may I be permitted to say that he was not far wrong in his assessment!

April–May 1962 when the Chinese were making their way into the North-East of India and into Ladakh was the time when in Madras I appeared for the final Masters degree examinations. Every thing was done to perfection those days, examinations held exactly on time, portions covered well in advance, no malpractices allowed during the tests and results published on time. The just and fair manner in which everything was conducted ensured that those who worked hard obtained their rewards without fail. I believe that even this great institution, and my alma mater, Loyola has suffered some decline in standards, but nothing compared to the systematic destruction of standards that has taken place elsewhere in the country in the sphere of higher education.

Having appeared for the Masters degree examination, job hunting was then very much part of the game, even though the civil services were a definite objective, as one can never be, one hundred per cent sure on this score. While therefore getting myself ready for the written examination especially with respect to subjects such as Mercantile Law and European history with which I had only a nodding acquaintance, I did apply for a variety of jobs, where I thought I could fit in. Many of my friends got themselves into educational institutions as tutors or lecturers though none of them considered these as anything other than stopgap arrangements. My targets were the banks, the oil companies, etc. but nothing emerged months. Indeed, I found the whole process quite bewildering and mysterious and totally lacking in transparency. One appeared for interviews one after another apparently conducted by functionaries at different levels in the hierarchy, but invariably there would be total silence at the end of it all. No one bothered to inform you whether you were found fit or not and so for what reasons. As to how one got selected at all in these organizations I could not fathom, but some did get selected probably on account of what was known as 'influence'.

All this only made me more and more serious as far as efforts to get into the civil services were concerned, as here at least while competition was severe, given the fairness of the procedures one could be sure that merit will ultimately prevail. In the event I suddenly found that I had cleared the written papers not with flying colours (as my performance in the statistics paper was poor) but with sufficient credit to be eligible for the personality test for the IAS and IFS. This success was truly morale boosting for the family, as my father had passed away while I was still a student in the MA first year class and the family had to carry on, dependent on the earnings from past savings and the rent from the second house built by my father.

I had never been to Delhi before and having lived all the while in the south, especially in Madras, all through the college days, I had to take special measures to equip myself with a proper woollen suit with a decent matching tie so that I could create the right impression during the interview held in the cold climate in New Delhi in February 1963. My mother made me travel by air costing a tidy sum for the family, which it could not really afford, but she felt that I should reach Delhi without undue strain.

One entered the portals of Dholpur house, Shahjahan road, the abode of the Union Public Service Commission, with great anxiety and nervousness, as so much depended upon the half-an-hour or so you spent trying to answer the volley of questions thrown at you by an assembly of august personages many of whom belonged to the legendary ICS. When one gets into the waiting room there is the tendency to compare yourself with the others, to see how many look smarter than you and appear more self-confident. I had found in my previous encounters with the interview process that it is better to keep aloof and not get perturbed by comparing myself with those around. I kept to this strategy and very soon my turn came for entering the chamber of the bigwigs waiting to get at you. The first thing I noticed was that the room number was thirteen and given the circumstances in which one is placed and the superstition surrounding this particular number, my heart did miss a beat. Once I entered the room, I noticed that the board did have some really weighty individuals. Hus ein Zaheer was the Chairman, K.P.S. Menon, an ICS, who had served the country in a number of capacities including as ambassador to Moscow, A.N. Jha, another ICS officer with a formidable reputation as brilliant civil servant and a Sanskrit scholar of distinction were personalities I could immediately recognize and did not help in reducing the tension building up inside me.

While asking me to come in even before offering me a seat, K.P.S. Menon tried to upset my balance by asking me as to why I wore thick spectacles and if the defect was congenital. This did not improve matters for me. Fortunately, the Chairman offered me a seat for which I thanked him. This brief respite enabled me to collect my wits and I got back to Menon answering his question by saying that I had myopia, a fairly common defect, that it was not congenital and wearing spectacle did not prevent me from pursuing any activities normal for my age including a good bit of tennis. This seemed to satisfy the board and I was able to breath a little more easily. K.P.S. Menon was practically the only member who grilled me throughout about Ignatius Loyola—as I had studied at Loyola College—the ecuminical council and then on to communism and Karl Marx and further to my interest in military history. I felt the discussion on Communism clearly went my way, as I was asked as to why the United States had not become a Communist country as predicted by Marx, who had postulated that capitalism carried within it the seeds for its own destruction motivated as it is by endless greed. My answer was that the capitalists had not only read Marx but heeded his warnings and changed their exploitative ways, finding that labour productivity greatly improved when workers are paid well and looked after well. Also, due to wide disbursal of shares the workers themselves were becoming capitalists. My answer invited fairly vigorous shaking of heads from both the Chairman and Menon. After some questions on the anti-Bengali riots in Assam by one or two members, KPS turned the heat on me about to the latest book I had claimed to have read the memoirs of Field Marshal Montgomery. I was on pretty familiar ground here and discussed at length the Montgomery strategy of a single big thrust into the heart of Germany leading to direct attack by the allies from the west as opposed to the multipronged thrust advocated by the Americans and the kind of uneasy compromises that had to be agreed to. I expressed the view that the British were right and their plan would have enabled the western powers to reach Berlin before Stalin.

With a few more questions the interview was over and when I got out of the room, I really could not be sure whether I had done well or not. I went to the Constitution Club for lunch with a family friend and as I was entering the place I saw two members of the interview board. One of them recognized me, smiled and asked if I was going back home on that day. Though it was a purely polite and inconsequential inquiry, given my frame of mind, the question had a very unsettling effect on me as I took it to be a form of bidding me goodbye and indeed a goodbye to my chances of finding a berth in the services.

Altogether, the whole experience did not give me any great confidence as to the prospects of employment in the public service and throughout the journey to Madras my mind was in a continuous state of agitation. On reaching Madras, I called on my maternal granduncle who had a distinguished career in the judiciary and a voracious reader—his son is the famous management guru C.K. Prahlad—and narrated the entire interview to him. He listened to me very patiently and made me repeat the more important parts. After cogitating over the matter for what looked to me an eternity, he beamed and said that I had performed very well in the personality test.

His assessment turned out to be pretty correct and when the results came out in late April 1963 I had made it into the IAS and my marks in the personality test contributed very significantly to my success. The only remaining hurdle was the medical examination where once again I was made to feel quite nervous because of my low weight. My mother made me take some Durabolin injections, which after a four week torture improved my weight by just two pounds. Medical examination did not cause any problems and very soon I got my formal appointment letter signed by Sri. K.S.N. Murthy, the then Under Secretary to Government of India beginning with the words, 'the President of India is pleased to appoint', and so on the sixth of June, 1963, at the age of twenty two and a half, I became formally a member of the Indian Administrative Service.

# 2

# THE CIVIL SERVICE IN INDIA AND THOUGHTS ON GOVERNANCE

We owe it to the British to have given this country a civil service system which can adequately answer the requirements of good governance. A United Nations study, compiled in the late 1950s outlined the essential ingredients of a good civil service emphasizing that; recruitment should be based on merit and achievement, it should be by an independent body with full autonomy, the recruits should be adequately trained, they should have the opportunity to operate in an environment where performance is recognized and career advancement adequately provided for, and outstanding performance properly rewarded, the civil service should be politically neutral, capable of giving independent objective professional advice to the politicians, the civil servant should enjoy a reasonable degree of security and protection from undue political interference, the civil service should attach paramount importance to the principles of equity, justice, total impartiality, administering the system in a fair and equitable manner while ensuring that rule of law prevails. The focus of the UN study was no doubt the lack of an efficient and responsive civil service system in most newly independent countries of Africa and the adverse consequences that followed. It is but fair to say that India was fortunate in having a system which answered almost all requirements outlined by the UN study. The Indian Civil Service and the Indian Police were, without doubt, effective instruments in establishing and running a system of governance in the entire country based on rule of law, much superior in quality than anything that this country has known except perhaps when *rama rajya* prevailed. While governing the country in an efficient manner the system ensured that justice and equity were available irrespective of caste or creed based on sound principles of law. In a multi-ethnic, multi-religious, multi-cultural country, the importance of this cannot be overemphasized, especially when we remember the intensity of caste and religious loyalties that prevail in our society. The contribution of this instrument in the political and economic integration of the country needs also to be noted.

There is no doubt that the ICS was meant to serve British interests more than anything else. India was after all a colony, and a colony was meant to be exploited. The British concerned themselves only with those aspects of development which reinforced their authority and improved the means of exploitation, such as building of the railways which greatly enlarged the scope of transporting raw material from India to England and the post and telegraph system which greatly helped in knitting the country together improving communications between the remote parts of the country and the provincial capitals and Delhi, thereby reinforcing the Central Government's authority over the provinces and the districts. It appears that when the British came to India the population of India was some seventy million and the country was not particularly backward or poor, judged by the comparable conditions elsewhere and indeed was known for the wealth of her natural resources. That is why one European power after the other showed such great interest in colonizing India. When the British left, however, while the country's population had gone up five or six fold to nearly 400 million, abject poverty stalked the land.

Nevertheless, that the Civil Service was an effective system of governance is well established. If the British had realigned their priorities paying greater attention to the economic development of the country, the civil service would not have been found wanting. The British governed this whole country with just about 2000 ICS officers and in the last decades of British rule, this elite corps of officers contained a sprinkling of Indians many of whom served the country with great distinction. By all accounts, they were with an occasional exception, able and incorruptible, determined to administer India in its own best interests though it is they who decided invariably what those interests were. They however kept themselves aloof, exercising their authority from a distance, convinced as they were that they 'belonged to a race which God had destined to govern and to subdue'.

One cannot, however, deny that the system ensured speedy and fair justice, systematized land revenue administration, and functioned with total impartiality in its dealings with all segments of the society. B.K. Nehru, a very distinguished member of the ICS, in his autobiographical book entitled *Nice Guys Come Second* tells us of a very interesting anecdote. It appears that when he got into the ICS his father advised him to go and pay respects to a member of the local muslim elite in pre-partition Lahore. When he did so, this revered gentleman asked him as to what he intended to do now that he belonged to the ruling class. Nehru without hesitation stated that he planned to ensure that justice and fair play was available to all and he wanted to work for the welfare of all members of the community entrusted to his care without any discrimination. The old man quickly lost patience apparently and asked him as to what use would he be (perhaps to him and his ilk) if he cannot help his friends and harm his enemies. This episode to my mind brings out in clear terms the vast gap in the perception of various stratas of our society as to what the civil service should and should not be. As we have progressed, as an independent country, these perceptions to my mind have sharpened with our masters—the politicians—veering increasingly to the view taken by the Lahore gentleman who had little patience with advanced concepts of impartiality, equity and justice.

When the British left the country, the fate of civil service came into the hands of our founding fathers, many of whom had suffered in the hands of the ICS and the IP. Strong voices were indeed raised that this legacy of the British should be thrown out. Krishna Menon had at his acerbic best sarcastically denounced the ICS as 'not Indian, not civil and indeed not a service'. The nation owes an immense debt of gratitude to that Iron Man of India, Sardar Patel, who fully grasped the value of the civil service in administering the complex and turbulent nation that he and his colleagues had to handle. He had, I believe, the support of the Prime Minister.

Apart from everything else, I feel that their experience in the Interim Government and in coping with the gigantic problems following the partition in particular had made them realize the importance of an organized civil service. Dominique Lapierre and Larry Collins in their epoch-making *Freedom at Midnight* inform us that while the leaders of independent India had the wisdom of asking Mountbatten to be the first Governor General of India, when communal passions threatened to engulf large parts of the country, when large scale massacres were taking place and when a seemingly endless flood of refugees were crossing the border from both sides, the leaders of independent India who apparently, due to lack of experience, could not cope with the problem turned to Mountbatten asking him to provide the leadership required at that hour. It appears that Governor General, quite against his will, displayed the kind of administrative and organizational skills that were required in those difficult circumstances, like mobilizing resources, allocating responsibilities, setting priorities and regularly monitoring developments all round. He set up a control room in the Viceregal lodge now turned the residence of the GG. He made the airforce track refugee columns, organized reception centres and camps which provided immediate relief to those in need. I dare say that this experience strongly influenced the leadership in deciding upon the question of constituting a civil service structure for independent India. The leadership also at this time came into close contact with some of the finest brains in the ICS such as H.V.R. Iyengar, B.K. Nehru and Girija Shankar Bajpai who handled their responsibilities with unsurpassed competence, and this could also have influenced their minds.

Basically, we retained the civil service structure that the British had established almost entirely. Except for the change in names almost everything else remained. No doubt, while the ICS and the IP were not answerable to the representatives of the people, the newly constituted services were true public servants answerable, at the state and the central levels, to the political executive, who in turn were answerable to the legislatures. This again was very much on the pattern prevailing in the UK where the permanent civil service is very much answerable to the political executive of the day.

The Iron Man of India, while piloting the All India Services Act in the Parliament, cogently argued the case for an organized civil service in India on the pattern established by the British. He laid stress on the need for a civil service not only for administering the vast country but also on its vital role as a neutral instrument of governance in a multi-party democracy, where parties with different ideological persuasions can succeed one another. It would have been a tragedy if the benefits of governance were reserved for only the adherents of the ruling party's beliefs, a normal and in no way unusual a possibility and the civil service was an instrument which could provide a corrective in such circumstances. Sardar Patel event went to the extent of designating the civil service as a reasonable check with respect to the over-zealousness of politicians. Whether the civil service has been able to come up to the high expectations of the Sardar is indeed a question that deserves close examination.

It is my conviction that in spite of the heavy devaluation that has taken place in the authority of the civil service and serious decline in the esteem with which it was regarded, the services continue to be an invaluable instrument of governance. There is a good deal that is wrong with the civil service of today and corrective action in several spheres such as accountability, decentralization, etc. need to be taken, but to my mind we have reached the present sorry state of affairs because after the initial years of independence there has been a continuous trend of down grading the civil service by the nation as a whole and the leadership in particular. While the situation in the Central Government is better in many ways, in several states the services have been so badly treated and today they play but a peripheral role in governance and are unable to play the kind of role envisaged for them, namely, adherence to the principles of rule of law and natural justice and sound financial management, impartial dispensation of justice, quick and non discriminatory redressal of grievances and acceleration of socio-economic development. The consequences are quite visible in terms of a general breakdown of law and order, insurgency and rebellion in several parts, misuse of public funds on a vast scale, slow if not negative economic growth, private armies ruling the roost, criminals in legislatures and even as ministers, and above all, the poor getting a raw deal.

It cannot be denied that in a multi-cultural, multi-ethnic, multi-lingual and multi religious society, such as ours, the civil servant who is enabled to function as per law is an effective instrument in ensuring that justice as envisaged in the Constitution of India is available to the ordinary citizen. The young subdivisional officer or District Collector, one who is from outside the state, invariably takes an impartial view as per law and does not get swayed by narrow considerations of caste or creed. He is able to view issues with an all India perspective and does not get influenced by regional considerations. If he can resist the pressures brought upon him to depart from such principles, he is greatly respected. There have been quite a few cases in recent times where people have organized protests against transfer of officers, whose sense of justice and fair play and whose commitment to development had won them the regard and admiration of the local populace. Moreover, in the remote areas of the country it is only the young IAS officer who thinks of the nation. All others think only of their tribe or community or caste and this tendency is getting reinforced all the time, especially when current trends in politics underline the advantages of adopting narrow sectarian postures.

The value of the civil service as a great instrument of national cohesion and integration has not been highlighted adequately. When we witness the growth of fissiparous and centrifugal tendencies all over the country and demands for seccession being voiced in several quarters, when we find that the instruments of governance have fallen into disuse, leading to the prevalence of near anarchic situations in parts of the country and the political class playing an active role in reinforcing such tendencies, it is the civil service which can and has indeed played a significant role in correcting the situation. My contention is supported by the fact that when the situation in a state or a region gets really out of hand, President's rule is imposed and if there is an able Governor supported by two or three competent advisors, it does not take a long time to bring back normalcy. Punjab is a very good example where competent officers such as Ribeiro and K.P.S. Gill fought and won a serious battle against an insurgency movement with strong secessionist tendencies actively backed by a foreign power. The political class either kept dormant or, at least in some cases, championed the cause of the insurgents. Even the judiciary in Punjab almost collapsed.

To hold this vast country together, to ensure that the laws of the land prevail in all parts of the country and uniform standards of administration and financial prosperity are observed and to ensure that non-discriminatory systems of justice and grievance redressel are available to every citizen in every part of the country, the civil service is absolutely invaluable. The preservation of the unity and integrity of the country is, I dare say, contingent to a large extent upon the efficacy of the civil service.

It needs to be noted that in the post-1990 period the Indian political system has become highly fragmented. Gone are the days when the same political party held office both at the centre and the states, thus introducing new complications in centre, state relations and making it more difficult for the centre to enforce its authority, even on issues of national importance. Not only this, it also appears that a single party gaining a clear majority in the nation's parliament is becoming increasingly difficult. Coalition governments seem to be inevitable and coalition politics has unfortunately meant giving greater importance to the interests of the political party, to the detriment of the coalition and, indeed, national interests whenever necessary. Each of the partners pursues its own separate agendas and the task of arriving at a consensus among the coalition parties and among the different parties ruling the states is indeed a formidable one.

In such a situation the linkages forged by the organized civil services, in particular the All India Services, assume an altogether new dimension in ensuring a degree of cohesion, uniformity in standards and observance of the laws and the Constitution of the land, while conflicting interests are sought to be resolved.

Also, when political instability occurs, it is the civil service as an institutional mechanism spread through the length and breadth of the country which can ensure that there is no breakdown of law and order, that basic services continue to be available to the common man and the ordinary citizen's life is allowed to proceed without undue disturbance. The laws of the land have adequate provisions to take care of these requirements and have empowered the civil service to act under law.

It is worth recalling that in the post-World War II France, there was acute political instability for almost a decade with governments changing very frequently and one coalition after another taking office for brief periods, while France had to cope with the aftermath of the war. In these circumstances, it was the well-organized civil service of France which enabled the country to carry on, regardless, ensuring that the post-war reconstruction programme did not suffer and the ordinary citizen's needs were adequately taken care of. Incidentally, the near exact equivalent of the office of the district magistrate that we have in this country is to be found in the office of the prefect in France, the prefecture being the equivalent of our district.

Unfortunately, the leadership, particularly in the states, have not only realized the utility of the civil service as an effective instrument of governance and a mechanism to ensure orderly development of the society, but, to my mind, have in a sustained manner reduced the role of the civil service. It needs to be noted that states which have allowed the civil service to play its due role have recorded much better progress than those which have actively down graded the civil service. States such as Karnataka, Maharashtra, Gujarat and Andhra Pradesh can be cited as examples where the civil servant has been properly utilized.

The deterioration that I have referred to is both within and without. For a variety of reasons there has been a steady decline in the quality of the intake into the civil service. Firstly, the rigour of the UPSC examination has been progressively diluted, in particular the personality test. When the services were constituted the personality test carried 400 marks and you had to get a separate minimum out of this 400 to get into the services. This meant that pure theoretical bookish knowledge was not good enough and one had to impress a very distinguished set of people with your presence, your ability to formulate articulate and defend a particular point of view, your ability to remain calm and collected when provoked and of course your general knowledge of awareness and understanding of current issues. All these skills are of great importance throughout one's career in the civil service. Due to some unknown 'wisdom' the separate minimum was abolished and theoretically even if one gets no marks in the personality test one could sail through, if one had done exceptionally well in high scoring subjects such as mathematics. Further, the maximum marks, first reduced to 250, recently have increased to 300. Again, originally one had to write five optionals to qualify for getting into IAS/IFS. This meant that a higher effort was required for these two services, but again this was changed and all appeared for one set of optionals and the rank obtained was the sole determinant for the entry into the IAS/IFS. Secondly, the number of times one can appear and the maximum age for appearing have been tinkered repeatedly with. Consequently, even one who has passed 30 years can also get into the service and he may find himself serving as an assistant collector under a collector who may himself be not more than 30. Severe interpersonal problems are bound to arise in these circumstances. Further, at the age of 30 one's ability to learn is on the decline and one's attitudes are more rigid. The task of moulding this material into a proper civil servant becomes all the more difficult.

It needs to be added that while at least the Union Public Service Commission has managed to retain quality as far as its members and personnel are concerned, the state public service commissions have been thoroughly politicized. The processes have been vitiated by nepotism and corruption and, consequently, the quality of intake for the state level services has declined, progressively.

From about mid eighties, the services have also failed to attract the best brains of the country. No doubt, with the diversification of the economy this is bound to happen, especially when compensations provided by the non-governmental sector is way above what the civil services offer. The best brains are also leaving the country, finding greener pastures abroad.

While the quality at the induction stage has suffered, with regard to performance levels as well, there has been a perceptible decline, primarily because the institutional mechanisms vital for extracting high performance have fallen into disuse. The basic instruments for ensuring high performance is a system of rewards and punishment. The annual confidential reports and disciplinary action when required are supposed to be the instruments through which rewards/ punishment are meted out. They form a vital element in ensuring a high degree of accountability on the part of the civil servant.

Generally speaking, rewards for high performance is not available in the civil service of today. In the ICS it was there and one understands that Girija Shankar Bajpai became a Secretary in the Government of India after completing only thirteen years of service in the ICS. He was knighted as well. No such thing can happen in India of today. Obviously the outstanding qualities of Bajpai were given due recognition. Also, Bajpai was appointed to some of the most important posts in the country. More or less, the same is true of B.K. Nehru who became Secretary to Government of India after twenty odd years of service and functioned as India's ambassador to the US, Governor of Assam, J&K and Gujarat. It appears that he narrowly missed becoming Secretary General of the United Nations.

While rewards for outstanding performance have indeed vanished, we have today a situation where honest and hard working officers, meritorious in their performance, suffer the ignominy of repeatedly being thrown out of jobs, sidelined into innocuous posts and made to look as if they are wanting. There have been cases where officers have had to face humiliation and physical assault for performing their duty and adhering to rules and implementing the law of the land. Many, no wonder, seek the path of safety by keeping quiet and turning the other way while violations of law are rampant.

As to punishments once again the whole mechanism has become almost inoperative. As it is under Article 311 of the Constitution, a civil servant enjoys a very high degree of protection. Some regard this as undue protection. Successive judicial pronouncements have reinforced this protection as a result of which to punish an erring official, one has to go through an unbearable torture. The advantage is to a large extent with the erring official. If he is placed under suspension, after the lapse of a short time, he is entitled to seventy five per cent of his pay and many suspended officials coolly take a second job. Monetarily, he is possibly better off. The prescribed procedures are lengthy and time consuming and weighed heavily in favour of the official proceeded against, and at any time during the proceedings the erring official can approach the administrative tribunals which can and do grant stay orders. The disciplinary authority has to defend itself in these forums. If after all the exhaustive and exhausting processes are completed and a punishment is indeed imposed, the erring official invariably approaches a court and, once again, the disciplinary authority has to defend itself. If he does not succeed in the lower courts, an appeal is invariably filed adding to the problems of the disciplinary authority. Little wonder that the number of disciplinary authorities willing and able to go through this process is diminishing. There is an increasing tendency of avoiding getting embroiled in such complicated processes and consequently there is hardly any penalty for non-performance and dereliction of duty and nay even for corruption.

An added and indeed unfortunate complication has been brought in by the induction of the caste virus into service matters. If the official proceeded against happens to be a member of the reserved categories, invariably allegations of caste bias fly about thick and fast and petitions are submitted to the commissions set up to look after the interests of such categories. All kinds of allegations are made in such petitions and the disciplinary authority has to spend a lot of time countering these allegations. The extreme wariness displayed in dealing with disciplinary matters concerning reserved category officials is, I suppose, eminently understandable. In the process a particular category of officials are virtually placed outside the pale of disciplinary procedures.

Even the writing of ACRs has become quite a routine. The

tendency is to write bland fairly neutral CRs, as adverse remarks invariably invite representations, which may include allegations of bias of one category or the other.

One of the most demoralizing developments in recent times is the policy of reservation, even in promotions. In one stroke the whole basis of career advancement namely merit, performance and achievement has been thrown overboard. Those who do not get their due promotions, in spite of good and even outstanding performance feel heavily demoralized. All this has already had a deleterious impact on the performance levels in the government.

It needs to be noted in this context that the system of reservation is available to even those whose parents have entered the services and high offices in the government on the basis of reservation. They suffer from none of the handicaps which can justify the unequal and privileged treatment. This deprives the truly deserving of the benefits of reservation.

It needs to be highlighted that the Article 335 of the Constitution lays down, "The claims of the members of the SC and ST shall be taken into consideration consistent with the maintenance of efficiency of administration in the making of appointments to services and posts in connection with the affairs of the Union or of a state."

Gandhiji had also attached great importance to efficiency as a criteria for public appointments. He had no hesitation in stating "For administration to be efficient it must be in the hands of the fittest. There should be certainly no favouritism. If we want five engineers, we must take the fittest five even if they were all Musalmans or all Parsis. The educationally backward communities will have a right to favoured treatment in the matter of education in the hands of the National Government. But those who aspire to occupy responsible posts in the Government of the country can only do so if they pass the required test". No one can dispute Gandhiji's anxiety and commitment to the advancement of the disadvantaged segments of our society. No Indian before him or since his time has done more for the liberation and advancement of the backward classes in the country. As in so many other things, the wisdom of Gandhi as regards efficiency in administration has been forgotten by our rulers. The tragedy is that even the dictum contained in the Constitution is given so little importance.

We have, therefore, landed ourselves with a system where

accountability as a principle of sound management has been virtually buried. The science of management indicates that for the efficient performance of a given task, the leader has to be given the freedom to choose his team, implying that he will choose the best available talent, that he has the right to demand the highest possible performance and has also the right to weed out of the inefficient. None of these advantages are available to the leaders in the bureaucracy. They have to make do with a team given to them selected not necessarily on the basis of their knowledge or expertise to handle the particular set of responsibilities, cannot hold them accountable for their performance and cannot deal effectively with the inefficient. He is still expected to deliver the goods.

This, already highly unsatisfactory, situation has been made even more difficult by the attitude of the politician in dealing with the bureaucracy.

The fine and delicate relationship between the elected representative and the professional civil servant has been thoroughly analyzed in the existing literature on the subject, but very few of our political masters have taken care of understanding the relationship and fostering the relationship in a healthy way. The civil service is a necessary and performance enhancing adjunct to the political executive, to give impartial professional expert advice based upon law, rules and regulations and in the process enable the politician to implement policies for furthering the nation's interests. The civil servant has the right to point out as to why a particular course of action is desirable or not, pointing out the adverse consequences of the particular action, considered undesirable.

The minister is expected to respect such advice and act accordingly, but if he in his wisdom decides to act against the right advice of the civil servant, then the civil servant has no alternative but to comply with the minister's decision. If the matter is sufficiently serious, he can possibly resubmit the case with new arguments, but if the minister stands by his decision, the civil servant has to comply. No doubt, in this process the responsibility is taken by the minister who may be hard put to defend himself before the legislature.

In practice, however, the political executive has increasingly tended to expect the civil servant to only say yes. A civil servant who argues a case on the basis of rules, etc., is dubbed as inconvenient, tactless and rule minded and often sidelined and given innocuous responsibilities. The situation in the Government of India is no doubt much better. At that level, the quality of the political executive is definitely superior and the vigilance exercised by the parliament and the press is quite rigorous. While there are variations from state to state, as regards the manner in which the civil service is treated, there is little doubt that in states like Bihar and UP officers have had a very raw deal. Consequently, officers prefer to work in the Central Government and do everything possible to remain there as long as possible.

The basic reason for this sad state of affairs is, it appears to me, the growing divergence between the objectives of governance as viewed by the politician and as perceived by the civil servant. Increasingly the sole obsession of the politician is winning the next election. So long as this purpose is served well by his actions, he does not care much about performance of the governmental machinery, application of sound principles of administration, observance of canons of financial propriety and even welfare of the people. Often constitutional propriety is also given the go by. If winning the next election does not seem possible, the tendency is to use the limited time available in office to get as much out of the system as possible, for personal gain.

In a constitutional democracy such as ours power emanates from the people and, constitutionally speaking, the people judge the desirability of continuing with a particular party based upon its performance every five years. However, over the years performance as the main ingredient for determining the eligibility of a government to continue in office has surely and steadily declined. Bihar is a prime example to show how little performance matters as a criterion for reelection. The Constitutional system that we have adopted, in particular, the first past the post method of winning elections, encourages our politicians to think in terms of winning and retaining the loyalty of a narrow segment of the electorate in the constituency. For this purpose, appealing to sectarian considerations based on caste, language, creed, etc. and generating and aggravating a sense of insecurity among different segments and presenting oneself as the sole defender of the interests of that particular segment of the electorate who are made to feel insecure, are all part of the great game. Added to this lethal mixture is the enmeshing of the interests of politicians and criminals of money power and muscle power. Money is required not only for the party, for the running of and winning of elections but also for buying legislators to gain a majority, if required. When there is such a dire need for money, financial integrity, probity and rectitude in public service naturally find no space.

The civil servant who has been schooled with respect to administrative efficiency and cost benefit considerations and told that in spending government money he shall exercise the same degree of prudence he would have exercised had he been spending his money, that governmental action should not only be fair but seen to be fair, that such action should result in the greatest good of the largest number, finds himself at odds with this situation. The politician finds such a civil servant an obstacle and tries to ignore him or by pass him, or even get rid of him.

It would, therefore, appear that while performance, as the determining consideration for winning elections, has been declining in importance the politician has found methods which are in fact superior in their effectiveness when it comes to running and winning of elections. Moral questions have no place in such a situation. Consequently when performance is, if at all, of secondary importance, the civil service as an instrument for increasing the effectiveness and responsiveness of the system of governance is greatly reduced in importance. The civil service is useful only to the extent of dressing up dubious actions with a cloak of legality, if not legitimacy, so that inconvenient questions from the judiciary or the press can be dealt with. Also there have been cases where, as an action became too hot to handle, the blame could be easily put on the civil servant for not having tendered correct advice.

Lest it appears a presentation of a one-sided picture, let it also be said that along with the decline in the quality of the average civil servant and the weakening of the systems calculated to extract high performances, there is also the growing trend of the civil servant acquiesing in the acts of the politician. For every civil servant who attaches importance to canons of financial propriety and stands by principles of probity and rectitude in public service there are at least two others who are prepared to look the other way. While the majority may not actively participate, the purpose is served by keeping quiet. This trend can only get reinforced when honest advice based on law and calculated to ensure financial integrity is ignored and in fact frowned upon and those tendering such advice are treated badly.

The forms in which an officer considered inconvenient, though his knowledge and competence may be unquestionable, is badly treated may vary. Given the fact that a punishment as such within the meaning of law cannot be imposed on a civil servant without due process, the two main forms are frequent transfers and placement, in innocuous appointments where the officer's talent is wasted and he gets thoroughly demoralized. Without adequate workload he develops a guilty conscience that he does not deserve that salary he takes home. Frequent transfers prevent officers from contributing their best and causes great difficulties in the personal life of the officer. Also, such transfers unnecessarily increase establishment expenditure. When the system rewards only those who refrain from tendering impartial objective advice, fertile ground is created for the proliferation of supine yes men and indeed those who actively aid and abet wrongdoing. Frequent transfers and extremely short tenures play havoc with the efficiency of the system as there is no stability in the administration and opportunities for "growing in the job" are effectively denied. In some states transfers have, it appears, become an industry as money power is freely used to achieve given objectives, of either getting rid of an inconvenient soul or placing a favoured officer in "lucrative" positions.

It needs to be qualified that all that I have stated are the broad, visible, readily observable trends in several parts of the country. There is no doubt that in several areas there prevails a situation where both the politician and the civil servant operate on the same wavelength and each respects the other's role attaching importance to clean and efficient administration. Where such a situation exists the results are definitely superior in terms of better standards of governance and benefits to the people at large.

Even the press, generally speaking, is unsympathetic in its attitudes towards the civil service. Outstanding work done by civil servants, in spite of all the odds stacked against them, finds mention, if at all in an obscure column of the fourth page so also the ill treatment of honest hardworking officers. On the other hand, innocuous gossip of so-called goings on in the corridors of power is published without proper verification. For God knows what reason, the press invariably refers to even the most senior civil servant as a babu, in a derogatory tone, hinting broadly that the babu can never do any good and can be counted upon to bungle everywhere and everything. The term babu is of colonial coinage employed by the British to distinguish the clerk from an officer and indeed an Englishman from an Indian as the Englishman was always a 'sahib'. The general picture of a babu is that of a being clad in native costume, plodding away in a hall filled with characters of the same ilk concerning themselves with routine matters, playing no part in decision making as such. On the other hand, sahibs were elevated creatures taking decisions and superior in every way to the babu.

By painting the entire bureaucracy with this quite derogatory brush, I am afraid, the press is bringing down the civil service in the esteem of the people.

The overall situation, it would appear, does not engender much of an optimism for the present and for the future. There is little doubt that the instruments of governance have ceased to function in parts of the country. Take the states in the North-East. In the case of Manipur, administration as an instrument for providing the people, at large, a set of services does not operate. There are no doubt the constitutional functionaries—the Governor, the council of ministers—and a fairly big hoard of government servants, but their writ runs over a very limited area. All of them have to be protected at considerable expense. There seems to be no effective control over insurgency activities and one hears of allegations of links between insurgents and politicians. The government servants have to pay a share of their wages to the insurgents and the few traders that are there buy peace by paying protection money. The politics of the state, on top of everything else, is so volatile with loyalties changing every other day that stable administration cannot be provided, and, what is worse, such political games bear no relevance to the common man who finds that his peace and security is better served by coming to terms with the particular insurgent group in control of the area. Can one expect investment, improvement in the standard of living and quality of life in such circumstances?

While the North-East has indeed some special problems, states like Bihar have witnessed a similar phenomenon of instruments of governance becoming non-functional. Many states are in a financial mess and in Bihar salaries of certain classes of government servants are not paid for months, telephones do not function and even paper for running government offices is, it appears, difficult to get. Police stations do not record complaints, very little, if at all, is done by way of investigations and to bring criminals to book. Policemen cannot travel as their allowances are not paid, and the most of the state's vehicles including those for fire fighting are in disrepair.

Various accounts emanating from the state indicate that the state as an instrument of governance has indeed withered away. As one travels in and through the state there are visible signs of deterioration everywhere in the state of the roads, the buildings and the grinding poverty so visible all round. Law or order does not seem to exist and one hears that police stations do not register cases if the complaint is against particular castes who claim to belong to the ruling class. Private armies roam around the countryside with immunity and the naxalities hold sway over substantial swathes of territory. Bihar is the only state in the country which records a negative rate of economic growth and has the largest percentage of people below the poverty line i.e. 43 per cent, as compared to a mere 6.2 per cent of the Punjab, 14 per cent of Gujarat, 8.7 per cent of Haryana, 20 per cent of Karnataka. The absolute number is growing alarmingly as the only thing that is growing unchecked and relentlessly in Bihar is the population. Vast sums of money have allegedly been misappropriated from the state's resources. The educational system is in shambles with the vice chancellors looting the universities. All the principles of good governance as well as the system of checks and balances enshrined in the Constitution have no place in the state and still winning elections is no great problem for the ruling class.

A related issue that needs mention is the parlous state of the finances of many states. Populist postures have made the states go on increasing their unproductive expenditure. Employment within government and wage bills have ballooned with no relationship between remuneration and productivity. Socialism and welfare economics have made governments to enter into all areas of a citizen's life and the citizen in turn has come to expect government to do everything. Insurgency and security concerns have vastly added to the problem of ever increasing non-productive expenditure. In quite a few states, treasuries operate only for a few days in a month to disburse salaries. Pensioners have to wait. Development expenditure is also basically for meeting salaries of persons, employed for executing schemes while the schemes themselves do not see the light of the day.

Population on the other hand keeps increasing and so are the expectations of the people. We have also conditioned the minds of our people to believe that payment is not expected with respect to services provided by the government. Our electoral politics is a competition in populism and promises and more promises are made, all the while. Fulfilment of promises is not of any great consequence, and, with resources disappearing, it is not possible for governments to fulfil promises. Consequently, when corrective action is sought to be taken, albeit hesitantly, very little is achieved.

I have tried to advocate, in this context, a theorem which I call the doctrine of reciprocity. Briefly, if in a welfare state the citizen expects the government to look after him from the cradle to the grave the government has an equal right to expect the citizen to behave responsibly. In concrete terms, if government has to provide education, healthcare and employment opportunities to its citizenry, this cannot be without reference to the resources at the government's disposal and more importantly in the face of ever expanding demands in an irresponsible manner by the people. In other words, government has the right to impose norms with respect to the growth of population. Citizens cannot expand individual families without limits and expect the government to provide a series of services all free, and also create employment opportunities. They themselves would not contribute anything towards the national exchequer by way of payment of taxes. No system can withstand strains caused by such mismatch between expectations and the ability to satisfy such expectations.

The unlimited growth of population has also another dimension in India, which some economists have called 'demographic fatigue'. Governments given their resource base, size of the administrative apparatus and the increasing inefficiency of the system, are finding it increasingly difficult to deal with the problems such as natural calamities, whose scale has been escalating exponentially because of the relentless increase in population. Cyclones and earthquakes result in much larger number of casualties and relief to all those who require it does not reach in time or in full measure.

During my various terms of office I have endeavoured to include these ideas in speeches I had to prepare for various dignitaries but no one was prepared to incorporate this theme in their speeches. They invariably considered it too risky, underlining the fact that somehow our leaders are so hesitant to tell the people the frank truths, get them to face facts, prepare them to pay the required price for bringing about substantive improvements in the situation.

In a state like Bihar or Uttar Pradesh which has a long border with Nepal, from where Pakistan's intelligence agencies have been active and along the border there is a perceptible growth of fundamentalist outfits supported by Pakistan and other Islamic countries, this 'withering of the state' and lack of policing has sinister implications. No wonder, Pakistan nationals entering India with valid travel documents manage to disappear without a trace and infiltration from across the border has assumed alarming proportions. It has already brought about a significant demographic transformation along the eastern borders of the country.

The external dimension of the decline in the quality of governance of the country, brought about by a systematic undermining of the mechanics of governance and the failure of the leadership to appreciate the vital need to pay attention to all aspects of governance and not merely the task of getting reelected by means which reduces the importance of performance, has to be viewed very seriously. The world is changing at a rapid rate and nations have to continuously face new challenges. Gone are the days when the ability to perpetrate violence on an adversary was the determining factor in the ability of nations to enforce their will on each other. Open wars with armies marching across frontiers have become outdated. The currency of the day is 'threat to use force rather than actual use of force'. This, combined with 'coercive diplomacy', use of trade sanctions, denial of technology, denial of economic aid, use of the media and the increasing role of intelligence to undermine the stability, sovereignty and integrity of nations by taking advantage of the weakness of institutions of governance, lack of internal cohesion and exploiting real or artificial grievances and sources of dissatisfaction are all weapons of today's wars. Very significantly the wars are not fought, won or lost in open battlefields, but on conference tables these days.

Nations, therefore, watch each other much more intensely, through humint (human intelligence) and techint (intelligence acquired through the use of technology–monitoring communications, use of satellites, etc), keeping track of economic and military as well as technological capabilities, the personality of its leaders, the belief systems, and strengths and weaknesses of institutions. What counts today is not military might alone, but economic strength, technological superiority, political stability, far sightedness of leaders and presence or absence of institutional mechanisms which can withstand international pressures.

The vulnerability of a nation to external threats of the subtle kind, which is the currency of today, increases sharply with the weakening of the state through a combination of unimaginative and shortsighted leadership and undermining of the effectiveness of the institutions. Today, India does face a situation of this nature and consequently the ability of external powers inimical to our interests, to exploit our internal divisions and weaknesses aid and abet insurgency movements, violate our borders, alter the demographic composition along our borders and let loose their intelligence agencies to undermine our security, has progressively increased.

It needs no emphasis that we have hostile neighbours who have nuclear teeth and missile power and who have not missed any opportunity to exploit our vulnerabilities, taking full advantage of our divisions and the declining capabilities of our institutions.

Alvin Toffler in his seminal work entitled 'Power Shift' has brilliantly analysed as to how today ' knowledge is power' and nations who are able to exploit knowledge to their advantage are able to dictate terms to their adversaries. There has been a significant transition in the source of power of nations from the ability to perpetrate violence—read strong armed forces—to wealth and now to knowledge as the weapon for dominating others. This indeed is the weapon of the twenty first century. No doubt, a nation which has all the three elements in good measure in its armoury is a super power as is the case of the United States. However, possession of knowledge in today's world is a vital instrument in creating wealth as knowledge greatly increases the productive power of both capital and labour and once one has knowledge and wealth, one can command the ability to perpetrate violence. As stated earlier, it is enough today to have the ability to threaten the use of force and one need not necessarily resort to the use of force.

Such a line of reasoning would demand that a nation which wishes to be strong and reduce its vulnerability to external threats, should very actively promote knowledge and encourage promotion of excellence in all spheres of human endeavour. Indians today are acknowledged, the world over, as highly capable and intelligent, but as a country our performance, except in certain limited areas, is far below world standards. The value added per employee in India is arguably the lowest in the world and something like one tenth of an average German worker. Productivity per unit of labour and capital in this country has not been increasing but, actually, declining as evidenced by the worsening of the capital output ratios through successive Five-Year Plans. We are spending more and more to obtain less and less.

A nation can afford to ignore these significant shifts in the nature of international relations only at its peril. Increasing the capability of the institutional framework to deal with these threats is of paramount importance and measures to arrest the decline in the quality of governance need to be taken without any loss of time. By opting for mediocrity in the systems of governance, we are, I am afraid, undermining the nation's long term security.

In the process of devaluing the institutions of governance we have also undermined the faith of the people of India in democratic institutions. Gone are the days when people talked about *Bhay* and *Bhakthi* (fear and faith) towards the government. The failure of institutions to perform functions required by law has made people believe that liberties, with the laws of the land can be taken with impunity. Crime does pay and punishment for crime is the exception rather than the rule. The higher you are placed in the society and, in particular if you belong to the political class, punishment can be postponed indefinitely, if not avoided altogether. Even in cases involving very large sums no politician has actually suffered incarceration. Discriminatory application of law, which means violation of the principle of equality in the eyes of law and equal protection to all citizens, has resulted in people losing all respect for law and for the agencies maintained at great public expense to enforce law, and unless there is respect for law, maintenance of law and order, civilized and orderly conduct of the affairs of the society are a near impossibility. There has been an increasing tendency to justify escaping punishment under law by referring to the so called 'court of the people' whose vote in favour is cited as acquittal, a not guilty verdict, on the basis of which further depredation can be indulged in.

Concern for this state of affairs is not lacking and some efforts have indeed been made to correct and reverse these highly undesirable trends. T.S.R Subramanium, the Cabinet Secretary in the period 1996–1998, an eminent civil servant of the UP cadre with impeccable credentials—yes the officer who was thrown out of the office of Chief

Secretary, UP only because of the accident of his birth—started a process for improving the effectiveness and responsiveness of the government. The right to information, the drafting of a citizen's charter, simplification of procedures, improving the morale of the civil service by removing the threat of frequent transfers and instituting a system of postings based on competence, record and specialization with fixity of tenure were all discussed at the highest levels—conference of Chief Secretaries and Chief Ministers. Unfortunately, the process did not have much of chance as the states were least interested in such matters and indeed some suspected that this process would loosen their hold over the civil services. The effort also did not address some of the basic issues in order to face today's complicated challenges, such as how do we improve performance levels, improve the efficiency of the delivery systems and redressal grievance mechanisms, encourage excellence in performance by a system of recognition of outstanding work and punishment for inefficiency and corruption, and how to restore the lost balance in the relationship between the civil servant and the politicians.

No doubt, the post-1991 economic reforms programme has brought about a fundamental change in the way in which we view government. There's a very welcome trend of making people less and less dependent upon government. Hopefully, the trend will continue and be intensified. What is required along with this is the improving of the efficiency of the system of governance in those core areas where governmental action is inevitable. These developments in the country have taken place at precisely the time when the phenomenon of globalisation is taking an increasingly firmer grip over the international economic relations. As the world gets increasingly integrated and trade and financial flows multiply, individual countries have to prepare themselves to face international competition of increasing intensity. We cannot take shelter inside protective cocoons. If nations are to survive and prosper and since competition can be vicious having wide ramifications, excellence in performance at all levels is absolutely essential. With the process of internal economic liberalisation and market orientation well under way, much of the heat of competition will have to be faced by the private enterprise, who, I am sure, is capable of fighting the battles and winning them.

However, even in the changed circumstances, the role of government remains very important. Some believe that while there is a definite change in the nature of tasks to be performed, particularly in the commercial fields, role of the government indeed increases. Success is contingent upon both government and business, acting in tandem, keeping national interest uppermost. There is very little room for mediocrity in such circumstances.

Governments have to continue playing a vital role in the core areas of governance, such as maintenance of law and order, national security, external relations and providing the regulatory framework for smooth functioning of business and orderly development of the economy. Managing the macro economic balances of the country and avoiding both overheating of the economy as well as fighting recessionary trends call for a proactive role on the part of the government. Further, in the Indian context, given the state of social and economic development and the emergence of regional sectoral as well as social imbalances, the government has to play a vital role with respect to education, healthcare, poverty alleviation, infrastructure development and development of backward segments of the society. Development experience the world over has shown that market mechanisms are inadequate tools for achieving the broader objectives of economic growth, such as quality of life, environmental protection, equity and justice, greater participation in public life, gender equality, etc. Substantial and sustained development needs, also, to focus upon structural aspects such as good governance, transparent decision, formulating efficient legal and judicial procedures and sound regulatory systems. Effective development requires the build up of a harmonious relationship between different levels of government, private sector and the civil society. A country which can achieve all this can definitely aim at a higher growth trajectory and solve its problems at a fast pace and with least difficulty.

The world's political and economic development scenario is witnessing two significant trends which appear on the surface to be running in two different directions. The first is, as mentioned above, the phenomenon of globalisation. The second is, as designated by the World Bank, the phenomenon of localisation. Apart from greater integration of the world economy, expanding trade financial flows and massive advances in information and communication technologies, national governments have had to, at the same time, also surrender parts of their decision making powers to super national bodies. The World Trade Organisation is a prime example where if you have to participate in the process of world trade you have to open up your own markets, and observe an internationally determined trade and tariff regime.

At the same time, with growing consciousness of ethnic identities and the desire, indeed, anxiety of local communities to participate in the decision making process, development of sub-national governmental structures have to be brought into being. India is currently going through this difficult experience where the challenges are: how while participating in a world system you manage to safeguard your national interests and while yielding to the demands of local level institutions, how you ensure the unity, sovereignty and territorial integrity of the nation.

To meet the new challenges the ability and competence of the nation's institutions, to formulate and articulate appropriate responses and withstand pressures while negotiating with super national bodies and local level institutions and to work out satisfactory arrangements, is of vital importance.

Given these new challenges the worry is whether the country's institutional framework is capable of successfully tackling these. The decline in standards which has been observed as the general trend does not give room for optimism.

A recent development in the country that needs to be noted in this context is the constituition of the third tier of government, namely, the *panchayat raj* system for the rural areas and local self-government institution for the urban areas. While urban local bodies have been in existence even prior to independence, the panchayat raj structure is essentially a post-Independence creation. The provisions made in the Constitution in 1992 were calculated to infuse new strengths into this third tier and is a bold attempt to tackle the problems of instability and financial inadequacy. The tendency of the state governments to keep these bodies out of action for indefinite periods is sought to be effectively curbed. Also, reservation for women in all these bodies is a great step forward in the process of empowerment of the weaker segments of population.

As is the case with many of India's experiments, the measures initiated with respect to the *panchayats* and urban local bodies have indeed been inspired by noble ideas. However, earlier experiments with regard to decentralisation did not meet with uniform success and several states simply abandoned the experiment. The main problem has been the quality of leadership with non-merit criterion as the basis of selection, combined with poor financial management and populist postures calculated to ensure continuity and winning of the next election. It would have been desirable to make education as a qualification for standing for elections. Unfortunately, these ills have not been addressed adequately even in the new dispensation under the Constitution. Nevertheless, reports from some parts of the country speak of encouraging developments, with genuine people's participation in the process of decision making, articulation of ground-level development needs and a greater degree of accountability on the part of those concerned with implementation. The system does seem to bring about the much needed participatory relationship between the people and local level instruments of governance and should satisfy the growing aspirations of the people to have a say in decision making and holding elected office bearers accountable for their performance. Very surprisingly, Bihar, which is so backward in so many respects, has taken the revolutionary step of making a provision for recall of *panchayat* functionaries by the people if there is unsatisfactory performance.

While detailed analysis of the benefits of this system of decentralisation against costs incurred have not, it appears, been attempted, the limited experience so far indicates that the problem of mismatch between resources mobilized and expenditure requirements continues to bedevil the system. As is the case with most state governments, there is extreme reluctance to mobilise local resources, as such steps, it is believed, may spoil the chances of reelection. On the other hand, there is great enthusiasm to give away freebies and make any number of promises. As a result, the third tier of government continues to be abjectly dependent upon the state governments. There is also the danger of financial irresponsibility at this level jeopardizing the macro economic stability at the state level, as local governments which have borrowed heavily and spent unwisely may have to be bailed out by the state government whose own financial health is very delicate, to say the least.

One other problem that has emerged, consequent upon the introduction of the *panchayat* electoral process, is the fact that the decision making process at governmental level has become a hostage to a third set of elections. As it is, elections to the Parliament, the state assemblies and the frequent by-elections have made chief ministers hesitant to take decisions, which even remotely are suspected to harm the electoral prospects of the party. Since *panchayat* elections are regarded as one more barometer to gauge the inclinations of the electorate, so-called 'unpopular' measures, such as much needed tariff revisions for power, are not taken.

The broad conclusion that seems inescapable from the above analysis is that there has been a continuous decline in the quality of governance in the country and the ability of the country to tackle successfully the new and complicated internal and external challenges cannot be taken for granted. The major causes for this decline are: the undermining of the effectiveness of the institutional mechanisms established to deal with such issues, and inability of the political masters to adequately appreciate the value of institutions as performance enhancing instruments, combined with the devaluation of performance itself as the most important criterion for continuation in office. To my mind, the basic reason for this is the decline in the quality of leadership at all levels and the flawed constitutional system that we have adopted with respect to the process of selection of leadership. Mature democracies elsewhere in the world have advanced as the process of selection of leadership invariably throws up the best possible leaders who are educated, capable of understanding the complex issues that need to be dealt with in today's world and who appreciate the value of institutions. Also, where the leadership failed or is corrupt, retribution followed quickly in terms of electoral defeats and political oblivion, and if the misdemeanour is of a criminal nature, the law enforcement machinery took adequate care of the matter.

On the other hand, we have a situation in the country where while for every job there is a prescribed minimum qualification in terms of education and experience, even the highest office in the land as per our constitution can be held by a person with no education. Further, given the electoral process adopted by us especially, the first past the post system, merit and competence is of hardly any importance. All that is required is to command the loyalty of a narrow segment of the electorate on the basis of caste, community, or creed. To keep winning, one has only to reinforce the separate identity of the group loyal to you while keeping the rest of the electorate divided again on caste etc lines. As to performance as a criterion for reelection, this has been heavily devalued and criminal acts do not invite speedy punishment.

Indeed, people, who have been convicted by courts of law, do win elections.

So, it is little wonder that we have a leadership class which is not even capable of understanding the complex issues that need to be tackled, leave alone the ability to tackle effectively these problems. It will be worth illustrating this with an incident—amusing for some, sad for a majority—that took place in 1997 during a meeting convened by the Prime Minister I.K. Gujral, of all chief ministers to discuss the question of evolving a more effective and responsive administration. Chandrababu Naidu, the dynamic and visionary Chief Minister of Andhra Pradesh, made a computerized 'power point' presentation on a big screen dealing with a number of issues relating to effective governance, comparing the situation in India with that in Singapore. The presentation was very well received. The hall had been darkened for the duration of the presentation at the end of which one of those present stated in Hindi, 'aab hum Laloo ko sunna chahte hain' meaning that we want to hear Laloo Prasad Yadav, the then Chief Minister of Bihar. Laloo's response was classic -'andhera ho gayaa tha tho hum so gaye the' meaning that since it had become dark he had gone to sleep. This was the kind of interest that was displayed with respect to a subject of such paramount importance.

Not very different is the story of the meetings of the National Development Council where the nation's economic future is supposed to be discussed and decided upon where while learned finance ministers talk about growth rates, capital output ratios, quantum of savings, management of the nation's macro economic balances, many of the responses reveal little or no understanding of the gravity of the issues under consideration. At the end of it all, a pre-drafted resolution is adopted basically endorsing the government's proposal and this is supposed to be the blue print for the nation's progress.

An issue related to the legislators having no qualification to perform their tasks is the phenomenon of legislators failing to legislate. Even Parliament, that great institution, which is supposed to represent the will of the people, spends less and less time upon legislative business and on debating national issues of grave import. An even more astounding recent development is the tendency of a group of parliamentarians to continuously disrupt proceedings by resorting to strong armed tactics, making a mockery of democratic processes, devaluing the institution in the public eye while costing the exchequer crores of rupees by disallowing the Parliament to function. The parliamentarians are undermining the faith of the people in democratic institutions. All this can be seen on the television, and the world looks at us with disbelief when we keep claiming that we are a great democracy.

The situation in the state assemblies is no better. It is not unusual for legislators to hurl furniture and microphones at each other. Legislative business occupies an increasingly smaller proportion of the time spent by legislators in transacting business. On the other hand, legislators are increasingly demanding and getting a share in purely administrative activities. Legislators are active in getting officers transferred and getting postings considered 'lucrative'. Legislators want to play a rôle in appointments and getting jobs for only those who are their favourites. Legislators are appointed as chairmen of various public sector corporations where they interfere with appointments, award of contracts, purchases and indeed in whichever field they can derive one advantage or the other. They have to be given cars, telephones, personal staff, petrol, etc. which casts a burden on the finances of the corporations. Efficiency and profitability considerations find no place in such a situation.

Even politicians who have lost elections insist on playing a role in the field of administration, especially if they happen to be a part of the ruling party. Apart from the usual role in taking up cases of postings and transfers, such defeated candidates have been able to procure lucrative jobs in the public sector undertakings, and atleast in one state even within the government. In Sikkim, for example, offices such as chairman of the power department, of the transport department are given to such worthies even though there is a full-fledged cabinet minister and a secretary for running the department. That this is an extreme form of political patronage and a waste of public money is no one's concern.

The question that needs to be asked is whether we would have been better off, had we decided to prescribe educational qualifications for our legislators and for the political executive. Also, can we change the present electoral system which seems to throw up leadership of uncertain quality. M.S. Gill, the venerable Chief Election Commissioner, has given expression to his concerns in this regard especially, the first past the post system, but hardly anyone else seems to be concerned about this basic ill of the system. Even the

Venkatachalliah Constitution Review Commission has not so far said anything concrete on this subject, perhaps on the ground that they are not supposed to talk about the basic structure of the Constitution. Indeed, on and off, concerns have been expressed about the criminalisation of politics and the role of money and muscle power, but nothing has been done about these.

Interestingly, some of these concerns had occupied our minds even when we were probationers in the National Academy of Administration in Mussourie. We, who belong to the 1963 batch of the IAS, were the last batch of officers to have had the privilege of calling on Prime Minister Pandit Jawaharlal Nehru early in 1964, just a few months before he passed away. To meet such a historic personality as Panditji, about whom one had heard and read so much, and whose deep and sonorous voice over the All India Radio was an inspiration and whose pictures in the papers and newsreels (no T.V. those days) was eagerly lapped up, was regarded by all of us as an elevating experience. We were, after all, meeting a man who had been an idol of worship for millions of Indians. He had been described as the 'light of Asia'. As a student in Ooty, and in the college at Madras, I was one of those who had stood along routes to see Panditji, elegant as always, pass by in his motorcade or to hear him speak at public meetings.

My heart did miss a beat when he entered the room where we were all waiting, as suddenly we were in the company of possibly the greatest man of his times in our eyes. He did look somewhat bent and distinctly old, but when he sat down and started talking, he held us enthralled. He spent a good 45 minutes with us, though he kept looking at his watch and reminding himself that he had to meet the President. He dwelt briefly with our tasks in the states and repeatedly emphasized the need to learn the local language quickly. He then invited questions from us and that is where the relevance of this narration comes with respect to the theme of this chapter, namely the politician civil servant relationship. My friend, Ajit Singh Chatta of the Punjab cadre (who retired as Chief Secretary of Punjab) asked Panditji about the need for politicians to undergo training. The PM replied that they do go through a serious learning process in the school of life and politics. Sreenivasan of the Madras cadre asked about the neutrality of the civil servant. The PM indicated that neutrality did not mean that the civil servant be out of tune with the economic and political philosophy of the party in power to the extent of failing to implement the policy. I made bold to ask the PM as to whether we should not have made education a qualification for exercising franchise in view of our people growing increasingly aware of only their rights and not their duties. The PM very patiently explained as to how throughout the freedom struggle the people's role in future governments was repeatedly stressed and as to how they were informed what freedom meant, that the people had the right to choose their governments and change the same. Having made these promises and raised their expectations it was impossible to deprive them of this fundamental right by laying down preconditions.

Panditji was indeed an idealist of great proportions and he perhaps could not have imagined to what extent manipulation of ignorant voters can take place and how religion, caste, etc can be exploited to achieve electoral ends. However, I still feel that we could have at least prescribed some credible qualification for becoming legislators and ministers. In the first years of independence we had a great deal of idealism among the elected representatives, a vast majority of whom had been schooled in Gandhian thought and the ideals of freedom struggle. A very high level of patriotism prevailed and corruption was virtually non-existent. There was a strong urge to do good to the people. Also, there was willingness to learn the art of administration combined with respect for impartial, objective, professional, expert advice. Panditji himself set a fine example by showing great and sustained interest in building enduring institutions. Almost like a schoolmaster, he frequently addressed chief ministers on all kinds of matters of public importance, to educate them and to goad them to act. Even such a topic as the poor design of the ordinary broom employed by the housemaid, which compelled her to bend and sweep for hours together, causing great strain to the spinal chord did not escape Panditji's attention.

The second and more especially the third generation of leadership had very little use for these ideals. Not only were they not knowledgeable but also with an arrogance matched only by ignorance did not want to learn. "We know everything" and "who are you to teach us" became the common theme. Where however educated legislators get elected and educated men become ministers there is a substantial qualitative difference in the manner in which they respond to situations and the way they appreciate problems and seek material solutions. On the other hand, when politicians without adequate knowledge refuse to go by expert advice, the quality of decision making suffers. Increasingly, non-objective considerations prevail and influence peddling and money power take a grip on the system.

Also, politicians without education find themselves uncomfortable while dealing with knowledgeable professionals. They tend to break the hierarchy, preferring to deal with lower level functionaries, causing serious damage to the system. I have known chief ministers who would prefer to deal with the officers in charge of police stations, by passing all the middle and senior level echelons of the police system. This plays havoc with the discipline of a uniformed service and the head of the police at the state and the district lose control over the force. The officer in charge of the police station, who gets to deal directly with the chief minister, becomes a menace assuming the role of direct agent 'helping friends and harming enemies'. He does what he pleases and no one can discipline him and there have been cases where such men are known to run extortion rackets misusing the name of the chief minister and others, if necessary, and doing very well for themselves in the process.

As to the other important issue of electoral reform, namely recognition of the failure of the first past the post system to serve our national needs, and the kind of reinforcement that this system has provided with respect to sectarian, regional separatist tendencies, I feel a review is called for and we must consider whether a presidential form of government would not be to our advantage. I am of the view, till the time of Indira Gandhi, and even some early part of Rajiv Gandhi's tenure as Prime Minister, we did have in effect a presidential form of government. The nation voted for Nehru and Indira Gandhi with one party ruling the entire country. The writ of the Prime Minister ran through the length and breadth of the country. Nehru and Indira Gandhi appealed to the whole nation and not to any sectarian or caste interests. Religion played no part in the electoral process. Individual candidates stood in the shadow of the awesome personality of the Prime Minister and they got elected because of the all pervading electoral appeal of Nehruji and Indiraji. Indiraji went on to greatly centralize the decision-making process and the PMO became an all-powerful institution. All the above, I suggest, are distinctly presidential in character.

A presidential system would, I feel, elect a leader of the whole nation by the participation of the entire electorate, and such a leader will have to have a truly national appeal and a national personality. He will have to pay attention to every part of the country to get elected and regarded as a leader in whom all sections of the people can have faith. He cannot afford to be seen as promoting only the interests of a particular part of the electorate. Such an argument will also apply to the state governors directly elected by the people. The governors will have to be truly representative of the whole people of the entire state and cannot afford to pander to the interests of a particular segment of the electorate. The president can be a true symbol of the whole nation and can be a great unifying influence.

The second advantage would be in terms of stability as the president and the governors enjoy fixed tenures and one can limit the number of tenures as is the case in the United States. The present danger of chief executives of the country and the states—read prime minister and chief ministers—being voted out of power due to shifting loyalties of legislators can altogether be avoided.

Further, as in the US system, the chief executives can have the freedom to choose their team from the talent pool of the whole country and not confine themselves to the particular political party they belong to.

Doubtless, the particular alternative system that the nation may consider adopting will have to be deliberated and decided upon by the people. We adopted the British West Minster model and our experience over the last fifty odd years has shown that this model has not been able to throw up leadership, especially in recent times, quite capable of dealing with the nation's problems with the required far sightedness, that political instability is seriously hampering the nation's efforts to advance, that the system has resulted in reinforcing divisive tendencies while criminalization of politics and politicisation of criminals has taken roots in parts of the country.

It needs to be stressed that the present West Minster system evolved over nearly two centuries and the people had to fight for and earn their right to vote. It was a gradual process with the build up of sound democratic institutions, maturing of the economy and, most importantly, the attainment of universalisation of education. Universal suffrage came about along with universal education, that is when people were ready and prepared to exercise this unique privilege in an intelligent, rational and informed manner guided by national considerations. Those who came to be elected were invariably men of knowledge with significant academic achievements.

It is therefore of great importance for the country to consider most urgently a suitable modus vivendi for dealing with the ills that plague the political system. We can ill–afford continuance of a situation, where there is so much cynicism and erosion of the faith of the people in the system.

As to the civil service, I feel that the quality of the service needs to be greatly increased. Specifically, I would advocate restoration of the original position with regard to the personality test, namely, higher marks and a separate minimum. The examination system should be more rigorous oriented to recruit the right talent. There seems to be no point in doctors and veterinarians trying to get into the services. So much of the nation's resources has been spent in training them in a specific field of specialisation and little purpose is served by making them chase decoits or dealing with financial rules.

Further, after the initial years of service, officers must be enabled to specialise in specific areas of governmental activity. In the old days there used to be the finance and commerce pool. Distinguished ICS officers such as L.K. Jha, B.K. Nehru, K.B. Lall belonged to the pool where officers with suitable academic background, aptitude and potential were retained in the Central Government to grow in particular ministries dealing with, for example, external, economic and commercial relations. They did not have to revert to the states. Such a system of merit and achievement as the sole criteria can be established, both at the centre and the states. Training programmes which already exist can be more closely tailored to answer to the needs of sectoral specialisation in the system. Further, officers should be encouraged to improve their academic achievement by granting facilities to enter institutions of excellence, both within and outside the country, to do specialized research and improve their knowledge base to deal with current issues.

The other immediate reform that needs to be undertaken is to free the bureaucracy from the threat of politically motivated transfers. In the central government because of the prescribed procedural requirements and the committee system transfers are by and large free from interference and officers are assured of a reasonable tenure. The exception in recent times is with respect to the Secretary level posts where competent officers have been given short shrift. In the states with MLA's arrogating to themselves a role in the transfer of officers, the situation has indeed reached undesirable proportions. The Government of India has indeed been concerned about this situation and has repeatedly advocated giving officers a minimum of three years as tenure. It has also suggested that while the post of Chief Secretary and Director General of Police can be filled up as per wishes of the Chief Minister keeping in mind considerations of seniority and merit, all other postings and transfers should be decided by a committee of Secretaries headed by the Chief Secretary. Such a system does indeed exist in the UK where the civil service is almost completely insulated from political interference. These ideas have, unfortunately, found no takers in the states.

# 3

# IN THE CIVIL SERVICE

B.K. Nehru in his biographical *Nice Guys Come Second* has quoted a particularly cynical wit to summarize the life of a civil servant as *'BA pass kiya, nowkhari khiya, retire hua, pension liya aur mar gaya'* 'passed BA, got into service, retired, got pension and died'. While to some this may be acceptable as an adequate summation of the life of a civil servant, for me, however, it appears that this is comparable to the view taken by some of the science of statistics and by some others of the bikini where 'what has been revealed is interesting but what has been concealed is vital'. I refer particularly to the bit called *'nowkhari kiya'* because behind these two innocuous words lie a whole world of extraordinary experiences as was indeed the case with Nehru himself, who had a truly brilliant career in the ICS having held a number of high offices including that of ambassador and governor and had made original contributions in the field of economic diplomacy. Incidentally, Nehru was the Governor of Assam when I was the Deputy Commissioner in the district of Cachar and I shall refer to my experiences with him at the appropriate place in my narration.

In June 1963, as mentioned at the end of Chapter I, I became formally a member of the IAS, the first act of this being what is designated as 'joining' the service for training in the National Academy of Administration, now known as the Lal Bahadur Shastri Academy, in Mussourie in the state of Uttar Pradesh, now Uttaranchal. One had to sign what is known as the 'charge report' in triplicate, as evidence that you have indeed assumed office. Unless this all important document is executed and reaches the Accountant General and he in turn takes cognizance of this event and authorizes you to draw your pay, you may do your work but will get nothing in return. This was our first introduction to the ways of the bureaucracy. At that point of time the emoluments were a princely four hundred rupees per mensum, the same I believe the ICS were given in the nineteen twenties. More than half of this went towards your mess bill. Some time later we were granted a dearness allowance of twenty rupees per month.

The Academy was an altogether new world with a dress code, emphasis on etiquette, decorum and officer-like conduct. You were thrown in the company of some of the finest talent in the whole country coming from every state. There was a great deal of idealism in the hearts of the young men and women with a lot of pride as to their achievement. The foundation course where you worked along with members of the IFS, other All India Services and the Central Services did give room for building up a great deal of comraderie and life long friendships. A good bit of romance was naturally in the air and striking a friendship with a lady probationer was considered a distinction and was something upon which quite a few worked diligently. Three or four successful marriages came out of such efforts. One also came across visits by senior civil servants with eligible daughters in search of 'suitable boys'. The IFS at that point at least considered themselves a class apart and were distinctly snooty.

The training part was a fairly leisurely affair, with lectures meant to provide the theoretical knowledge on subjects like public administration the Constitution, the laws of the land mainly criminal and civil procedure codes, the evidence act and the penal code, and a bit of economics and history thrown in. While this was the core, a large number lectures on a wide variety of subjects such as music, art appreciation and even the *Bhagavat Gita* were also organized. An excellent library, overlooking the mountains, gave us plenty of material to browse and ponder over. Horse riding and physical training was compulsory for the IAS and the IPS officers and while quite a few enjoyed horse riding, a large number went through this part of the training as if they were being taken through the purgatory, some trying to mitigate the torture by bribing the horses with sugar cubes. The lady probationers had a particularly harrowing time, though docile horses were reserved for them. In the very first encounter with the horses one understood that the horse took no time to estimate the competence, ability to exercise control and willpower of rider and thereafter treated you with calibrated nonchalance. If the horse had little respect for your talents, it merely tolerated your presence on its back and took no notice of your commands. With difficulty one managed to stop the horse when others stopped.

The horses, no doubt, obeyed the instructor Nawal Singh, an impressive ex-army type with a formidable moustache, whose voice and commands they clearly recognized and acted upon, ignoring whatever else the chap on their backs tried to convey. When he shouted 'turret' meaning 'trot' the horse instantly obeyed without regard to the frame of mind of the unfortunate probationer precariously perched on top of the horse or preparedness on his part mentally and physically for the sudden acceleration, from walk to trot. It was quite an achievement to balance yourself on the beast for a whole hour, having realised that the beast gives a damn to you, and would gladly throw you down, as also give you a kick for good measure if you happen to fall conveniently behind him. At least one of my friends had the distinction of having been kicked by a horse even while standing in front of the horse, he having fallen low in the estimation of the horse quite early in the proceedings.

I managed to go through this trying experience with minimum damage, and even remember to have enjoyed a ride on a couple of occassions. I passed the required examination in the very first attempt an accomplishment which eluded quite a few, an examination which apart from riding the disobedient horse and making him do a variety of things, included the dangerous operation of saddling and bridling, when your chances of being kicked or bitten by an irate horse who did not like your face or the way you took liberties with his person and the more sensitive parts thereof, multiplied exponentially and the equally dangerous feat of jumping a hurdle. Quite a few flunked in these departments, the horse and the probationer failing to maintain contact through the jump, and consequently failing to cross the hurdle together. Many of us have had the ignominy of being berated by our venerable horse-riding instructor as to how we hoped to control a district, when we had, so comprehensively, failed to gain control of a mere horse.

Almost immediately after reporting for duty at the training school, all of us were whisked away for a trip of Jammu and Kashmir—our first ever trip at government expense. It was summer time and the Kashmir valley was in full bloom with tourists all over the place.

We called on the then Chief Minister Bakshi Gulam Mohammed and the Sadar-e Riyasat Karan Singh in his magnificent palace. Peace seemed to prevail at least on the surface but one did hear from the locals and the ponywallahs that they harboured great feelings of kinship towards Pakistan, religion being the great binding factor. The reputation of the government, especially with regard to rectitude in public life, did not seem to very high. Bakshi did play an important role in bringing about greater integration of the state of J&K with the Indian Union and a number of central acts were extended to the state during his period. The story goes that Bakshi agreed to the extension of the AIS act when he was on the look-out for a suitable boy for his very eligible daughter and someone mentioned to him that IAS officers were a favoured lot in this regard. He found that in J&K there were no IAS officers since the AIS act had not yet been applied to the state. He then waived off all objections to extending the act if that would give him a good son-in-law. In the event he did get Mir Nasrulla as his IAS son-in-law who worked in the Ministry of Home Affairs and ultimately became the chief secretary of J&K.

During the tour, we were taken to quite a few places in and around Srinagar and there can be no two opinions about the grandeur of natures alluring endowments on this state. Shahjahan's words 'if there is paradise on earth it is here, it is here' rang so true from everything one saw in that blessed vale.

The major component of the tour was attachment to the army formations deployed in J&K. We were taken to a place called Sambha, a brigade headquarters, and attached to a battallion. The heat was quite unbearable and one had to go through the rigours of daily physical training, visits to numerous shooting rangers where one fired all kinds of weapons, LMGs, MMGs, mortars, grenades, etc., ride in tanks and lectures in various defence related subjects. Bone chilling however was what is called 'battle inoculation' where actual conditions in battle are simulated all around with ear-splitting noise from all corners, accompanied by smoke and dust, and you consider the chances of survival extremely slim. Equally nerve-racking was the patrolling at night, when in utter darkness you walked and walked for interminable hours, not knowing whether you are going to step on a mine or going to be ambushed, and indeed whether you had strayed into Pakistani territory. We were indeed close to the border, but I am sure the Captain who made us go through this exercise knew his bearings very well.

Suddenly after we had lost all hopes of returning in one piece, somewhere around four in the morning we hit a road and were made to halt much to our relief. Some even laid themselves on the road and had a short nap. Soon enough we were bundled into a truck which arrived from nowhere out of the darkness without lights and we were brought back to our battallion head quarters.

This part of the training served the very useful purpose of familiarizing us with the way the army is organized, the way it functions with the various levels of command and control and the vital importance of close liaison between the civil administration and the army formations in terms of crisis. We also saw at first hand the very difficult conditions in which the formations had to live and be ready for combat all the while. Though at that time the Indian Army was just recovering from the debacle it had gone through with China and one heard of complaints of lack of equipment and preparedness especially for high-altitude warfare, generally speaking we found that the army was very proud of its traditions and one got the impression that the officers were competent well trained professionals, willing and able to get on with their difficult responsibilities. In later life at the district level—during the 1971 war—at the state level and in the Ministry of Defence, I had to deal with the armed forces on numerous occassions, and my experience has invariably been pleasant and professionally satisfying.

In order to get the officers acquainted with what is happening on the development front all over India as also give them an adequate exposure to the historical and cultural heritage of the country, a fairly long train journey was organized through a major part of the country called the Bharat Darshan. One had the opportunity to see very many of the 'temples of modern India' living almost entirely in the compartments of the railways for weeks together and shunted from one place to another. As part of this travel and see programme one also went through brief attachments to the Civil Defence establishment at Nagpur and Panchayat Raj Institute at Junagadh, Gujarat. Calling on national and state level leaders were also scheduled and it was during this period that we had the privilege of meeting Pandit Nehru and the then Vice President Dr Zakir Hussein. I also recall Dr Sampoornanand the respected Chief Minister of UP, who had given us tea along with his MLAs. He was not happy that we failed to mix around adequately with the MLAs. The CM of Gujarat Balwantarai

Mehta and that of Rajasthan Dr Mohanlal Sukhadia created very good impressions on our young minds.

It was also during these travels that I met my future wife. My father-in-law Shri O.K. Moorthy, who was in the Ministry of Home Affairs, managed to track me in New Delhi and whisked me away from the New Delhi railway station. He was an anthropologist of distinction and contributed a great deal in formulating policies and programmes for the welfare of tribes, scheduled castes and backward classes. He worked closely with Verrier Elwin, the anthropologist who specialized in studies relating to tribes of the North-East and Heimendorff, who had worked with great distinction among the tribes of Madhya Pradesh. Both Elwin and Heimendorff refer to my father-in-law in their published writings.

Many in the IAS and IPS displayed what appeared to my mind undue anxiety, as to the state cadre to which they will be allotted, since they were keen to work in their own home states. Getting posted to state far away from the one they came from was looked upon with considerable apprehension. I, for one, thought that to serve in one's own state would rob you of the wider and more interesting experience of dealing with people whose language, culture and social mores you could with profit learn. The whole point of entering an All India Service was to develop an all-India outlook and greatly widen your mental horizons. When eventually the state allotments were announced, there were some oohs and aahs, but these died down pretty soon.

This paved the way for teaching of the language of the state to which you were allotted. Given a fair bit of grounding in Sanskrit I had no difficulty in learning Assamese, though it was only when you actually landed in the state that you could acquire adequate proficiency in the language. One eventually found that in Assam you had to, besides Assamese, also learn Bengali and indeed pass examinations in both the languages. You were also encouraged to learn one of the tribal languages Khasi, Lushai, etc., with cash incentives. All this brought into sharp focus what a complicated state Assam was, from the administrative point of view, and how the linguistic differences could often be the cause of deep seated animosities and conflicts, even resulting in bloodshed and worse.

Mussourie, all in all, was a very memorable experience as an institutional mechanism which helps young minds to go through the process of transformation from that of a student to that of a responsible officer who will be called upon to face myriad challenges throughout his career. At least during our time, the emphasis was very much upon building character, a good value system and quite clearly to stress that you belonged to an elite corps, which commanded authority and respect all round, and it was incumbent on your part to use the authority for the greatest good of the largest number of your countrymen and women.

It is worth noting that this batch ultimately produced two cabinet secretaries, three politicians of which two were Union Ministers, twenty odd secretaries to Government of India and around fifteen chief secretaries, besides a foreign secretary and director of Central Bureau of Investigation—not a bad record for any batch. Of the two politicians, one Bhagey Govardhan has passed away and the other under a cloud with allegations of shady deals. The third, Mani Iyer, is still hoping to become a Minister.

# 4

# ASSAM

In the hot summer of 1964, we were dispatched to our various states and I took the long train journey to Guwahati in Assam, across the hot and dusty Gangetic plain where the landscape appeared to be parched and dry awaiting eagerly and thirstily for the arrival of the monsoon. The landscape dramatically changes once you reach Siliguri and, though a great deal of denudation has taken place now at that time, when the train took you through the dooars, the tea gardens and into Assam hour after hour, one was greeted by greenery all round. Thick foliage seemed to touch the tracks, and the population concentration was also very much less than that in the plains of UP and Bihar. On the northern side all along the route to the foothills of Himalayas, dominate the scene.

The word 'Assam' is derived from the word 'Ahom', which refers to the dynasty which ruled over much of Assam from about A.D. 1228 right up to 1826, when the British walked into Assam. In fact, the word Assam is regarded by some scholars as nothing but the English rendering of the native word 'acam'.

Some claim that the word means unequal or even undefeated—a reference possibly to the westward expansion of the Ahoms subjugating all the kingdoms then existing right up to the Manas river. The Ahoms also defeated the Mughals in the famous battle at Saraighat near Guwahati, thus ending the temporary occupation of a portion of western and central Assam by the Mughals. They had come right up to Goregaon, near Sibsagar, then the capital of the Ahoms.

The Ahoms entered Assam under the leadership of Chukhapa through the Patkai range of hills in far east Assam in A.D. 1228 and established a small principality by subjugating local tribals such as Morans and Barahis. The Ahoms belong to the Thai ethnic group and Chukhapa was a Prince of a Shan state in Upper Burma. The Ahoms managed to extend their rule westward steadily and in the process reduced, if not eliminated, the power of the earlier rulers, mainly the Chutiyas who controlled the north-eastern extremity of Assam, the Kacharis, who had the control of central and southern Assam and the Rajbanshis who controlled western Assam. The Ahoms also reduced the extent of the kingdom of Kamtapur, and the rulers were ultimately sent out of the present political boundaries of Assam into the Cooch Bihar area. At one time, the Kamta power covered the districts of Goalpura and Kamrup of Assam along with the Cooch Bihar and Jalpaiguri districts of West Bengal.

The Kachari kingdom, which engulfed the greater part of central and southern Assam, had to retreat in face of Ahom advances and first shifted its capital to Dimapur (now in Nagaland) and then to Maibong in north Cachar hills and ultimately to Khaspur in the district of Cachar. The term Kachari is applied to several tribes such as Bodo Kacharis, Dimasa Kacharis.

The Ahom system of administration had some very interesting features. The ultimate power rested with the king, but a variety of functions were entrusted to a hierarchy of officials, the kingdom having been divided into administrative areas called Bilats entrusted to a few nobles. A clear chain of command was established and it appears that the society was geared to wage war at short notice. The areas administered by the Ahoms enjoyed peace and order and brought under one umbrella diverse ethnic groups. Apart from political unity, a high degree of social, cultural and linguistic integration was achieved. Significantly, the Ahoms conducted a census of all males and introduced what can be termed as compulsory national service under the 'paik' system. Groups of four adult males were formed as a 'got paik' and each member had to serve the state or nobles by turn for three months each, in lieu of the state providing three acres of agricultural land free of tax. These paiks were organized into guilds and a system of leadership was introduced. A *Bora* was the leader of twenty paiks, a *Saikia* of hundred and a *Hazarika* of a thousand. A *Barua* or *Phukan* controlled over three thousand paiks.

In times of war or emergency all the paiks were liable to be called for military service.

The leaders of paiks mentioned above such as Saikia and Hazarika were called chamuwa. Above these chamuwa were higher grade officers named Baruas, Phukans, Rajkhowas, Borbarua, Borphukan and Gohain as also three ministers Buragohain, Bor Gohain and Bor patra Gohain who generally belonged to the Ahom noble families.

Some scholars have termed the paik system as a form of bonded labour. However, the system provided the necessary manpower in times of war and for carrying out public utility works in times of peace. The privileged classes such as nobles, members of the royal family, high officials, religious heads were exempt from compulsory service and were also favoured with large land grants and paiks attached to them. Some of the intermediate class of officials had to pay taxes for the right to cultivate the land enjoyed by them. In today's Assam, one finds a large number of people with names such as Barua, Saikia, etc., and these names are not confined to the Ahom community.

The title is possibly inherited from ancestors who held offices under the Ahoms. Interestingly, there was a title called Tamuli Phukan, an official in charge of the betel gardens of the king.

When the Ahoms came into Assam they carried their own religious beliefs. They, however, seem to have come under the influence of the three competing Hindu belief systems, namely, Sakhtism, Saivism and Vaishnavism. While originally the kings carried Ahom names, gradually Hindu names were adopted and the later kings of the 17th and 18th century had switched over to Hindu names such as Rama Sinha, Chakradvaja Sinha, Rudra Sinha, etc. It was Jayadhvaja Sinha who first formally embraced Hinduism getting himself initiated into Vaishnavism.

The revenue administration of the area seems to have been influenced by the Mughal methodology. Koch kings had officers with titles such as dewan, vazir, mazumdar, nawab, sikdar, gomastha, choudhry, patowari, talukdar, etc. During their brief occupation of parts of Assam the Mughals divided the area into sarkars and parganas. This system called 'pargabandhi' system was retained by the Ahoms. They divided the parganas into taluks each under a talukdar while the pargana was under a choudhari. Each taluk was further subdivided with 'lats' placed under a thakuria. A lat has several villages and had a set of functionaries as kakati (accountant), gao barik (an attendant), gomastha, a clerk cum surveyor and revenue collector. Above these were officers such as majumdar for maintaining land records and settlements of land, sikdar for collecting revenue, bujarbarua as a sort of area chief of one or more paraganas. They also possibly were responsible for maintaining public order.

The Ahom language, a branch of the Thai language, was also gradually replaced by Assamese as the court language during the reign of Pratapa Sinha.

Hinduism in various forms had been practised in Assam well before the Ahoms took control of Assam, but the bulk of the population being non-Aryan was observing localized religious beliefs. From about the twelfth century, however, with the patronage of kings and nobles Hindu beliefs started spreading all over Assam. A large number of temples are to be found all over Assam belonging to one or the other belief systems namely Sakhtism or Vaishnavism.

The most remarkable religious movement in Assam termed neo-vaishnavism, initiated by Srimantha Shankardeva in the early part of the sixteenth century, has left a permanent imprint on the social and religious life of Assam. Shankardeva was a great religious reformer, who, while basing his teachings on the *Bhagvatha Purana* and the *Bhagavat Gita,* preached a simple monotheistic Vishnu religious cult, and managed to synthesize the various belief systems being practised by different sects and tribes. Eschewing elaborate rituals, necessitating the intervention of priests, neo-vaishnavanism sought to establish a direct relationship between the devotee and the supreme being, namely Vishnu. Simple prayer services and a code of conduct for individual and social life formed part of the system. Interestingly, the new philosophy was propagated, utilizing culture-oriented media such as dance, music, drama and literature. Every village came to have an orchestral party known as *gayan bayan* and were trained practitioners of religious music. The establishment of village prayer halls 'namghars' where villagers could gather and sing hymns in praise of the lord and listen to religious discourses and a series of 'satras' or 'mutts' where religious and spiritual life was organized and encouraged, greatly helped in the spread of the neo-vaishnavite philosophy. As one travels across Assam, the *namghars* found in most villages bear testimony to the lasting influence of this great reformer and his followers who, for nearly two centuries, carried on his work with missionary zeal. Shankardeva tried to reconcile the competing belief systems, highlighting the fact that 'hari' and 'hara' are ultimately one and the same. He assimilated into the Hindu fold tribal practices prevalent in Assam, highlighting the principle that all forms of worship ultimately lead one to the highest goal. In this he was true to the spirit of the *Gita* where the Lord advises against the denigration of the beliefs of the common people and not to weaken the religious devotion of any kind (*Bhagavat Gita,* Chapter III verse 26).

The translation of a great deal of Sanskrit religious literature into the language of the people by Shankardeva himself and his followers established spiritual equality, and brought religious thought close to all sections of the people.

Shankardeva's notable disciples include Madhadeva, Damodardeva and Harideva. Nearly five hundred *satras* were established in Assam by Shankardeva and his followers and they are usually presided over by *Satradhikars.* Along with the Shankardeva's school of vaishnavism, in the latter part of the sixteenth century, the Chaitanya branch of vaishnavism also started making an impact, emphasizing as it did on pure devotion as a path to salvation.

In today's Assam all three branches of Hinduism are being practised with a large number of temples for Shiva and Shakti has also for the followers of the vaishnava traditions. The great temple at Sibsagar, with a beautiful tank, is a fine example of Shaivite architecture. The shakti cult with animal sacrifice is also fully represented with the Kamakhya temple in the Nilachal hill at Guwahati as the centre for this tradition. Human sacrifice was also practiced, though with the advent of vaishnavism, this practice has gradually died down. Durgapuja, which is observed all over Assam, continues to be an occasion for animal sacrifice practised even by the Nepalese and the tea garden tribes.

The Kamakhya temple in Guwahati with its association with Parvathi or Gowri is regarded as one of the holiest of Hindu shrines and attracts devotees from all over the country. Adishankara, the greatest exponent of advaita philosophy had designated Kamakhya as one of the nine holiest places of worship in the whole of India, and, legend has it that he had visited the place. There is a statue of Adishankara in the Kamakhya temple.

The Kamakhya temple is located in the district of Kamrup which was the ancient name of the area before the advent of the Ahoms. According to folklore this signified the place where 'kama' regained his 'rupa'. The story goes that Shiva after the death of his wife Sati carried on a penance which greatly frightened the other gods as the penance would have made him immensely more powerful than what he was. So they sent Kamadeva, the god of love, to break his penance. Shiva was indeed disturbed but having being enraged, he reduced Kamadeva to ashes. He was able to regain his forms eventually after severe efforts, in the area near the Brahmaputra and hence the name Kamrup.

I have devoted a few paragraphs to briefly describe the rich history of Assam and its age-old cultural and religious links with the rest of India in order to widen the knowledge about this part of the country, as also to draw pointed attention to the great and bewildering ethnic diversity of the region. While I have mentioned about the various kingdoms in the planes of Assam, the hills of Assam contain a variety of tribes, who going by the language spoken by them belong to the Tibeto-Burman group originating from East Asia. The Khasi language has resemblance to the Khemr language of Laos and Cambodia. The Constitution of India lists fourteen hill tribes of which the kuki have thirty-five sub-tribes. Further, this list includes nine plane tribes. The states of Meghalaya, Manipur, Mizoram, Tripura, Nagaland and Arunachal Pradesh contain a large number of tribes each speaking a different language and displaying varied cultural characteristics. Meghalaya, Nagaland and Mizoram were all parts of Assam at the time of Independence. Meghalaya has seventeen different tribes, Manipur twenty, Mizoram fourteen, Arunachal Pradesh twelve, Tripura nineteen and Nagaland fifteen.

The region had witnessed, therefore, well before the British stepped in, migration of ethnic groups both from the east and the west. The Ahoms had succeded in integrating those sub-nationalities through a strong administration, spread of the language and absorption of cultures with a composite, all-embracing, regional identity. The process did not, of course, cover several of the hill tribes, such as the war-like nagas who not only ferociously fought among themselves with head hunting, a standard practice, but repeatedly raided Ahom territory. The Ahoms built a kind of boundary wall called 'ladoigarh' which can be seen even today in the Sibsagar area of Assam. The Nagas were told in no uncertain terms that they should not cross the wall and if they do, swift retaliation would follow. The Nagas it appears got the message.

The tribal life of the North-East has very many extraordinarily interesting features. In many ways their social and economic organization is far more sophisticated and democratic than what is to be found even in the so-called forward communities in the rest of India. The system is highly egalitarian with no stratification among members of the tribe. The Mizo driver who has been driving you around the whole day expects to be treated as an equal in the evening, strumming his guitar, singing a song or two and partaking a meal. Social cohesion was of a high order, and the whole community came to aid the needy whenever and wherever required. If a man falls ill he will be carried from village to village to the nearest hospital, all villages on the way lending relay carriers. Free mixture of the sexes is quite common and women enjoy a very high status in the tribal society. Some of the tribes such as the Khasis are matriarchal, the youngest daughter inheriting the property. After marriage, it is the bridegroom who moves into the house of the wife. Women generally are more hardworking and with property being inherited by them, their economic status is often quite superior to the males. Bride burning, dowry deaths, ill-treatment of the daughter-in-law, mistreatment of widows and indeed the practice of taking dowry are unheard of in the North-East. Infanticide of girl children is also unheard of. In fact, the birth of a girl child is a joyous occasion in some tribes. Divorce is available to women without much of a hassle, and among the Khasis it is enough if the woman places her husband's shoes outside the front door for him to be declared *persona non grata,* and to marry his wife's mother if she is widowed. Widow remarriage is quite common. Though officially discouraged, many of the tribes practise *jhum* cultivation which involves slashing and burning of hill slopes as a method of clearing the forests and undergrowth and sowing paddy or the other crops. This practice was when acceptable population was sparse and land abundant the as the area deforested was abandoned after two or three crops and the village moved to another area, which allowed the deforested area to be able to recover over a period of time, given the abundant rainfall and sunshine in the area. Once population pressures increased, this cycle was shortened, leading to serious problems of soil degradation and erosion forcing the government to discourage this practice.

From the point of view of social and economic organization, however, it needs to be noted that when a land/hill slope was selected for clearing and cultivation the whole village worked on the project.

No individual parceling of land took place and ultimately the output was shared among all the villagers, according to need. Individual greed had no place in the system.

The attitudes towards many aspects of social life such as marriage, divorce, etc. were extremely liberal. It is said that when Christian missionaries started preaching the Gospel to the Mizos they were asked to worship God. The Mizos hadn't bothered about God earlier and naturally enquired as to the need for such worship. The answer was that God will pardon their sins. Now the Mizos hadn't heard of sin either, there being no word for sin in the Lushai language. The purity of mind of the Mizos and their belief systems had to be corrupted first in order to civilize them by inventing sin, about which they were totally innocent before.

Many of the tribal languages did not have a script of their own and had adopted the Roman script. The Khasi and Lushai languages are written in the Roman script while the Bodos had accepted the Assamese script. Among the Nagas rudimentary Assamese, called Nagamese, is the language for inter-tribal communication.

Christianity has spread to many parts of the North-East. Nagaland is now wholly Christian while the Khasis and Mizos have attained over 80 per cent literacy rate with women's education receiving due share. With the reservation in government jobs, many tribes have been able to get into the Central and All India Services, the Mizos benefiting the most. Compared to the tribals of central and eastern India, the tribals of the North-East, it will be observed, are educationally, socially as well as economically, far more advanced.

This brief discussion on the tribes of the North-East is once again intended to draw attention to the extremely diverse ethnic composition of the region and the consequent complexities in administering the area. During the Ahom period followed by the British, the assimilative, absorptive and, above all, accommodative process of evolution of a composite culture proceeded forward, along with strong institutions, political unification and good governance, all of which helped in maintaining order and resolution of conflicts in an impartial and evenhanded manner.

Assam possibly is the last part of the Indian sub-continent to come under the British. The Ahom power started to decline from about 1770 when what is known as the Maumaria revolt, which was basically a conflict with religious overtones between *sakta* elements and the mass-based *vaishnava* school. Added to this was the effort by the people to escape from the rigours of the 'paik' system which, as already mentioned, was a form of bonded labour. These conflicts created conditions of widespread civil strife and anarchy, causing serious economic distress among the populace. Taking advantage of the decline of Ahom power and the chaotic conditions, starting from 1816, the Burmese launched a series of invasions accompanied by large-scale violence and extreme inhuman cruelty perpetrated by the invaders.

The Ahoms, in order to avoid total liquidation, invited the British to come to their aid and with superior organization and weaponry, the British succeeded in driving the Burmese out of Assam. They then proceeded to incorporate this area into their British Indian Empire, extending their jurisdiction right upto and including the whole of Nagaland (which was not part of the Ahom kingdom) as well as all the areas of present-day Mizoram, Manipur, Tripura and Arunachal Pradesh.

Pax Britannica was introduced all over the area with uniform laws and standards of administration. Tribal customary laws were respected and in areas such as Nagaland, existing tribal institutions were more or less left intact.

The already complex ethnic diversity of the region, with a very large number of ethnic groups with their own languages, cultural mores, traditions, religious practices and systems of social and economic organizations, was further complicated during the British period, with further waves of immigration primarily from the west. That this area had long-standing links with the rest of India is well known. The *Mahabharata* refers to participation in the Kurukshetra war by an army under the leadership of Bhagadatta, which mainly consisted of *kiraatas* and *mllechas*, people of Mongoloid origin and Austroasiatics. The various royal clans ruling parts of Assam such as Kamtapuris, KochRajvanshis, Kachaaris and Ahoms were also influenced by Hindu religious thoughts and a steady flow of Hindus into the area had been going on. The pre-Ahom ruling dynasties carried names such as Pushyavarma, Stalasthamba, Brahmapala and Dharmapala and as early as 6th century A.D. Bhutivarman had encouraged the immigration of brahmins and kayasthas. Koch kings had names such as Naranarayana and Shukladhvaja and patronized both the *shakti* and *vaishnava* cults.

While the migrations from the west were small in number and

confined to certain classes of people, who generally enjoyed royal patronage, the arrival of the British introduced an altogether new dimension to the flow of people, namely, that of economics. When the British type of administration started taking root, an army of civil servants and clerks was required and the Bengalis readily answered this requirement, as they had already received the benefit of an English oriented education. The Assamese caught up, sometime later, with the establishment of colleges in the Brahmaputra valley. When tea cultivation started, this required a large number of labourers. The Assamese refused to participate in tea cultivation as they were basically self-sufficient, with enough paddy land, a pond for fishing and a loom for weaving cloth. Initially, tea cultivation was a highly hazardous operation as the land suitable for cultivation was full of jungle with an abundance of tigers, rhino, elephants, snakes, leopards, wild boar. Also the area was, and still is, highly malaria-prone and many a British planter and a large number of labourers imported from Orissa, the Santhal Parganas and even Andhra Pradesh, fell victim to this debilitating disease and to the predators. Fairly brutal practices were employed to get the labour to come over and clear the area facing all the hazards and to prevent them from running away. Today, as one travels through the Brahmaputra valley and notices lush green beautifully manicured tea gardens on both sides of the National Highway, what should be borne in mind is the heavy human cost that was involved in this endeavour.

The spread of tea cultivation and indeed the establishment of a tea industry in Assam created the need for a large number of traders, suppliers, transporters and who, but the marwaris, could fit the bill. They spread their network right into the tea gardens and gradually into the village economy of Assam. Money lending was very much part of their business and in the absence of any credit mechanism they provided the much-needed lubrication for turning the wheels of the economy. The discovery of oil and gas brought new demands for specialised skills. The marwaris today control almost the entire business operations in the area and have also bought up the tea gardens from the British.

The opening up of the countryside increased the availability of cultivable land, and from the over-populated East Bengal came Muslim immigrants. They provided cheap labour at various stages of agricultural operations, and the Assamese landowners were quite happy to obtain this type of assistance, relieving them of the burden of the more onerous operations. Active encouragement of Muslim immigration from Mymensing district of East Bengal was provided during the time of Sir Sadullah who was Chief Minister of Assam during the late 1930s and early 40s, under the 'grow more food' campaign. Lord Wavell, the then Viceroy, during a visit to Assam was forced to remark that Sadullah's programme resulted in 'grow more Musalmans than grow more food'.

Bihari labour, Nepalese and immigrants from Uttar Pradesh are all to be found in various parts of Assam, as they could get ready employment and arable land, both in short supply in their own provinces.

The North-East, and in particular Assam, is indeed a land of immigrants and today when one hears so much about 'insiders' and 'outsiders' and 'indigenous' and 'nonindigenous' people, it needs to be stressed that except for a miniscule minority, all had come into the area at one time or the other. There is, of course, nothing unique about this as in many states of India, people from outside come, live and work and become part of the cultural milieu.

This vast and continual admixture of population and cross-fertilisation of cultures has given the Assamese society a truly composite and cosmopolitan character. As a consequence, Assam has not witnessed the kind of rigidities of the caste system to be found in other parts of India. Untouchability has never been practised in the area, nor for that matter 'sati'. Illtreatment of widows is not heard of and the status of women is far superior to that in the rest of India. Female children are as valued as male children. Tolerance of other beliefs has always been very much in evidence. It would perhaps come as a surprise to many that Jyoti Prasad Agarwala, a Marwari, is regarded as a national poet of Assam. His poetry, termed Jyoti sangeet, is considered by many as the Assamese equivalent of Rabindra sangeet. It is indeed a great pleasure to listen to Jyoti sangeet, and Assamese a beautiful language with an almost feminine softness when spoken, mellifluous to the ear, was taken to great heights of poetic beauty by Jyoti Prasad. He went into raptures about the natural beauty of Assam.

When the movement against illegal immigrants started in 1979 with the All Assam Students Union (AASU) at the vanguard, the students had taken to singing Jyoti Agarwala's songs as testimony to their patriotism. It is a great pity that this accommodative process, that had been going on for a long time, has come to halt in Assam in the post-Independence era and the region has descended into a poisonous atmosphere of suspicion, animosity and conflict.

The above account of Assam's history, tracing the development of a multi-ethnic, multi-cultural, multi-linguistic and multi-religious society, in the area would serve as a useful backdrop for recounting my experiences in this fabled land.

Of course, when I landed in Guwahati, in May 1964, my knowledge on Assam was indeed minimal. All that I knew was that Assam had been described as the land of the red river and blue hills. Indeed, in the summer time the Brahmaputra, the only male river in the whole country, all others being feminine, swells to enormous proportions, floods vast areas in the plains and indeed assumes reddish colour bringing down as it does the top soil from the hills through its very long journey across the Tibetan plateau and then through the plains of Assam. The hills, because of abundant greenery, assume a distinct blue hue, especially in the evenings. The landscape is breath takingly beautiful, as in the north, the Sela range of the Himalayas dominate the scene while in the south the Khasi, Jayantia and Mikir hills rise, contributing to the formation of a long valley through which the Brahmaputra majestically flows. A large number of tributaries pour into this great river, bringing down huge quantities of water and silt during the monsoon.

Nature has been extremely benevolent to this area, endowing it with resources which include oil and gas, coal, uranium, gypsum, bauxite and a variety of forest produce—teak, plywood, cane, bamboo, etc. It has huge potential for generation of hydropower. The soil is fertile with abundant, and indeed, excessive rainfall and the area can easily be turned into a granary for supplying large quantities of food grains to the country. Assam has the world's highest concentration of tea gardens and is easily one of the largest, if not the largest, producer of high quality tea in the whole world. The area is of immense importance from the strategic point of view, bordering, as it does, China/Tibet, Myanmar, Bangladesh and Bhutan. Nepal is not very far either. The extremely sensitive Siliguri corridor extends into Assam.

When I landed in the Circuit House in Guwahati, the red river and the blue hills are objects that immediately hit your eyes. Night falls fairly quickly in the far east, even in summer. Rains and high humidity are to be taken for granted, and swarms of bloodthirsty mosquitoes of the extra large variety with excellent camouflage, night-attack capabilities along with heat-seeking and targeting capability made your life difficult leading you to take shelter inside the mosquito net as early as possible. Modern-day military aircraft designers may have learnt quite a few lessons from the mosquitoes. Apart from the mosquito net, none of the other defences seem to work in Assam. One had been warned of the possibility of malaria, and it is with considerable apprehension, one took every possible measure to avoid being stung quite painfully by these deadly creatures. Fortunately, they left you in comparative peace during the day, though an odd character, depending on how bloodthirsty he was attacked you, even during the day.

Since at that time Shillong was the capital of Assam, one went to pay calls on the senior officers and high dignitaries. Vishnu Sahay was the Governor and he gave us an excellent lunch in Raj Bhavan. He was earlier the Cabinet Secretary, with a very distinguished career in the ICS. B.P. Chaliha was the Chief Minister, a true Gandhian and a thorough gentleman. A.N. Kidwai of the ICS was the Chief Secretary, and he functioned in the true Lucknavi Nawabi style. He was extremely good to his officers, very informal, of easy access, he showed genuine concern for the good of the officers and earned the respect and loyalty of all those who worked with him.

Shillong was a lovely hill station, and had been made the capital of Assam by the British who preferred the cool hills to the heat and humidity of the plains. The Ward lake, right in the centre of Shillong, is surrounded by beautiful bungalows and manicured lawns for ministers and senior officers and one wondered if ever there would come a time to live in these luxurious surroundings. In the event with the formation of Meghalaya, with Shillong as its capital, I did not have a chance to occupy any of these houses though many of my friends did.

In the Raj Bhavan at Shillong, above the main entrance, one finds a bold inscription which reads 'My country is greater than my uncle'. For those not familiar with the history of Assam these words may sound strange but these were spoken by the famous Ahom General Lachit Borphukan who decisively defeated the Mughals at the famous battle of Saraighat near Guwahati and drove them out of Assam never to return. The Mughals had invaded Assam no less than 17 times, and had succeeded only in occupying a part of the country, and that too for a short period. In this battle, while the General was inspecting his battlements and defences, he found that his uncle who was responsible for a part of the defences had not taken measures meeting his exacting standards. He considered his uncle's conduct as prejudicial to the interests of the Ahom kingdom and though the uncle's conduct was more an act of omission than commission, Borphukan, without any hesitation, proceeded to dispatch him with the words *'deh momaithkoi dongor'*, 'my country is greater than my uncle'. We have here Assam's own version of 'Deutschland deutchland uber alles'

Back to Guwahati, after all the too brief sojourn in Shillong, the first act was to call on the Deputy Commissioner of Kamrup district. In the Academy, the deputy commissioner is built up to the status of a demi god, presiding over the lives of anything between 10 to 20 lakhs of souls, even at that time. He is responsible for everything that happens in his district: law and order, land settlement, land revenue collection, land acquisition, civil supplies, natural calamities, civil defence, elections and, indeed, quite a few development activities such as agriculture and irrigation. He represents the Government and the President in the district being the most visible symbol of the awesome majesty of law. In Assam the DC was known as *'zilar borsaheb'*.

Schooled as I was, as regards correct and proper protocol, I got in touch with my predecessor in office, M. Gopalakrishna, Assistant Commissioner and conveyed to him my desire to call on the DC. I thought that he would have notified my presence to the DC and fixed up a time for me to formally call on the great personage. Gopal asked me to come over to his office with the intention of guiding me to the DC. Being very particular to see that I observed all the requirements of the prescribed etiquette, I wore a proper summer suit, though it was very uncomfortable in the hot climate of Guwahati, carrying my calling cards and a little notebook to write down in case any words of wisdom happened to fall my way during the encounter with the DC, all part of the discipline instilled in you during the training. The DC was K.K. Phukan, an officer promoted from the Assam civil service to the IAS.

The office of the DC in Guwahati, where Gopal had his cubicle, is located along the river Brahmaputra and when I entered the building, in my finery, I was assaulted by the all-pervading smell of lime, betelnuts and betelleaves chewed by everyone present and a fair portion of the mixture along with saliva spat on the walls in particular in the corners of staircases which had been coloured almost red due to incessant splattering, by the local gentry, passing up and down. The office was a crowded place and it appears that everyone had some business or the other to transact being aided by lawyers who wore black coats.

I must have looked flustered when eventually I got into Gopal's room as he calmed me down, having correctly assessed the kind of impact the building, his surroundings and walls had on me. Gopal was quite relaxed in dress more suitable for the weather and informed me that we are to meet the DC in his bungalow. Not knowing that the DC's bungalow is as much a place of work as the office, I was a bit taken aback wondering how the DC can spend time in the bungalow during office hours.

The DC's bungalow is a large colonial structure with a wonderful view of the river. I accompanied Gopal with nervous anticipation, under the impression that a time had been allotted for the meeting. Apparently this kind of a scheduling was alien to the work culture of the DC and when I got to the verandah of the bungalow, pulling out my calling cards, I saw for the first time the DC's bungalow office partly hidden by a green screen which had been used quite liberally by all and sundry to wipe their hands to get rid of the surplus lime and betel juice sticking to their hands. Behind the screen there was a motley crowd of men occupying the chairs, busy thrusting some file or paper in front of the person sitting behind the desk, who, I presumed, was the DC. I had difficulty digesting that this indeed was the DC for the man behind the desk was wearing nothing but a vest and a lungi, the extreme of sartorial impropriety in my opinion. My opinion did not seem to matter at the moment at least and before I could get myself oriented to this unexpected situation, Gopal pushed me into the room, where somehow two chairs were vacated for us, the ACs considered superior to at least the clerks.

Though Gopal introduced me to the DC, he took no notice of me and continued to sign in a mechanical fashion the various papers thrust before his eyes. Suddenly he woke up to my presence and said that it was somewhat unfortunate that I had landed myself in Guwahati as the judiciary had been separated from the executive in the district and consequently my judicial training could suffer. I did not fully grasp the implications of these weighty words, and around me part of the motley crowd was preparing to leave, having possibly satisfied the procedural requirements prescribed by managing to get the DC's signature, when suddenly the DC deemed it proper to order for tea, possibly in honour of the newly arrived AC. This encouraged those who were preparing to depart to stay back and when eventually the tea tray arrived, several hands descended on the train, the cups vanishing all round leaving nothing for me or Gopal. A second round was ordered by the DC who possibly felt that the AC deserved a better deal and soon cups of tea were placed in front of us. I being still very conscious of etiquette would not touch the cup waiting for the DC to ask me to take the tea. Nothing of this sort happened and Gopal understanding my predicament gave me a hefty nudge into my left rib cage and told me that if I did not take the cup, either others will lunge for a second helping or the tea would get cold. I, then, proceeded to drink the tea and the DC having possibly had enough of signing the papers, leaned back and for the first time, took a closer look at me, and realising the stark contrast that my attire presented to his quite basic and rudimentary outfit thought that an explanation was in order and stated that he had a few heat boils and hence the vest and lungi outfit. The other notable individual inside the room was a Taimur who was then subdivisional officer (sadr). His wife was already in politics and rose to become Assam's Chief Minister for mercifully a brief and not very glorious innings.

Gopal indicated that we may leave and since I was in a complete daze, I followed him without realising what I was doing. A whole world built in my mind on the basis of all that I had learnt in the academy had crashed all round me. Gopal took charge of me and stated that I should not attach disproportionate importance to this divergence in perception between me and the DC with respect to etiquette and decorum, and should concentrate upon learning the job for which I was appointed, learning the language and passing all the required examinations.

Gopal had a hearty laugh at my discomfiture and related the story to quite a few officers with some embellishments and consequently I acquired a reputation for being quite British in my outlook and tastes. My accent which invited comment added to this reputation.

I was put through attachment to various branches of the DC's office, and soon, my training requirements with respect to judicial responsibilities were sorted out with the high court permitting me to do judicial work three days a week. I started with the glorious title of magistrate, third class, known in Assamese as *'poali hakim'* or child magistrate. The lawyers gave a boost to your ego by addressing you as 'your honour'. Most submissions had to start with the phrase, 'may it please your honour', a very colonial subservience. I found judicial work not only very interesting but of great help in training my mind in the fine art of weighing evidence, application of the principles of natural justice and exercising my judgement in a balanced manner to arrive at correct conclusions. In later official life, this training proved to be of immense value. It also helped me in greatly improving my knowledge of Assamese, as all the proceedings had to be conducted in that language including recording of oral evidence.

I would say, without hesitation, that I learnt a great deal more from Gopal at that stage about various aspects of administration than anyone else. He was already a role model, very organised in everything that he did, quite knowledgeable even at that stage and meticulous in dealing with official problems. He had already served in the Andhra Pradesh civil service and brought with him a value system and self confidence which was worth emulating. Even at that stage, he behaved like a senior officer and when he lifted the telephone to answer calls with the words 'assistant commissioner speaking' there was a distinct tone of authority and it is quite possible that the person at the other end of the line got the impression that he was addressing someone a shade higher than the Deputy Commissioner himself.

I soon adjusted myself to the ways of the DC and at least twice a week I used to meet him in the morning so that, without the usual hangers on, I could get his attention. He periodically did a review of the progress was making, and in the event, when it came to recording my confidential report, a document vital for my confirmation in the service, he did rate me quite high.

I had a lot of leisure and since my brother-in-law was in the NF railway at that time, I could play a lot of tennis in the beautiful floodlit courts in the Maligaon railway colony. I was still quite an eligible bachelor and I was not unaware of the fact that there were a few hearts that were aflutter in the colony trying to corner me through their parents and even directly—all part of life I suppose.

On one of my by-weekly visits to the DC's bungalow, the DC, who usually presented a picture of absolute calm seemed a little flustered, the reason being that he had to meet the Governor Vishnu

Sahay, who had come down from Shillong for a brief visit. Possibly, as a prop for him, he asked me to come with him to the Circuit House. Those days the Governors were still carrying on the British tradition of flying their own standards and when we reached the Circuit House the Governor was already in the verandah. Sahay was a very tall man, with a graceful presence and my keen eye noticed that his daughter was not far away, possibly intending to accompany the Governor wherever he was going. The DC introduced me to the Governor who immediately said that since the DCs were usually very busy, he would take me with him, so that the DC could continue to attend to his various responsibilities. I have no idea where the Governor was scheduled to go and the DC did not tell me either. In a jiffy, I found myself sitting in the car wedged between the Governor and his daughter. I thought that the pilot and the ADC would no doubt know where the Governor was headed. These stupid characters took the Governor to the Guwahati Museum, whereas he was expected in the History Department of the Cotton College to have a look at ancient historical records called buranjis, in Assamese. The Governor did ask me during the brief journey—'we are going to the buranji place, isn't it?' My knowledge on this score being limited, I kept quiet. The Museum director came out in a flurry and apologised to the Governor mentioning that he was not expecting him, as no one had informed him of the visit.

Since the entire responsibility of conducting the Governor to the right place fell squarely on my shoulders, I ran out and made some quick enquiries to find out the right destination. I got back to the Governor in double quick time and informed him of the mistake. Throughout, Sahay was not at all disturbed and behaved admirably without losing his cool. He could have easily berated me for rank incompetence and worse, and indeed reported the matter to the government and this could have had lethal consequences. It was however his daughter who deemed it proper to pull me up with 'aah, you goofed it up'. I manage to deliver the Governor in the right place very shortly, but not before word of the goof up had reached the DC and he scurried down to accompany the Governor for the last few yards. He did not want to take any more risks and kept company with the Governor for the rest of the visit. The Governor busied himself, looking at the various documents spread before his eyes for his inspection, but his daughter lost her patience very quickly and departed leaving her father behind, glancing at me with mischievous glee as she got into her car.

Assam was then just recovering from the shock of the 1962 Chinese invasion. There was a lot of apprehension as to what would happen if the Chinese decided to come down the hills again. A big programme of building roads to the border had been taken up and the presence of the armed forces in the area was being enlarged. There was in the mind of the Assamese a feeling that they had been left alone during this unfortunate period. The statement by Prime Minister Nehru in a radio broadcast that 'his heart goes out to the people of Assam' was to my mind badly misinterpreted to mean that Assam was being abandoned. A lot of adverse comments were heard on this score, quite unjustifiably, in my view.

Assam had again to face hostilities this time, in the winter of 1965 in the form of 'Operation Gibralter' launched by General Ayub Khan to grab Jammu and Kashmir. India had to cross the international frontier, opening a new front in the western sector, resulting in all-out hostilities. Suddenly, one saw anti-aircraft guns being installed and civil defence measures taken. Fortunately, nothing much happened in the eastern sector except when one day all of a sudden all the AA guns on the Brahmaputra bridge opened up targeting what was suspected to be an intruding enemy aircraft. It was a false alarm. With the Tashkent agreement, peace was restored.

Before Tashkent, however, the Prime Minister, Lal Bahadur Shastri visited Guwahati and I, as part of the DC's team, was involved in reception arrangements in the Circuit House. I was deeply impressed by Shastriji's humility, ability to communicate and accessibility to all. He had already earned the gratitude of the nation by taking the bold decision to open the new front in the Punjab–Rajasthan sector of the Indo–Pak border which was a masterstroke resulting in the total failure of Ayub Khan's nefarious intentions. His stature, at that time, was immense and people came in large numbers to give him an enthusiastic welcome at all the places he visited.

Periodic communal riots in neighbouring East Pakistan exposed Assam to a continual influx of refugees. Relief and rehabilitation consequently became a serious and substantive responsibility of the district administration. It was indeed sad to see the uprooted people housed in temporary shelters and given just the basic necessities. Many, particularly women and children, looked acutely malnourished and there was an air of despair and hopelessness. The only thing that kept them going was the fact that they enjoyed comparative safety, having faced frenzied mobs which targeted them only because of their religious persuasion. After quite a period of uncertain existence, these refugees were airlifted to Dandakaranya in Orissa, where they were given land and rehabilitated. Throughout the history of East Pakistan and even after the creation of Bangladesh, the Hindus have been victims of communal fury. At the time of Independence, East Pakistan had approximately 25 per cent Hindu population which has been progressively reduced to around 11 per cent now. The agony of this minority is so graphically and poignantly portrayed in Taslima Nasreen's *Lajja* (shame) in Bengali.

In West Pakistan, of course, having for all practical purposes eliminated religious minorities, they have now turned their attention to Islamic subsects who are considered not pure enough and hence deserve ill treatment. There is no *'lajja'* for all this in Pakistan. India's record in sharp contrast is far far superior. Yes, there have been communal riots in some areas but the population of minorities has more than trebled since Independence and empirical evidence clearly suggests that the most important minority is recording a growth rate faster than all other segments. All minorities enjoy constitutional guarantees and our secular ethos ensures that these guarantees are actually honoured, with the courts playing an important role. In a democracy where numbers matter, no political party can be seen to be anti-minority. In spite of all this, Pakistan dares to pillory us accusing us of ill treatment of minorities and we ourselves are often quite defensive on this score. Some minority organizations such as the Student Islamic Movement of India have been allowed to get away with rank anti-national statements and even anti-national activities.

My training was near completion and I faced the prospect of being posted as a sub-divisional officer. Before this happened, I got married in Delhi. That I married before the end of my period of probation raised a few eyebrows as in this period you are liable to be booted out of service. It becomes infinitely more difficult to get rid of you once you have successfully completed your probation.

More eyebrows raised and possibly to greater heights, when it was discovered that I was marrying the granddaughter of the then Governor of Kerala, V.V. Giri. As everyone knows, he became President of the country when the Congress party was going through fundamental changes. Had he not become President, Mrs Gandhi—who backed him even though he was not the official nominee of the Congress party (N. Sanjeeva Reddy was)—may not have continued to hold her office. The country's history may have been altogether different, and it is possible that the old guard would have preserved the Gandhian values better. It cannot be gain said that with the sidelining of the old guard, a new breed of younger Congressmen emerged, especially after the advent of Sanjay Gandhi, who were not schooled in Gandhian values and were far more concerned with the exercise of raw power.

Giri, however, did very much belong to the old Gandhian tradition, extremely soft spoken, always kind and considerate with not one trace of arrogance about him. In all the offices he held, he made it a point to be always accessible and endeavoured to help everyone seeking his intervention. I have seen him interrupting even his meals to meet someone with the words "I don't know what distress has brought him to my doorstep. He would not have come all the way if he was not in dire need."

My wedding was attended by President Radhakrishnan, who presented me with an autographed copy of his world-renowned work on the *Bhagavad Gita.* A whole lot of VIPs were there including the Home Secretary L.P. Singh. Years later, when I was appointed as his Secretary, while he held the office of Governor of the northeastern states, he recalled having attended a wedding.

# 5

# ASSAM–GOLAGHAT

The subdivision of Golaghat lies in what is called upper Assam and was then part of the district of Sibsagar. This has now become a fulfledged district. I was posted as Sub-Divisional Officer in the latter part of 1965, and all of a sudden, with only basic preparation, I was thrust with the responsibilities of head of an administrative unit of around 4000 square kilometres and a population of over four lakhs. Unlike other states of the country, the SDOs in Assam enjoyed administrative and at that time judicial powers, almost equal to that of the district collector. One was expected to deal with all matters, quite independently and also in most matters directly with the government. There was no requirement of having to go through either the district collector or the divisional commissioner. This arrangement had both plus and minus points: while on the one hand it made you think and act on your own and take a great deal of responsibility on your shoulders at a very early stage in your career, on the other hand due to lack of experience, you could land yourself in deep trouble.

Golaghat was basically a very peaceful subdivision. Unfortunately, in later years it had become one of the prime centres of ULFA's activities. I had the good fortune of having a good set of officers and the staff were a truly competent lot, well versed in rules and procedures. I spent the initial weeks learning from them the finer points of administering the area, touring the subdivision, inspecting the subordinate offices and interacting with the other subdivisional departmental heads. S.D. Phene was the Deputy Commissioner, an officer of outstanding ability, highly methodical and very quick in decision-making. He had a very fine value system and an exemplary code of ethics which called for absolute integrity in all dealings. He was one of those rare breed of officers who managed to preserve his ethics and value system throughout his service life, no mean achievement. It was a privilege to have worked with him and I learnt a lot from him. He guided me at the required times without giving the impression of imposing his views on any occasion.

Crisis management is part of the job of a district officer and my first brush with this area of responsibility came fairly early in my tenure with the Naga underground blowing up a compartment of a train passing through my subdivision, late one evening. I could hear the explosion right in my bungalow and was wondering what it was all about when the telephone rang informing me that not far from the subdivisional HQ an explosion had taken place in a train and the needful had to be done immediately. The call had come from the railway control room. I gathered at once whatever resources were available, police, doctors, para-medical staff, ambulances, stretchers, fire-fighting equipment and proceeded post haste to the spot of occurrence. We could reach the place within about half an hour, and since it was winter time, with the ground dry, we could get right upto the train. I ordered that train should be surrounded to protect the passengers and their possessions. I found that a third class compartment had been blown up skyward by a powerful explosive placed inside on the floor of the compartment concealed as luggage. The roof of the compartment had been ripped apart and the inside severely damaged causing several casualties and injuring many more. The force of the explosion and the fire that followed had killed and charred many hapless passengers, a few had been totally dismembered.

I faced a dilemma whether to ask all the passengers to disembark in order to search for any more explosives or to allow them to remain in the compartments to save them from exposure to the cold. The Superintendent of Police of the district, S.K. Chakravarthy, who had by this time reached the spot, firmly ruled in favour of the former course of action, as he felt that it would be entirely inadvisable to risk further casualties in case more explosives were indeed on the train. A thorough search was conducted and one more box containing explosives was found in another compartment. Fortunately, it had failed to explode.

The medical team attended to the wounded and sent off the more serious cases to the nearby hospitals. The dead were taken to the morgue in Golaghat for identification by the relatives. Fortunately, only one compartment had been damaged and I was anxious to see that the passengers, whose journey had been so violently interrupted, were enabled to continue their journey and reach their destinations. Also, through traffic had to be restored at the earliest, as the railway line was a vital blood line for essential supplies to the whole of upper Assam and neighbouring areas, and for the movement of defence personnel. The railways took over this responsibility with the GM, NF railway himself reaching the spot by midmorning.

I sent a detailed report to the government advocating introduction of checking all passenger luggage along the route not only with respect to the railways but also buses.

This violent introduction to the 'Naga Problem' made me take immediate interest in the security situation on the border with the state of Nagaland. Nagaland had become a part of British India by the middle of the nineteenth century and was administered as a district of the state of Assam. The Naga tribes of some twenty odd separate ethnic entities were fiercely independent, and apart from continuous inter-tribal warfare, had the nasty habit of perpetrating violence on the inhabitants of neighbouring areas. The British responded to this kind of violence with punitive expeditions and subdued the tribes. They also converted them to Christianity.

When Independence dawned, the Nagas did not want to be part of India and an armed rebellion was launched. The Indian Army had to be deployed to deal with the situation. After protracted negotiations with representative elements the Central Government decided to grant statehood to the Nagas as a way of satisfying their political aspirations, while preserving their separate ethnic identity.

This step forward of making the erstwhile Naga hills district of Assam into a full fledged state of the Indian Union did satisfy a substantive segment of the population. However, the demand for independence did not die down. Zapu Phizo, a firebrand Naga leader and an impressive orator who could speak several Naga tribal languages, organized an underground movement launching a guerilla war. Assistance was sought and obtained from the Chinese in substantive measure. The Nagas were told by Phizo that before the British takeover, they had never been part of India and their civilizational characteristics are distinctly different from that of the Indians.

I shall deal with this issue in greater detail in a subsequent chapter on internal security, but as Sub-Divisional Officer of Golaghat my immediate concern was to safeguard the lives and property of the villagers along the interstate border. I toured the area and visited all the border outposts established and manned by the Assam armed police battalions, for the purpose of ensuring the safety of the villagers from the depredations of the Nagas.

The problem I found was twofold. One related to the activities of the underground which had constituted itself into the so-called Naga Federal Government with its own parliament or council, called the 'Tatar Hoho', which indulged in harassing the villagers and forcible collection of levies. Officers of this set-up were active in the area. I have seen their tour reports, submitted in duplicate, very bureaucratic! The other was the claims of the official Nagaland government to large areas of Assam including reserve forests along the border. At the time of the constitution of the state of Nagaland, it had been clearly notified that the boundaries of the new state will be the same as that of the erstwhile Naga hills district of Assam. The Nagaland government, however, refused to accept this position and laid claim to large areas of not only Assam but also of Manipur and Arunachal Pradesh. This dispute was adjudicated upon by a commission appointed by the Government of India under the chairmanship of K.V.K. Sundaram, and, since the report rejected the Naga claims it has never been made public.

The ground level problem for me was the repeated efforts by the agencies of the Nagaland government to encroach upon Assam's territory and erect buildings for something or the other. I asked the border outposts to keep strict watch on this front and report to me at the very first instance any attempt to erect structures. At least on two occasions I personally went down to the border, dismantled the partly erected structures, seized and confiscated the materials and brought these along. I immediately notified the government of my actions. Loud protests were lodged by the Nagaland government to both the Assam government and the Centre.

Apart from the problem of floods in the summer time and an occasional calamity such as a fire in the bazaar area of the subdivisional HQ, life in general was peaceful. I found myself quite busy with judicial work as, in this district the judiciary had not as yet been separated from the executive, and as a Magistrate first class it was interesting to deal with 'committal proceedings' which is part of the process of trial of serious cases of crime such as murders. Violent crime was rare and took place mainly in the tea garden areas during drinking bouts. Kidnappings happened more often and, given the fairly liberal attitudes in the society, the girl or even the parents raised fewer objections than an aggrieved relative, who had possibly his own designs regarding the girl.

I had my brush with the student community during this time who even those days considered themselves not subject to ordinary rules of law. They conducted themselves as self-appointed guardians of the society's interests and conscience and felt entitled to go on one agitation or the other. The political parties had started to use them for their own ends.

All this was quite strange to me, schooled as I was in the discipline of a Jesuit institution, where our only interests were the lecture hall, the library and the tennis court, and politics, if at all confined to debating clubs and agitations, could not even be dreamed of. My opinion of the students had suffered when the local college had invited me for the college week as the chief guest and I was quite annoyed when the function started five hours late.

When, because of drought in several parts of the country, the prices of foodgrains started showing an upward trend, the students of Assam started a statewide agitation. In Golaghat the students attributed the rise in prices to hoarding and black marketing by the traders, the Marwaris—regarded as undesirable 'outsiders'—and wanted to raid their godowns. This I could not permit. I had myself directed the staff dealing with civil supplies to inspect all the godowns, but the students were not satisfied alleging collusion between the traders and the supply staff. This allegation was not altogether without foundation. The answer was more intensive supervision, which I organized, but trained as I was with respect to observance of the provisions of law in all governmental actions, I could not countenance students going around checking godowns. I belonged to the school which believed that the students were supposed to study and pass examinations. In one or two districts, the Deputy Commissioners had got the students involved as witnesses. Strictly speaking, this was outside the framework of law but this measure helped in avoiding student unrest. I had not yet got used to the idea that the students of the North-East were an altogether different kettle of fish demanding and obtaining roles which had nothing to do with studies, but with regard to a whole lot of issues which had strong political overtones. Some students even then had clear political ambitions.

In the event of considerable build-up of tension, I had to promulgate orders under section 144 of the CrPC, make quite a few arrests, order a lathi charge and bring the agitation under control. I was indeed unpopular with the students and they boycotted the Independence Day parade where I was taking the salute. My whole effort was to uphold the law and my Deputy Commissioner fully supported me.

Life, apart from these infrequent but interesting diversions, was pleasant indeed and did not, it appears differ very much from what would have been the case when the British were there. We still carried a lot of the vestiges of colonial rule. The representatives of the people, the MLAs of Golaghat were gentlemen to the core, meeting you on occasion, to make an odd request or two. They never interfered with the workings of the administration and indeed volunteered to help you, on and off. One had a fine bungalow, a good set of servants and all the authority given by law to get on with one's job. What is important was the fact that one had all the freedom to exercise the authority given by law without any undue interference from the government or the politicians. With communications quite primitive, the state headquarters hardly bothered you. The police wireless telegraphy was the quickest method of communication and this was used primarily to report about events that had gone by and the steps already taken to overcome a particular situation or problem. I do not recall a single occasion where I asked for instruction from my superiors as to the manner in which a particular problem was to be dealt with.

Golaghat had a large number of tea gardens and, it appeared to me that, the remnants of the British Raj were very much alive and vigorously kicking in these very picturesque places. A large number of gardens were still in British hands carrying names such as Williamson Magor, Goodricke, etc., and so there were a generous sprinkling of British managers who seemed to carry on, as if nothing very much has changed as far as their way of life concerned. Polo in the Dhansiri Club, tennis in the various garden clubs on beautifully maintained lawn courts, open air garden parties, an occasional game of cricket in the cold season, horse riding, innumerable well-trained servants in impeccable uniforms and white gloves taking care of everything in the large airy bungalows set in the midst of well-tended gardens, surrounded by manicured tea bushes and shade trees as far as the eye can see, were all very much in evidence in Golaghat. Yes, tiger shooting, pig sticking and fox hunting, which were part of life earlier, had gone out of fashion. In their eyes, the SDO and the Deputy Commissioner still occupied the position they had prior to Independence and were treated with due deference. I did play a good deal of tennis in the tea clubs during the weekends.

Labour unrest was rare and there was only one occasion when I had to spend a while in a tea garden with some police force to deal with any contingency, when.a strike was called which lasted for not more than two days. The tea labour had been brought from all over India and fairly well organized, the trade unions taking good care to get a series of benefits such as fair wages, rudimentary housing, basic healthcare, education for the children and some cultivable land and in some cases even fuel. This, however, is a comparatively recent phenomenon, especially after Independence. The earlier lot of labourers had to undergo untold sufferings due to malaria, difficult climate and wild animals. There is no count of the lives lost in the process. No doubt, the British planters of that period had to go through the same vicissitudes and many a life was lost whilst still very young.

Tea cultivation and processing are labour intensive, involving plucking of the green leaves at the right time, allowing the moisture to evaporate in large airy multilayered withering sheds, gently grinding the leaves to release the juices, allowing the ground leaves to ferment for a few hours and thereafter fire the leaves in specially designed ovens to arrest the fermentation. The end product is the all-too-familiar brown tea consumed all over the world. Before packing, the tea is graded into leaf grades, broken grades and dust categories. The leaf grades fetch higher prices and the best varieties contain the tips or buds, and are known by the colourful names tippy, golden, flowery, orange, pekoe no1, no2, etc.

Often, as the gardens and indeed many villages were quite near the reserve forests inhabited by wild elephants, raids by the mammoth creatures resulting in the destruction of houses and even loss of life were quite frequent. If a herd had during such raids happened to taste the rice brew, prepared by the villagers one could be sure of a return visit. A good deal of noise was usually made on such occasions with demands for compensation and permanent measures to drive away the elephants. The fact that humans had encroached upon elephant territory was not stressed upon. Elephants and trees have no votes.

The world-renowned Kaziranga National Park, which is the habitat of the 'Great Indian one-horned rhinocerous' was within my jurisdiction. Trained elephants take you into the park. Once when due to poaching a rhino had been killed, I had to go deep into the jungle to conduct an on-the-spot enquiry and prepare a report for the government. I could start on my journey to the spot where the rhino was lying deep in the jungle only around 2 pm and could reach the place around 5.30 pm, when darkness was descending. It took about an hour and a half to get all the details and complete the enquiry and since the return journey was through the dense forests we had just traversed, I was quite apprehensive as to how we will get back without getting lost or getting mauled by any of the predators known to reside in the area. The forest officers who had accompanied me however showed no concerns of nature, as they knew that the elephants had an excellent sense of direction and would without fail reach us back to the very spot from which we had started. Though the journey took a bit longer through complete darkness and thick jungle all round, the three elephants merrily walked along at a leisurely pace and without any problem reached us to the place from which we had started that afternoon. Of course, the elephants showed no inclination to interrupt at any stage their propensity to consume the variety of plants and vegetation so abundantly available within easy reach of their eminently elastic trunk. From the elephants' point of view the trip would have been, I am sure, quite enjoyable and rewarding.

Poaching of rhinos is a serious problem, as for some strange reason the horn of the rhino is considered an aphrodizlac by the Chinese. It has been scientifically established that the horn is nothing but a clump of hair, which serves as a defensive and offensive weapon for the rhino. The belief however persists and the horn continues to command a high price, making it worthwhile for poachers and smugglers to risk killing the rhino.

Somewhere midway during my tenure as SDO, Lal Bahadur Shastri, who had gone to Tashkent for negotiations with General Ayub Khan in the aftermath of the Indo–Pak war of 1965 unexpectedly passed away. I immediately took the measures required to be taken on such occasions as per standing instructions. While I was sitting in my office awaiting implementation of all these measures, the manager of the State Bank of India walked in and said that while he was taking steps to close the bank, he found a large number of villagers had come from far away places with cheques issued to them against paddy procured from them under government's own purchasing programme, and if their cheques are not paid they would be put to a great deal of inconvenience. The villagers had no way of knowing that the Prime Minister had died and the banks would not function when they started their journeys early in the morning. The manager indicated that if I allowed the bank to function for a couple of hours as an exception the villagers' problem will be solved. He assured me that no other transaction will be undertaken.

Since this was an eminently reasonable request I readily agreed, and the villagers got their money. I do not know in what twisted and distorted fashion this act of mine was reported by mischievous elements to the government, as a few days later I got from the government what in official parlance is known as a ' bamboo', stating that my action, though for understandable reasons, amounted to disrespect to the memory of the late Prime Minister. I was cautioned against such 'misguided enthusiasm'. The government had not bothered to ask for my side of the story or even a report from my immediate superior, the Deputy Commissioner, before reprimanding me. My representation against this step was ignored. To this day, I hold that I did nothing wrong, and I had shown no disrespect to the late Prime Minister or any one else.

Golaghat also saw me conducting, for the first time, a general election. This is a massive administrative and management exercise, involving definition of goals, mobilization and rational allocation of resources, training and deployment of personnel, arranging for transportation on a large scale, setting milestones, supervision and monitoring of progress, maintenance of law and order, and submission of various reports, the entire effort designed to ensure free and fair poll. The Election Commission has, over the years based on experience during each poll, laid down a very detailed drill for the conduct of elections and if the instructions are scrupulously followed nothing really can go wrong. I assumed the very dignified appellation of District Election Officer and Returning Officer and without me formaly declaring the results, after completion of poll and signing of the prescribed certificate, the MLAs and MPs cannot take their oaths of office. Though it was the very first of my many experiences in the conduct of the polls, the entire affair went through without a single hitch. The really tricky part in a state like Assam at that time with poor road communication system was to ensure that all the ballot boxes with votes cast inside them, were brought back safely to the subdivisional headquarters at the end of the day, from all the polling stations, spread throughout the subdivision, including some really remote and hilly areas. I had to spend a good seven or eight hours, after the completion of the poll, in a state of great tension, until the last of the ballot boxes had reached safely and these were locked up in the presence of the contesting candidates or their agents, and armed guards posted.

One other distinguishing feature of the subdivision of Golaghat is the fact that largest river island of the world—Majuli—is part of this administrative unit. It was administered as a revenue circle by a sub deputy collector, the equivalent of a taluk in the rest of India. One had to reach this island by crossing the river Brahmaputra, and while the area is relatively dry during winter, the whole place gets submerged throughout the monsoon period. Travel by boat is all that is possible. The residents, I found, were quite used to this, reaping a rich harvest of fish all the time. The famous Kamalabari Satra is located on this island.

# 6

# DEPUTY COMMISSIONER, CACHAR

I left the Golaghat subdivision in 1967 and, as is the practice, got a posting in the state headquarters Shillong in the revenue and forest department. This helped me learn the procedures involved in decision-making at the governmental level. I had the privilege of working with J.N. Das, a father figure, an embodiment of kindness and consideration, always smiling, ever mindful of observing the correct procedures and a great and patient teacher. He was an acknowledged authority on revenue law.

Acute housing shortage in Shillong compelled junior characters like me to hire private accommodation at heavy rents. Making both ends meet was a real struggle. Shillong gets very cold in winter and lighting a fire is unavoidable if you want to keep yourself reasonably warm, especially in the evenings. But we could afford to buy the fuel—mainly coal—for only the first fortnight of the month. After about six months of such difficult existence the Chief Secretary was kind enough to give us a government house named 'ekanth cottage' overlooking the Shillong racecourse, called the polo grounds, and the golf course. The racecourse was but a poor imitation of the grand courses of Bombay or Calcutta, with only a few local ponies, of indifferent pedigree, taking part. They were very temperamental and would often refuse to obey their riders and even abandon the course, if they found anything more attractive outside. Our resources, of course, did not permit us to go anywhere near the races.

Life however became a little more comfortable as one had to pay less than fifty per cent of the rent paid for the private house. My wife, who had borne all the privations with fortitude, was greatly relieved.

Much to my surprise my name was sent for a Ford Foundation fellowship, sponsored by the Calcutta Metropolitan Planning Organization (CMPO) for a one year course in metropolitan and regional planning. I was selected after an interview by a few Americans who were part of the Ford Foundation. This was prior to the Marxist takeover of West Bengal and when the takeover took place the Americans were sent packing. The great attraction of this course was the promised world tour, ostensibly to obtain exposure to the experience of advanced countries with respect to urban planning, all paid for by the Americans.

Six months were spent in Calcutta, studying the nightmarish urban problems of the city, the impossible imbalance between demand and supply of every basic civic amenity, the congestion, poverty and squalor in the large and innumerable slums, the urban decay, the near breakdown conditions of urban transport, the several municipalities all waging turf wars, the ever-increasing population and the meagre, if any, investment to tackle effectively these problems. Dr B.C. Roy, the urbane learned and farsighted Chief Minister, had got the Ford Foundation involved in preparing a concerted plan for tackling the growing problems. The idea was to vastly improve the state of civic amenities in Calcutta, while creating satellite towns in an effort to decongest the city. Haldia as a new port city, Kalyani as a new township development of Durgapur, Asansol and Siliguri as counter magnets were all to be taken up. A new bridge across the Hooghly was also planned. At that time, West Bengal was one of the more industrialized states with jute, engineering and tea as major contributors. It had a good seaport, though even here problems had started making themselves felt.

All plans require money and political will. After Dr B.C. Roy, both have been in short supply and West Bengal has gone into a steep decline and today ranks low in the order of industrial and social development. With the emergence of militant trade unionism industries have been driven out and Calcutta's problems have remained largely unattended. Except the second Howrah bridge and the metro, no major project to ameliorate the city's woes have been undertaken while the quality of life has continuously declined—one more case where winning elections is not contingent upon performance.

After studying all aspects of the pathetic state of affairs in Calcutta the six-month period spent overseas, when I saw city after city in Europe and the Middle-East thriving, having made massive investments in infrastructure, urban transportation and housing, with standards of living and quality of life of a very high order, the experience made me sad and angry. Right policies can still bring about substantial improvement in the situation. Patrick Moynihan, who at one time was the US ambassador to India, pointed out that at the end of World War II there were three great urban settlements in the Orient—Singapore, Calcutta and Rangoon. Singapore followed the right policies and is where it is today. The other two are not even pale shadows of their glorious past, entirely due to wrong policies.

This interlude greatly expanded my mind where, apart from travelling all over Europe right upto Scandinavia, I could undergo short courses in the London School of Economics, The Institute of Social Studies in The Hague, Netherlands, the Middle East Technical University at Ankara, Turkey and the Doxiades Associates in Athens, Greece. Almost a month was also spent in Yugoslavia studying the Tito model of communism which operated on the principle of greater autonomy for the enterprises.

By late 1969, I was posted as the Deputy Commissioner (DC) of the district of Cachar in southern Assam. Cachar was regarded as one of the most difficult districts to manage, with the population divided almost equally between Hindus and Muslims, prone to communal riots, heavily populated and, most importantly, with a long and troublesome border with the former East Pakistan, now Bangladesh. This district was part of the Surma valley division of Assam before the partition along with the district of Sylhet which is now in Bangladesh. It has the North Cachar hills and the Jaintia hills in the north, the Manipur hills in the east and the Mizo hills and the state of Tripura in the south. This bowl-like structure, a gigantic amphitheatre as it were, opens up into the Sylhet district and to the plains of Bangladesh on the western side. Sylhet, which had a large Hindu population, became a part of Pakistan on the basis of a referendum by a very narrow margin. On the day of Independence, since it was not yet known if Sylhet would be part of India or Pakistan, the Indian flag was hoisted in the district and subdivisional headquarters, only to be replaced by the flag of Pakistan a few days later. Distinguished civil servants like Sir B.N. Rao, who later became one of the architects of our Constitution, had administered this district as a member of the

Assam ICS cadre.

The language spoken in Cachar is the same as that in Sylhet, called Sylheti, a modified form of the Bengali language. I could however get away with my very bookish Bengali.

The district had over twenty-four lakh people, even in 1971 when the census was taken, packed into an area of around six thousand sq kms. The population has exceeded thirty lakh now. The towns contained most of the Hindu population while the villages were inhabited overwhelmingly by Muslims except where there were tea gardens. There were several tea gardens, nowhere in comparison to the scale and beauty of the gardens of the Assam valley and the tea produced was also quite inferior in quality. Nevertheless, the gardens did make a significant contribution to the mainly agrarian economy of the district.

I found the transport situation I found to be the proverbial 'Achilles heel' of the district. There was only a single metre gauge railway line which connected the district with the rest of the country. This went through the northern hills and was frequently prone to disruption. This was supplemented by a narrow road, hugging the hills, even more unreliable than the rail link. Through these two arteries had to be transported all the requirements of not only my district but also that for Tripura, Mizoram and part of Manipur. All through the rainy season these links can snap at any time. Consequently I had to keep a nervous eye on this front monitoring the stock situation regarding essential supplies including petrol and diesel almost on a daily basis. There was an airlink but this was mainly for passenger traffic. The airport actually belonged to the airforce.

The Mizo insurgency had not yet been fully controlled, and along this border the villages were vulnerable to the activities of these insurgents. The Naga insurgents were also active along the northern side, using the thick jungles to get across to East Pakistan from where they were able to get weaponry quite freely. These groups could also disrupt communications by sabotage.

The economic condition of the people of Cachar was poorer compared to that of the Assam valley primarily because the land area could not support the burgeoning population, and the economy was not growing and diversifying. Except for tea, there was no industry worth mentioning. The per-capita land availability was low and declining, and standard of nutrition was poor. Repeated communal riots in East Pakistan brought in waves of refugees. Realizing the need to increase foodgrain production, Cachar was granted the Intensive Agricultural Development Programme (IADP), where fertilizers, pesticides, scientific agricultural practices and irrigation were applied in a coordinated manner as a package. Farm yields showed increases but were quickly swallowed up by the increase in population. Dependence upon supplies from outside the district kept increasing. Malthus would have been impressed by the way his theories were being validated in this place.

The Hindus were better educated, and the number of educated unemployed kept multiplying. The only possible area of employment was the government, and there was hardly a day when I did not have to meet people asking for jobs.

Another problem with the district was also that the people faced an identity crisis, not knowing where they reall, belonged especially after the partition. Before the partition with the combined strength of the Cachar and Sylhet districts, the people of the area had a substantial say in the affairs of the state, commanding tangible political clout. Partition drastically reduced their representation in the political set-up. Further, the economic outlets to East Bengal and then on to the rest of India were suddenly closed. The British had favoured the educated class from this area to work in the government offices but with the growth in education among the Assamese there was stiff competition and indeed the Assamese viewed the Bengalis as a threat to their employment prospects. Anti-Bengali disturbances in the Brahmaputra valley can be attributed partly to this perceived threat posed by the educated Bengali.

After Independence the emphasis on Assamese as the official language and the emerging xenophobia of the Assamese placed the people of Cachar at a disadvantage. The Assamese tended to emphasize more the differences between their language and Bengali though both have the same script, similar grammar, same numerology and have Sanskrit as the base. Culturally as well, though heavily influenced by Bengal, the Assamese tended to lay increasing emphasis on the differences. The Bengali was regarded as an agent of cultural imperialism, and by the late seventies of left extremism.

The Cachar Bengalis, no doubt, felt closer to East Bengal and by extension to the rest of Bengal through language, cultural and religious practices, poetry, music, etc. Rabindra Sangeet worship of

Kali and Durga and the practice of Sakti cult dominated the scene.

To be sure, Cachar was never part of the Ahom kingdom. This area was ruled by the Kachari kings who, in the face of the Ahom advance, retreated from their capital at Dimapur (now in Nagaland) first to Maibong in the North Cachar district and, ultimately, to Khaspur in the Cachar district. Heavy migration from East Bengal has also fashioned the character of the population to be distinctly different from that in the Assam valley.

These accidents of history have thrown the people of Cachar into the political lap of Assam while culturally and linguistically their affinity is so much more to Bengal. Consequently, Assam treats Cachar as a poor cousin. The Congress party is a binding factor, ensuring a degree of fairplay, but with the rise of regional parties advocating Assamese identity if not chauvinism things have become more difficult. The most visible manifestation of this is the lack of development in the district, impoverishment of the people and serious lack of employment opportunities. Thoughts relating to gainful exploitation of the district's resources and mitigating the unemployment problem have been articulated sporadically and indeed have received sympathetic consideration from the central government. Consequently, apart from a medical college, the district has seen the establishment of a regional engineering college, a central university, a sugar mill and a paper mill. No private investment, however, has made its way here and it will be of advantage to exploit the water resources and the gas reserves for the diversification of the economy.

Some have articulated the view that Cachar should be merged with Tripura, where the population is now predominantly Bengali, most of whom have come as refugees after the partition. This can solve the problem of identity as also improve the economy of the region but this solution is not favoured by the Muslims of Cachar. The uneasy relationship of the Cacharis with the rest of Assam therefore continues.

With all the above-mentioned factors, economic, political, ethnic and religious in full play, one thing that was not in short supply was trouble of every character. On top of all this at my time the Congress party which ruled the state was vertically divided in the district. Moinul Haq Choudhry, a dynamic personality, with considerable following in the district was out of favour with the state Congress, as he was suspected of practising communal politics. He was an MP and became a Minister in Mrs Gandhi's cabinet. His opponents, patronized by the state Chief Minister, were represented in the district by Altaf Hussein Majumdar, a Minister of the state cabinet. The district administration had to be extremely wary in such a situation where every action was viewed with suspicion by one faction or the other, and each faction wanted the administration to favour it and harm the other. I maintained strict neutrality between the two factions but even the showing of ordinary courtesies, as per protocol requirements to a Central Minister, was often mistaken and mischievous reports conveyed to the Chief Minister. The local Congressmen played both sides of the game as they were averse to taking any risks. It was amusing to see their genuflections before the Central Minister and before the Chief Minister on their frequent visits to the district. Touching the feet is a common practice in the area and the same set of characters would do this to the Central Minister with exaggerated reverence claiming *'sir aami aaponar padadhuli khawarjonye aaschi'*–an expression of extreme humility meaning bowing down and consuming the dust of the feet of the person venerated. A little later the same performance will be repeated with the same exaggerated reverence before the Chief Minister. The Superintendent of Police (SP) Subramaniam and I used to wonder as to the amount of damage they were doing to their digestive systems by such repeated consumption of *'padadhuli'*

The general public, while generally submissive, were at the same time very emotional, prone to fly off the handle quite easily. Agitations and slogan shouting were easy to organize, given the level of unemployment and with the severe tensions beneath the superficially calm surface trouble seemed to be round the corner all the while calling for vigilance of a high order.

As I settled down to my job and learnt more and more of my volatile district, I realised that I was really sitting on a simmering cauldron of dissatisfaction and potential conflicts, which was prone to, reach boiling point, without much warning. The lid of the cauldron had to be kept in place quite firmly and coolants poured periodically in order to keep the temperature under control.

Fortunately, I had three competent Superintendents of Police-during my twenty-six month tenure and a good set of magistrates and police officers. The DSP—Special Branch Sen was an absolute wizard who, while sitting seemingly idle in the verandah of his house, knew well in advance what was happening all over the district, what plots were being hatched and by whom and where and what kind of trouble can be expected.

My first SP was Madan Ram Choudhry, a senior and experienced officer. A huge man whose very appearance was enough to instil a degree of fear in the mind of potential trouble makers. He was deeply into the 'shakta' cult and was consorting with some tantrics in the district. He was busy building a Kali temple where he had installed a 'shakta' priest who was possibly an accomplished tantric. Though this side of his personality did not, in any way, impact on his competence and performance as an SP, nevertheless, I thought that such a pursuit was somewhat unusual to say the least. He also had great faith in the efficacy of various precious and semi-precious stones, and was invariably wearing an array of rings on his fingers. Since different stones had different influences, he would wear different rings to deal with different situations, or alter the combinations. While dealing with law and order situations in particular, he was careful in choosing the right stones and take time to ensure that he had the right combination. Since generally he was successful in dealing with situations of this nature, I suppose the stones did have a role to play. The experience seemed to only reinforce his faith in the efficacy of the stones and their influence on his adversaries, all in all quite a colourful personality. He rose to the rank of DGP of Assam later in life.

He was followed by S.V. Subramaniam, a sober, correct and disciplined officer along with whom I dealt with a number of difficult situations. Sonowal again a very collected, calm, and too mild an officer succeeded Subramaniam.

The advantage with Subramaniam was that all secret conversation could be carried on in Tamil between us with eavesdroppers left clueless.

Maintenance of law and order was a major, almost daily concern. I attached great value to there being a perfect equation between the DC and the SP and instantaneous action at the very first sign of trouble. I intended conveying a message to all concerned that effective action will be taken against trouble makers, while the administration will be absolutely evenhanded in all its dealings. I was particularly sensitive to communal trouble and exercised great vigilance on this front. At the district HQ and the two subdivisions we managed to organize small rapid action forces which could take off for the troubled spot at very short notice. It was essential, I felt, to convey an impression of strength and resolve all round so that no one had the courage to take liberties with law. Fortunately, those days there was absolute freedom to act, as per law and no one including the local politicians interfered in this sphere of governance. Consequently, during my tenure except once no communal trouble occurred and even the other law and order situations could be dealt with effectively with no damage to life or property. I had asked my subdivisional officers at Karimganj and Hailakandi to create and convey the same message of strength and determination.

The Divisional Commissioner was my immediate superior and since he wrote my annual confidential reports it was incumbent on my part to keep him in good humour. On most matters, I had the authority to deal directly with the government, keeping the commissioner informed of all important matters. The commissioners, however, came to the district frequently for inspection. The officers, under whom I served, allowed me all the operational freedom I needed, and from the government as well there was seldom any interference. The initiative squarely was on my shoulders and problems had to be solved on the spot. This experience greatly sharpened my wit, judgement, as well as decision-making powers. Given the nature and variety of the problems I had to deal with, and the tendency on the part of the people to get agitated as well as the fractured nature of the local politics, I had to finely balance considerations of speed with exercise of due caution in all matters. I may have committed a blunder or two but overall, I was very much in command.

The local politicians were different from the mild and helpful kind that I had dealt with in Golaghat and tended to worry you quite often trying to influence the DC to take courses of action which would further their political objectives. In fairness it must be said that they observed certain limits even here, but I had no hesitation in taking an independent stand and invariably stood my ground. I was not, therefore, popular with this breed who, periodically, complained against me to the Chief Minister. I had the support of my Commissioner and the Chief Secretary and hence was quite safe.

It appeared to me that, given the state of communication and the structure of administration, my position was not far different from those colonial administrators, so vividly described by Somerset Maugham who, in his writings, talks of the Malay East Indies where island administrators acted independently to attend to the various problems of the locals, be it disease, food shortages or disputes with an impartial and even hand, his only contact with the external world being the weekly boat, which brought in mail and supplies. European rubber planters were possibly the equivalent of Assam tea planters.

I attached great importance to accessibility of the general public to the head of the district as, I believed, if a man is given a hearing even if his problem is not solved, he refrains from agitational postures. To be sure, over fifty per cent of the people who came had problems which were difficult to resolve, such as demands for land, employment, etc., which were in such extreme short supply.

From around eight in the morning on all days, including holidays and Sundays unless I had to be away on tour I received the people providing them an opportunity to air their grievances and place their demands, for nearly two hours. A good portion of the problems such as requests for various permits, land disputes, grant of building material, and such controlled commodities could be dealt with in these meetings. I made it a point to be in my office known still as the DC's court—exactly at 10 a.m. so that the others observe the office timings scrupulously, and in the office as well while attending to various matters the general public had access to me. I took about an hour off for tennis in the evening, three or four times a week, but sat in the bungalow office till around 9 p.m. for disposing the files, which poured in daily. This intensive interaction with the public enabled me to keep my ears close to the ground and hear all the rumblings in the entire district.

Except for the floods and an occasional tension in one part of the district or the other, the first part of 1970 passed off quite peacefully. Suddenly, one day in the month of August the local Indian Airlines office informed me that their regular afternoon flight to Guwahati—a Fokker friendship aircraft—which had taken off on time had not reached its destination even though twice the journey time had expired. The plane had ceased contact with the tower of the Silchar airport fifteen minutes after take off. The worst was feared and the problem, as usual with all the problems of the district, landed squarely on my lap. It was monsoon time and with very cloudy skies aerial search was not immediately possible. I, nevertheless, alerted the airforce and having ascertained the normal flight path, organized ground search parties, all along the northern boundary of the district. I also alerted all the police stations and para-military posts in the area.

I set up a control room for keeping in touch with all concerned and kept myself ready to deal with any eventuality. I hardly slept that night, worrying myself about the fate of the passengers, most of whom were from Silchar. The relatives of the passengers gave me no peace, demanding immediate location of the plane. The airlines conveniently receded into the background.

Nothing could be found the next day either in spite of sorties by the airforce and intensive search by the ground parties. Given the fact that the airport was located in a bowl-like structure with hills on all sides, all aircrafts were required to gain a height higher than the tallest peak in the area by, if necessary, taking a full circle of the valley airspace itself before venturing to cross the hills. The pilot in question had apparently failed to execute this manoeuvre and, given the heavy cloud cover, had in all probability crashed into the hills along the northern fringes of the district. With this possibility in mind I got in touch with my neighbouring districts requesting them to mount search operations, which, given the thick jungles in the area, was no easy task. None of this mattered to the relatives and friends who started appearing at my doorstep in an agitated frame of mind. They were losing hope of finding their near and dear ones alive and were naturally getting increasingly impatient. When, by the third day also, nothing concrete emerged, the general public were getting really agitated and the students got into the act declaring no confidence in the district administration. The students wanted to go and search the area themselves. I permitted this knowing that their exertions would be of no avail.

Tension was increasing by the hour on the fourth day with the students abandoning their classes and gathering in front of my bungalow and the office of the airlines. Violence was very much possible in the increasingly charged atmosphere, and I had to take the usual precautions against breakdown of law and order. Emotional and prone to lose their cool the local population had to be handled with great care, taking due account of their legitimate sorrow over the unforeseen developments and the great sensitivity of the issue. After all, their near and dear ones had been snatched away in an entirely unexpected manner—a tragedy of great poignancy—and they were in a very disturbed state of mind. Maximum restraint and great patience was required to deal with the situation. I accordingly instructed the SP to ensure that while the police were indeed deployed as a preventive measure, use of force was to be resorted to only if there was an emergency and extreme provocation.

Suddenly, as I was dealing with the various delegations, joined now by the press and agitated relatives, some of whom wearing the distinct attire worn for performing the last rites, the airforce informed me that the wreckage had been found. They gave me the grid reference and a quick look at this revealed that the aircraft had crashed not in my district but in the neighbouring North Cachar hills district, where my friend Bhaskar Barua was the DC. This was no relief for me and in fact complicated the situation further because one had to traverse very difficult terrain full of jungle to get to the spot. There were no roads or paths to reach the spot where the plane had fallen. At least it was now clear that the plane had indeed crashed with no survivors and efforts could be made to get the remains of the passengers for completing the last rites. I immediately contacted Bhaskar and requested him to send parties to the site and gather the remains so that these could be sent to Silchar where the relatives were waiting with growing restlessness.

Early next morning I took a helicopter to visit the site, saw for myself the wreckage, took some photographs and returned post haste. The news that the wreckage had been located and that there were no survivors increased the agony of the local populace, who now demanded immediate recovery of the remains. Tension soared to new heights and huge crowds started gathering near the airlines office which was adjacent to my bungalow. Tempers were high and high pitched voices belonging to trouble makers were heard goading the mob towards irresponsible acts.

I now learnt that Bhaskar himself had proceeded to the spot bracing the elements and, worse, the hordes of leeches capable of sucking aman dry. I assumed that he would, no doubt, do his best in the very difficult circumstances.

The mob was restive and the airlines officials rushed to my bungalow as they rightly apprehended violence at any moment. The SP and I decided to talk to the people to calm them down. We walked down the road in a purposeful manner. The crowd was large and more were arriving. In order to be more visible I stood on a table and spoke to them in a calm and collected manner outlining all that had been done so far and assuring them that the neighbouring DC had himself marched to the spot in deference to their requirements. While a measure of calm was being restored, some hot-heads demanded that I speak to Bhaskar in their presence so that the latest situation can be ascertained and some sort of a time frame could be settled.

I had no problem in doing this, my only doubt at that time being whether Bhaskar had returned to his HQ after the perilous journey. Fortunately, he was back and I enquired if he had taken steps to despatch the remains. What Bhaskar told me in reply was a real bolt from the blue as he, being highly conscientious, had decided to cremate the remains as he found them in an advanced state of decay. But I could show no signs of dismay on receiving this shocking piece of news, as the crowd that had anxiously and angrily surrounded me would have gone berserk, if this became known. One false step or show of the true state of my troubled mind could put me in deep trouble. Therefore, I kept up the conversation with Bhaskar, repeatedly asking him that he should immediately send all the remains and that the people of Silchar were extremely agitated over the delay, without showing any of the torpor that was going on within me. Somehow, Bhaskar understood the gravity of my plight and stated that he would again go to the spot, gather all that was available and send the same. Since it had rained in the area I felt that there could still be some substantial remains left for him to get hold of. I, in turn, told him that I will send my Additional Deputy Commissioner at once to help in the transportation of the remains. We agreed that by straining every nerve we will get the remains to Silchar by the next morning travelling overnight from his place.

I conveyed this to the seething crowd who had heard at least all that I had said, without betraying even a trace of the terrible predicament in which I had been placed by Bhaskar's quite justifiable, though from my point of view hasty and indeed dangerous, act. Fortunately, there was an immediate visible reduction in tension. The airlines officials were a relieved lot, having watched the high drama from the sidelines, and quite appreciative of the patience and understanding I had displayed. The SP throughout this episode stood next to me but by employing some sign language had managed to get quite a few lathi-carrying policemen into the crowd and near me in order to deal with any contingency.

I hurried back to my bungalow and despatched K. Bora, my ADC, and he, poor soul travelled through the night on a really bad road and having received whatever Bhaskar was able to transport from the site, returned without wasting any time. I had confirmation that the party would reach Silchar in the morning. Bhaskar was true to his word and had gone to extraordinary lengths to gather all that was possible in the circumstances at considerable risk to himself and his party. There was no question of individual identification and the relatives agreed to a common funeral and cremation.

Now that there was really nothing to be done except quick disposal of the remains, tension in the town evaporated in no time. I had kept the government informed, twice daily, and received all the assistance that I required. In particular they were effective in informing Bhaskar the grave situation I was facing and his help was crucial in overcoming the situation. When after the remains had reached, I spoke to the Chief Secretary, N.K. Rustomji, informing him of the improvement in the situation to near normalcy and how relieved I was. He gave me an invaluable piece of advice namely to ensure that I and the SP participate in the last rites. He told me that such a gesture would go down very well with the local population. This indeed happened and our presence was very well received. Someone, somewhat foolishly demanded that I make a speech and though it was hardly the occasion for such an act, I managed to speak a few words in Bengali, conveying my sympathies to the bereaved families. I was, indeed, exhausted having had no sleep for nearly five days, at a stretch.

Soon thereafter to participate in a periodic conference on border management with the Government of East Pakistan, I had occasion to travel to Sylhet. I had first to go to the state capital Shillong and then drive down the hills to the plains of Pakistan and on to Sylhet. The conference was a routine affair but gave us an opportunity to have a look at the economic and political conditions in that country. Pakistan was under military rule and the presence of the army was quite visible. Economic conditions were not very different from that on our side, with the heavy burden of the ever-growing population and unsatisfactory pace of economic and social progress. Visible, however, was the open hostility towards India, the main grievance at that time being India's decision to build the Farakka barrage. The propaganda was that the perfidious Indians were deliberately and unfairly denying East Pakistan of its due share of water flowing in an international river. Sylhet had nothing whatsoever to do with Farakka, but this did not matter.

The last part of 1970 saw considerable political uncertainty in the country, with Mrs Gandhi splitting the Congress and calling for general elections, on the platform of *'garibi hatao'*. All of a sudden, the entire machinery of the district had to be geared to conduct elections. Sufficient experience had been gained in the conduct of elections and I anticipated no serious problem. All that was required was mobilization of resources and close coordination and monitoring of the entire process.

Mrs Gandhi herself visited the district, flying in and out in a helicopter spending all of four hours, which included a lunch. Irrespective of the duration of the visit, all measures regarding law and order had to be taken and equally importantly all aspects of VVIP security as laid down in the Blue Book. Though it was strictly speaking an election meeting, my hands were nevertheless full. The Chief Minister had reached a little earlier and all the local Congressmen were in attendance. Mrs Jyotsana Chanda, the sitting MP, was again contesting. A very large crowd had indeed gathered more to see the PM than hear her. We had kept the crowd away from the landing area of the helicopter, and until she finished her speech and drove up to the Circuit House for the lunch, the arrangements were well in tact. While the PM was having lunch, I suddenly noticed that the crowd had somehow broken the barricades and surged forward towards the helicopter. I apprehended that to get the PM back to the helicopter would be almost impossible, a piquant situation indeed. I bolted from the Circuit House, located the SP and with great difficulty succeeded in making a passage through the crowd, and posted a line of policemen with lathis to prevent any breach of the passage. My anxiety was that the PM should not leave the Circuit House before the passage was clear especially as she was travelling in an open jeep. I got back to the Circuit House just in time, as the PM and the CM were beginning to descend the stairs to get into the waiting vehicles. Fortunately, the crowd behaved and once the PM was safely inside the helicopter I could breathe more easily. The crowd dispersed quickly when the helicopter rotors swung into action, raising a whole lot of dust.

Though she was possibly fighting the battle of her political life and the outcome of the elections was no way certain, the PM gave the impression of absolute self-confidence, fully in command, a real leader, whose appeal to the masses was unmatched. They looked to her as their saviour and truly believed that she would indeed banish poverty. The local Communist Party Marxist controlled telephone staff to coincide with the visit of the PM, gone on strike on the alleged ground that one of the local Congress MLAs had misbehaved and insulted a staff member. The demand was that he should be arrested at once. This could not obviously be done and when this was mentioned to the PM she merely smiled.

The elections went off peacefully and the Congress won most of the seats.

Across the border in East Pakistan at this time, the rise of Mujibur Rahman as a charismatic leader, a fiery orator, championing the cause of the Bengalis against the domination of the Punjabis of West Pakistan and the army, had become more and more prominent, portending altogether new developments in the politics of Pakistan. In Karimganj, the border is just across the Kushiara river and one could see the flags of Mujib's Awami League fluttering atop many buildings and houses. I had made it a point of familiarizing myself with the entire border and while supervizing the poll arrangements, I had visited all the border outposts manned by the Border Security Force (BSF). My particular concern was the frequent—sometimes days together—exchange of fire along the border at places like 'Latitilla' and 'Dumabari'.

The border between the two countries was what was part of the well-known 'Radcliffe award' at the time of the partition of the country, and ran a zigzag course. Where the river Kushiara is passing through, the middle-of-the-river was the border. The river itself runs a somewhat meandering course. River erosion during the flood season was common. At one spot where a village called Tukergram is located the middle-of-the-river principle is not observed for a short distance. The boundary line takes a jump across the river at a point where the river takes a turn from its north–south course to an east–west course. Having crossed the river the boundary line takes a north-westerly course and then veers to the south to join back at the rivers mid-point, and in the process encircling a small area of around six or seven sq kms. This area belonged to India as it was inhabited by Hindus and was called Tukergram. The BSF had established a post in this village.

Unfortunately, for the poor souls inhabiting this small area, the river was continuously changing course, pushing itself north-westwards thereby eating up substantial portions of land every year. The meagre holdings of these villagers were being progressively reduced. Corresponding land was being thrown up on the opposite side. As per the revenue laws this newly thrown up land is 'Sarkari', that is of government. This however was being illegally cultivated by the villagers of the adjoining village who happened to be mainly Muslims. When I visited the Tukergram village I immediately understood the plight of the villagers and could foresee that if the river continued to behave in this manner, the entire village will be lost. As it is, an already-poor lot was being driven to utter despair. The solution was to give them the land that was being 'created' on the opposite side, due to river action and I quickly got a survey organized of the newly-created land, prepared a list of families who had either lost their holdings or whose holdings had been severely reduced. I instructed that the surveyed land be allotted to these villagers of Tukergram and they be given proper *'pattas'*. They occupied the lands and built their dwellings, but no sooner had they completed this, they were attacked by the neighbouring villagers who had viewed my actions with disfavour and who were illegally cultivating these lands. These marauders burnt all the houses during the night. I sent the police but the whole village had disappeared. I made the settlers rebuild their houses but three days later they were attacked again and their houses torched. The settlers were naturally panic-stricken.

Now this had become a test of wills, and I was made of sterner stuff than what the criminals had imagined, determined not to allow this ugly situation to continue. I called in the BSF commandant, briefed him on the nature of the problem I was facing and asked him if he could establish an outpost right in the heart of the newly-created settlement and afford protection to the settlers. I could not spare the local police, because of other commitments. Also, the BSF were feared more. The commandant agreed and within a few days a post was established and the settlers came back. The villagers dared not attack them again.

I reiterated my instructions that the villagers who had indulged in crime and arson should be brought to book. Raids were conducted but the police found that the villagers had disappeared.

I did not want this episode should to be given a communal colour though attempts were indeed made in this direction. The local MLA Maulana Abdul Jalil Choudhry took up the matter and initially championed the cause of the raiders to give it a communal colour. Some telegrams had been sent to the government maligning me. The MLA met me in a delegation along with some of the villagers and I patiently explained to him with a map the legal basis for all my actions and as to how I had only helped a set of people who had suffered from nature's fury and were on the fast track to becoming destitute. In fairness, I must say, after listening to me he agreed with me and assured me that he will, in turn, explain the matter to the villagers, so that there is no further trouble. I however insisted that action against the criminals will continue.

Some eight years later when I was commissioner of the division of which this district was part, it gave me immense pleasure and satisfaction to revisit this village and see that the settlers had established themselves very well. A Durga mandir had been built and the BSF post remained. I had saved scores of poor people from certain disaster and given them a future.

At about this time, while naxalism was spreading its lethal tentacles in the state of West Bengal, reports had started reaching me that this virus had entered the district and recruitment of cadres was taking place. Inflammatory literature was being distributed and even arms were being collected. Slogans had appeared right in Silchar in an effort to propagate the pernicious extremist creed, championing the cause of the poor, calling for the annihilation of the rich, denigrating democratic institutions and calling for their overthrow. One slogan in Bengali read *'aamirdher chamda theke garibdher jootha thouri hobe'* 'from the skin of the rich the shoes of the poor shall be made'. Another stated *'Parliament aamirdher adda gruho'* meaning 'Parliament is nothing but the house of gossip of the rich'.

The SP Subramaniam and his team had done an excellent job in collecting accurate information about the activities of these naxalites, keeping close watch over their movements, their dens and a complete list of activists was soon ready with detailed dossiers. We decided to strike at once. In one fell swoop during the night, spread throughout the district, nearly ninety per cent of those involved were nabbed under the National Security Act, on charges of attempting to wage war against the government established by law. A few diehard elements had indeed come from West Bengal to build up the movement and these were also taken in. With this swift and very timely operation naxalism was finished once and for all in the district. Had this measure not been taken, we could have been in big trouble, with a long-drawn battle on our hands as had happened in West Bengal. States like Andhra Pradesh, Bihar, Madhya Pradesh, Jharkhand and

Maharashtra even today are expending resources in combating this menace of left extremism. The economic and social conditions of the district at that time, I have no doubt, provided a fertile ground for left extremism to take strong roots.

The events across the international border were now gathering momentum and a veritable storm was brewing. The call for general elections by the military ruler of Pakistan, General Yahya Khan, had resulted in the Awami League of Mujibur Rahman gaining a majority in the nation's National Assembly. Mujibur Rahman should have rightfully assumed the office of Prime Minister of Pakistan but this was not acceptable to the army or the political elite of West Pakistan, and the by-now-familiar drama of suppression of East Pakistan started, being enacted across the border. Sheikh Mujib was imprisoned and the army let loose a reign of terror on the hapless population. It was easy to see the Pakistan Army's terror tactics from the border outposts in my district.

By March 1971, this inhuman suppression had triggered an inevitable exodus of the terrorized population into India, all across the international border. The subdivisional officer, Karimganj, reported within the first part of March that refugee influx was a daily occurrence and the numbers were increasing every day, to nearly a thousand per day. All had abandoned their possessions and were indeed destitutes. We decided to accommodate the refugees in school buildings as we had no other place readily available. The numbers were swelling by the day and we could not have kept them in the open when the rains were already upon us. We had no tents at our disposal.

No one could estimate as to how many the district will be called upon to shelter and, suddenly, a massive administrative effort had to be organized. Based on past experience, we quickly mobilized personnel for camps—each school for the time-being designated as a camp—arranged for supply of foodgrains, edible oil, salt and fuel. Most schools had water supply facilities and rudimentary sanitation. Where required borewells were dug and sanitary facilities provided. I organized mobile medical teams to take preventive measures against the outbreak of communicable diseases and to attend to the sick.

The arrival of refugees continued unabated and soon there was not a school left in the whole of the Karimganj subdivision. The subdivisional administration was stretched to the limit. Funds, fortunately, were no problem as by then the government machinery had been geared up to ensure a continuous flow of funds. My main worry was—given the tenuous transportation links with the rest of the country—to ensure adequate availability of all essential supplies. The situation in neighbouring Tripura was far worse, with a much larger flow of refugees, and massive supplies that had to be sent to that state through the only rail line connecting the whole area with the rest of the country.

Karimganj was now full and overflowing, and I had to inevitably transport the new arrivals to the Silchar area, filling up school after school, and made all the arrangements for the supply of food, water, fuel, sanitation and healthcare. Eventually all the schools in the entire district got filled up with refugees.

It was becoming increasingly clear that the refugees would be with us, for some months, at least. The students of the whole district were now on a forced holiday and no exams could be held. It was most undesirable to keep the schools occupied indefinitely. This matter had received the attention of both the state and the central governments and plans were made to build camps with substantial capacity with standard designs and provision for dispensaries, small hospitals as well as a school for the children. Water supply sanitation, storage for essential supplies and security were all provided for.

Fortunately, bamboo, which is a versatile construction material, was available in plenty in the district and we proceeded, post haste, to build planned colonies, selecting suitable sites near water sources. Within a month, we could start the process of shifting the refugees from school after school. I took steps to thoroughly disinfect all the schools, repair the damages and get them whitewashed before the children were allowed to come in. Soon normalcy was restored on this front. Care had been taken to build in excess capacity in the new camps so that fresh arrivals could be straightaway accommodated in the camps. The government was particular that the refugees be kept segregated and not allowed to mix with the local population. They were to return to their homeland at the earliest opportunity, and the possibility of their finding shelter on a permanent basis among relatives was to be avoided.

Though there was a fair sprinkling of Muslims who had come away, the majority of the refugees were Hindus, as the Pakistanis had targeted them for special treatment, joined by local communal elements. They were not at all sure if they would ever go back to their homes. While every effort was being made to attend to the needs of the large number of refugees, I started receiving requests from local political leaders asking for one thing or the other for the refugees. For the moment the local people's own needs seemed to receive less attention. This was reflected in the way local politicians viewed the whole problem, and, regrettably, there was a strong communal angle in this. The Hindu politicians were not prepared to believe that the refugees will go back and some, I dare say, did not want them to go back. They therefore represented to the politicians a potential vote bank, and why not start building up a following among the refugees by acting as their advocate? I found this quite irksome and quite firmly discouraged such tendencies.

The Muslim leaders on the other hand were not sympathetic to the refugees and their presence in the district was viewed with distaste, if not hostility. Indeed, reports indicated that the Muslims in general were not in favour of the struggle in East Bengal the reason being the declaration by Sheikh Mujib that the new nation will be a secular country where all religions will be respected. The twisted logic of this stance was difficult to understand, but this hostility assumed an ugly dimension as time went by, especially at the time of operations against Pakistan.

While I had more or less placed the relief operations on a sound footing and the flow from across the border had assumed manageable proportions, the possibility of armed conflict between India and Pakistan was increasing with every passing week. Already a full army division was in the district, but this formation was concerned primarily with the operations against the Mizo rebels. A new division was now inducted into the district drawn from Nagaland commanded by Major General Krishna Rao, who later became Chief of Army staff. A whole lot of weaponry was being brought in including amphibious tanks. This deployment brought in new requirements, and land had to be provided in several places for the various units. General Rao was kind enough—brushing aside protocol I must say—to come to my bungalow and discuss his requirements. I had all the powers required under the Defence of India Act and Rules to provide him all that he wanted. Lieutenant General Sagat Singh was the Corps Commander and the SP and I called on him to ensure that there is full cooperation and coordination at all levels.

The airforce establishment, under Group Captain Lata, had also started gearing itself for operations, and liaison with them as well was organized.

My main concern, in this context, was the organization of full scale civil defence measures and the maintenance of the morale of the civilian population. The people, in general, were ready to bear the consequences inherent in the situation as there was a lot of sympathy for the struggle in East Bengal. Rabindranath Tagore's *'aamar sonar bangla, aami tumai bhalo bashi'*—My golden Bengal I adore thee' was on everybody's lips. The Awami League politicians, who had fled East Bengal and taken shelter in the district were well received. Nevertheless, the protection of the population against enemy action had to be organized and the morale of the population, especially in the border areas, had to be maintained so that there is no panic evacuation of areas choking of communication lines and consequent hampering of the movement of the armed forces.

I set about organizing the whole range of civil defence measures, with the division of the district into civil defence wards, appointment of civil defence wardens, training of personnel, gathering of fire fighting and rescue equipment, enforcement of blackout regulations. Trenches were dug all over the place. Blackout drills were conducted, and all houses made to paste black paper on glass windows. Sand bags were piled up where necessary. Our son, who was all of three years, got into the act, appointed himself a warden of sorts and kept yelling at everyone to put off their lights as otherwise Pakistani bombs will fall on their heads. I kept lecturing to gatherings in the border areas, advising against panic, painting an optimistic picture, and assuring the people that the Army was fully geared to deal with any eventuality and that they should carry on their normal activities. I stressed repeatedly that they were privileged witnesses to, and indeed participants of a truly historic event, the birth of a new nation in the subcontinent after a heroic struggle against tyranny and oppression.

Several Awami League leaders had taken shelter in the district and were, in as unobtrusive a manner as possible, recruiting volunteers for their armed wing the 'Mukti Bahini' and giving the recruits training. These members of the 'Mukti Bahini' would sneak across the border to carry out various acts calculated to weaken the Pakistan army's fighting potential, such as damaging installations. Reports reaching me indicated that the Pakistan army was intent on retaliation, and had managed to recruit some elements from within my district to train them in planting explosives for damaging vital installations and communication lines. This added an altogether new and dangerous dimension to the already overflowing set of problems I was burdened with. The railway lines, the innumerable road bridges, electricity installations all were vulnerable. I organized village defence parties to guard the road bridges, enlisted the services of the railway police and the BSF to patrol the railway lines and posted static guards at all vital installations.

At several places the railway line ran very near the international border, and it would not take a long time for someone, with even rudimentary training, to bury explosives under the track and get back to East Pakistan. We did identify such points, but in spite of all the precautions, two instances of sabotage occurred. In one, an anti-tank mine was placed under the rail track and anticipating that an explosion on the rail line will invite relief teams one more mine was buried on the adjoining road. The moment the engine of a goods train touched the track at the spot where the mine was buried an explosion was triggered throwing the engine and three bogies off the track. The track also was damaged; fortunately, there were no casualties as the train carried no passengers and the driver also got away with a few broken bones. The SDO, Karimganj, within whose beat the explosion had occurred, had, post haste, sent a team and an ambulance, and this hit the antitank mine buried on the roadside. Though the vehicle was partly damaged, the passengers, who were all in the front seat, escaped unhurt.

The other incident took place near Karimganj railway station, once again an explosive device was placed under the railway track. The device went off prematurely ripping off a length of the track. No other damage took place. Another more powerful explosive device was discovered in the Silchar station, but was diffused before any damage could be caused.

I intensified supervision, all along making my officers go out on night patrol, and I myself undertook patrolling on a few nights.

With respect to the blowing up of the track resulting in the derailment of a goods train, we got information that some youths, from a nearby village which happened to be on the river, across which was East Pakistan, had been recruited and trained to carry out disruptive activities by the Pakistanis. The very efficient DSP–Special Branch, was able to zero in on two young men who had received such training and had been foolish enough to come back to the village. These were promptly arrested and interrogated. One of them made a statement indicating that he had actually planted the anti-tank mine on the railway line and on the roadside. Since this amounted to a confession, as required under the Code of Criminal Procedure, he was produced before a magistrate who observing all the required procedural formalities recorded the confession. This was very important, as such a confession is admissible as evidence in a court and can lead to conviction. In the course of the confessional statement recorded by the magistrate the young man made a startling revelation namely that before going across the border, he had been sheltered by the local MLA Maulana Abdul Jalil Choudhry about whom I have mentioned earlier in the episode relating to 'Tukergram', and on his return as well, with the mines, he had been harboured by this MLA. This MLA was of the ruling Congress party, and the statement recorded could prove to be highly damaging. This MLA because of his religious persuasion was always seen in Arab dress even within the assembly, presided over a mosque within his premises and ran a madrassa. In view of the seriousness of the matter, it was brought to my notice and I very carefully went through the confessional statement and satisfied myself that the confession was not under duress, that all the procedural formalities had indeed been followed and it can stand rigorous judicial scrutiny.

I discussed the matter with the SP Subramaniam and we decided to register a case and send a detailed report immediately to the government. The MLA, who possibly got wind of the development, made himself scarce getting away to Shillong in order to escape apprehension and use his political connections to thwart the course of law.

As expected, alarm bells rang in the concerned departments of the government. The Chief Secretary rang me up and told me that I was to await government instructions before taking any action. The CM summoned me and told me the same thing in sharper language. What followed was a charade which seriously undermined my faith in the whole system. I had viewed the matter very seriously, as after all what had occurred was an act which amounted to abetment of a serious criminal offence, at a time of national emergency, an act detrimental to national defence and security, sabotaging of a vital communication link, an act calculated to help the enemy and in congruence with his designs. All this apparently was of no consequence for the powers that be, and their effort was to somehow rescue the MLA and for this a cunning subterfuge was employed, which totally surprised me and the SP.

Within twenty-four hours of my conversation with the CM, we found that the Deputy Inspector General (Special Branch) arrived in the district. He bypassed the SP, severely berated the DSP (SB) Sen for having allegedly got on to the wrong target—his theory was that the sabotage was the handiwork of the naxalites, laughable to say the least—and worked on the junior operatives with whose help he managed to contact the saboteur who had confessed, and influenced him to change his story, avoiding any reference to the MLA. He also managed to produce the accused before another magistrate and got a confession recorded, which, while being identical in all respects to the original confession, totally omitted any mention of the role of the MLA.

It was disgusting to see these diabolical machinations with respect to a matter whose gravity was enormous. With one neat but nefarious and foul stroke the basis for further action on our part was removed. Needless to say that those who had done their duty sincerely, honestly, courageously and in the interests of the nation were outraged and demoralized. The MLA in question never again had the courage to face me.

With all this keeping me occupied, I had also to keep very close track of the overall supply situation, and, indeed, build up a buffer stock to meet any eventuality. Black marketing, hoarding and price rise were matters which required continuous vigil. When sugar prices showed a sharp upward trend, out of tune with the trends elsewhere in the country, I suspected foul play and raided godowns of sugar dealers and detained them. Pressure was brought on me not to proceed against them, but I refused to oblige.

I was also keen that normal functioning of the administration is not disturbed, and saw to it that the common man's problems continued to be attended to without much delay. Indeed, during this period, I had also to organize and conduct the census operations, an immense task involving mobilization of a huge quantum of manpower and a great deal of paperwork. Even a family planning drive was organized under government instructions.

Amidst all this, one night, the railway employees went on strike on the alleged ground that an engine driver had been assaulted by

CRP men. What had happened was that in Badarpur junction—around twenty kilometres from the district headquarters—from an incoming train, the CRP men who had alighted were unloading their weapons but before this could be completed the engine driver started the train. One or two jawans got on to the engine and possibly after an argument stopped the train. This was enough for the railway employees not only to stop this train and refuse to work, but stop all the trains and go on a strike throughout the district. Chaos prevailed on the platform and the railways passed on the buck to the DC and SP.

Both of us reached the station. The railway employees demanded that the CRP men and their Commandant should be arrested and the railway employees should be provided with foolproof security. We could not accept such demands and while I kept talking to the railway employees the SP quietly managed to send away all the CRP men with their weapons. He did not want the CRP men to get agitated and complicate the situation further. We then kept arguing with the railway staff telling them that their complaint against the CRP will be registered, that an investigation will be carried out and action as per law will be taken. There was no evidence that the driver had been assaulted, and basically what had happened was nothing worse than a case of chain pulling. We pointed out that this incident did not justify going on strike inconveniencing hundreds of passengers, and bringing the whole system to a halt. After several hours of patient negotiations some sanity was brought about and the employees agreed to resume duty if written assurance was given by the District Magistrate promising adequate security to all the railway employees. This was essentially a face-saving device and I readily agreed to this. While preparations were then commenced to start the trains and send the passengers to their destinations, the local Municipal Board Chairman suddenly appeared from nowhere and said that he will not allow the trains to move unless food was provided for all the passengers. He was clearly out to create mischief and I requested the SP—in Tamil our handy code language not understood by the locals—to take him into another room where his proposal could be discussed in detail meaning that the chap was not to be allowed to come out. This achieved, within half an hour or so, I saw to it that the trains on the platform departed. The honourable chairman was allowed to come out well after all the trains had gone, and we, ourselves, had departed.

It was early morning when I reached home.

Given the situation prevailing in the district, it was but natural to expect VIPs and VVIPs to come and review the situation and the way problems were being taken care of. The Union Minister for Industries Moinul Haq Choudhry, who was from the district, came quite frequently and so did the Chief Minister Mahendra Mohan Choudhry. The Union Minister of State for Relief and Rehabilitation visited all the refugee camps. The Governor B.K. Nehru and the Cabinet Secretary T. Swaminathan also came and most importantly the PM, Mrs Gandhi, herself came twice to the district. Her visits were memorable in many ways, especially her second visit as war clouds were gathering at a fast pace.

For the first visit of the PM, I got barely forty-eight hours notice but, fortunately, the PM was spending only a few hours in the district as she was making a stop on her way to Tripura, where the number of refugees was very large and their condition was a cause for concern. The PM, after being received at the airport, was taken to a nearby refugee camp, spent about an hour there and got back to her plane. Because of the short notice the VVIP car from the State headquarters did not arrive and I had to quickly spruce up my own official car give it an extra coat of polish, give the driver a new uniform and place the car for the PM's journeys. The PM did not seem to mind, and she sat next to the driver in the front seat, while the CM, myself and the PM's security officer occupied the rear seat with me wedged in between the CM and the security officer, Mrs Gandhi's very Grecian-looking head not far from my nose.

The problem, however, was that the CM was inclined to dose off the moment the car got into motion and he would recline on my shoulder. I had a very uncomfortable hour, trying my best not to wake him up and incur his wrath, while answering the volley of questions coming from the PM. I was very nervous as to when she will turn her imperious head and find that the CM had dosed off, but, fortunately, throughout the journey she kept chatting with me and occasionally even with the driver in a totally relaxed fashion. Even if she had noticed the CM in a comatose state, which I suspect she indeed did, she chose to ignore it.

The second visit was longer and involved, arrival early in the morning, travel through the day, a night halt at Silchar and departure next morning. She was accompanied by K.C. Pant, then Minister of

State for Home, Mrs Padmaja Naidu and B.N. Tandon, the Joint Secretary in the PMO. Apart from the CM of Assam, the CM of Meghalaya and a number of ministers landed in the district. It was the height of monsoon and while waiting in the airport for the PM's arrival grave doubts whether the PM's plane would be able to land at all were expressed, as there were low very thick clouds all round and visibility was poor. The pilot, however, had other views and the PM landed well in time and looked distinctly cheerful and relaxed. We had lined up helicopters to take her to the camps she intended visiting, but the weather conditions were such that the pilots refused to fly. A huge convoy of cars were lined up and throughout the morning the PM drove from one camp to another, spending around half an hour in each of them.

Throughout this journey, I noticed an extraordinary phenomenon, namely, while the rain poured relentlessly whenever the PM was in the car travelling, whenever she stopped to go round the camps the rain would stop, to resume again with equal fury the moment she got into the car. This happened throughout the day in all the places she stopped and I did not have to use the umbrellas and raincoats that had been kept handy. The ground, of course, was very slushy but on the wooden planks placed for the party to walk the PM managed to walk gingerly without any assistance. Throughout the day she kept asking me about the facilities provided in the camps, the places from which the refugees had come and whether they had been subjected to any atrocities. She seemed quite satisfied with the facilities that we had managed to provide to the refugees in the district.

Lunch was at the Karimganj Circuit House; while the others partook of the repast that had been arranged, the PM had brought her own little carrier and quietly had this in the privacy of her room. After meeting a couple of delegations, she addressed a public meeting where once again the rain behaved in the manner it had throughout the morning, there being no precipitation while she spoke. This pattern was repeated during the visit to two other camps. The PM then expressed the wish to visit the divisional headquarters and address the officers and jawans. This involved only a minor diversion from her route on the journey back and was quickly organized.

By four thirty in the evening when light was already fading and while the rain continued to pour she reached the divisional headquarters and proceeded to the helipad where the jawans had assembled. Again, while she stepped out and spoke to the jawans for some twenty minutes there was not one drop of rain. The jawans who were waiting were all soaked to the skin. I had kept an umbrella ready and when at the beginning of her address, I felt a drop or two on my shoulders I took the umbrella near the PM but she waved me aside. After the address the PM was taken to the mess for a tea and she gaily chatted with the GOC and other officers. The rain had resumed and continued thereafter.

I am still to find a rational explanation for this extraordinary behaviour of the rain throughout the day. Did Mrs Gandhi have something special about her?

We reached the Silchar Circuit House by about six and I sought her permission to call three delegations who wanted to meet her. There were a large number of requests but considering the time available and the strain that the PM would have gone through, I had cut down the number to just three. I could see that she was having a headache—migrane as I was informed by her doctor Dr Mathur—but she still agreed to meet those waiting. She emerged from her room within half an hour after a shower, looking fresher, in a crisp cotton sari, but still rubbing her head. She listened to the people who met her patiently, but when one of them had the temerity, to argue, that India should recognize Bangladesh at once, she justifiably lost her cool and told the delegation that she knew precisely what to do when. She kept rubbing her forehead all along, as the headache was possibly getting only worse.

The PM thereafter retired to her room. I am not sure if she had anything much to eat. I could turn my attention to the other guests. K.C. Pant wanted that both his dinner and next morning breakfast should be sent from my house, as he was very particular about hygiene and was averse to taking any risks.

The PM was leaving early next morning and, fortunately, the weather had improved a great deal. She had a meeting with the members of the Assam cabinet, and drove to the airport for her departure.

The Cabinet Secretary T. Swaminathan came at a very short notice and I was able to take him to one of the newly-constructed camps, which housed some ten thousand souls. By this time, the total number of refugees in my district had crossed the two-hundred thousand mark. He questioned me closely about all that we had done for the refugees and the overall security situation. He complimented me on the manner in which the camp he visited had been built and organized. He was impressed by the neat rows of barrack type structures all made out of bamboo and other locally available material, as well as the facilities that we had given to these people, and the regularity with which all essential supplies were provided.

The country as a whole had borne the burden of some nine million refugees who had been evicted forcibly from East Pakistan, with very little assistance from either international bodies or other countries. I, sitting in a remote corner, never felt the impact of any such external aid. I wonder if the UNHCR which is so much in the news these days extended any assistance.

The Governor of Assam, B.K. Nehru, came accompanied by his wife, a Hungarian Jew, known to be very fussy about cleanliness and with a sharp tongue. She had particular interest in health and family planning matters, and often grilled the Deputy Commissioners on such matters. A very distinguished career was behind Nehru and it was a great pleasure to converse with him. Saddened by the division of Assam into different political entities, he authored the concept of the North Eastern council as a mechanism to preserve and foster the economic integration of the region. Even at that time, he was an advocate of lessening the role of government in the economic sphere, withdrawing from all non-essential areas that government had unnecessarily entered into only to make a mess of it.

The Governor also visited the refugee camps, was given a civic reception, and a dinner by the tea gardeners. He took particular interest in the intensive agricultural development programme. He had planned to depart by train and a saloon had been arranged. Though the train to which the saloon was to be attached was to leave late at night, the Governor told us that to get him to the saloon by ten p.m. and leave him so that he can rest in the saloon. Following his instructions my wife and I reached him to the saloon in time. The saloon was a metre gauge contraption, and Mrs Nehru who had got into the saloon first and carried out a quick inspection, came out with a somewhat disturbed expression on her face and addressed her husband, 'Brij, do you know there is only one bed in this saloon and don't tell me that I have to sleep with you tonight'. We barely managed to hide our embarrassment but apparently making this kind of remark was nothing unusual for this distinguished lady. My colleagues in other districts have had experiences not dissimilar to this. When I was posted in Australia, some time later, her sister Carlotta, who had settled down in Australia, became a good friend of ours, and there was a good deal of similarity between the two sisters.

Apart from the VIPs, I had to handle a regular flow of press correspondents, quite a few representing international magazines such as the *Time* and *Newsweek*. I believe they highlighted the refugees problems in a sympathetic manner the world over.

The winter of 1971 was gradually coming in, and the impact of the cold weather on the hapless children in the camps caused me considerable anxiety. The local Red Cross and the Ramakrishna Mission were able to gather some woollen clothing but this supply was entirely inadequate. The American missionary doctor Dr Kenoir and his wife offered to import second-hand woollen clothing from the USA, and true to their word, they airlifted a large quantity of children's clothing. The sizes were, of course, far too large for the children in the camps, and my wife took up the responsibility of getting the clothes altered by engaging a host of local tailors. For a fortnight or so, except my office room the entire bungalow had been converted into a large tailoring shop with everyone tripping over and trampling mountains of woollens. She then distributed the clothes to a large number of grateful children in the camps.

By October and early November 1971 the possibility of armed conflict with Pakistan was looming large, while on the other side of the border the Pakistan army was busy settling scores with the Mukti Bahini. Firing and open fights were increasing, with the Pakistan army bent on keeping its grip on the territory. On occasion, the conflict resulted in firing into Indian territory, and I was apprehensive of casualties among the civilians.

One day, early in the morning, I got a message from the SP that a border outpost at a place, called Suterkhandi, manned by the BSF, had come under attack by the Pakistan army. Apparently, the Pakistanis had suspected that some Mukti Bahini cadres had taken shelter in the BSF post and was attempting to flush them out. The initial report indicated that the BSF personnel had suffered casualties, and the post was being vacated. The problem was that the Suterkhandi post was hardly ten kilometres away from Karimganj town, connected by an excellent road, and the SP rightly apprehended that the Pakistanis could, in hot pursuit of the Mukti Bahini, reported to be on the road, enter Indian territory, come to Karimganj, cause havoc and get back. There was no force that could prevent the Pakistan army from doing this. The task of taking on such an assault which could violate the international border by firing on the BSF was clearly that of the Indian army. I therefore contacted the GOC at once and informed him of the report I had received and my apprehensions in this regard and requested him to take immediate action.

Since we felt that the situation could assume grave proportions and the civilian population could go into a panic, both the SP and I drove straight to the divisional headquarters and met the Colonel general staff, told him all that we knew and the fears that we had. His reaction was at best lukewarm for reasons he did not specify and we could not gauge. We however stressed repeatedly the need for the army to react and teach the other side a lesson so that they do not repeat such a violation of the international border.

The SP and I quickly drove down to Karimganj in order to handle any eventuality and travelled right up to the border. We met the BSF personnel, who had had informed us and had left the post with injuries. Firing was still going on intermittently. Only junior officers were there and they had not succeeded in contacting their own commandants, and no reinforcements of the BSF had so far been arranged.

I decided to speak to the Chief Secretary, and after giving him the details of the incident and the possibilities, urged him to take up the matter with the army authorities in Shillong and New Delhi, as also the Ministry of Defence. I then made a second trip towards the border to a spot as near the outpost that had come under attack as possible, and I could see, with my bare eyes, the Pakistani army personnel in battle gear on the other side of the border. Through the binoculars I could see their weapons. If they decided to make another foray there was nothing to stop them. Since there had so far been no reaction whatsoever from our side—a good five hours had passed since the first report of the attack—I spoke to the CS again and informed him of what I had personally seen. I thought it appropriate to speak to the CM as well to suggest that he speak to the Prime Minister. The firing was still sporadic, and it was well past noon when the BSF commandant came in with reinforcements and it was only by 3 p.m. that I could see an army column moving in. The Pakistanis had by then withdrawn. This delay had denied us a fine opportunity to retaliate effectively against a blatant violation of the border. By our continuous presence in Karimganj throughout the day, the SP and I had however succeeded in ensuring that there was no panic among the civilians, who could see and hear the firing that was going on.

A couple of weeks later, a senior general from the army HQ had come to look into the matter and he met the SP and me. What came out of this enquiry, I do not know. The CS however mentioned to me, some time later, that the army was of the view that I had over reacted. I have no doubt that my fears were quite justified.

The month of December 1971 witnessed the outbreak of armed conflict between India and Pakistan with an air attack on our bases in the west. From my district large scale attacks were launched by the Mukti Bahini crossing the river near Karimganj into Jakiganj in the Sylhet district. The Indian army followed and firing all along the border erupted. Within a matter of hours the defences on the other side were breached and the army and the Bahini could penetrate deep into enemy territory. The firing had caused minor damage to a few buildings along the river, but there were no casualties. I reached Karimganj at once, and in order to prevent any panic imposed curfew, activated the entire gamut of civil defence measures and enforced blackout as a precaution against possible air raids. These measures were taken with respect to all the towns of the district.

Jakiganj was captured within forty eight hours and with this the threat to Karimganj town vanished. Lt Gen. Sagat Singh, the Corps commander who had come to Karimganj took me across the river into the captured territory, a memorable experience for me to travel into a war zone. Bodies of Pakistani soldiers were still on the roads. Gen. Sagat Singh was briefed about the operations and all the while gunfire was audible from various surrounding points. Within a week the whole of Sylhet was liberated.

Air superiority had been achieved in the Eastern sector, within a week of the commencement of hostilities and the threat of air attack by the Pakistan airforce consequently ceased. I could therefore lift the blackout regulations immediately.

My concern at this point was the population, inhabiting the liberated areas who would surely be in need of essential supplies. Some kind of organized efforts had to be mounted and I reflected these concerns to the state government and discussed this with the Chief Minister who was on a visit. No instructions in this regard had come so far. It would have been quite undesirable to allow the liberated areas to be without regular supplies.

The government responded quickly by deputing a team of officers to visit the areas liberated, make an assessment of the quantum of requirements and organize supplies for the people across the border. I undertook a visit to Sylhet, where I met the Deputy Commissioner, who, though part of the 'ancient' regime, had been allowed to continue by the new set-up which itself was just starting to assume a formal shape. I also met several Awami League members of the national assembly. They were all highly appreciative of the assistance rendered and being organized for the liberated areas. The Indian army was busy with mopping-up operations, de-mining of roads, restoring communications and providing healthcare. In the two or three schools that I was taken to, I saw huge quantities of ammunition including heavy artillery shells, that had been stored by the Pakistan army but had been abandoned during the hasty retreat.

The airforce in Silchar, which was operating Hunters and Gnats, repeatedly conducted raids into the enemy territory and in coordination with the army, speeding up the process of achieving total victory, liberation of East Bengal and the birth of Bangladesh. I was invited by the airforce to their control and operations room to witness the conduct of air attacks. It was fascinating to see the briefing of the pilots about their missions, the take-off of the jets, monitoring of their progress by ground control, the success of their missions and return to base.

On one mission the pilots, while yet to cross the border, fired on a bridge located within the district by mistake and, unfortunately, a car which was crossing the bridge was severely damaged resulting in the death of a businessman on a visit from Calcutta. This was extremely sad and unfortunate—euphemistically and ironically termed 'death by friendly fire'—but the airforce took good care providing compensation and flying the body to Calcutta.

Soon enough this great chapter of India's history was drawing to a close. General A.A.K. Niazi of the Pakistan army surrendered in Dhaka, and the liberation struggle was over. On my part I got busy organizing the much-awaited return of the refugees to their 'Sonar Bangla'. We started with those who had come first and from camps which had large populations taking care to get together people from the same village.

Cachar had a large number of locally published newspapers. At my time there were no less than thirty-five and the majority of these appeared only once in a while. Many were basically one-man operations, the editor, printer, publisher, correspondent, advertising and circulation manager all rolled into one. Their content and credibility were of a low order and only served the basic purpose of keeping some souls employed by raising their revenues out of government advertisements for which they competed fiercely. Some indulged in scandal mongering. Speculation about official transfers were a frequent news item and the transfer of the DC was a hot subject especially if he had spent about two years in the district.

As the year 1971 drew to an end, rumours about my exit were rife. I had myself formally requested the government to send me to the Government of India and by February 1972 I had got my posting orders as Under Secretary in the Ministry of Defence.

I have always held that the office of the Deputy Commissioner is a unique institution and the job is easily the most interesting and exciting in the whole country. No other job in government calls for the exercise of such a degree of initiative and drive, poses such a variety of challenges, necessitating the employment of all your mental faculties testing you all the while, and offers you so much opportunity to do things which can directly benefit the people. It is an office which necessitates display of high qualities of leadership, to get the best out of a multidisciplinary team, gives you so much Independence to act while it provides you with so much job satisfaction. In my case, given the particular circumstances existing at that time in the district I had to handle, and the special problems it had, as also the particular period in the country's history in which I had the opportunity of serving, the tasks and challenges were indeed extraordinary and called for the deployment of all my mental and physical reserves. I look back at this period with great satisfaction, especially to the time when over two hundred thousand souls, who had lost everything, and who had been tortured and damned, were enabled to obtain the basic requirements of life, their well being which was my daily concern. I also take pride in the fact that I participated in the national endeavour of liberating an oppressed people and in creating the new nation of Bangladesh, supporting and supplementing the nation's war efforts, while safeguarding the civilian population from possible consequences of enemy action.

The only regret that I have is that the services rendered at a time of national emergency, at grave personal risk, were not given due recognition. My colleagues who worked in the neighbouring districts of Khasi hills and Garo hills, both on the international border, who did exactly what I was called upon to do were given the Padma Shri as the government of Meghalaya took up their case as indeed the government of Punjab, with respect to officers who had served in the western border. The government of Assam took no such initiative and consequently, Madan Bezbarua, who had also performed equally onerous duties in the Dhubri district of Assam, and myself were denied this honour. A commendation letter was all that was given.

# 7

# GOVERNMENT OF INDIA—AUSTRALIA

After all the adventure and excitement during the period in the district, I landed in the corridors of the Central Secretariat with the exalted title of 'Under Secretary' to the Government of India in the Department of Defence Production. While in the United Kingdom, the permanent under secretary is indeed a weighty individual, with a Knighthood to boot, in our system the under secretary is very much an underdog. He is consigned to the under world, namely the lowest and most ill-kept part of the building, often having to share a small room with another soul, occupying a similar inglorious station in the highly stratified and hierarchically determined pecking order, which is so much an integral part of New Delhi's life.

From the position of a district collector, which carried a good deal of the trappings of office, it was a big come-down in my case, as I occupied my small single-windowed room in the hutments near the main South Block buildings, where an assortment of lesser mortals were expected to discharge their responsibilities. A horde of monkeys seemed to be in command of the corridors, and neither they nor, for that matter, anyone else showed any respect towards you—a sharp contrast to all the fawning that is so much part of the collector's life. The monkeys were absolutely fearless and if they decided to walk in the corridors, it is you who had to exercise all the caution required in order to avoid a possible attack by the quite unpredictable creatures. On top of this, with the electricity supply being uncertain, your life was made miserable during winter by the coal-fired chimneys which were seldom cleaned, as a consequence of which the files, tables, chairs, etc. were all coated with coal dust and at the end of the day you got home, remotely resembling a coal miner, with a fair sprinkling of coal all over you.

In summer, the pecking order comes into play with full force. The poor mite of an under secretary is entitled to a water cooler which had to be periodically filled with water. If there was power, it succeeded in cooling that part of your body which is nearest to the cooler while everything else remained unaffected, at near-boiling temperatures. A deputy secretary is entitled to a desert cooler which, given continuous supply of electricity, kept the entire room in a tolerable condition. It is only when you become a joint secretary that air conditioners are allowed—not to mention good room heaters in winter. The additional special and full secretaries worked in near-freezing conditions, even when the temperature outside soared to 45 degrees Celsius, a cool head considered vital for decision-making at these levels.

On the housing front as well, rigid rules governed your entitlement, the remotest, smallest and most ill kept, reserved for the lesser mortals. To get even this, one had to cringe and crawl before the arrogance of those in the directorate of estates, who treated you as a worm. Often the only accommodation that was available was in the hostels, basically a one-bedroomed affair. Of course, there were quite a few who were more equal than others, who managed to get reasonable accommodation, not too distant from the office and these were invariably officers who belonged to the select breed of private secretaries to the Ministers.

Under Secretaries in the Government of India, I found, also participated very little in the process of decision-making. Sending reminders, attending to routine matters and recording the proceedings of the innumerable meetings formed the bulk of the workload. When Parliament was in session, handling of 'unstarred questions' was entrusted to you. I was dealing with the defence public sector undertakings, namely, Bharat Electronics and Bharat Earth Movers, and in the aftermath of the 1971 war with Pakistan, the US sanctions had drastically curtailed the availability of foreign exchange—that is free foreign exchange, as against the Russian roubles of which no shortage was felt. These companies consequently had to fight for every dollar that is available in the kitty to meet their import requirements, and I did play the role of a facilitator in getting their cases through the intricate channels of the Ministry of Finance.

This phase of official life did not last long and with a promotion as Deputy Secretary, I was shifted to the Ministry of Foreign Trade, bringing about a distinct improvement in the quality of my life. I was dealing with, in the beginning, the state trading organizations, Africa and Latin America and later on with jute. The Ministry was divided into territorial divisions and commodity divisions and the task was to increase and diversify India's exports to various countries. A great deal depended upon generation of an exportable surplus by the nation's agriculture and industry while ensuring that the highest quality standards were observed. Competitive pricing and strict adherence to delivery schedules were vital considerations. Given the fact that we were highly protectionists at that time, providing our industry and agriculture, a large sheltered market with no external competition and in many cases not even internal competition, exports as such were of only marginal interest to most industries. Our exports were confined to primary products and raw materials. Indian industry was highly uncompetitive and our share in world trade was in no way significant. Imports, however, outstripped exports by a substantial margin and in the usual bureaucratic style, the Ministry busied itself producing volumes of papers on export promotion strategies, and sending delegations with the ostensible purpose of conquering new markets for India's products. The rupee trade with the Soviet Union, of course, flourished because of the special relationship with the former USSR. The Russians were, it seems, ready to accept our prices, quality and indifferent delivery schedules. One often heard the words 'political price', which apparently did not have much of a relationship with such mundane considerations as cost of production.

Everyone in the Ministry was also busy travelling abroad and in this even the lowly under secretaries got a fair share of the jaunts. The joint secretaries were, no doubt, the most frequent fliers to attend various conferences of international organizations such as GATT, ESCAP, UNCTAD, etc. and leading trade delegations. I myself travelled to Africa, Tanzania, Kenya, Zambia, Latin America, Brazil and Europe. I participated in an UNCTAD-organized seminar on 'Generalized System of Preferences' in Brazil's newly built capital, Brasilia.

Even though we were as a country quite inward-looking, chanting the mantra of economic autarchy with the public sector striving to achieve the commanding heights of the economy, given the fact that we were heavily dependent on oil imports and capital goods imports, as well as technology, in order to enable the country to meet its foreign exchange requirements a strong export effort was very much called for. The Yom Kippur War had resulted in a tripling of the crude oil prices and this further aggravated the imbalance between imports and exports. Consequently, the Ministry was trying to intensify export efforts, which in the true bureaucratic style consisted of more meetings, more strategy papers and more exhortations to the industry to redouble their efforts. No one considered loosening the hold of the government over industry, deregulation, delicenzing, etc. to give the industry freedom to expand, introduce competition, improve quality and reduce costs. These were the hey days of socialism when we were busy nationalizing the coal industry, the banks, and stifling the industry through legislations such as MRTP, FERA, etc.

Everyone in the Ministry was always very busy holding meetings or preparing papers. In fact, the standard response for any problem was usually 'take a meeting and prepare a paper'. The word decision was seldom used and carefully avoided by many and instead everyone took a 'view' which of course can be changed subsequently. There were indeed some brilliant minds involved in all this. I had the good fortune of working with Y.T Shah, who, earlier as Joint Secretary in the Department of Economic Affairs of the Ministry of Finance, had acquired a formidable reputation and had come to the Ministry of Foreign Trade as Additional Secretary and eventually became the Secretary. He was considered a favourite of no less than the austere and awe-inspiring Morarji Desai. A very punctilious and meticulous, as well as a cerebral, officer, he was known for his short temper and intolerance towards sloth and inefficiency. If you did not appear before him at the exact time—to the minute appointed by him—with the required material meeting his exalted standards, you ran the risk of being physically thrown out of his room. Many in the Ministry had indeed gone through this painful process. He, however, commanded respect all round by his knowledge, efficiency, grasp of complicated issues and ability to match the wits of the so-called experts and wizards from international organizations.

In my particular area of responsibility, namely jute, the emergence of Bangladesh as a 'friendly' country presented peculiar problems. When we had East Pakistan to deal with, as an unfriendly competitor to our raw jute and jute products, we had no hesitation in offering effective competition in terms of price, quality, etc. With

Bangladesh, we were not supposed to compete and indeed accommodate them to largest possible extent. Bangladesh was merrily undercutting us in the international market, but any similar action on the part of our industry received howls of protest on the ground that jute and jute products were, for all practical purposes, the only exportable commodity of Bangladesh and we had an obligation to protect this industry and help Bangladesh earn the much-needed foreign exchange. Not only this, Bangladesh also expected us to buy raw jute and jute products from them at prices higher than at which internal products were available and at which our industry was prepared to buy. On one occasion, a delegation from Bangladesh had arrived to sell raw jute for which there was indeed a requirement, as the jute crop that year was considered somewhat below target. The Bangladeshis knew this and quoted prices well above affordable limits. Our industry was not in favour of buying the jute at these prices and three days of discussions at the official level produced no agreement. The Bangladesh delegation, through its High Commission, managed to get the ear of the Prime Minister, Mrs Gandhi, who generous as she was towards Bangladesh, agreed to the price asked for by them and a fiat came down to go ahead and buy the jute. The government had to bear the extra cost.

Throughout our dealings with the Bangladeshis, one found a distinct note of hostility in them even in those early days. Having so intimately participated in the historic process of emergence of Bangladesh as an independent nation, during my district days, and having witnessed the atrocities perpetrated on the civilian population in East Pakistan and having experienced at first hand the great sacrifices India had made while looking after the nine million refugees who had come over as also in the process of liberation of the suppressed, I thought there will be a modicum of consideration, accommodation, friendliness and indeed gratitude from the new nation. This was apparently there but very short-lived and even during this period there were quite a few elements who were not favourably inclined towards India. Within three years of independence, Sheikh Mujibur Rahman, who almost single handedly fought against the discriminatory policies of Pakistan and who played such a pivotal role in the liberation struggle, was brutally murdered and almost all members of his family also butchered in one fell swoop by pro-Pakistan elements. Since then, Bangladeshi politics has invariably seen the interplay of anti-India forces and anyone remotely suspected to have pro-India feelings is put on the defensive. The creation of Bangladesh was expected to substantially take care of our security concerns on the eastern front, but this, if at all, proved to be unfortunately very temporary and successive regimes in that country have taken a series of steps to rebuild their ties with Pakistan, and continue to provide assistance to the insurgency movements of India's North-East and generally adopted a non-cooperative attitude in resolving bilateral issues. Even the Sheikh Hasina regime, which has been in power for the past few years, has had to be very cautious in its dealings with India, as anti-India elements keep up a constant tirade against the PM, accusing her of being unduly accommodative towards India. The return of the BNP government in Bangladesh indicates continued sway of anti-India elements in the country.

Normally, deputy secretaries to the Government of India are not permitted to attend the meetings of the union cabinet but once since a matter relating to jute namely fixing of minimum support price as per recommendations of the agricultural prices commission was to come up for discussion in the cabinet, the Secretary dragged me along. Mrs Gandhi was about to come into the room in the Parliament House where the meeting was being held, while other members of the cabinet and the officials including the Cabinet Secretary had already taken their seats. The meeting to my eyes was an eloquent testimony of the hold that Mrs Gandhi had over her cabinet, the awe in which she was held by her Ministers and the supreme authority she exercised over all aspects of the nation's governance. At that time, she had reached the absolute pinnacle of her power having so successfully orchestrated the birth of Bangladesh, having destroyed the credibility of Pakistan's military rulers, taking on the likes of Richard Nixon and reducing them to impotence, having been honoured with the Bharat Ratna and having made India a nuclear power. The moment she entered the room, all chatter stopped and absolute silence fell. The Cabinet Secretary started the proceedings, with a signal from her. She took only partial interest in the proceedings putting in an observation here, and a word there while she kept scribbling on pieces of paper, with her spectacles at the lower edge of her very roman nose. Strange and amusing was the behaviour of the ministers, who, whenever she raised her head from her scribblings and directed her gaze towards one of them, seemed to visibly shrink back, their voices getting lowered by several decibels and exhibiting a noticeable degree of fear and subservience. One heard that many would not have their cups of coffee in her presence, as they could not keep their hands steady.

She had absolute command over the entire country and wielded an authority which surpassed even her father's. The London *Economist* had described her as the Steely Empress of India and someone else had stated that her boldness had proved that 'she was twice the man, her father was'.

This was of course before the declaration of Emergency, the rise of Sanjay Gandhi and all that followed, resulting in a very substantial reduction in her stature.

Since I was dealing with jute and since at that time a proposal to open an office in Brussels to deal with problems relating to the emerging European Union was being considered, I was asked if I would be willing to start the office in Brussels which was supposed to be part of our mission to the European Union. The office was supposed to be a joint industry–government effort to be organized on the model of the one in New York. In view of this, I started learning French and had made quite some progress. While the Ministry was keen that I should proceed to Brussels, there were indications that the industry would prefer someone with actual hands-on experience in the industry itself. I thought this to be fair and hence requested that my name be withdrawn.

I met Y.T. Shah, the Secretary, who had taken a liking to me, observing that I could meet his exacting standards, and while conveying my reservations as regards Brussels, requested him to consider my name for a posting to Sydney or New York where the Tea Board had its offices and where the incumbents had completed their tenures. Y.T. Shah very readily agreed to my request and very soon I had my orders to go to Sydney. I could claim that having spent considerable periods in tea-growing districts of Assam, I had reasonable knowledge of the industry. Marketing of the product was an area I had to fully familiarize myself.

T.S. Broca, the Chairman of Tea Board, put me through a routine visiting all the tea growing areas, Darjeeling, Assam, the Nilgiris, talking to the tea company executives and studying the prospects in the Australian market. I had also to look after the New Zealand and the Fiji Islands markets as well.

Late in 1975, I landed in Sydney which along with Melbourne

were the centres for commercial activity. The High Commissioner to whom I was reporting was stationed in Canberra—the nation's capital; whereas in Sydney itself there was a Consul General.

The Australian tea companies were importing substantial quantities of tea in bulk from India, price being the overriding consideration. They compromised on quality and if India's prices were considered high, they unhesitatingly switched over to tea from Sri Lanka or even Indonesia, not to mention Kenya. India was placing considerable emphasis upon value-added products, namely packaged tea and tea bags. We wanted to increase the foreign exchange earnings and, equally importantly, establish a distinct India brand identity in the market. One had to, however, tread cautiously as the market was not large, the Australian population at that time being a mere 15 million. Any largescale import of packaged tea could invite the wrath of the Australian tea packers who had an established market for their brands leading to a reduction of bulk tea imports. Keeping good relations with the bulk tea importers was essential, and the induction of value-added products could be only a gradual process. I aimed at the upper end of the market with attractive packaging of the product, especially as gifts. The Australians believed in giving gifts on a variety of occasions and I tried to cash in on this attractive habit and succeeded in introducing a number of brands of the Tea Trading Corporation of India, of Duncan and Williamson Magor.

To popularize tea drinking as against coffee which commanded a macho image in Australia, I kept highlighting the health benefits which were supposed to accrue, undertaking tours, addressing Rotary Clubs and schools all over Australia. For the first time, I also managed to achieve considerable exposure on television, while cultivating the press, quite assiduously.

The Emergency in India received a great deal of adverse reaction in the very liberal and democratic Australia. How could India of Gandhi and Nehru resort to draconian measures, curb the freedom of expression, gag the press, suppress dissent by violent means were questions raised in various forums. The defence put out on the basis of briefings by the High Commission were received with large dose of scepticism.

Australia has been truly described as the lucky country. With a small population, large geographical area, enormous natural resources like coal, iron ore, uranium, plenty of good arable land and a very

European work culture, Australia was a prosperous country by any standards. That it began its present life as a penal settlement, where convicts were sent to serve out their terms, was no doubt mentioned quite often, only to draw attention to the great advances that the country has made since those early days. Not mentioned, however, is the brutal and inhuman manner in which the original inhabitants of Australia were treated by the white settlers. These aborigines were shot down as if they were no more than wild animals, their lands forcibly taken away, their traditions and belief systems trampled upon, their children separated from their parents and denied any share in the governance of the country. One could see them reduced to abject poverty, living in isolated pockets without basic amenities and prone to a high degree of alcoholism and a variety of diseases. Deprived of education and chances of advancement, their future looked bleak. Very few of the human rights activists, who make such a song and dance of the so-called violations in India or China, have anything to say about the white man's cruelty to fellow human beings, merely because the pigmentation on their skin is different from his. Only very recently there have been some voices in Australia who have been demanding restoration of aborigine lands, respect for their traditions and belief systems, giving them education and working towards a better future for them.

The Australians, I also found, had a fairly serious identity problem. They were very European in their origins and in their cultural mores, not to mention language and religion. They are very proud of their heroic participation in the European struggles of World War I and World War II, recalling their stellar role in the battles at Gallipoli and against Rommel in the Sahara. Anzac Day is celebrated with great fanfare and ex-soldiers are an honoured lot. General and later Field Marshal K.M. Cariappa, who after being Commander-in-Chief of the Indian Army, took office as High Commissioner of India in Australia, was very fondly remembered as a great figure and had addressed a whole lot of ex-servicemen's clubs all over the country.

The Australians had built up strategic relations with the United States. Protected by the oceans, the Pacific ocean on one side and the Indian Ocean on the other, Australia faced really no threat, except briefly during World War II from Japanese.

Despite all this European orientation in terms of geography and with respect to trade and economic interest, Australia however is firmly placed in the Orient. They would very much like to be regarded as part of Asia and the Far-East, to play a greater role in Asian affairs, using their economic and technological strengths, building bridges and strategic relations with their Asian neighbours. They have become members of the ASEAN group but at the same time are wary of losing their European identity, while the Asian nations themselves are not yet ready to accept Australia as one of them.

While for a long time, Australia followed a white Australia policy encouraging immigration only from Europe, offering a variety of incentives for them alone, the static and indeed declining population and high levels of prosperity in western Europe has virtually brought to a halt this flow of immigrants. Asians now form the bulk of immigrants and, though still a small percentage of the overall population, the complexion of the Australian society is undergoing distinct changes. Alarm bells are already ringing and the far right is calling for an immediate halt to Asian immigration. Economic forces, however, are likely to prevail and if the Australian economy is to grow and prosper, there seems to be limits beyond which the white Australia policy cannot be carried on.

It needs no great emphasis that the white man because of his adventurous character, capacity to perpetrate violence and inflict cruelty on people with darker skin colour, has managed to occupy a disproportionate share of the world's geographical area—the world's real estate. When he colonized large parts of the globe, his ability to use force with greater lethality was the only determining factor. The indigenous peoples did not impose passport or visa restrictions, and were subdued or eliminated by the use of brute force alone. Prosperity of the white man is to a large extent due to this inequitable distribution of land and natural resources of the world, heavily in favour of the whites. The world's poor who occupy a relatively smaller portion of the world's geographical area and command lesser quantum of natural resources, have to reduce their rates of growth of population, if they have to improve their living standards.

Quite strangely, the Australians have a love–hate relationship with the English. Their cultural and civilizational characteristics are very English and they tend to imitate English lifestyles, admire English poetry, drama, opera and literature. Indeed, the more English an Australian is, the more advanced he is regarded. The monarchy still commands great respect and the many efforts to delink Australia from the monarchy and make it a Republic have not so far succeeded. The umbilical cord with England, the mother country is still very much intact. At the same time, efforts to establish a distinct Australian identity continue and the English are derisively referred to as 'the Pommies'. This antagonism surfaces quite strongly during sporting events, especially cricket when beating the English becomes a national passion, almost the moral equivalent of war. English is spoken but with a distinctly Australian accent.

Strangely again, the Australians have not been able to decide what should be their national anthem. 'Waltzing Matilda', 'Advance Australia Fair' and two other songs are still vying with each other and the required majority in votes repeatedly polled has not been given to any of the four songs.

The Indian population in Australia is miniscule but highly prosperous, consisting of mainly doctors and engineers and some professors and teachers.

The workload that I had can at best be described as barely adequate, with lots of leisure. I found the staff in the Consulate as well as the High Commission in Canberra, leading an equally leisurely lifestyle, while those in the tourism office and the Air India office seemed to have even greater leisure. The State Trading Corporation manager, however, seemed to be very busy.

Australia being a great sporting nation excelling in cricket, tennis, rugby football, golf, yachting and what have you, sporting facilities of excellent quality were available for everyone. The entire citizenry appeared to be health freaks and one could see groups specializing in jogging on the roads every day. Everyone seemed to play one game or the other and lead very healthy lifestyles. Apart from city dwellings, most had large farmlands where sheep and cattle were raised and owning five to seven thousand acres was nothing unusual. Very many had yachts and going out into the sea during weekends was their favourite pastime. Spending time on the beaches, on the golf courses and outdoors is a national passion and weekends normally from Friday afternoon to Monday afternoon are taken very seriously.

Since New Zealand and the Fiji Islands were within my beat, I visited these places quite a few times. New Zealand, though very picturesque, was colder with rains pouring down all the while and generally speaking less prosperous than Australia. The New Zealanders were less thorough in disposing off the native population and the original inhabitants, namely the Maoris, appeared to be far more numerous than the aborigines of Australia and also comparatively better off. They have been able to fight for their land rights more successfully, and have evolved a unique lifestyle combining European and their own native customs and traditions.

Fiji Islands has a large population of people of Indian origin who had been brought in by the British as indentured labour. They now control the entire business and sugarcane farming. They have reached high levels of prosperity and have been looked upon with hostility by the indigenous Fijians. Through a system of tribal chiefs called 'Tuis' and through constitutional safeguards the natives retained political power in their hands. The armed forces and the police were also manned by them. Ratu Sir Kamisese Mara was the then Prime Minister, 'Ratu' being a chief of chiefs. It was said that all Ratus are Tuis but not all tuis are ratus. In recent times, Fiji has witnessed considerable political turmoil as Indians have started entering the political arena and the constitution is being changed to bring about a more balanced and equitable political arrangement. This has invited hostile reactions from the Fijians, with a coup to boot. At that time, however, there was peace all round with a thriving tourism industry.

In Fiji, our High Commissioner Bhagvan Singh, whose own ancestors had reportedly been in Fiji as indentured labour, was a really dynamic representative and had developed an excellent rapport with the Fijian government. It appears his views were heard with respect by the Fijians and he had adopted a lifestyle totally in tune with the local habits, which made him a very popular figure.

He also represented India in a nearby island called Tonga, famous not only because the international dateline passes through this tiny island in the South Pacific, but also for the immensely obese population. The king of Tonga was an enormous mountain of a man whose breakfast consisted of four suckling pigs. His other meals would only be of larger volume and greater variety. I had the pleasure of meeting him in Sydney airport, on his way to India on an official visit, and the lift to the VIP lounge could just about accommodate him and no one else. His Majesty, therefore, had to be sent up on his own, while the rest of us including some Tongans had to climb the stairs. The accompanying Tongans were not much smaller than His Majesty and after the very first few steps, they were gasping. His Majesty who had reached the designated floor and with great difficulty managed to squeeze himself out of the lift but had to wait quite a while for his compatriots to join him.

Fiji, Tonga and the nearby islands such as Samoa—French American etc.—are inhabited by people belonging to the Polynesian race and have a unique civilization. R.L. Stevenson in his novels on these south sea islands has evocatively described the life in these islands and it was a wonderful experience to see firsthand this joyful, carefree, egalitarian and very colourful civilization so filled with songs, dances and festivities round the year. Nature has been kind to these islanders and the growth in tourism has worked wonders in uplifting their standards of living.

# 8

# ASSAM AGAIN

I had now spent a little over six years out of my parent cadre and it was time for a return to Assam. When I left India in 1975, the Emergency had been imposed by Mrs Gandhi and much has been said justifying her decision and indeed much more as to why the Emergency need not and should not have been imposed and the damage that it had caused to India's image abroad and to Mrs Gandhi's own stature. The rise of her son in the politics of this country and the kind of changes that took place in the philosophical and ethical underpinnings of the Congress party have also been widely discussed and commented upon.

By the time of my return from Australia in March 1978, a good deal had changed, as regards the political situation in the country. Mrs Gandhi had been unseated and Morarji Desai was presiding over the destiny of the country. The Shah Commission hearings were unraveling the excesses of the Emergency, particularly on the family planning front. While the intentions were of the right kind, the implementation of the programme in several parts of the country had given it a bad name. The whole effort consequently received a severe setback with very adverse fallout with respect to control of the unacceptably high rates of growth of population. The nation is paying a very heavy price as the number of people below the poverty line continues to be very high, our levels of unemployment and malnutrition continue to be unacceptably high, our per capita income remains low and most achievements of the nation are swallowed up by the population growth.

Changes had taken place in Assam as well, and the Congress

yielded power to a new conglomeration led by Golap Borbora. One however found that many Congressmen had just switched their loyalties and were again ministers. The Chief Minister was quite inexperienced in statecraft, and the overall effectiveness of the administration was in question. A little earlier Sarat Sinha, an able, austere and principled Chief Minister, had given Assam an efficient administration with the assistance of Rana K.D.N. Singh as Chief Secretary who, with wide experience in the Government of India and UN bodies, gave the kind of support that an organized bureaucracy is supposed to give. He made the system work and deliver exacting standards by his own conduct. He was much admired all round.

The capital of Assam had been shifted from Shillong to Guwahati and the Secretariat was housed in makeshift structures. Apparently, these structures were being used as godowns earlier, and with a number of partitions, rooms of various sizes were created with no particular regard to the functional requirements of running offices in an efficient manner. For years, these near-dilapidated structures have served the secretariat of the state of Assam, greatly inconveniencing the officers and the staff, damaging their morale and conveying a poor image of the government to the public, robbing it of the air of strength, dignity, power and authority a government is supposed to project and command.

The adjacent housing colony was poorly planned, congested and could easily be mistaken to be a slum. A particularly miserly or sadistic genius of an architect had determined the dimensions of the rooms to be such that furniture of normal sizes could be accommodated only if the occupants themselves stayed outside. The houses were placed so near each other, with thin brick walls, that you could not only hear but clearly understand the neighbours' quarrels. The planners had probably calculated that this would be a good incentive for people to avoid domestic strife of the noisy kind at least!

Notwithstanding these inconveniences, I was keen to bring the work culture that I had learnt in my tenure in the Centre and in Australia, which was definitely superior to the leisurely and laid-back style in the secretariat of Assam to the areas of responsibility that was entrusted to me, namely, welfare of plains tribes and backward classes. I had hardly settled down to my responsibilities when my name was proposed to the Governor of Assam, L.P. Singh, to be appointed as his Secretary. Singh was impressed by my record and I was soon inducted as Secretary for the state of Assam.

Normally, the governors have only certain constitutional responsibilities. However, in the case of the North-Eastern states the governors have been invested with certain special responsibilities with respect to law and order and economic and social development of the tribal areas. L.P. Singh, an officer of the ICS, with a legendary reputation for his knowledge and skills and had vast experience in the Government of India where he had distinguished himself as an outstanding Home Secretary. While indeed observing the constitutional norms for his conduct, he wanted to play a very constructive role through a process of gentle persuasion, suggestions and advice on crucial matters concerning the state's administration. He appointed himself as a one-man thinktank, worrying himself about the problems of the state. He expected his Secretary to prepare detailed papers after studying all aspects of a given problem, which engaged the attention of the Governor and incorporate the Governor's own ideas on the subject and the solutions he proposed. He would take great pains in polishing up and refining the studies. These would then be sent to the Chief Minister for his consideration and action.

L.P. Singh took his responsibilities with respect to the tribal areas very seriously and took great pains in finding a solution to the Naga tangle. He was also the Chairman of the North-Eastern Council, a body specially created for accelerating the economic advancement of the whole region.

He was therefore a pretty busy Governor and, given his own habits, attitudes, interests and inclinations, worked at a pace almost equal to that in his Home Ministry days. He did not spare himself nor his subordinates. He was very fond of reading and rereading the Constitution and the regulatory laws. Given his reputation as a very hard task-master, impatient, with a very short temper, to work with him was considered a punishment by some. He was however kind to me and within the first two or three weeks I made the necessary adjustments to bring my own working habits to be fully in tune with his exacting standards. After that he was openly appreciative of my work.

I had made it a point to keep him fully informed of all developments in the state—political, economic, administrative—and was prompt in preparing studies that he wanted in keeping with his philosophy of acting as the think-tank of the state. My papers were of acceptable quality and received encomiums from him. The Governor on one occasion went to the extent of stating that 'he was beholden to me for the excellent contribution' that I had made in preparing a paper on the status and future of higher education in Assam.

L.P. Singh had taken particular interest in Naga affairs and was instrumental in bringing to fruition the Naga peace accord. It was a truly exhausting process, and it was only due to his great knowledge of the area, enormous patience and understanding of the complex issues involved that success could be achieved. He had because of this significant achievement, earned a place in the history of the North East.

The Governor was a delightful conversationalist and was very happy to talk about his Home Ministry days and when he was in Bihar. He had become the Chief Secretary of Bihar at the age of thirty-five and thereafter worked wholly in the Government of India. I however found that when it came to international relations or economics his knowledge was limited. With my experience in the Ministry of Foreign Trade and in Australia I detected a window of opportunity in this—an escape route, as it were—whenever the going got sticky for me. I held forth on matters such as Brazil's economic development or the Australian immigration policy or Indo–Peru relations, thereby diverting the Governor's mind.

For me it was indeed a rewarding experience to have had the privilege of working with such a distinguished civil servant of the old school and the lessons I learnt from him did serve me very well in my career. I had also seen in action the other equally distinguished civilian B.K. Nehru and both were men of extraordinary calibre and achievements. In terms of clear thinking and written expression Nehru was definitely a cut above. One single dictation was enough for Nehru to produce a perfect piece of art, whereas Singh will go through two or even three drafts before producing an equally fine masterpiece.

Questions have however been raised about L.P. Singh's attitudes and inclinations with respect to the 'the anti-foreigner agitation' launched by the All Assam Students Union from 1979 onwards, and all the turmoil that followed. I shall deal with this matter in some detail a little later in this chapter.

By July 1979, the government deemed it proper to promote me to the super time scale of the IAS, as a vacancy had occurred, with respect to the office of the Commissioner of the Hills and Cachar division. I had just completed sixteen years of service. This meant that I had to leave the Governor's office and the Governor agreed to my relief; I was told with considerable reluctance.

I had hardly settled down in my new saddle when the political situation in Assam started becoming unstable. At the same time the Central Government was also facing an uncertain future. Soon the Golap Borbora ministry lost its majority and yielded place to a hotch-potch conglomeration led by Jogen Hazarika. This new set-up had even less coherence than the earlier one and a general drift was noticeable all round. More or less during this period Charan Singh became the Prime Minister. The events were clearly leading towards a general election in the country.

While Desai was still the PM due to the demise of an MP from the Mangaldai constituency—Hiralal Patwary—a bye-election had to be conducted. This had to be preceded by a revision of the electoral rolls. For some time now the issue of entry of the names of illegal immigrants into the electoral rolls was being widely debated and the press had started playing this up as an issue of vital importance for the future of Assam. The students under the banner of the All Assam Students Union (AASU) jumped into the fray, making it a subject which deserved their full-scale intervention. The students had played a key role in a number of agitations, be it for a refinery or for a railway and had emerged as a strong force capable of bringing life to a standstill in Assam. They could decisively influence the outcome of any agitation, and no political party could afford to annoy them. The students had become quite conscious of their power. On occasion, the political parties were even prepared to ride piggyback on the shoulders of the students. They also seemed to command considerable resources. The local press invariably supported their campaigns. The students had become, it appeared, true champions of Assam's interests and were a weapon strong enough to take on the Central Government where necessary. With representation in each and every educational institution, fiercely loyal to the AASU, the students had acquired a formidable and well-organized machinery capable of launching state-wide agitations at short notice. Since the students were generally seen as espousing causes considered to be in the interests of Assam, successive governments showed great reluctance to apply harsh measures allowing the students to have their way taking only minimum precautions to avoid violence. 'Neglect by the Centre' was a favourite and popular theme and any agitation which focused on this angle invited widespread support and the government was happy to be a mute spectator.

It is in this fairly charged atmosphere where the powerful students body was focusing upon the issue of illegal immigrants that the above mentioned bye-elections for the Mangaldai constituency had to be taken up. As luck would have it, the Chief Secretary wanted me to take on the responsibilities of the Chief Electoral Officer (CEO) in addition to those of the divisional Commissioner. The heat was squarely focused on me, as a full-scale agitation by the students backed by the press and a very large section of the population was well on its way. I would now have to get ready to face the challenge squarely, calling up all my reserves of physical and mental energy.

The demand voiced was that all foreigners must be deleted from the electoral rolls and only genuine Indian citizens should be permitted to exercise their franchise. It would be worth examining the dimensions of this problem, as it has a history of its own, has international ramifications and serious national security implications.

On the face of it, the demand had all the elements of legitimacy, as after all what was being asked for was nothing but the implementation of the provisions in the Constitution and those of the Representation of People's Act. Both clearly lay down that a person who is not an Indian citizen is not entitled to exercise his or her franchise.

The big problem in Assam, as is the case with other border states, is in determining who actually is and who is not an Indian citizen. The provisions in the Representation of People's Act and the procedures for inclusion and non-inclusion do not constitute and are not meant to be foolproof methods for determining the citizenship of all those residents on Indian soil, especially when the numbers involved are large and, as in the case of Assam, it is so difficult to distinguish a citizen from a non-citizen due to ethnic and racial similarities, everyone claiming to be a blue-blooded Indian. An added complication is the role of vested interests and political parties who favour inclusion of even those of doubtful nationality in the electoral rolls, as this increases the number of potential voters in their favour.

The primary document that constitutes the beginning of the process of preparation of the electoral rolls is the enumerator's slip where the enumerator—normally a school teacher or a clerk in the local government office temporarily drafted for the purpose of enumeration—is supposed to include the name of the resident, so long as there is no prima facie evidence which casts a reasonable doubt about his citizenship. Normally possession of a ration card, inclusion in past electoral rolls, possession of immovable property are deemed adequate to establish eligibility for inclusion. The word of the village headman or the local revenue official goes a long way. Inclusion rather than exclusion is the rule. If anyone has doubts about a person's citizenship he is supposed to file an objection before a duly designated Electoral Registration Officer, who, through a quasi-judicial process, pronounces a verdict in favour or against inclusion. No doubt, at this stage, a more rigorous scrutiny is undertaken and the burden of proof is upon the person whose citizenship is challenged.

The whole spirit of the law regarding elections is that it is not the responsibility to determine the finality of a person's citizenship. In fact, inclusion of a person's name in the electoral roll or even exercise of franchise is not proof enough for determining a person's citizenship.

The question of determining a person's citizenship falls within the ambit of another piece of legislation namely the Foreigners Act under which the police have powers to detect and deport illegal immigrants.

Now in Assam, for a variety of reasons, the implementation of the Foreigners Act has been extremely difficult, controversial and lax. I have referred to the problem of immigration from East Bengal in Chapter III, which had been encouraged before Independence. East Bengal was a source of cheap labour and with a heavy concentration of population in that area and decreasing per capita land availability the newly opened-up spaces in Assam offered a great relief to the poverty stricken and land hungry masses. The Assamese themselves seem to have raised few objections to this influx at that time as these immigrants were prepared to work for the Assamese landholders at a pittance of a wage and for long hours. They were also employed in road building projects, flood protection works, etc. where the Assamese themselves were not too keen to work.

After Independence, because of periodic communal riots, bouts of Hindu refugees came to Assam. Strangely, there was greater resentment towards this kind of influx than what was the case with respect to the pre-Independence flow and Assam witnessed periodic anti-Bengali riots. At the same time illegal immigration of cultivators for economic reasons did continue, inviting several concerted measures by the Central Government in consort with the state government. A fullscale outfit for preventing, detecting and deporting infiltrators from East Pakistan was created, a village-wise register called National Register of citizens was created—all those not in the register deemed as suspected illegal infiltrators—watch posts established in all sensitive areas and detection and deportation teams organized in all the districts. The Police could act under the Foreigners Act and indeed thousands of illegal immigrants were deported to East Pakistan right up to 1971. The then Chief Minister B.P. Chaliha was quite conscious of this problem and its long-term implications, but some of his own colleagues such as Debkanta Barua and Moinul Choudhry strongly opposed such operations. At one stage, the differences on this score became so serious that Chaliha had to drop these ministers from his Cabinet. It was no secret that people like D.K. Barua regarded the immigrants as convenient vote banks and he is reported to have stated that the Congress party will always win so long as it had the votes of 'the Alis and coolies', namely the immigrant Muslim and the tea garden labour supported by the Bengali and the deswali, that is, the Bengali immigrant and the Bihari.

Prior to the creation of Bangladesh, fairly satisfactory procedures for detection and deportation of illegal immigrants were in place and the police, especially when they had the leadership of a dynamic superintendent of police, could achieve significant results. The situation changed substantially with the creation of Bangladesh as this newly created country was supposed to be 'friendly' and given our foreign policy objectives, measures considered harsh were discouraged.

The problem of infiltration is not confined only to Assam, but has assumed serious proportions in all bordering states, including West Bengal. Enough documentary evidence is available of the continuing large scale influx termed a silent invasion and demographic aggression and by now the illegal immigrants have penetrated right across India and are to be found in Mumbai, Delhi and many try to go through to Pakistan.

A number of factors have been identified as responsible for this phenomenon. While prior to the creation of Bangladesh Hindu migration was larger, primarily due to religious persecution, along with a substantial Muslim influx due to economic reasons after 1971 immigration of Muslims has been steadily rising. This is due to the very high concentration of population in Bangladesh, high rates of growth of population, shrinking per capita availability of land, little or no diversification of the economy, low rates of economic growth resulting in unbearable rates of unemployment and poverty squalor and misery. Political instability, poor standards of governance and periodic civil unrest are additional factors. Bangladesh was at one stage designated as an 'international basket case' and indeed one of the LDCs —least developed countries.

While the above can be classified as 'push' factors encouraging outflow, there are also what can be called 'pull' factors. These are mainly economic, social as well as religious.

Compared to the abject poverty in Bangladesh with poor prospects for employment, getting a remunerative vocation in India's North-East is not difficult. Hard physical labour for low wages is something the immigrant is prepared for; there were many vocations which the local people did not like to get involved in, which demanded this kind of skill such as rickshaw pulling, earth digging, road building, etc. There were not many takers among the locals for even such trades as carpentry, shoe repair, cane and bamboo works, etc. With the Centre pouring in large amounts of money into the area in answer to the charges of neglect by the Centre and the intense road building activity that had to be taken up to meet defence requirements, all meant plenty of demand for cheap labour. Land, though becoming increasingly scarce, was still available if one can get it from the gullible tribals or be sufficiently adventurous to encroach into the reserve forests. Corruption among the land revenue staff was useful for getting over the land revenue regulations, prohibiting transfer of tribal land to non-tribals, and the forest staff could also be equally effectively persuaded to look the other way. Political patronage was not difficult to obtain, either, if you showed sufficient inclination to patronize a particular candidate or a party which is on the look-out for increasing their vote bank.

Even at the time of partition, the characteristics of the population on both sides of the border was not very different. Those Muslims from the area, who went to East Pakistan immediately after partition, returned as a consequence of the Nehru–Feroze Khan Noon agreement and relatives with religious affinity had no hesitation in giving shelter to those seeking a better and more secure economic future and helping them in getting them any document that could help in establishing their citizenship. Those functionaries, trying to check citizenship in border areas often get into hot waters with a whole lot of villagers supporting the claim of illegal immigrants at times even violently. Corruption does play a role in all these matters.

The effectiveness of the Border Security Force in checking and deporting illegal aliens has often been questioned. Stories of corruption abound, not only with regard to illegal immigration, but also relating to cattle smuggling, traffic of arms and narcotics. Further, ever since about 1989, because of the vast increase in the force requirements in Kahmir the number of BSF battallions, deployed along the Indo–Bangladesh border, have been cut down quite substantially, thereby reducing the ability of the force to effectively patrol all sectors of the border and check illegal activities.

The other pull factor is religious. Evidence is available of the role of religious organizations on both sides of the border, aided generously by nations such as Saudi Arabia and Iran, to alter the religious character and composition of the population, all along the international border. Reports point to the ease with which lands are purchased by the immigrants from Hindus and of Hindus moving away from the border areas. Proliferation of mosques and madrassas, and Islamic universities financed by Saudi Arabia have been noticed along the border. The sonorous bells of the Hindu temples have been replaced by the call of the muezzin. This has happened particularly on the West Bengal border and in the Dhubri and Goalpara districts of Assam. The population pattern in the highly sensitive and strategic Siliguri corridor has already undergone substantive changes, with an increase in the population of those whose loyalty is at best untested and at worst suspect. One cannot ignore the long-term security implications of these developments. In Assam, reports have indeed emerged of the coming into being of armed outfits such as Muslim United Liberation of Assam, who command considerable resources and even weaponry. The area has also thrown up credible evidence of the spread of ISI activities. ULFA, which started with the so-called ideal of safeguarding the interests of the Assamese seems now to have wholly slipped into the stranglehold of the ISI.

While the above factors have been in full play, political patronage has become a very important factor in encouraging the influx. In our democracy and in the particular type of electoral system we have adopted numbers play a critical role in winning elections and with the progressive and unabashed use of caste, creed and ethnicity to gather votes the immigrants have become increasingly important for winning elections not only in Assam but in West Bengal as well. Political parties, therefore, facilitate obtaining ration cards, identity cards, land documents and entry into the voters lists. In Assam, as of now, in at least 40 out of 127 constituencies the votes of immigrants determine the outcome of elections.

Studies after studies conducted by various government agencies have drawn attention to the menacing proportions that unchecked influx has already assumed and the kind of socio-economic strains that are being caused thereby, and the short term and long term political consequences for the border states. Since 1971, it has been estimated that 14 million Bangladeshis have crossed over to India. Every day some 500 souls cross over to India. Between 1981 and 1991, no less than 1.6 million people had settled down in the border districts of West Bengal. Press reports indicate that during election time political parties vie with each other to get their votes and also encourage those who are already in to bring their relatives. All are promised Indian citizenship.

Bangladesh does not even bother to admit that her citizens enter India illegally. Why should they when our own parties refuse to call a spade a spade. Some intellectuals of Bangladesh even talk of the North East of India being the natural *lebensraum* for the growing population of their country. Where else are we to go, they ask. It may be recalled that Jinnah's concept of Pakistan did include Assam. If, God forbid, as a consequence of global warming and consequent rise in sea level parts of Bangladesh do get submerged under the sea, a possibility which cannot be ruled out or ignored, the *lebensraum* theory may well come into play. As it is, large parts of Bangladesh go under water in the rainy season.

In the case of Assam, the Assamese in general and the students in particular have been ringing alarm bells expressing grave concern over the possibility of the Assamese being reduced to a minority in their own state and the complexion of the governments being determined by the votes of the immigrants. Steps to combat the influx have however been tardy to say the least. Indeed the staff, sanctioned under the scheme for checking influx fully financed by the Centre, have been withdrawn and deployed for other duties.

The agitation launched by the students in 1979 focused pointed attention on this problem and one expected a coherent response from both the state and the centre. Developments on this score will be covered in the later part of this chapter.

I have dealt with the issue of illegal influx in foregoing paragraphs in some detail in order to provide a suitable backdrop for going into the events that took place in Assam from the middle of 1979 onwards.

As mentioned earlier, the focus was on the revision of electoral rolls for the Mangaldai constituency, when I assumed charge as the Chief Electoral Officer (CEO) of Assam. The Chief Election Commissioner S.L. Shakdhar had, a little earlier in a conference of CEOs, drawn pointed attention to the problem of large-scale entry of ineligible noncitizens in the voters' lists in Assam and this had provided a good deal of ammunition to the students.

In Mangaldai, because of the active interest taken by the students and others a large number of objections had been filed and the district administration had enlisted the services of a large number of officers to act as Electoral Registration Officers, who were supposed to dispose of these objections. I visited the district and found that, broadly speaking, the objections and claims were being disposed of in a fair manner, based on objective criteria. This however raised the hackles of those who feared a reduction in their captive flock of voters and both the state government and the Government of India were hammered with telegrams, alleging unfair elimination of genuine voters. I had submitted my reports to the state government, who therefore did not react but the Centre took a somewhat alarmist view and the Joint Secretary in the Home Ministry K.M.L. Chabra was sent to Assam. During his visit he could not find fault with the procedures put into practice. In any case, the subject matter fell within the exclusive province of Election Commission of India who found nothing wrong with what was being done.

Suddenly, certain fast-paced developments took place in Delhi, with the government losing its majority and countrywide elections to Parliament had to be held.

My cup of woe was now full. The Jogen Hazarika Ministry was directionless and ineffective and I could get no support from this quarter. Constitutionally, I was mandated to conduct elections and I was answerable to the Chief Election Commissioner. The administration was supposed to place, at my disposal, the necessary resources. The DCs in their role as district election officers cum returning officers were duty-bound to carry out my orders as regards revision of electoral rolls and the conduct of elections.

On the other hand, in the towns and villages all over Assam, a veritable storm was brewing, assuming menacing proportions every day. The announcement of the general elections seemed to lend a new urgency to the movement of the students and it was made known that a 'do or die' battle was beginning. The demand clearly was that the electoral rolls in Assam contained an overwhelming number of illegal immigrants, who being non-citizens, were not eligible to vote and unless all of them are removed from the electoral rolls no elections should be held in the whole of Assam. The students were articulating the deep seated fear of the Assamese that political power was slipping away from their hands and illegal aliens were already in a position to determine the outcome of elections. The students threatened a sustained agitation to ensure that elections were not conducted in Assam until their objectives were achieved, and they wanted that steps be taken at once to clean the rolls.

Prafulla Mahanta and Brigu Phukan, who were then leaders of the AASU, suddenly emerged as supremos of the movements and the media built them to the status of demi gods and saviours of Assam from the invasion of foreign nationals. The *Assam Tribune* and the vernacular *Aajir Asom* daily carried on a virulent tirade against the foreign nationals, targetting the central Government for having failed to tackle the problem, all these years supporting the view that polls should not be held in Assam till the last foreigner was taken out of the rolls. Indeed, it was projected in no uncertain terms that was the duty of every one in Assam to join the agitation and prevent the conduct of elections. Further, participation in the struggle was made out to be the acid test as regards the patriotic credentials of all residents of the state, and anyone not fully participating pronounced a traitor.

So effective, sustained and virulent was the propaganda that in the entire Brahmaputra valley the educational system collapsed, with students and teachers participating in the daily processions, protest marches enforcing bandhs and disrupting all normal activity. Attempts at paralysing government offices were frequent. The agitation had assumed an emotional and feverish pitch, with the entire intelligentsia joining the fray. Lawyers, doctors, teachers, journalists, all deemed it proper to join the agitation and women came out in large numbers.

The agitators wanted to project that their struggle was non-violent and they were observing the Gandhian principles. Often portraits of Mahatma Gandhi were carried by the protesters. Normal life was disrupted, repeatedly, and given the platform that the agitators had adopted compliance with the diktats was complete. To be sure, the hill districts of Assam were only partially affected and the Barak valley was practically untouched by the agitation. This, no doubt, angered the people in the Brahmaputra valley.

The Jogen Hazarika administration, which had been reduced to the status of a helpless onlooker, gave up the very feeble efforts to deal with the situation. In the handful of discussions held by the CM, the AASU did not bother to participate and those who came only denounced the politicians, declaring that they would not allow holding of elections until all the foreigners were removed from the electoral rolls. It was very disturbing to see the kind of virulence and anger displayed by the intellectuals who normally were placid and gentle in their dealings.

The Union Home Minister Y.B. Chavan visited Guwahati in an attempt to talk to the agitators and to bring about a degree of normalcy, so that elections could be held. The students who were thoroughly committed to their cause and who were so completely convinced of the righteousness of the course they had set for themselves and the State were in no mood to listen to anyone and least of all to Chavan, who, as a Congressman, was suspect in their eyes as a champion of the immigrants. They spoke to him in manner so arrogant, discourteous and insulting that we were squirming in our seats. The meeting had to be ended abruptly and Chavan returned to Delhi, empty handed. In any case the lame duck administration at Delhi, facing a general election with uncertain prospects was in no way capable of tackling such a serious problem.

In the face of this, I had the onerous responsibility of revising the electoral rolls and conducting the elections. The bulk of the government servants had already expressed solidarity with the students, though they had not yet gone on strike. This happened a little later. In spite of daily disruptions, I was able to get the DCs and SDOs get on with the job of enumeration of eligible voters. In accordance with the relevant provisions of law, I had given detailed instructions to ensure that only Indian citizens were enrolled. Given the overall atmosphere and possible over enthusiasm by some officials, I had to caution against omission of genuine voters.

I had to face a situation where every day there was the prospect of this process coming to a halt, as the students were now increasing the tempo of agitation and were pressurizing the government servants to join them. I was trying to convince those who cared to listen to me and through them the students that here was an opportunity given to them to achieve the very purpose for which they were agitating, namely preparation of a clean electoral roll. Wide publicity was given regarding filing of objections, which was a legally permissible means to eliminate from the rolls all those whose nationality was suspect. By sheer luck, I was able to complete this phase, namely enumeration and publication of the draft rolls all over the state. My message regarding the need to utilize the opportunity available under law had possibly reached some ears and, consequently, a large number of objections were filed in all the districts. There were also quite a few claims for inclusion in the electoral rolls.

I got busy organizing the process of hearing and disposing of all the claims and objections. In spite of very great pressure on the government officials to abandon their posts and join the agitation, the hearings went on in all the districts. I was extremely nervous as to when and where this will come to a grinding halt and was in daily contact with all the DCs. My luck held once again and all the claims and objections were duly disposed of and I was ready to publish the final rolls.

The Chief Election Commissioner, who was closely watching my travails and who was being kept informed of the kind of extreme pressure under which I was working and the explosive situation that was building in Assam, conveyed to me his appreciation promising all support.

Since there was a high degree of participation during the stage of disposal of claims and objections, I felt that we had succeeded in satisfying the desires of the students. My hopes in this regard soon vanished and there was an intensification of the agitation.

The Jogen Hazarika ministry had, in the mean time, collapsed and President's rule had been imposed. The politicians of all hues were a frightened lot, not knowing what stand they should take. The Congress and the communists were at a particular disadvantage, as agitators squarely held them responsible for encouraging influx and building vote banks. The other political parties who in any case had little following became inconsequential. Grave doubts therefore arose as to however can an election take place, calling for aspirants to campaign and appeal to the electorate. This was not however my immediate worry as suddenly an eventuality, which I had all along feared, namely strike by the government servants, landed on my head. The problem on hand was the printing of the final electoral rolls and the government printing press workers in sympathy with the agitators refused point blank to take up this work. With considerable difficulty we managed to get the rolls of a few constituencies printed, working at night, but in a large number of cases I had to take the help of private presses and at least in two districts the rolls had to be published in a handwritten form. In Guwahati, the staff refused to do even this I had to take the help of literate constables, put them in a sheltered place to complete the job. In the event, I succeeded in publishing the final rolls well on time.

The mood of the agitators in the meanwhile was getting increasingly hostile and while claiming that the movement was non-violent the agitators were preparing to prevent holding of election by direct action. I had now become the target of the agitation, and I was warned that I was in some personal danger. The fact that the state was now under President's rule did not make any difference to me or the agitators. Government servants were now openly espousing the cause of the agitation, the press highlighting it as one more achievement. Even senior officers had started talking irresponsibly of secession from India if the Central Government failed to solve the problem to the satisfaction of the agitators.

Chief Secretary B.S. Sarao, who had just taken over, was of no help to me. All the advice that I got from him was to take it easy, not to get worked up, listen to music and visit a gurudwara, none of which could be of any direct assistance to me in the discharge of my constitutional responsibilities. I was determined to do all that I could to see that the constitutional requirements are all fulfilled without fail and the machinery for conduct of elections functioned against all odds.

The stage was now set for the formal publication, in the official Gazette, of the Presidential notification calling upon the nation's electorate to elect their representatives to the house of the people, that is the Lok Sabha. This is a step of vital importance and had to be done precisely on the date fixed by the Election Commission. Again, a battle was on my hands as the government refused to print this. Indeed they had gone on an illegal strike and all official work had come to a standstill. With the government servants openly supportive of the movement and the AASU getting all the information regarding our efforts to fulfil the formalities volunteers were keeping watch over the movement of the election staff and the press. The Presidential Notification had to be printed in a private press in the night, thanks to the initiative of the Joint CEO, Sharma. Thus, this constitutional requirement was also fulfilled.

The fury of the agitators was increasing every day and maintenance of law and order became the single most important preoccupation of the government. Since I had now become an important target, for me to get to the office was a daily ordeal. The agitators wanted that I and the election office should cease functioning, as we were seen to be the real culprits still standing in their way, trying to thwart their efforts to prevent the holding of elections. Every morning groups of women would gather in front of my house and in fact lie down to prevent me from leaving my premises. Slogan shouting and threats of dire consequences, if I go to office, were not unusual. The agitators often got the timings of my departure wrong as I deliberately varied this and succeeding in departing before their arrival. My car would often stand in front of the house creating the impression that I was still inside whereas I would traverse the distance on foot. Unfortunately, my methods became known and I was waylaid at least on two occasions. The agitators fortunately confined themselves to the use of abusive language. I was advised that I should not continue this practice and in the last stages of the election process I was given a police escort.

With the publication of the President's Notification the stage was set for the other steps in the election process, namely filing of nominations, withdrawal, scrutiny, finalization of lists of contestants printing of ballot papers and actual polls. The timetable for all this had been finalized and duly published as per legal requirements. I was now in constant touch with the state administration, planning the actual conduct of the polls, getting the lists of polling personnel prepared, issuing appointment letters, etc. With increasing non-cooperation by the government staff in the entire Brahmaputra valley and daily calls for boycott of elections and physical intimidation, completion of each of these stages would have become an excruciating experience. It was fortunate that the DCs and SDOs did not throw up their hands but continued their preparedness to get these remaining processes completed.

One expected now the political parties to come forward and participate in the democratic process, but they had all but abandoned the field. The AASU and its companions dominated the scene. The student leaders Prafulla Mahanta and Brigu Phukan had been built up as folk heroes by now the only saviours of Assam. Their daily statements were given wide and prominent publicity by the press and were taken as commands for instant compliance. There were no doubt several self-styled advisers behind the scenes with varying shades of militancy narrowing the space for accommodation reasonableness, dialogue, compromise and a solution for the problem.

The Barak valley was free from the impact of the movement, though some attempts were indeed made to get the support of the students and others of this area as well. Every stage of the election operation in this area had gone through without any hitch and campaigning by aspirants had started.

The debate regarding the foreigners issue was becoming more and more virulent, with all kinds of arguments being thrown about in the media and the press. The students did not distinguish between the refugees and illegal immigrants and wanted everyone removed from the rolls and deported. This meant that even those who came to Assam, from the date of the Partition, were the targets. Armchair intellectuals, who argue that immigration was inevitable in conditions of economic disparity and who quoted the example of the US–Mexican situation, invited angry reactions. The reply was that the US was a rich country and could well afford to take on the extra burden.

Assamese were hard put to find land and employment to their own people and these were now being snatched away by the immigrants. Further, it was pointed out that the East Pakistanis, and as inheritors of this legacy the Bangladeshis had demanded their own homeland on religious grounds, arguing that they cannot live under the hegemony of another religion and having realized their aspirations, attended as it was by largescale violence, why should they come to that very country towards which they had expressed such strong reservations. The burden the immigrants cast on the resources of the country while contributing little or nothing towards the nation's advancement and the plight of the tribals who in spite of the laws to protect them were being driven out of their traditional lands were all repeatedly stressed. The real fear, of course, was the future political consequences of the demographic changes. The effort was to reverse the trend and ensure the dominance of the Assamese over the politics of the state. The intelligentsia were so convinced of the correctness and rationality of these arguments that anyone even mildly trying to advance counter arguments met with violent reactions. Dissent therefore ceased to exist, for all practical purposes.

It was becoming increasingly clear to me that conduct of elections in the Brahmaputra valley could be achieved, only if a miracle occurred. My worries on all these matters were being conveyed through daily memoranda but the help available was nil. I had to plough my lonely furrow. I now sought a meeting with the Governor to pour out my woes and to seek his intervention. He was, constitutionally speaking, entirely responsible for the administration of the state and it was his duty to ensure by all possible means that elections were held in the state, which was under President rule.

When I met the Governor I spoke in some detail about the problems I was facing, the measures I had taken to overcome them and the assistance I needed. I also described the fears that I had regarding conduct of the polls in the Brahmaputra valley. The response from the Governor was, however, surprisingly lukewarm. He offered me no particular assistance, but on the contrary, asked as to why I was so keen to conduct elections. What was the point when the people of Assam did not want elections, he queried. He hinted that even where elections could be held, namely the Barak valley, polls should be kept in abeyance. This was very disturbing to me. I had in a manner considered this question in my mind and had felt that so long as there was a constitutional requirement it was my duty, as a civil servant, to hold the same. If anybody has a particular point of view, the electoral process in a democracy gave him a more than sufficient opportunity for the viewpoint to be aired, public opinion mobilized in an effort to achieve prevalence of that point of view. While the students might have a grievance, there was nothing to prevent their participation in the political process. We had given them all the means legally available to register their point of view and get them to participate in all the processes involved. Preventing holding of elections was not the answer to the problem. I also had this thought that using the Assam example as a precedent any other powerful political leader could, by paralysing the state through violent or non-violent means, ensure that elections were not held if he perceived that he might not win the elections. These views were shared by the CEC who was keen that no unhealthy precedent should be set up.

I briefly gave the above arguments to the Governor, but he gave me no particular assurance. I am not sure what considerations the Governor had in his mind in taking this particular stand, but I for one could not deviate from the path laid down by the Election Commission.

The process of holding elections had to be carried forward and I instructed all the DCs and SDOs to ensure that they were available for candidates to file their nominations on all the days fixed for this purpose. The law and order machinery had been geared up to prevent any picketing by the agitators as also prevent intimidation of intending candidates. So effective however was the call for the boycott of the polls, and so intense and widespread the fear generated that in the entire Brahmaputra valley not one nomination paper was filed. It was only in the Barpeta constituency that an attempt was made to file a nomination. The political parties had been reduced to a state of utter helplessness by the overwhelming mobilization by the students. They had failed to prevent the electoral machinery from discharging its responsibilities, but rendered the whole effort meaningless by compelling the potential candidates to stay away from the electoral process.

In the Barpeta constituency, however, Mrs Abida Ahmed, wife of the late F.A. Ahmed, former President of India, wanted to file her nomination and the Centre had apparently made up its mind that come what may her nomination must be filed. Her agents were therefore to be escorted to Barpeta, a road journey of some three hours, by a special team consisting of no less than the Divisional Commissioner M.C. Narasimhan and the DIG K.P.S. Gill. Almost half a company of armed police had accompanied the team. The agitators had set up roadblocks at quite a few places and at one point a considerable crowd had physically occupied the road to prevent the party from proceeding further. A lathi charge had to be ordered to clear the way. The party thereafter proceeded to Barpeta and returned after filing the nomination.

It appears that while the crowd was being disbursed one Khargeswar Talukdar, while running away fell in a nearby pond and died. No firing had been ordered at all. The escort party was not aware of this incident. By the evening however the news of this death had spread like wild fire with the allegation that the death was due to police firing. The movement it was immediately propagated had claimed its first martyr. The agitators were now set to reap all the dividends they possibly could out of this. The body of Talukdar was brought to Guwahati next morning and emotions were built up to a frenzied pitch. No one cared to hear the two senior officers or to verify the facts and the version of the agitators was accepted as gospel truth. The officers were now accused of murder, and the city went completely out of control with lorry loads of students going from place to place baying for the blood of the officers and seeking revenge. The district administration had collapsed as the whole machinery of the government confining itself to the secretariat. Its writ did not seem to run anywhere. A sort of madness had gripped the whole populace, reminding one of Shakespeare's *Julius Caesar* 'Oh justice thou art fled to brutish beasts and men have lost their reason'. Sympathetic doctors had given a post-mortem report confirming the version of the student agitators.

For three continuous days this death was built up as an event of monumental proportions a national tragedy, portraying the victim as a great martyr. The movement had taken over the body as its property and Guwahati's Judge's field was turned into a place for the outpouring of grief and for a public funeral. Men and women in large numbers in their traditional attire poured into the area to hear emotional and inflammatory speeches exhorting the people to carry forward the struggle increasing its intensity. Cries of '*Khargeswar Bopa thoi amar holi* ('Khargeswar thou hast become immortal') rent the air.

The character of the movement had, by now, undergone subtle changes. The foreigner alone was not the target any more and all non-Assamese were now considered enemies of the movement. One of the senior police officers H. Bhattacharya played a very dubious role in this whole episode. Narasimhan and Gill had to go through a harrowing experience with murder cases filed against them and the judiciary playing a partisan role. No local lawyer would take up their defence. The state government also did not come to their rescue. The officers had to ultimately move the Supreme Court to get their cases transferred out of Assam as there was no chance of a fair trial in that state.

Though the nomination papers of Mrs Ahmed had been filed, the Returning Officer, for very valid but technical reasons, rejected the papers. No one appealed against this decision. The task now was confined to the conduct of elections in the Barak valley, and if possible in the hill districts. The AASU now directed its attention towards these districts and mobilized all that it could to prevent holding of elections in this area. They succeeded in paralysing the administration in the hill districts and though a couple of nominations had been filed and accepted, I had to reluctantly request the CEC to hold in abeyance holding of elections in the hill districts.

All steps had however been taken to conduct polls in the Barak valley constituencies and campaigning was in full swing. The Governor was of the view that even in these districts elections should not be held. He possibly and quite justifiably felt that holding elections in that area could reinforce the already deep divide between the two valleys and may exacerbate the known animosities between the communities inhabiting the two valleys. While I could understand his concerns, my task was to fulfil the constitutional obligations and the mandate of the Election Commission and since the people of Cachar had opted in favour of allowing the democratic process to be carried on and desired to elect their representatives to the Parliament, there was no way I could prevent this process and, indeed, it was my duty to see that their desires were fulfilled.

The government press at Guwahati would not print the ballot papers for the two Barak valley constituencies and I had to transport the special paper meant for this purpose to Silchar and get the ballot papers printed in private presses at that place.

Both the DIG of the range Bhattacharya and myself travelled to Silchar in order to ensure smooth conduct of the elections. Bhattacharya had by now become well known for his open support for the AASU agitation and there were doubts as to the kind of role he will play in the conduct of elections in the area. Fortunately, he behaved correctly and the poll arrangements went ahead smoothly. On the polling day while the voting went on without much of a problem almost upto the close of the polling time, all of a sudden some youthful supporters of one of the contestants, namely S.M. Deb, sensing victory, very foolishly, went and attacked a shop belonging to a supporter of the opposing candidate Mrs Rashida Chaudhry. She was the wife of the late Moinul Choudhry, a well known figure in the district, who had been a minister at the Centre. This uncalled-for exuberance was given a communal colour at once, and rumours spread like wild fire that a mosque had been attacked.

Both the DIG and I had only a few minutes back reached the Circuit House and were joined by the DC and the SP of the district, all of us feeling that the day had been won, when this news reached us. We immediately rushed to the police station and found that panic was setting in. Silchar town is inhabited by Hindus whereas most of the surrounding villages had Muslim population and the information that reached us was that the mobs which had been inflamed by rumours of an attack on a mosque were marching towards the town with all kinds of weapons intent on revenge and mayhem. '*Allah ho akbar*' and 'nara-e-taqbir' could be heard at a distance. The Hindus feared the worst. There was no time to be lost and since no chances could be taken with a communally explosive situation I decided that curfew must be enforced at once and applied very strictly. The DC and the SP acted with great alacrity and despatched and used the public address system to impose curfew. They mobilized all the available resources to send armed police to all the areas of the town and to the approaches to the town to prevent the mobs from entering the town. Violent mobs were approaching the town and had gained ingress in some areas. Firing was ordered in three places resulting in some casualties. Though it took a few hours for the panic to settle down strong and timely action in the crucial first hour of the crisis saved the town. The mobs, it was gathered, had come with kerosene, petrol, etc., to commit largescale arson. It was almost midnight before calm was restored, while the curfew was kept in force and all ingress routes sealed by strong police presence.

The next day near normalcy appeared to have been restored and the DC and I were confabulating whether counting could be organized. Fortunately, in all the confusion during the night, all the polling parties had managed to return and the ballot boxes had been stored safely. It was felt that the curfew could be relaxed for a while and the DC issued the necessary orders. Hardly an hour had passed when information reached us that the neighbouring villagers were preparing for another attack on the town. Curfew had to be again imposed and enforced very strictly. Counting of the ballots was not possible in the circumstances and the CEC was informed of the situation seeking their approval for the postponement of the counting. It was only after

48 hours of curfew that near normalcy could be restored. In the meanwhile precautionary measures had to be taken to prevent spread of communal violence. Karimganj was quite peaceful but Hailakandi, the other subdivision, experienced a great deal of tension and an army column had to be sent to that place. In Silchar as well on the express instruction of the Governor, a flag march by the army had to be organized.

During the counting that was taken up on restoration of normalcy no particular problem emerged and S.M. Deb won the contest with a fairly comfortable margin. I advised him to keep the celebrations very quiet if at all.

The developments in this area were being watched closely by the AASU which had sent representatives to the disrict. Though they did not meet me they sent a longish letter threatening me with dire consequences for my 'unpatriotic' acts. It was indicated that I will receive a very hot reception when I return to Guwahati. My wife had received a few threatening calls and she kept the government informed of this.

Fortunately, when I flew back to Guwahati, the day after the announcement of the results I could reach home without anyone waylaying me. I was told later that the AASU had considered putting me on trial before the people's court and punishing me.

My task was now over and I prepared a detailed report for the Election Commission. The CEC was indeed pleased that I had not failed to fulfil any of the constitutional requirements. In a formal letter of commendation he wrote that 'Rao had to discharge his onerous functions under trying circumstances. It is highly creditable that he did not flinch an inch from the chosen path set for him by the Election Commission. The events have clearly proved his mettle and dedication to duty even at considerable personal risk to himself. He has really set an example to others as to how one should act in furtherance of a national cause even against heavy odds. The services rendered by the officer should be duly recognized and suitably rewarded'.

Before officially communicating this commendation to me the matter was put up to the Governor who while agreeing to the communication, strangely commented that I could not be said to have served a national cause. This part of the CEC's letter was therefore omitted by the government in their letter to me. The government also ignored the suggestion that the services rendered should be duly recognized. It is possible that the Governor felt that given the strong feelings against conduct of elections it would be appropriate to play down what I had done. After all civil servants are supposed to do their duty without expectation. Perhaps there was also something wrong with my stars.

I shall only briefly deal with the subsequent history of this movement which during 1979 so dominated the scene and was characterized as a do or die struggle. Mrs Gandhi had again become Prime Minister and while the agitation continued during the whole of 1980 attempts were made to start a dialogue and find a solution to the problem. At times the agitation did take violent forms, with stoppage of the flow of oil out of Assam, disruption of rail traffic, etc. The administration was being carried on by the two advisers Ramamurthy and Baveja. The office staff were generally absent and the officers had to be ferried to the offices with police escort. Very little work was done.

At one stage there were indications that the students may agree to a solution involving detection and deletion from the voters lists all those who had come after 1971 and the Prime Minister visited Assam to get an agreement concluded, but the student leaders changed their mind at the last moment and the PM's visit could achieve nothing.

The Government of India in the meantime appointed H.C. Sarin as Principal Adviser with the idea that he would take over from Singh whose term as Governor had expired. Both belonged to the Bihar cadre of the ICS and established records. Sarin made a somewhat ill-advised effort to break the movement by floating an outfit called the All Assam Minority Students Union with communal overtones. This move received hostile reactions in Assam and the Governor also reportedly did not favour this idea. There were other issues as well on which Singh and Sarin did not see eye to eye and, consequently, the effectiveness of the administration was further lowered. For some reasons the Central Government could not decide whether Sarin should at all take over as Governor. Possibly, his ill-advised moves and growing unpopularity played a role. He had also made a highly undiplomatic statement about the role of school and college girls in the movement which was played up for all that it was worth to discredit him.

The politicians who had almost completely faded away were in the meantime bestirring themselves. The assembly had been kept in suspended animation. The fact that a Congress government had taken office in New Delhi gave a boost to the local Congressmen. With some encouragement from Delhi, a popular government under Mrs Anwara Taimur was cobbled up and took office. The agitation however continued though with reduced intensity and semblance of normalcy was brought and government offices started functioning.

No dialogue was however initiated with the agitators who were resentful of the formation of a government by elements which in their opinion was inimical to their cause. Tension surfaced periodically and alarming incidents of violence multiplied. In places, non-Assamese were forced to sell their belongings and leave the area. Officers from outside the state were treated with hostility and the students who considered themselves above the law resisted any attempts to enforce the law. The most tragic event of this period was the murder of the Commissioner of the Upper Assam Division E.S. Partha Sarathy. A dynamic and courageous officer, who had earlier been Chief Secretary of Pondicherry, had activated the administration in his area and prevented the students from targeting non-locals. He had achieved a measure of success in curbing the illegal activities of the students who were therefore angry with him. A plot was hatched to kill him and a pressure-activated explosive devise was placed right under his office chair. When he sat down in his seat on the fateful morning the pressure was enough to cause an explosion and blow him up. The entire official community was benumbed by this shocking incident. It is a great pity that the perpetrators of this dastardly crime are yet to receive their punishment. Indeed, some of them have been ministers in the state. It is a sad commentary on the functioning of the Assam police and that of the Central Bureau of Investigation that they have failed to prosecute the murderers and see that they are punished, even though some twenty years have gone by.

The Taimur ministry could not last primarily long due to internal dissentions and President rule had again to be imposed. L.P. Singh had left Assam and Mehrotra had taken over as the Governor. Elections were due early in 1983, and while the Government of India was determined to hold the elections, the AASU and all those who supported the cause, it appeared, were equally determined to resist. The agitation which had shown signs of flagging was revived with renewed vigour.

I had been by then posted in Delhi as Joint Secretary in the

Ministry of Defence but the CEC who was drafting the services of Assam cadre officers to function as observers in the troubled state enlisted me as well. The state government staff refused to work for the elections and the Government of India had to send a large number of staff members from Delhi and states like Bihar to work as polling personnel. All were frightened and expected to be attacked at any time. Massive protection had been organized. Nominations had been filed, mainly by Congressmen and the administration, through herculean efforts, managed to send all the polling material and staff to the various polling stations.

The election, however, was an absolute farce as no elector turned up any booth all over the state. In a few cases, a handful of people were persuaded or pressurized to come out. Armed escort had to be provided to them. The votes cast per booth amounted to but a few and those who got these votes were declared elected. Notwithstanding this charade of an election, a government was indeed formed under the leadership of Hiteswar Saikia.

While the administration during the conduct of elections was totally preoccupied with the task of ensuring that somehow the poll is held even for namesake, the Lallung tribals in the district of Nowgong, who had longstanding grievances against those who had come and occupied their lands, mainly Muslims, taking advantage of the preoccupation of the law enforcing machinery with the elections, massacred the Muslims for two consecutive nights in the now famous Nellie area. When the administration finally woke up the damage done was already severe. The incident was so serious the PM herself airdashed to the area to show her concern and initiate some remedial measures.

As to why such an election was conducted, at such a great cost, and achieve what ends, is not clear. I who was in Dibrugarh as an observer could see that the election had only increased the anger of the people and they were getting convinced that no one was really interested in understanding their concerns and taking measures to solve the main problem for which they were fighting tooth and nail. The blame was now placed on all Indians, who were regarded as unsympathetic and hostile, interested only in the exploitation of Assam's rich natural resources. Secession from the Indian Union, violence as the only means of solving the problem were talked about by even the more responsible sections of the community. This needs to be taken note of as a backdrop for the rise of militancy in Assam.

The Central Government was now getting increasingly embroiled in the more dangerous developments in the Punjab and was able to pay much less attention to the problems on the eastern front. Mrs Gandhi herself was perceived to have lost some of her sure touch and charisma and the fear that was noticeable when she came to power evaporated. Practically nothing more was done by the Centre, during her tenure as PM, which tragically ended in October 1984.

The Hiteswar Saikia government tried to carry on bravely and the Chief Minister, who was a very shrewd and crafty politician, was able to reduce the intensity of the movement, marginally improve the performance of the government as also improve the law and order situation. The government's legitimacy was however highly questionable, and except for a few, the Assamese boycotted the government.

Rajiv Gandhi had taken over as the Prime Minister and he wanted the Assam problem to be given a fresh look. A serious dialogue with the students and their advisers was initiated. An earnest effort was indeed made to understand the concerns of the Assamese, while explaining the practical problems in meeting all their demands. The Home Secretary R.D. Pradhan played a key role in making the students come around handling the talks with great sagacity and patience. The Chief Secretary of Assam Shrimati P.P. Trivedi also played a very important role.

Though the student leaders kept changing their minds, the effort was to bring the students into the political mainstream, with emphasis on strong measures to prevent all further infiltration, while initiating a series of steps for the economic and social advancement of the state. The preservation of the rich cultural heritage of Assam was also to be given due consideration.

Rajiv Gandhi was very keen to make a formal announcement of the break in the deadlock over the foreigners' issue in Assam from the ramparts of the historic Red Fort on Independence day 1985 from where his illustrious mother and grandfather had addressed the nation, so many times.

Work on arriving at an agreement was therefore being proceeded with at a frenetic pace and could be finally concluded only well after midnight of the fourteenth of August. A few loose ends were yet to be tied up, but the accord was final enough to merit formal announcement by the PM next morning.

The famous Assam accord gave priority to cleaning up of electoral rolls, with particular reference to post-1971 immigrants, while deportation was given lower priority due to the enormous practical problems. The Saikia ministry was to be sent out and the students invited to contest the new elections to be held shortly. Considerable pressure, it appears, was exerted over them to join the Congress but they preferred to retain their regional identity. A few sops such as the Indian Institute of Technology, a new oil refinery, more institutions of higher learning, permanent measures for flood control, etc. were all part of the promises made by the Central Government. Fencing of the border with Bangladesh, issue of identity cards for genuine voters were also to be taken up.

In the event, the student leaders formed a regional party—the Asom Gana Parishad—, contested the elections held in the latter part of 1985 and achieved a resounding victory.

I had again been deputed by the Election Commission as an observer, this time to Sibsagar. The Commission had taken every possible step to ensure that only genuine voters were enlisted. In the poll, there was overwhelming participation by the people all over Assam. The voters came out in strength and women, in their colourful traditional attire, could be seen everywhere.

When the AGP government took office it was widely expected it would take concerted measures to tackle the 'foreigners' problem. There was some fear in certain interested quarters that the measures may result in a drastic reduction in the size of their vote bank.

While Rajiv Gandhi was indeed sincere in his efforts to get Assam back on its rails and his credibility as a young Prime Minister who talked about taking the country forward towards the new century on the basis of technological progress bringing a new vigour into the government, as in the Shah Bano case, he probably came under severe pressure from his own party men, particularly from Assam, who feared a disappearance of a large chunk of their traditional supporters. After all, Congressmen had openly claimed that they could win elections so long as they had the support of 'Alis and coolies'.

The result was the enactment of the by-now-notorious Illegal Migrants (Determination by Tribunals) IMDT, Act. By this act, the Central Government took away with one hand what it had given the Assamese by the other. It sent out all the wrong signals to the people who were already smarting under a severe sense of alienation. They were now forced to conclude that the Government of India, the Parliament and by extension indeed the people of India were not interested in their travails and were prepared to sacrifice their future for the sake of votes of the immigrants. Their apprehensions that they will be reduced to a minority in their own state and that political power would pass into the hands of foreign nationals were it appeared to them as of no consequence to the rest of India. Examples of Tripura and Sikkim were quoted, repeatedly, where immigrant Bengalis and Nepalis had reduced indigenous people to a minority and political power had irretrievably and irrevocably gone into the hands of immigrants. Many regard this enactment as possibly the most important cause for the rise of militancy in Assam, the rise of the ULFA and the Bodo Security Force. The ULFA came into being almost immediately after this enactment.

Some may regard this reaction as an expression of Assamese xenophobia, but it is worth analysing the reasons for the reactions of the Assamese. The IMDT Act's provisions were such that it protected the immigrants rather than help facilitate their deportation. There are indeed extraordinarily peculiar features of this Act which a considerable body of opinion hold as unconstitutional.

The first distinctive feature is that this Act applies only to Assam, not to any other State of the Union, not even to the other states of the North-East though this enactment is that of the Parliament of the nation. To be sure, the states in the North-East also have a problem regarding illegal aliens. In Nagaland there are a large number of immigrants who work as labourers. In these states it easier to detect the illegal immigrant as he looks distinctly different from the local tribal. If one day the Nagas decide to throw out the immigrants which is easy, given their propensity and capability to perpetrate violence, the entire lot may land on Assam's head. Tripura has a big problem of immigrants and the rise of tribal insurgency in the area with the formation of the NLFT is directly attributable to this. The Assamese naturally ask as to why this Act is applicable only to Assam whereas everywhere else the Foreigners Act applies and was indeed in force in Assam as well. This Act is in force just next door to Assam, namely Meghalaya. The Assamese have been asking for sterner measures than what is available under the Foreigners Act for strengthening the defences against the 'silent invasion' whereas the Central Government has responded to their demands by a drastic reduction in the severity of the legal provisions with respect to the immigrants from Bangladesh, and indeed extended a high degree of protection to them.

The second feature is that, unlike the position in the Foreigners Act, the burden of proof has been shifted from the foreigner to the law enforcing agency. Hence the police have to get all the evidence they possibly can to prove that one is a foreigner while he needs do nothing. It is not difficult to imagine how difficult it is to obtain concrete proof in Assam, given the composition of the population in the border areas.

Third, even if the police have a solid case they can do nothing except to submit the case to the Tribunals established under the IMDT Act. The police have been rendered toothless in one stroke. Tribunals, notorious for their lengthy procedures, take their own time and in the meanwhile the foreigner has every opportunity to disappear. Also, the degree of proof demanded by the Tribunals is so difficult to obtain.

Fourth, even if it is finally established before the Tribunal that a man is indeed a foreigner he is expected to be given one month's time for him to get prepared to depart. He is therefore given another opportunity to disappear.

Fifth, this Act applies only to immigrants from Bangladesh and not to any other foreigner, not even to the Nepalis who can be dealt with under the Foreigners Act. How can two different acts dealing with the same subject in the same geographical area be in force is a big, but unanswered, question.

It may be added that apart from the difficulties in obtaining the kind of conclusive proof that the courts usually demand the number of tribunals set up were woefully small, and cases filed by the police after a great deal of effort are not dealt with expeditiously. There is also the provision of appeal against the verdict of the tribunals.

It would therefore be clear that the whole purpose of this Act is to make it as difficult as possible to detect and deport illegal aliens from Bangladesh alone. The students had agitated for strengthening of the defences against illegal immigrants and erection of new barriers but what they got was a drastic reduction of even the existing legal mechanisms.

In spite of all this, there are those who defend this legislation vociferously on the ground that this is necessary to prevent harassment of genuine Indian nationals. Why such concern is shown to the so-called Indian nationals only in Assam and not anywhere else in India, not in other north-eastern states or West Bengal or Bihar, is not explained. In effect, the process of identification of immigrants and their deportation has been brought to a standstill, with a few cases for form's sake being referred to the tribunals more as a justification of their existence and to show the effectiveness of the IMDT Act. On the other legislation has sent a clear and unequivocal signal to the potential immigrants from Bangladesh, that they are welcome in Assam and there is a law in place making it impossible for the police to detect and deport them and they are well protected.

Arguments have been advanced that under the Constitution the Central Government has the responsibility to defend every part of India from external aggression, which includes the kind of 'silent invasion' and 'demographic aggression' that is taking place in Assam. Instead of doing this, it is alleged, the IMDT Act actually facilitates this type of aggression and protects the aggressor, while the interests of the indigenous people are being sacrificed.

The students and the AGP government have been pressing the Centre to repeal what they perceive as a pernicious piece of legislation. So far this has not happened even though the then PM Narasimha Rao in a public meeting admitted that certain provisions of this Act need to be amended. The NDA government has been sympathetic but has been unable to do anything because of its position in the Rajya Sabha. Strangely the AGP government, which came to power on the platform of taking measures to deal effectively with the foreigners issue, has become progressively ambivalent in its postures and considerably diluted its enthusiasm, with respect to this issue. Strangely also, nothing has been done to effectively challenge the legal and constitutional validity of the IMDT Act in the courts. Even though reports have appeared that some public interest litigation has been initiated, no one seems to be pursuing this matter vigorously. The recently constituted Subramaniam Committee on National Security in its report has referred to this problem and has recommended repeal of the IMDT Act.

So after all the sound and fury of the anti-foreigners movement that started in 1979 and which involved so much disruption so much sacrifice by the students who lost precious years of education what exactly has been really achieved? Very little one may say. The reasons are worth looking into.

As analysed earlier, the problem of immigration from East Bengal is at least eighty years old and is extremely complicated with economic, social and religious factors operating. The students were impractical in demanding a solution to this problem in one stroke.

Second, there was a lack of clarity in their objectives with various influences working on them not allowing them to settle for an implementable solution. At the height of the movement an agreement could have been reached when Mrs Gandhi came to power, with 1971 as the cut-off year, for detection and deletion from the electoral rolls. This opportunity was lost due to the indecisiveness on the part of the students.

Third, by viewing all non-Assamese as hostile the movement lost a great deal of the sympathy it had initially generated. The Assamese started projecting a xenophobic image trying to hit out against all kinds of imagined enemies. Fourthly, when violence was being progressively resorted to, especially after the murder of the Commissioner of the Upper Assam division E.S. Parthasarathy, the movement could be easily discredited as one that had been taken over by extremist elements who were now pitting themselves against the Indian State and were not amenable to reason.

Fifth, once they entered politics, the student leaders lost much of their idealism and spirit of sacrifice, getting used to the trappings of office and interested in remaining in office, which meant reluctance to take on any substantial segment of voters.

Sixth, with no experience in the art of statecraft and poor educational background, the AGP could not provide effective administration, became directionless exercising little or no control over the institutions of governance and failed to attend to the ground-level problems of the people. The government's credibility was eroded in no time.

Further, the rise of the ULFA, whose links with the AGP were not unknown, the soft attitude the AGP displayed towards this militant outfit, and the fact that the ULFA was permitted to operate with impunity in several parts of Assam, running a parallel administration indulging in violence, all resulted in the basic objectives of the movement getting completely lost, ULFA's violent creed demanded secession and independence for Assam and this invited hostile reactions.

After all the years, therefore, the Assam movement instead of removing the basic fears of the Assamese has led to a series of negative developments. Assam has now been in the grip of insurgency and violence for years bringing the process of economic development to a halt. The educational system has been damaged. Investments have been greatly reduced and creation of employment opportunities has been negligible. I shall deal with the ULFA problem in greater detail in a subsequent chapter on internal security but note has to be taken of the adverse fallout of students' movement at this stage.

There are, however, some very thin silver linings in the otherwise gloomy scenario. Some definitive action has indeed been taken by the Centre to prevent further infiltration from Bangladesh. The entire Assam–Bangladesh border has been fenced. Though not foolproof, combined with effective patrolling, it is at least a signal that there is a modicum of seriousness with respect to checking influx. Madhav Godbole, when he was Home Secretary, took great pains to speed up completion of border fencing. Serious efforts have also been made to provide unique identity cards to genuine Indian nationals and permit voting of only those who possess the identity cards. Successive chief election commissioners have taken great pains in ensuring preparation of clean electoral rolls and a series of guidelines have been issued in this regard. At the time of revision of electoral rolls, particularly in Assam, a number of senior officers have been invariably deputed to supervize the process and ensure compliance of the CEC's instructions.

It would, therefore, appear that the Election Commission has tried to address the concerns of the students, to the extent possible, and legally permissible. Therefore, while the illegal aliens may not face deportation they would not be able to exercise their franchise at least. Also, it is gratifying to note that in recent times Bangladesh also seems to be succeeding in her efforts to reduce the rate of growth of population and improve living standards. The fertility rate, the average size of the family, infant mortality, have all shown a decline *albeit* marginally. Women's empowerment, the reach of family welfare services, the use of contraceptives, all seem to be gaining ground. The micro credit system enabling women to become economically semi-independent has been widely appreciated. The country has to, however, contend with opposing forces of religious extremism which are attempting to thwart these processes. They oppose liberation of women. If, however, the positive developments are speeded up, may be one day one may witness the disappearance of the main reason for emigration, namely economic. One hopes that this day comes sooner than later.

Further, some recent statistics seem to suggest that the favoured destination of the immigrants is not Assam any more. The number of infiltrators towards Assam seems to be declining whereas more are coming through the West Bengal border and getting into not only Bengal, but into Bihar and Orissa and all the way to Maharashtra. Would this be due to the violence of ULFA and the Bodo Security Force or the border fencing or the tightening up of the electoral registration system? The Government of Maharashtra tried to deport a number of foreign nationals but West Bengal refused to allow them to go through its territory. The illegal migrants have been noticed in substantial numbers even in Delhi.

The 2001 census also reveals that Assam's rate of growth of population in the decade 1991–2001 has been less than the previous decades i.e. 1.73 per cent per annum as compared to 2.17 per cent in 81–91 and 2.12 per cent in 71–81, and a high 3 per cent in 61–71. The growth is also below the national average of 1.93 per cent for the period 91–2001. There may be some room for cautious optimism, here.

I must admit that a good deal of what I have written in this chapter is based purely on my memory. No one has so far attempted to write an official account of this turbulent period of Assam's history, and one cannot have access to official papers, given the limitations imposed by the regulations relating to secrecy. When and if an official history is written, I am sure what I have stated will be found to be a fair and a truthful account.

# 9

# GOVERNMENT OF INDIA AGAIN

As mentioned in the last chapter, by 1981 I found myself in the Government of India, first as Managing Director of an organization called National Federation of Industrial Cooperatives, and, then, as Joint Secretary in the Department of Defence Production. Compared to the travails that I had gone through in Assam, life was peaceful and orderly with little or no excitement.

The Federation of Industrial Cooperatives was meant to assist cooperatives in their production and marketing activities including exports. Cooperation as a management philosophy is highly idealistic and requires an extraordinary degree of self-abnegation. Very successful cooperatives have been organized in Sweden, Denmark and the UK and in our own country industries like sugar have been run on cooperative basis. The cooperatives that I had to deal with had none of this idealism and the cooperators were actually individual traders who masqueraded as cooperators to take advantage of generous government subsidies. They never bothered about quality or price and wanted that their products must be taken over by the Federation merely because they were members. If profits were made, this had to be shared with them, but if losses were made they did not bother to look at you.

This was quite a disgusting experience for me. The cooperators, I also found, believed passionately in travelling abroad and wanted to be financed by the Federation. Cooperation among cooperatives was supposed to be guiding principle and the International Cooperative Alliance, a world body of cooperatives, keeps organizing meetings and conferences ostensibly to fulfil this objective.

During the brief period that I spent in this organization, as part of some delegation or the other, I went to Helsinki, Stockholm, Copenhagen, London, Moscow and then to Dar e-salaam and Arusha, in Tanzania. In all these places, speeches were made in various languages, dinners were eaten, visits to cooperatives organized and cocktails attended, all apparently resulting in nothing. Our cooperators, who with such enthusiasm got into the bandwagon, fighting for their place with considerable ferocity, I found hardly participated in any of the proceedings. Most knew no English, and were clueless as regards French, German or Dutch. Strangely, they were not even interested in sightseeing and most of the time confined themselves to their hotel rooms. Cognac, I found, was their favourite and substantial amounts were consumed. Shopping however was their forte and here they must have surpassed delegations of other nations by a wide margin. Some paid attention to their health problems.

Moscow, however, was important for us as we were indeed exporting substantial quantities of woollen garments and tea. The Russians tolerated our inefficiencies, but were quite particular about quality and price and since the quantities were substantial and purchased on a sustained basis, our cooperatives could be pressurized to improve their performance standards. Ludhiana cooperatives, in particular, come up to the standards and benefited a good deal as a result of the contacts with the Russians.

Fortunately, I was able to get out of this organization soon enough. The cooperators did not like my ways and I did not like their ways and this mutual animosity was enough to ensure my early exit.

The Ministry of Defence was an altogether different kettle of fish. Of all the functionaries in the Government of India, generally speaking, the Joint Secretary has the longest tenure, a good five years and this enables the officers to properly learn the job, develop a certain amount of expertise and indeed contribute a great deal with respect to policy making and implementation. When I entered the Ministry, R. Venkataraman was thc Defence Minister. He was followed by P.V. Narasimha Rao and then S.B. Chavan. All three of these were men of outstanding merit and acumen, with great ability to grasp complex issues of national security, deeply interested in national self-reliance, defence preparedness and indigenous production of defence equipment. With their vast experience in the Government of India, dealing with a variety of subjects, they commanded the respect of the armed forces and the Civil Service and provided the right kind of leadership to an important and sensitive ministry.

I was dealing primarily with the Defence public sector undertakings, as also in the first two years with the Defence Quality Assurance Organization. The quality assurance set-up was modeled on the UK pattern, being independent of both the producer and the consumer. It was a surprisingly large establishment, dealing with a wide variety of goods required by the armed forces, from clothing to ammunition, from heavy vehicles to electronics and small arms to heavy guns. A number of specialized directorates operated each with considerable expertise, with respect to quality assurance methodologies.

The ordinance factories came under the purview of the Defence quality assurance mechanism, and it had been decided that a good part of the quality assurance work relating to stage and inter-stage inspection should be handed over to the ordnance factories themselves. The problem was the disagreement over the number of employees to be transferred, as a consequence of this decision, from the quality assurance set up to the ordnance factories. A number of discussions between the two organizations produced only a good deal of acrimony. I was asked to serve as a one man arbitrator and decide how many in each of the categories should be transferred to the ordnance factories. This task gave me the opportunity of visiting almost all the ordnance factories, study their production procedures and problems relating to quality control. What was at stake was very high, because there can be no compromise, whatsoever, as to the ultimate quality of the product; in a battle there is nothing called second best.

After a detailed study I gave an award with respect to each of the factories, and to my great surprise and immense satisfaction the award was accepted by both parties, without a murmur.

The Defence public sector undertakings, with which I was concerned, were responsible for producing a wide variety of the requirements of the services. The company called Midhani employed the most sophisticated of technologies—vacuum induction melting, vacuum arc refining, electroslag refining powder metallurgy, etc. and was capable of producing highly complex super alloys for use in the aircraft and other industries capable of withstanding very high temperatures and pressures. Midhani stood for Mishra Dhathu Nigam, the Hindi version of 'Super Alloys Establishment', and those not familiar with this translation thought that the company was either a

Sindhi family concern or belonged to Mr Mishra, so common a name in large parts of India.

Intense cooperation between the Defence Metallurgical Research Laboratory and Midhani had been achieved, and it was a pleasure to get to know the high standards of work that was being carried out under the able leadership of Dr P. Rama Rao in DMRL. Dr Rama Rao, who is now the Vice Chancellor of the Central University in Hyderabad and was earlier Secretary in the Department of Science and Technology, managed to combine outstanding scholarship with a high degree of humility. In Sanskrit such a person is described as '*vidya vinaya sampanne*' i.e., a person accomplished both in learning and humility, a rare blend indeed.

When Midhani had to get a certain complex material processed in Krupps of Germany they surprisingly failed to meet the stringent specifications laid down. What was involved was rolling of rings through the use of centrifugal forces, totally avoiding any welding and observation of certain pre-heating procedures. Dr Rama Rao was sent to the Essen–Bockum plant of the Krupps to sort out the matter, and the processing regime he prescribed obtained the desired results. I had also visited the plant at that time, and witnessed the process. The Germans were all admiration for Dr Rama Rao. Incidentally there is a very interesting exhibition on the history of the Krupps and while all their many achievements are on display, there is a total blackout of the period 1933–45. Everyone knows the role the Krupps played with respect to the rise of the Nazis and during the War. There is also the beautiful family abode of the Krupps called the Villa Hugel where every summer a grand music festival is organized.

Dr S.K. Gupta was the MD of Midhani and Dr Brahm Prakash, an outstanding metallurgist, was the Chairman. Both were professionals of exceptional merit and contributed a great deal to the progress of the company.

Bharat Dynamics Limited was responsible for manufacture of missiles and I negotiated and concluded a license agreement with a French German consortium for transfer of technology of a particular weapon system. The French were tough negotiators but once the agreement was reached, observed the provisions most scrupulously. This enabled me to visit their headquarters in Paris as also their plants in France and Germany. The plant in Germany in a place called Schroben Hausen had been in existence from World War II and is so well camouflaged that right through the war and the innumerable air raids of the allies, this plant was never located and hence never damaged.

The Defence shipyards, which also became my charge, were responsible to meet the country's naval requirements. The production was backed up by a credible naval design capability and a large part of the activity was based on indigenous design. For highly advanced vessels such as missile boats and submarines the license production route had to be resorted to. Even here, however, progressive indigenization was indeed taking place.

Mazagaon docks in Mumbai, which was the premier yard for warship production, has also diversified into the area of offshore oil platforms and was meeting a good deal of the requirements of the ONGC. I functioned as a Director of not only Mazagaon docks but also the Goa Shipyard and the Garden Reach Shipbuilders and Engineers (GRSE). These yards were also building warships

Our longterm strategic defence cooperation with the USSR meant, for those of us in the Ministry of Defence, fairly frequent and intense interaction with the Soviets. Visits to Moscow was on the cards every now and then and the Russians treated you very well on all occasions. The Generals of the famed Red Army with their particularly large brimmed caps, received you right outside the door of the plane. You were whisked away to the VIP area of the Sheremetyevo airport, and welcomed with champagne and caviar. Your immigration formalities were taken care of by the protocol people and you travelled to town in the large 'chaika' car built more like a tank than a limousine.

Though a communist country, equality was not meant for either the armed forces or the party in the USSR. Champagne, caviar or chocolates were available only for these special categories. The chaika and ZIL (Zavodnya Iiyich Lenin—or factory of Lenin) cars were meant for the privileged and these cars were given priority in traffic, often ignoring the red lights and waved through by the distinctly burly Moscow policeman, who obviously knew who is who.

Most ordinary Moscovites used the public transport, and if at all they had a car it was the pedestrian Lada for which there was a long waiting period. Everyone in Moscow seemed to carry a large bag all the while, because there was a general shortage of everything and, as it happened often, a particular item was more readily available in an area than at other times, one joined the nearest queue and filled up the bag. One found queues all over Moscow, very disciplined, orderly and very patient, all members carrying bags. For even vodka, without which the Russians could not apparently live, there were queues. Easily, sixty to seventy per cent of the queue consisted of women.

Moscow public transport was indeed superb and the underground system far superior to London, or New York or Washington. Reportedly built during Stalin's time, under the supervision of Krushchev, the stations had marble floors, good decor, paintings of quality and superb passenger amenities. You could commute from anywhere to anywhere in Moscow paying about two or three kopecks. This charge was not revised for decades, and indeed price of most essentials were held constant without regard to variations in the cost of production. Inflation, considered a capitalist phenomenon, had been banished in this workers' paradise. So also unemployment, considered again a capitalist disease, had no place in the dictatorship of the proletariat.

If one travelled in the underground at least forty per cent of the passengers, it was noticed, wore one uniform or the other. The USSR was a highly militarized country. No one seemed to communicate with anyone and smiling had probably been officially banned. All were reading or pretending to read one of the only two newspapers that the Russians were permitted to look at, namely *Pravda* and *Izvestia.* Both were under tight official control and published only such items considered by the powers that be, to be fit for consumption by the general populace. *Pravda* in Russian meant 'truth' and *Izvestia* means 'News'. So it was generally believed that what was truth was not news, and what was news was not the truth.

The television was also fully controlled and the Russians saw what their rulers had determined to be fit for them to see, and nothing else.

It was taken for granted that among those who received you at least one was from the KGB, the dreaded state security apparatus. His task was to keep a tab not only on you and such aliens but equally importantly on the other Russians themselves. Also taken for granted was that the car was bugged, your room was bugged and even the embassy was bugged. You were also cautioned that the driver may know more than one Indian language, and if you were trying to maintain secrecy by talking in Hindi or even in Tamil you may be in for a shock.

We were invariably treated as state guests of the mighty USSR, which meant that your room, food and transport was free. Of course, we also treat the Russians in a similar manner when they come to India, though with much higher standards of luxury and greater variety as regards food. The massive Hotel Russiya with about 2000 rooms, very near the Kremlin, was usually our abode for the duration of our visit. The rooms were not luxurious but very satisfactory and the menu everyday had been laid down well in advance, possibly as per the Gosplan specifications and probably by the Politbureau. No change was permissible and vegetarians were in for a rough time. If anyone wanted a change, it took about 72–96 hours for the system to churn, process the request through the all-too-rigid bureaucracy for the change, to be made effective. Often the whole delegation had to digest the change even if only one of its members had asked for it.

In Hotel Russiya and whichever other hotel we were put up, there would invariably be a 'floor lady' called in Russian as *dezeurnaye.* These specimens were selected in all probability for their extra large physical dimensions and engendered a degree of fear by their sheer size. It was believed that they were of the KGB and could be engaged in having a look at the documents you carried. Officially, however, they were to give you your morning tea, wake you up if you wanted and see that your room is kept clean and well supplied with linen soap etc. Given their size, very few if at all, took, I believe, the risk of getting themselves woken up by any of these amazons.

Moscow looked a place with very few avenues of entertainment. The Bolshoi theatre, the Circus and may be one or two other places were all that appeared to be there. The Bolshoi and the Circus were of course of outstanding quality. Fascinating to visit was a place called the 'Panorama', a huge circular painting with a radius of around one hundred and fifty metres which had captured in vivid detail a particular moment in the battle of Borodino during the invasion of Russia by Napoleon. The scale was vast but the dimensions of the figures were so precisely set that you had the impression of standing right in the centre of the battleground and witnessing all that was happening, the figures near you being more or less life-size and diminishing in size as the distance increased. Quite far was the figure of Napoleon himself and very near you, you could see a French soldier fighting a Russian, or a horse which had just been killed, or a canon that had fired.

Though the battle of Borodino was won by Napoleon, the Russian General Kutuzov had managed to inflict such huge losses on the French Grand Armee that Napoleon had to retreat, after only briefly entering Moscow. The rest, as they say, is history.

While generally speaking work went on during the week, the Russians invariably arranged for field visits during the weekends. Riga, the capital of the Baltic Republic Latvia, was a favourite destination. Latvia, along with Lithuania and Estonia were taken over by Stalin as part of the secret agreement between him and Adolf Hitler in August 1939. The three Baltic republics were non-Slavic, inhabited by people of the same stock as the Scandinavians and for a long time part of the Hanseatic league, a prosperous trading arrangement. The architecture, language and culture were quite similar to that in Scandinavia. One could see that the Russian occupation was highly unpopular. In the ninetees of the twentieth century all the three republics were able to become independent.

During the war the Nazis had occupied these republics in their drive into the Soviet Union and in the outskirts of Riga there still remains a concentration camp—buildings only fortunately without inhabitants—which evokes gruesome memories of the holocaust. The camp had Jews and other undesirables—*'unterminchen'* in German—who were exterminated as part of the so-called 'final solution'.

The long cavernous barracks where the inhabitants were kept have been preserved. What is remarkable is the memorial to the dead particularly the statues, one of which is that of a woman surrounded by three children, whose bodies are that of children but whose faces are of old men. The meaning sought to be conveyed is that these little children, during the short period they were on this earth, saw and experienced a whole tragic life. It is difficult to keep a dry eye while visiting this place. I have also seen other concentration camps in Germany—Bergen Belsen—and Trebelinka. The experience was equally saddening. One wonders how man's cruelty to man could assume such horrendous proportions.

Our purpose of visiting Riga was to see the naval establishment, and the commanding Admiral gave us a briefing and took us around the whole yard. At the end of the visit, very appropriately, he presented me with a largish bell which he called 'the peace bell' of Riga.

Stalin's imprint on Soviet life was still very much evident. Large buildings with a distinct architectural style, with a remarkable degree of similarity, built in Stalin's time, called the seven sisters, were to be seen in several parts of Moscow. Centralized state planning was still being practised with the same degree of rigidity as in Stalin's time. Indoctrination of the population, censorship and tight control of information was very much in vogue, so much so that there was not even a telephone directory in Moscow. It was, I believe, considered a secret document and possibly a device to prevent contact between foreigners and the Soviet citizens. The notorious KGB HQ and the Lubyanka prison, where people were said to 'disappear', could be seen right in the centre of the town, ironically very near it is the only children's toy store in Moscow, known as 'Disky Mir' or children's world. Allexander Solzenitsyn has so graphically described this prison as the Gulag Archipilago.

The rulers of USSR operated from inside the magnificient Kremlin. Built by the Czars, it houses the top echelons of governance serving as an awe-inspiring symbol of Soviet power. The Kremlin is encompassed by a high impenetrable wall, with a distinct imperial architecture of the Czarist era, and covers several square miles of space. A number of buildings are inside the high security area, regal in appearance, housing various wings of the Soviet government, all projecting an unmistakable image of immense authority, dignity and power. On one occasion, since a matter had to be taken up at the highest levels, I had the opportunity of getting into this historic and hallowed precincts. The corridors and rooms were on a scale not dissimilar to Versailles of France. The rooms were all elegant beyond compare with very royal period furniture, thick carpets and great looking paintings on the walls. There was nothing proletarian about the place from which the dictators of the proletariat lorded over the proletariat.

The long Brezhnev era had ended when our visits were taking place. This was followed by a succession of General Secretaries, Andropov, Cherenenko, etc. The Soviet paranoia regarding the health of their leaders is well known and their leaders' health was a closely guarded secret. The leaders never appeared in public except on May Day.

Though very seldom spoken about, it was not difficult to detect that the Soviet system was getting into serious difficulties. Stray comments made at unguarded moments revealed that the Soviet Union had to import large quantities of food, that her exports were declining, that the system of subsidies to her satellites was becoming unaffordable, that matching the US in the arms race was taking a heavy toll on the Soviet system leaving little or no investible surplus for the other sectors of the economy, and the economy was failing to generate a capital surplus, adequate to facilitate even a reasonable rate of economic growth. The USSR had been gripped by a disease which Paul Kennedy has described as 'imperial overstretch'. Political and strategic compulsions were making the country divert a disproportionate share of the GNP towards defence, and for fulfilling her imperial ambitions while the GNP was not growing fast enough to take care of all the nation's requirements. Modernization, upgradation of technology, improvement in the productivity of labour and capital could not be attended to, and the USSR, except in the defence and space sectors was falling way behind advanced economies. The state enterprises were least cost-conscious or quality conscious and failed to contribute anything towards capital formation. On both fronts, namely increasing savings and capital formation as well as upgrading the efficiency with which capital resources were employed, the USSR was failing to achieve the required advances, while it had to keep up the pretense of being the world's second super power.

Change, radical new thinking and drastic reorientation of the nation's direction was required, but old rigid and tired hands such as Andropov and Cherenenko could not be counted upon to bring this about.

It was during the Cherenenko period that Mrs Gandhi was assassinated. I was in Moscow on that day and so were the Defence Minister S.B. Chavan and the then Defence Secretary S.K. Bhatnagar. Both of them had to return, post haste, to New Delhi, while we continued our work. I was told by one of the officials in the Embassy that Cherenenko was to come to the Mission to sign the condolence register. No time was given but the day of the visit was communicated. Officials waited anxiously, having transferred the register from upstairs to a more convenient space near the entrance. All of a sudden without much warning the road was cleared and three or four large black limousines, used only by the highest in the land, arrived at top speed near the entrance. While high dignitaries like Arkhipov could be seen, from one of the cars, a wax-like figure was taken out by two large KGB men, made to stand, propelled towards the entrance and the table, its hand lifted and placed on the register. The wax figure did not have any facial expression worth mentioning, did not greet anyone and just about managed to sign the register. This accomplished, the figure was lifted, propelled again to the car and was driven away.

This was Constantin Cherenenko in charge of the mighty USSR, kept just about alive by the Soviet doctors. Every evening however on the television you heard of the frenetic pace at which Cherenenko worked for the welfare of his beloved people, taking this decision and that, giving directions everywhere and generally keeping the whole machinery humming. All this reminded one constantly of George Orwell's *'1984'*.

It must however be noted that in the Soviet system a very high degree of egalitarianism had been achieved. Leaving apart the privileged class of party bosses and the generals, the drive for distributive justice had ensured that the common man was enabled to obtain all his basic needs. Housing space, for example was provided according to need—a large family got larger space and high officials if their family size was small, got lesser space. Healthcare was available to all and children were taken very special care of. Workers enjoyed holidays at state expense.

Nevertheless, central planning had introduced such a degree of rigidity that there was no room for individual initiative, and more importantly for innovation. There was no incentive for better performance. Fixation of prices without any relation to cost of production or for the interplay of forces of demand and supply, maintenance of stability in prices over unduly long periods through massive subsidies and commitment to maintain full employment, with a wage bill unrelated to productivity, all ensured that there was little or no generation of surpluses. It must be noted that the Soviet system was only a pale shadow of the idealised version of socialism which involved equality, social justice, respect for the individual, widening choice and access to decision-making for every member of the community. The State was used increasingly as an instrument for social engineering, while the language of socialism, devoid of its content, was used as a means of legitimacy, both at home and abroad. The system was being utilized for constructing a politically determined future in which all spheres of activity, economic, social, legal, etc. were subordinated to the political criteria, regardless of its appropriateness. The rulers who perpetuated their existence by a system of total control could not accept any degree of social autonomy and consistently destroyed all manifestations of uncontrolled thought and action. Ideology deteriorated to a system which offered no choice proclaiming 'I have made the perfect bed for you to repose. If you do not fit, it is your fault and you must be chopped or racked till you do'.

Equally, importantly the system did not demand any accountability on the part of the rulers. Their continuation was not contingent upon generating the confidence of the people and retaining it. The question of seeking popular approval was not part of the system. The claim to legitimacy was being based on the sole fact of being legatees of the Communist revolution. When this claim lost credibility, the party continued its monopoly rule through the means of force and little else.

The inexorable laws of economics, however, would not permit continuance of this system and Mikhail Gorbachev started his well known *glasnost* and *perestroika* in an attempt to dismantle a system which had outlived its usefulness and replace it with a capitalist oriented one. The Soviet system seemed to operate well when there was a high degree of patriotism as was the case when Lenin was on the scene or at a time of national crisis as during World War II, when central planning and control enabled a high degree of mobilisation of the nation's resources and galvanized the system for winning the War.

The War had, no doubt, left a permanent imprint on Soviet life. No less than twenty million people from all the republics of the USSR were killed, many more millions wounded and rendered homeless. Every family had lost someone or the other. The Soviets make it a point to remind everyone that but for the sacrifices of the Soviet people, the Germans may have won the war. The Germans had reached the outskirts of Moscow, the spot is marked by huge tank barriers serving as a memorial, which can be seen on the way to the airport. Of course just outside Berlin there is a far more solemn and magnificent memorial for the war dead of each of the Soviet Republics.

West Germany, which I visited a few times, presented a stark contrast to the quite sober if not gloomy atmosphere that seemed to envelope Moscow. Capitalism had worked miracles and prosperity was discernible in every department of life. The 'antobahn' took you at high speeds to all the cities and travelling at 180 kilometres was nothing unusual. Cities which had been pulverized during the War had been all rebuilt with modern gleaming skyscrapers. West Berlin was full of life with business booming—again a contrast to the very sedate and quite dull East Berlin. The Kaiser Wilhelm Church on Kurfurstendam which was severely damaged during the War has been preserved as a bombed out ruin, as a War memorial, but everything else has been rebuilt—a tribute to German enterprise. Few perhaps recollect that the 'antobahn' was conceived originally by Adolf Hitler who viewed it as an instrument for welding his Deutschland together and for solving the unemployment problem that Germany faced at that time. This was followed closely by the development of the 'Volkswagen' the people's car meant to provide an affordable means of transport to the ordinary German. These were highly popular measures as in a very short time Germany was able to achieve near full employment. Of course, the rapid expansion of the 'Wehrmacht' also helped. The 'antobahn' concept was later borrowed by most European countries and by the USA under the Eisenhower administration.

On one of the visits I had occasion to drive on the 'antobahn' through Bavaria and on to Austria all the way to Innsbruck. This takes you through the fabled Tyrol with the Bavarian and Austrian Alps on the northern side and the Italian Alps on the south, snowclad all the way with picture postcard villages dotting the landscape. Tyrol is easily one of the most beautiful valleys in the whole of Europe and everything looked so enviably clean and perfect. It is along this very route that Hitler travelled frequently to his retreat at Obersalzburg, whenever he wanted a respite from all the tension he himself was creating. The mighty 'Wehrmacht' also rolled through this highway to effect the famous 'Anchluss'. On the way the German resort of Garmish falls, developed, with the usual German attention to detail and perfection. There is a cable car that takes you to the top from where the view is absolutely breathtaking.

One of the visits was for the purpose of reviewing the submarine construction programme. The Howald Deutsche Werft (HDW) company in Kiel, on the Baltic, was providing the technology. A license agreement had been concluded with this company which provided for building of the vessels in the Mazagaon Docks of Mumbai. The Germans, of course, had vast experience in submarine construction and though relatively speaking much less sophisticated, they were building a submarine every two days even in the last months of World War II under the dynamic Albert Speer, Hitler's armaments minister. I have had the very interesting experience of spending some seven hours inside the submarine constructed for the Indian Navy diving to a depth of some three hundred and fifty metres under the Kiel Canal which connects to the Baltic. Getting in and getting out of this vessel is no joke, given the highly constricted space inside and the vertical ladder with a very small opening. The submariners have to be quite slim and have to watch their weight all the while. One can get highly claustrophobic if one were to spend even a day inside one of these lethal contraptions, and it requires a high degree of training and special aptitudes to be a successful submariner.

On the Kiel beach, on display, is one of the World War II submarines as also the impressive and touching memorial to all the submariners, who lost their lives in the War, having caused such havoc to allied shipping during the War. Some of the orders, issued by Grand Admiral Raeder and Admiral Doenitz, are also on display. It was interesting to talk to one of the veteran submariners of World War II who had a number of 'kills' to his credit. His regret was that he did not have at his disposal the kind of sophisticated weapon system that is now available. He had no doubt that Germany would have won the War if such submarines had been given to him.

The HDW deal has been subject to considerable controversy and naval officers would often mention that they would have preferred the Swedish Kockum technology considered superior and more suitable to our requirements. Apart from certain technical difficulties, the fact that HDW had concluded a technology transfer agreement for this very vessel with Turkey, which had close relations with Pakistan, was a matter of concern.

All in all, the period in the Ministry of Defence was a highly enriching experience, widening my horizons, expanding my mind and enabling me to get introduced to new and technically oriented disciplines. I look back on this period with great satisfaction.

# 10

# SIKKIM

I was somewhat surprised, quite pleasantly I would say, when in early February' 1986 I was asked whether I would be willing to go to Sikkim as Development Commissioner. My term in Government of India was to come to an end by May that year, and in the normal course, I would have found my way to Assam, a prospect not very attractive at that point of time. The AGP government which was in office was yielding ground rapidly to the ULFA menace, with its violent creed. Apart from lack of experience and incompetence, the AGP showed a highly tolerant attitude towards the ULFA, unwarranted in the eyes of many, leading to a suspicion of links between the ULFA and the AGP. The ULFA cadres were being allowed a free run, openly indulging in violence, raising funds and progressively establishing a parallel administration. The government officers were seen to be complying with orders coming from ULFA cadres, building bridges, repairing roads, etc. while spending government money. The writ of the government did not prevail in quite a few areas and a general atmosphere of fear and insecurity was progressively taking over the state.

A full-fledged insurgency movement was being built up, with large-scale recruitment, running of training camps, acquisition of sophisticated weaponry, and plenty of resources flowing in. Non-Assamese became special targets of the ULFA. While the AGP government kept talking vaguely of a political solution, allowing the police little freedom to deal with elements, who were in the process of unleashing a civil war, murdering innocent people, the Central Government was also very slow to act. Though the Rajiv Gandhi government had a massive parliamentary majority, there was hesitation in dismissing a government which had failed in its duty of carrying on the administration of the state in accordance with the Constitution, and indeed could be accused of abetting an armed rebellion. It is possible that the AGP government which had come into being as a result of the Assam accord, whose main driving force was Rajiv Gandhi himself, it was felt, should be given a reasonable chance to prove itself. In the process, an insurgency movement, which could have been nipped in the bud by timely action, was allowed to grow into a monster. The administration in the state was in shambles and officers could work only with great fear, and that too in a limited way.

The circumstances in Assam were not exactly inviting and a tenure in Sikkim was no doubt a definitely more attractive option.

Sikkim became a full-fledged state of India in 1975. It was a kingdom ruled by the Maharaja of Sikkim, known also as the Chogyal or divine king. The last Chogyal was Palden Thondup Namgyal who was revered by his subjects, combining as he did temporal and spiritual authority.

Sikkim's history is shrouded in a great deal of mystery. Definitive information is no doubt available of the progressively expanding British control of Sikkim, and at the time of Indian Independence Sikkim was a protectorate. The British appointed political officer and the Dewan wielded considerable power and influence and had a great say in running the state. There was also a considerable presence of the Indian Army, greatly increased after the Chinese aggression of 1962. Sikkim's defence was the responsibility of India. When India attained Independence, Sikkim concluded a "stand still" agreement with India, and its status as a protectorate was continued. The Maharajah was treated as a Sovereign, given all the respect due to him and the Ministry of External Affairs looked after Sikkim affairs. The Government of India provided considerable financial and technical assistance to Sikkim. Indian officers functioned as Dewans and political officers.

Having established their hold over the whole of India, the British policy towards Tibet and the Himalayan kingdoms of Nepal, Bhutan and Sikkim was largely influenced by their anxiety to prevent any expansionary tendencies on the part of Tibet, while maintaining a reasonably friendly posture towards China. The British were highly conscious of the possibility of Czarist Russia making inroads into the areas north of their Indian empire, and as in the case of Afghanistan took great care to prevent any such thing happening. Since foreigners were not permitted to enter Tibet, the British treated the Tibetans with great suspicion, condemning them as a lawless lot.

With respect to Nepal, the British were happy not to interfere, keeping it as a buffer between their empire and Tibet. They concluded an extradition treaty, which worked well and used Nepal to get information on any activities by the Sikkimese or Tibetans which were considered prejudicial to their interests.

Bhutan was also left alone, the British merely taking such precautions as were necessary to prevent raids into the 'Doars' or gates, which had been earlier part of Bhutan, and in which tea cultivation on a large scale was being taken up.

Sikkim could not, however, in the opinion of the British, be either ignored as in the case of Bhutan or be treated on terms of comparative equality as in the case of Nepal. The British felt that Sikkim cannot stand by itself; it was bound to fall either to Tibet or to Nepal. Sikkim was therefore becoming a playground for competing interests of Tibet, Nepal and the British.

Sikkim had come under the sway of Tibetan Lamaistic Buddhism centuries before the British came in on the scene, and the Tibetan influence was all the while being reinforced with the acceptance of the Dalai Lama as a kind of appellate authority on religious questions, increase in trade ties, and marriage of the Chogyals with Tibetan women. Due to the influence of the Tibetan wives, the Chogyals even transferred their headquarters to the Chumbi valley, on the eastern side of the Jelepla pass.

In the meanwhile from the West and South, the Nepalese were making incursions into Sikkim and, by 1814, had taken over the Terai region. The British intervened on the presumption that Sikkim and the hills south and west of the Tista could become a province of Nepal. In 1817, they restored the Terai to Sikkim, and extracted guarantees against outbreak of hostilities. On the basis of the treaty of Titalya, the British 'assumed the position of Lords Paramount of Sikkim, with title to exercise predominant influence in that state' *(The Sikkim Gazetteer)*.

In 1835, the British made the Maharajah of Sikkim grant them title and possession of the hill station of Darjeeling and its surrounding areas. The imprisonment of Dr Sir Joseph Hooker, the botanist, by Sikkim, when he was on a botanical expedition, was enough for the British to punish Sikkim by annexation of the Terai. The harbouring of criminals and kidnapping of British subjects for slave trade provoked the British to send their troops upto Tista. The Maharajah agreed to the terms dictated by the British by the force of arms, concluding in March 1861 the Treaty of Tumlong, which among other things gave the British suzerainty over foreign policy, right of passage to troops. The transfer of the seat of government from the Chumbi valley to Sikkim proper was agreed to by the Maharaja. Sikkim also agreed not to cede or lease any portion of its territory, as also abolish slave trade.

The British were busy exploring the possibilities of expanding trade with Tibet, using the Sikkim route and had built a road upto Jelepla. Even on the question of succession, on the sudden death of the Maharajah in 1875, the Deputy Commissioner of Darjeeling seems to have had a decisive say.

The Tibetans were apparently unhappy with the steady growth of the British influence, and in a provocative act occupied a place called Lingtu inside Sikkim in 1886. The Maharajah, who was invited for discussions to Darjeeling, replied that he was not free to hold parleys as he had signed a treaty in 1886 which declared that Sikkim was subject only to China and Tibet. Apparently the China card was being played as a counter to the growing British influence. This change of allegiance was viewed with hostility by the British. They now assessed that the Lepchas and the immigrant Nepalese were friendly towards the British, and wanted their protection, while the ruling class was leaning towards the Tibetan side.

The British decided to evict the Tibetans from Lingtu having issued an ultimatum. The Viceroy even addressed a letter to the Dalai Lama explaining the reasons for the British action. After a ding dong battle the Tibetans were decisively defeated by September 1888. The British position as per the Treaty of Tumlong of 1861, was irrevocably reestablished. A convention, governing Sikkim–Tibet relations, was concluded in Calcutta on 17 March 1890. Earlier in 1889, T.C. White was appointed as Assistant Political Officer to 'advise and assist the Maharajah in the administration of the country'. The British, it appears, favoured increasing immigration of the Nepalese into Sikkim territory as a means of reducing Tibetan influence going to the extent of declaring that they desired 'the replacement of the prayer wheels of the lamas with the ritualistic practices of the Brahmans' *(The Sikkim Gazetteer)*.

The pre-British history of Sikkim is interesting from the point of view of understanding the extent of Tibetan influence on both the religious and temporal life of Sikkim, and it is worth recapitulating this, briefly.

Though shrouded by the thick mist of Lepcha tradition, certain definitive contours of the history can easily be discerned. It is clear that the original inhabitants of Sikkim were the Lepchas, with physical characteristics of the Mongolian race. Certain peculiarities of language and religion render it probable that this tribe is a very ancient colony from southern Tibet. The etymology of the modern name of Sikkim is also shrouded in some mystery. The Bhutias and Lepchas feel that the word is derived from the Sanskrit *sikhin* i.e., crested, a name applied by the conquering Gorkhas. This view is supported by the fact that the Gorkhas, who came from the west, sighted the Kanchenjanga and Kabur mountains right on the border with Nepal. Others think that it is a Sanskrit translation of the Bhutia word *demozong* or *denzong* meaning happy place, the Sanskrit equivalent being *Sukhi* (happy). The Lepchas themselves call Sikkim as *'Nye me el'* or paradise. It is also believed that the name is derived from the Limbu word *Sukhim*. The Bhutias call it the *bemyul denzong* meaning the hidden valley of rice.

Guru Padmasambhava, also called Guru Rimpoche, had a decisive influence on the course of events in Sikkim. It is in connection with the construction of a monastery in Tibet by the King, the Srong Detsan who favoured Buddhism, that Guru Padmasambhava made his entry into Tibet. All endeavours to build the monastery were frustrated by earthquakes attributed to demons. On the advice of Shantharakshitha, the Indian monk, the King sent for Padmasambhava who belonged to the Yogacharya school in Nalanda. With the *dorje* or *vajra,* the thunderbolt and spells from the Mahayana school of Buddhism, he vanquished the devils and built the monastery in AD 749, and established the first community of Lamas.

Guru Rimpoche is believed to have visited Sikkim, particularly the western areas, and started the process of establishing lamaistic Buddhism in Sikkim.

However, the full-scale conquest of Sikkim by Buddhism and along with it the establishment of the institution of the Chogyals—

the divine King—the dharma raja—with temporal and spiritual authority, took place only in the seventeenth century.

The arrival of Llatsun Chhempo meaning the 'great revered God' a high lama with the religious name of Kunzang Namgyal or victorious essence of goodness, with two other lamas named Sempah Chhempo of the Kartokpa sect and Rigdsin Chhempo of the Ngadakpa sect is considered to be of great historic importance. The three most holy lamas met at a place called Yoksum, now in West Sikkim, which in Lepcha means 'the three superior ones or noble beings'. The three wanted to convert the hitherto irreligious country to Buddhism and wanted to find a ruler to take on the responsibility of governing the country. Llatsun Chhempo then referred to a prophesy of Guru Rimpoche which had indicated that there will be a gathering of four noblemen who will arrange for the good governance of the country. The three lamas had come from north, west and south, and the prophecy had said that there shall be a fourth from the east named Phuntshog. This Phuntshog was discovered in the East of Sikkim near Gangtok. He was then conducted to the revered lamas, who crowned him by placing the holy water vase on his head and anointing him with the water, and exhorted him to rule the country religiously. He was given Llatsun's own religious surname of Namgye or Namgyal and the little of Chho-gyal-Dharma raja or divine king. Phuntshog Namgyal was at that time 38 years, and this event is believed to have taken place in AD 1641.

The throne upon which Phuntshog Namgyal was consecrated as the first Chogyal of Sikkim is still very much there in 'Yoksum' and is much revered by the Sikkimese. Also, at the spot is a huge stone, with the imprint of a foot indelibly stamped on it, believed by everyone to be that of Guru Rimpoche himself.

Thus started the Namgyal dynasty which governed Sikkim through the eighteenth and nineteenth centuries, right upto 1975, without interruption.

Note may be taken of the fact that Tibetan lamaistic Buddhism and its Sikkimese manifestation is based on the Mahayana school, whose main exponents, Nagarjuna and Shantha Rakshita, are held in great esteem. Elements of the earlier Tibetan Bon religious and tantric practices of the *sakta* school of Hinduism have been liberally mixed during the development of the religion.

The Tibetan religion has four main sects, the Nyingmapa or old unreformed school, the Sakyapa and Kargyapa or the semi-reformed school, and the Gelukpa sect the reformed school. The Dalai Lama is of the Gelukpa sect. There are subsects under each of these sects.

In Sikkim, basically, only the Nyingmapa and Kargyapa sects are represented with their subsects and large number of monasteries have been built over the years. Guru Padmasambhava is worshipped as 'a second Buddha' in eight forms called 'eight worshipful names of the teacher, the prominent of these being Guru Padma Jungne, born of a lotus for the happiness of the three worlds, Guru Padmasambhava the Sanskrit equivalent also called the 'saviour of the religious doctrine' and Guru Nyima od-zer, the enlightening sun of darkness.

The oldest monastery of Sikkim is Dub-de founded by Llatsun Chhempo himself. Monasteries such as Tashiding, Pemayangtse and Sanga Chholing were built at spots believed to have been consecrated by Guru Rimpoche. Pemayangtse is believed to have been designed if not actually built by Llatsun Chhempo, and its monks alone enjoy the title of 'la sang' and to its lamas is reserved the honour of anointing with holy water the reigning sovereign of Sikkim, the Chogyal. It is also believed that the Pemayangtse monastery was built by the third Chogyal, Chador Namgyal.

While the above monasteries subscribe to the Nyangmapa sect, the Karma Kagyu sect has three monasteries, Ralang, Rumtek and Phodong. Of these Rumtek had become the seat of the sixteenth Gyalwa Karmapa when he had to quit Tibet, and the Tsurpu monastery which until then was regarded the headquarters of the Kagyu order, because of persecution by the Chinese. The succession question relating to the reincarnation of the sixteenth Karmapa has become mired in controversy and consequently this monastery has been in the limelight for some time now.

This brief dabbling with the history of Sikkim that I have indulged in will, I presume, be of use in understanding the events of 1975. A good deal has been written about this by those who were participants in the drama. B.S. Das's account reflects more the official side of the story, whereas Sunanda Dutta Ray's *Smash and Grab* attempts to portray a picture of more 'wrongs' than 'rights' and quite sympathetic to the Chogyal's cause. The Bhutia Lepchas still refer to Chogyals period with great nostalgia and has little hesitation in stating that the 'takeover' by India was not justified. Even the Nepalese feel that they were not unfairly treated in the Chogyal's regime.

There are however inexorable forces—geo-political and geo-economic—which would have inevitably brought about the changes that took place. As mentioned earlier, the British had assessed that it was impossible for Sikkim to have stood alone, and would have had to face a takeover either by Nepal or Tibet. Bringing Sikkim under British protection guaranteed that this did not happen. The dependence of Sikkim on British India both for her security and for promoting her economic progress kept increasing all through the British period. After independence of India, the ties were reinforced, with India substantially upgrading assistance towards Sikkim's economic development.

Apart from the British legacy, several factors played a role in bringing about the events of 1975.

In the second half of the twentieth century, monarchy as a form of government was disappearing all over the world. Everywhere people were demanding and obtaining their due share in the process of governance. Participative democracy was the political philosophy, sweeping the world and represented the zeitgeist–or spirit of the times. Where it survived monarchy was merely symbolic and was increasingly seen more as a tourist attraction than anything else. Sikkim could not expect to escape this whirlwind of change, especially after her giant neighbour India had achieved such great advances in putting into practice the democratic form of governance.

Secondly, the population composition of Sikkim had so drastically changed with the Nepalese reaching the figure of 70 per cent, that for the minority Bhutia Lepchas, to continue to hold the monopoly of power through the Chogyal and the nobles called the Kazis, was getting to be increasingly anachronistic. The basically feudal character of the regime could not altogether be ignored. On balance it must be admitted that the Chogyal himself was conscious of this and had indeed introduced elements of participative democracy with an assembly. There were, however, limits beyond which even his good intentions could not carry him. Chogyals such as Sir Tashi Namgyal and the last Chogyal, Palden Namgyal, indeed had the welfare of all sections of the people at heart and paid great attention to spread of education, health services, conservation of forest resources, control of soil erosion, generation of power, exploitation of mineral resources and road building. Officers recall, admiringly, the way the Chogyals would closely monitor progress of development projects and how corruption was unheard of in the regime.

Thirdly, the takeover of Tibet by Communist China, the exodus of the Dalai Lama, and the suppression unleashed by the Chinese, introduced an altogether new element in the already fragile equation. A peaceful and isolationist Tibet, which just wanted the world to leave it alone, armed with nothing more lethal than outdated rifles, catapults and such medieval weapons of war was itself treated with suspicion and caution by the British, who took anxious steps to safeguard the northern frontiers of their empire. Note may be taken of the 1886 treaty by which Sikkim submitted to the authority of Tibet and China. A nuclear China, with missiles backed by the huge Red Army, capable of aggression, with the declared intention of abrogating all 'unequal' treaties and bringing back to its fold all territories lost when China was weak, was an altogether different proposition. This greatly heightened the anxiety of New Delhi, highlighting the urgency of securing the northern frontiers of India. India had already gone through a very unpleasant experience with China in 1962, and had become wary of the 'yellow peril'.

Fourthly, Mrs Gandhi, having humbled Pakistan, having made India a nuclear power and with supreme authority in her hands, had already earned the reputation of a leader willing and capable of taking decisive action. Though diplomatic ties had been reestablished with China, she showed no inclination to lower her guard on the northern frontier, and was very legitimately interested in reinforcing India's defences and taking adequate care of India's security concerns. In India's post-Independence history, she had emerged, at that time, as the one leader who could be counted upon to take action without hesitation, if the situation so demanded and could not be trifled with.

While these developments were coming into play, the Chogyal played his cards, it would appear quite unfortunately, in such a manner that his actions raised concern in Delhi. It was perceived that he was not sufficiently sensitive to New Delhi's security requirements. New Delhi was already peeved with the way Nepal showed a distinct inclination, to play India against China and was concerned with the rapid growth of the Communist influence in Nepal.

New Delhi looked with great suspicion the reported contacts with the Chinese by the Chogyal during the coronation of the King of Nepal.

The Chogyal's personal life had, at that time, taken on dimensions which seemed to reinforce New Delhi's anxieties and suspicions. His first wife Sangey Dikhi had died followed by the death of his son in a motor car accident. A shattered man, given to bouts of drinking, happened to meet Hope Cook, an American, in Darjeeling and decided to marry her. The marriage was attended by a number of Americans. Her influence, it appeared to New Delhi, encouraged the Chogyal to adopt more independent postures. Her book, proscribed in India, argues that she was only helping her husband in the discharge of his duties. She did take keen interest in education and women's welfare. She firmly denies having played any political role. New Delhi was however in no mood to take any chances on this score either.

The NBC of USA produced an interesting documentary on Hope Cook's life in Sikkim entitled 'Yankee Queen in Shangrila'.

Interestingly, Kazi Lendhup Dorji, who led the movement for establishment of full-fledged democracy in Sikkim, had a Belgian wife and rumours have it that she had taken a dislike to the Yankee queen—now called Gyalmo, divine queen of Sikkim, and she played quite a role in bringing about the change.

Students of history would doubtless agree that most of the pathbreaking events in the annals of world history have taken place because of the decisive and forceful personality of those leaders who are prepared to run the necessary risks and win the game. Here is possibly one more such care where the 'Steely Empress of India' was on the one side and on the other quite a weak and indecisive Chogyal.

In the event, a pro-democracy movement took shape demanding end of the Chogyal rule, merger with India, application of the Constitution of India to Sikkim and establishment of a representative government based on free and fair elections based on adult franchise and the principle of 'one man one vote'. A resolution to this effect was passed by the Sikkim assembly, and the Parliament of India duly adopted an amendment to the Constitution endorsing all the demands. Article 371 (F) while making Sikkim part of India, provides for a number of safeguards, particularly with respect to the maintenance of the political balance between the Bhutia Lepchas and the Nepalese.

While all this was happening, the Chogyal kept himself confined to his palace operating a ham radio appealing for help in his hour of crisis. His American wife had departed never to return again. A very sad man, he became a recluse and died not long after the merger. His son and heir an elegant, highly educated, very princely personality with impressive and cultivated manners, Prince Wangchuk Namgyal, resides in the palace and has become almost a monk going into retreats with great regularity. He is highly respected, but takes no interest in public affairs. Still a very eligible bachelor, will possibly continue to be so, more inclined towards monastic life than anything else. Wangchuk is the son of the last Chogyal's first wife. Hope Cook had two children, a son and a daughter. The daughter Hope Lizum lives in Sikkim married to a police officer. The son, who lives in the USA, visits Sikkim on and off. Hope Cook has reportedly married again and lives in the USA. The debate, whether India was right in taking the steps she took, has not altogether died down in Sikkim. The Bhutia Lepchas have found that political power has slipped out of their hands, though the safeguards provided under 371(F) reserving thirteen seats in a thirty-two member assembly, does ensure that they have a decisive say in the political life of Sikkim. Nevertheless, given the fact that democracy is all about majority rule, the Nepalese now have control over the politics of Sikkim. The Kazis may have lost some of their privileges, but no one has touched their large holdings of lands. Many have become top bureaucrats and continue to play a prominent role in the governance of the state.

The events, it appears, on balance was a case where India, while no doubt taking steps to secure her northern frontiers, merely helped along a historically inevitable process. Whether in this process the Chogyal could have been allowed to continue, with a review of the standstill argument and superior safeguards with respect to India's security concerns, remains a moot question.

To me the ultimate test is whether the people of Sikkim are better off today by casting their lot with India, economically and socially, than would have been the case had they remained semi-independent, or been taken over either by China or Nepal.

With respect to Nepal, the existence of pan Nepalism as a political posture if not a long-term objective is well known. For economic reasons outward migration of Nepalis in substantial numbers into Bhutan, into Sikkim, into the northeast of India, not to mention the trickle to almost all parts of India, is an age-old phenomenon. The Bhutanese, fearing a serious upsetting of the population balance, introduced the policy of 'Driglam Namza', namely Bhutanization of the polity, resulting in largescale eviction of the Nepalis. These 'Bhupalis' kept in camps in Nepal and along the northern borders of India have been almost forgotten by history. They keep trickling into

Sikkim. Nepali migration into Sikkim continues, as there is a huge demand for labour, for border roads and all the development projects that keep getting implemented. Sikkim has a fairly lengthy border with Nepal, and a formal claim to the territory of Sikkim was an apprehension articulated by the British as one of the reasons for their proactive policy towards Sikkim. An effort to take over Sikkim by the Nepalese cannot be regarded as that farfetched as it seems, on the surface. If it had happened the kind of political instability, fractured polity, the continued and perhaps growing clout of the leftists, of various shades of red and indeed of left extremism, the poor economic conditions in Nepal, high rate of growth of population combined with poor economic performance, all point to the distinct possibility of the Nepalese paying little regard to safeguarding the rights and interests of the indigenous people. In any case, Nepal would not have been able to pour in the kind of resources that India has provided to Sikkim, and may have only exploited the territory as one more outlet for her ever-growing population.

As to China, with its history and performance in Tibet, its extreme insensitivity to the feelings of the Tibetans, its sustained efforts to destroy the Tibetan religion and civilization, one would shudder to think as to what would have happened to Sikkim if the Chinese had walked across the Nathula and other passes. The beautiful monasteries and places of religious significance and indeed the rich religious and cultural life of Sikkim would not have been spared. As it is, the Chinese are yet to recognize Sikkim as a part of India, even though the matter has been raised at the highest levels. They have been trying to exercise an influence on Tibet's religious affairs by appointing their own Panchen Lama and recognizing the seventeenth Karmapa both developments considered by analysts as unprecedented, given the godless nature of the regime. Strong political motives can easily be seen behind their moves. The Chinese record of treating minorities, and total lack of respect for human rights, soundly criticized in various forums, with little or no effect on the regime, all inspire no confidence that Sikkim would have received fair treatment in Chinese hands.

In sharp contrast to these possibilities, with the integration of Sikkim, the state has witnessed unprecedented prosperity and progress, while her social fabric has been fully preserved and has been given all the opportunity to develop.

I have already mentioned that the political power of the minority, Bhutia Lepchas, has been largely protected and preserved in the new democratic setup through the instrumentality of the constitutional provisions under article 371(F). Twelve of the thirty-two seats in the Assembly have been reserved for the Bhutia Lepchas. They alone can be elected for these seats. One more seat is reserved for the 'Sangha' or the monasteries, a unique accommodation for the Buddhist clergy, who had a great say during the days of the Chogyal in the affairs of state, and who have been given due representation in the new set-up as well. The number of seats reserved is not proportionate to the size of the population, a principle of great importance in a democracy. This significant departure is an eloquent testimony to the great sensitivity that was displayed towards the requirement of the singular situation in Sikkim, and towards the special features of its history.

Given this arrangement, no government can be formed in Sikkim without the support of this segment of the population, and no government can survive if it loses their support. The Nepalese have been urging the Government of India that seats should be reserved for them as well in the Assembly—as was the case during the Chogyals time—but there have been no takers for this in New Delhi.

Secondly, the Bhutia Lepchas have been classified as scheduled tribes, more to preserve their unique culture than for their economic or social status. This entitles them to all the privileges enshrined in the Constitution of India and relevant laws, be it in government jobs, in education or with respect to special financial flows provided for in the Constitution for scheduled tribes.

Thirdly, the old laws of Sikkim have been allowed to be in force in the state. Protection with respect to land and as regards the criteria for government appointments have been constitutionally and legally recognized and guaranteed. Even Nepalis are not permitted to enter and reside in North Sikkim, a move calculated to preserve and foster the unique Lepcha culture and traditions, while non-Sikkimese cannot purchase land anywhere in Sikkim. Sikkimese can however possess immovable property anywhere in India. Also, only those registered as Sikkim subjects can get Sikkim government jobs. Further, the Inner Line Regulation ensures that no foreigner can enter Sikkim without a permit, in addition to the usual travel documents.

Fourthly, religious freedom has been guaranteed and the state of Sikkim has continued to have an ecclesiastical department to look after religious affairs, and provide aid to the monasteries. A practice and a system that was put into place by the Maharaja has been thus allowed to continue. It may be added that this department only handles affairs relating to the monasteries.

Fifthly, with respect to monastic life, training of monks and their welfare, the age-old practices have continued, with little or no change. Change, if at all, is to take place from within, with no interference from the official side.

Sixthly, the nobles have retained their land and possessions. No land ceiling laws have been applied in Sikkim, and since no transfer can take place to non-Sikkimese their economic status is substantially preserved.

Further, Sikkim, on the economic front, has been a huge beneficiary of Central plan and non-plan expenditure. It has been given the status of a special category state which means that its plan expenditure is fully met by the Central Government. It is not expected to show any surplus out of its own revenue earnings for the purpose of expending on the plan for creating assets. Further, ninety per cent of the Central Government's plan allocation is given as grant and only ten per cent as loan. In terms of per capita development expenditure, Sikkim occupies the first position in the whole country, way above many states. In the latest Five Year Plan, the figure is over Rs 20,000 per year, compared to a measly eight or nine hundred rupees in West Bengal. What is important is the prudent and productive utilization, of all the available resources, so that the State reaches high levels of growth and prosperity.

Educational opportunities have been opened up for the Sikkimese in a very big way. Reservations are provided for students from Sikkim in various technical institutions, in several parts of the country, in the engineering and medical disciplines. Of course, many study in various states, taking advantage of the usual opportunities available for everyone.

The officers, who had worked with the Chogyal, have all been inducted into the All India Services, and, with the vast expansion in the bureaucracy and manifold increase in plan expenditure, job opportunities have multiplied enormously.

Consequently, there is really no poverty in Sikkim. On the contrary, within ten years of the merger, the per capita income had more than doubled. Gangtok, which was not very different from a very small town with basically single-storied tin roof structures, prior to 1975, has been transformed to a bustling prosperous urban settlement, with multi-storied buildings, occupying every possible nook and corner especially along the high way. Many of the state government's employees, even of the lower grades, own huge buildings and enjoy elaborate lifestyles.

The conclusion can justifiably be that by casting her lot with India, Sikkim may have had a change in the manner she is governed, to the regret of an influential segment of the society, a process that had a certain historic inevitability about it, on balance, the gains far outweigh the losses.

When I reached Gangtok, in May 1986, my official concerns related purely to the field of economic development. Debates on the merger, if at all, were conducted in the very elegant drawing rooms of some of the officers, in gentle and dignified language, and with great dignity, reflecting the highly refined and civilized character of the society. Fine scotch was always available, and copious quantities were consumed with gusto by all present. This seemed to improve the manners, conduct and demeanour of the participants, rather than the other way about.

T.V. Rajeshwar was then the Governor and Nar Bahadur Bhandari, the Chief Minister. Having been the Director of Intelligence Bureau Rajeshwar was ideally suited to be the Governor of this strategic and sensitive state. Highly accomplished, well read, capable and articulate, the Governor, while observing all the constitutional norms, took keen interest in the welfare and progress of the state. A fine and very hospitable host, there were many occasions when I had the pleasure of partaking a fine repast in the Raj Bhavan.

The Raj Bhavan, an elegant and very colonial structure, which was earlier the residence of the Political Officer, occupies a high point on the longish Gangtok ridge and commands an extraordinary view of the entire Singalila range. The Kanchenjanga dominates the scene, a massive double peaked mastiff rising above 28,000 feet, with its companion peaks of Sinolchu and Mount Pandim, each of them having their unique contours, particularly at the top. In the winter time, when this range is visible throughout the day (and even during the night if the moon is shining), Governor Rajeshwar would generously get a select gathering to lunch, preceded by a variety of drinks. To sit and enjoy the meal in the emerald lawns, while the cool refreshing mountain air wafts across you, is an incomparable experience. A sojourn in a mountain resort in Austria may come close to this. Down the ridge at a lower point is the residence of the Chief Minister, earlier occupied by the Dewans of Sikkim called 'Mintogang'. Further down, at a still lower point is the palace of the Chogyals. Whether this difference in the elevation at which each of these buildings were located was intended to convey any particular message by the British, I am not sure.

'Mintogang' and the palace commanded breathtaking views of the mountain range. What appeared fascinating is the continuous change in the colour of the snow mountains. In the very early morning, when the sun's very first rays fall on the mountain, they assume a deep golden colour. As the morning progresses, this changes into shades of yellow, and then on to pure white. By about four, when the sun starts to get to the western side, gradually descending behind the mountains, they become grey in colour. In full moon, the mountains can be seen through the night with a silvery shine.

Nature has been exceptionally generous in her endowments to Sikkim. Greenery is abundant all over, with heavy rainfall from about May, right upto the middle of October. This fills up all the water bodies, and the numerous rivers and rivulets. The Tista system has its origin near the holy lakes, right on the Tibetan border, while the other major river, Rangit, flows right from the Kanchenjanga. In Sikkim, all rivers, streams, lakes, water bodies and mountains are holy and invested with divine power. The Kanchenjanga is the holiest, a guardian deity, as it were, worshipped in a special festival with monastic dances. The Chogyals would not permit mountaineering expeditions to clamber over Sikkim's holy mountains, especially the Kanchenjanga, and it is strongly believed that when apparently such a permission was wrested from a reluctant Chogyal in the 1970s misfortune of many dimensions overtook him.

Buddhist beliefs and precepts hold a very prominent position in the life of the people of Sikkim. The Nepalese do have their temples and follow Hindu rituals, festivals and religious practices. In terms of visibility and grandeur, the monasteries are quite matchless and monastic life and practices, and the everyday religious life of the Bhutia Lepchas occupy a predominant position. Festivals, monastic dances and various ceremonies occur in the calendar, with a frequency unknown elsewhere and are observed with elaborate, age old rituals with great public participation. The grandeur and colour is lent by the large presence of the monks, in their very eye-catching and brightly yellow and ochre costumes, very solemn in their appearance, invariably accompanied by the traditional drums, pipes and trumpets, very large in size. The masks and brocades worn by the lamaistic dancers have a unique character and carry a special appeal. While the purpose of the exercise may be deadly serious, such as gathering all the evil demons of the yesteryear and burning them at the stake, the atmosphere is gay and relaxed. The local brew 'chhang' is no doubt consumed liberally all round.

In every house there is always the 'chapel', a very revered room full of images of the Buddha, the Bodhisattvas and Guru Padmasambhava, colourful religious paintings called 'tankhas', prayer books, tables called 'choksis' and the butter lamps. Traditional carpets complete the picture.

The monasteries and the lamas exercise great influence on the people and they are invariably consulted on a variety of questions of life and death.

The death ceremonies are indeed elaborate and generally very expensive. The lamas have to release the soul on death, by observing appropriate procedures, a horoscope has to be cast to determine the time for the funeral and cremation. The body is made to assume the Buddha, sitting posture and is carried in a palanquin-like structure, in a colourful long procession, as per very-clearly-laid-down procedures accompanied by the chanting of 'Om mani padme hum'. The mourning period is as long as forty-nine days, followed by pilgrimages to holy places by senior members of the family. All the while, a great deal of food is prepared and distributed. Along the route, juniper bushes are burnt, ostensibly to keep the air sanctified.

In the cremation area outside Gangtok on the way to Nathula, the highest point is reserved for the royal family. A little lower is the area for the nobles, and below that is for the others. The marriage ceremonies are comparatively simpler. There is, no doubt, considerable eating, drinking and merry making.

Everywhere in Sikkim, on house tops, along the roads, on hilltops and ridges can be seen fluttering prayer flags of various colours, on which are inscribed prayers with great care. The idea is that winds will carry the prayers to the Gods.

Also to be seen are the prayer wheels, not only in all the

monasteries but also at various places, being driven by watercourses. Miniature ones can be seen in the hands of people, especially old ladies, walking on the roads. Rotating the wheels is a form of prayer, accompanied by counting of the beads and utterance of various litanies.

The monasteries of Sikkim are elaborate establishments, with an impressive and unique architecture. Big or small, their various features have a standard pattern, with the altar dominating the central hall. The biggest is the Rumtek monastery, commanding, as it does, large resources and has a beautifully designed marble-floored annexe, completed in 1988.

The monasteries serve invariably as schools for lamas. The tradition, it appears, has been to second one son in every family, for lamahood. The institution of the reincarnate lama or 'rimpoche' is very strong and a rimpoche is always expected to be in a monastery.

Near Gangtok, there is also a very large school belonging to the Nyangma tradition, where lamas, from not only Sikkim but several parts of the world, are students.

Volumes can be written on the religious life in Sikkim. This is not my intention, and the only purpose of briefly referring to this interesting aspect of the life in Sikkim, is to draw attention to the deep religiosity of the people of Sikkim, their strong and abiding faith in their ancient religion, its precepts and practices and the role it plays in shaping the life of the people.

What I found is that the belief systems had strongly reinforced the moral underpinnings of this very civilized and gentle society, instilled in them great respect for nature and her ways, insulating them to a considerable extent from some of the more corrupting influences of the modern world. Peace and tranquility is to be found everywhere. The character of the people has been moulded through the ages by a fine blend of the best elements of Hindu and Buddhist religious and philosophical thought. The Buddhist concept of '*vinaya*' or humility seemed to permeate all layers of the society which along with '*ahimsa*' has ensured a high degree of tolerance and accommodation for the viewpoint of others, other belief systems and customs and practices.

Exchange of a white scarf 'khadha' is standard practice on all occasions. There is a code even for this, when to retain the khadha, when to return it to the giver, whether it should be put on the shoulders or given into the hands. It is always presented with a respectful bow.

For me, having gone through so much of turbulence in Assam, with so much anger, animosity and violence, so much of intolerance, justifiable or not, to deal with the people of Sikkim was an altogether refreshing experience. Everyone who met you from the high to the low, showed such refined and cultured demeanour, great consideration and politeness employing an idiom and a language which would be the envy of the most accomplished of diplomats. It was a delight to deal with them, and if you were able to get their problems settled, they were most effusive in expressing their gratitude. It appeared that the Sikkimese had perfected the fine art of living in harmony with each other and with nature. To be sure, there are a number of communities, Bhutias, Lepchas, Nepalis and among the Nepalis, the Newars, the Tamangs, the Rais, the Magars, the Gurungs, etc., to name a few. All religions are also represented in the state, including Christianity and Islam. In spite of this, conflicts, at least so far, have not reared their ugly heads.

Nar Bahadur Bhandari was the Chief Minister when I landed in Sikkim as Development Commissioner. I was directly answerable to him. He had founded the Sikkim Sangram Parishad. The 'Sangram' part of it baffled me a bit, as the exact target and the purpose of the 'Sangram' has been kept rather vague. He was not in favour of the merger of Sikkim with India, and had reportedly suffered at the hands of the Central Reserve Police. With considerable experience behind him, he gave me the impression of a mature administrator, firm and decisive, capable of taking tough decisions. He had done a great deal for Sikkim, already commanding the respect of the people. He had full and firm control over his party and his ministers and was able to articulate his viewpoint with authority and knowledge. He was a fine orator holding his audience spellbound in Nepali, for even five to six hours, not only because of the content of his speeches but also because of his fine sense of humour. His English was pretty good, and his orders on file generally clear cut and precise.

My predecessor in office, R. Narayanan, a Madras Cadre IAS officer on deputation, had earned a fine reputation in the state for his integrity and hard work. My being also from the south of India was considered a plus point.

The CM, and indeed all the ministers, treated me with great courtesy and consideration and welcomed me, at all times, with a broad smile. Any number of cups of hot tea was always on offer, and given the very cold climate particularly in winter, tea drinking was almost continuous, throughout the day.

The Secretariat had a fine location, just below the palace, and commanded a grand view of the Kanchenjanga and her companions. The work ethic in the Secretariat could, if one is inclined to apply the most charitable interpretation, be described, at best, as leisurely. Though the working hours were officially from ten am to four pm—a far cry from Delhi's 9 am to 7 pm schedule—barely twenty per cent would reach the Secretariat by 10 am and leaving the office by 3.30 pm was more the rule than the exception. In any case no one stayed beyond 4 pm whether there is work to be done or not. They had wisely interpreted the 4 pm limit as an absolute prohibition to stay even a minute beyond 4 pm I got into hot waters while trying to finish the day's work by sitting in my office on occasion beyond 4 pm. While my staff showed their disfavour, by distinct body language, the chap who was responsible for locking up all the rooms told me in firm tones, after tolerating, in his view, my erratic and uncalled for behaviour for two or three occasions, that it was his duty to lock up all the rooms at 4 pm, and he had no intention of failing to carry out his onerous responsibility, whether I decided to foolishly be inside or not. The message was loud and clear, and I decided to carry my files home rather than get locked up!

Everyone in the Sikkim Secretariat was always dressed to kill. The CM set a fine example in sartorial elegence, wearing Yves St Laurent ties, suits which would have been the envy of Saville Row tailors, with matching shoes of the latest design. The ladies looked as if they were on a perpetual parade, competing with each other to win contests. The local 'baku' worn by the ladies is an epitome of elegance and the Sikkimese women added to this by a choice of fine shoes, variety bags and what have you. Smell of fine perfumes was not difficult to detect.

Holidays were taken seriously and every religion's, every festival, it appeared was a government holiday. Several new years are celebrated, and a few of them for days together. In the month of December, the holidays are more than the number of working days. I got into hot waters, when later as Chief Secretary. I attempted to reduce the number of holidays and increase the number of working hours.

From day one, Bhandari gave me absolute freedom to do my work. Throughout my period as Development Commissioner, he never interfered with my decisions and was always gracious to acknowledge the good work. He was a very shrewd judge of men, and possibly concluded that I could present Sikkim's case in New Delhi effectively, and get all the resources that could be obtained from the Central Government.

The planning department in Sikkim functioned more or less as an instrument for collecting and putting together the 'wish lists' of various departments. There was little or no strategic thinking with adequate theoretical and technical inputs. No methodology existed to evaluate proposals from the point of view of technical feasibility and economic viability, and once projects were taken up there was hardly any monitoring or evaluation. Cost and time overruns occurred with unfailing regularity. No one bothered to think about returns on investment, and the pricing system with respect to public utilities existed only in name. The tendency was to give the people of Sikkim everything free—free water supply, free electricity, free housing, free education, free text books, free uniforms, etc. Little or no attention was paid to maintenance of assets. Rural water supply was a prime example, where under the plan, villages were provided the required infrastructure, but within three or four years the assets had gone to seed. The villagers did not pay for the purified water and they expected the government to take care of maintenance, while they indulged in wasting the water.

I set about revamping the system, prioritizing Sikkim's development objectives, setting long term and short term goals, taking into account Sikkim's natural resources endowments, and stressing upon generating returns out of the investments. Given the terrain conditions and limited availability of cultivable land, and little or no scope for mechanization of agriculture, horticulture, floriculture, cash crops like cardamom and ginger and animal husbandry were to be given priority. Foodgrain production was not economical. The Nepalis had brought in the culture of terracing the land—a fine technique for controlling soil erosion in hilly terrain, and there was a regulation in place put in by the Chogyals, laying down standards for terracing. A good deal of paddy was indeed being cultivated in these terraced spaces, but the productivity standards were low. The terraced fields, no doubt, presented an extraordinarily pleasing sight to the beholder. Diversification of the economy, with emphasis on 'clean' industries and low volume high value items and full exploitation of Sikkim's potential for hydropower, I felt, would lead Sikkim towards self reliance and prosperity and take care of the unemployment problem. Sikkim had already advanced on the fronts of education and basic healthcare. Higher education and specialized healthcare required particular attention. Vocational and technical education, which had so far been neglected, had to be taken up.

Utilizing my contacts established, during my period in the Ministry of Defence, I persuaded the Chairman of Bharat Electronics, Bangalore, to consider setting up a plant in Sikkim. Given the advantages of climate and the dust-free atmosphere, I felt, manufacture of electronic components would be promising. Already HMT of Bangalore had set up a watch factory in Sikkim, where productivity standards were even higher than that in Bangalore. Captain S. Prabhala had my proposal looked into at top speed, and it was decided after a series of discussions, based on technical studies, that manufacture of 'discrete semiconductors' can be taken up in Sikkim. The idea was to build up a long-term partnership with BEL, for gradual and sustained technological upgradation and manufacture of a stream of products, if the 'discrete semiconductor' programme succeeded. An agreement was concluded under which the entire investment was to be made by the Government of Sikkim, while BEL was to provide all required technical inputs, training of personnel, supervision at the time of construction and managerial personnel until local talent is built up. Very importantly, the entire production was to be marketed by BEL.

I took this project as a personal mission and a challenge to ensure that there are no time or cost overruns. Taga Khampa, the Managing Director, an IIT product, proved to be a very able ally. By close monitoring, I was able to ensure that the project was commissioned exactly on time, and a little below cost. Nearly 150 people got new jobs, having been trained in BEL, even more importantly, Sikkim was introduced, for the first time, to high technology, capable of releasing growth impulses and several spin-off benefits.

I was according high priority to exploitation of the huge hydro power potential in Sikkim and encouraged taking up a series of generation projects. Quite a few mini hydel projects were taken up, while strengthening the transmission and distribution network. Rural electrification had already made giant leaps in Sikkim. My regret was that no one was prepared to upgrade the tariffs to come anywhere near the production costs.

Primary healthcare had been substantially upgraded in Sikkim. However, in the absence of facilities for specialized healthcare, the patients who required such care had to be moved to Delhi or Calcutta or even to centres in the South. Given the generous attitude of the state government, in Delhi, a full-scale establishment was being maintained, at considerable cost, with a building, for enabling sick people from Sikkim to get treatment in the various hospitals in Delhi. Often given the overcrowding in Delhi hospitals, the quality of health care received was not satisfactory. Also, whenever the road from Sikkim got blocked due to landslides, patients could not be evacuated. The only state-level hospital meant for specialized health care is in Gangtok, the Tashi Namgyal Medical Hospital, located right in the heart of the town very near the main bazaar. The facilities were limited and quite outdated.

This could not serve the growing needs of the present population and was really overcrowded. It had not been designed, keeping in mind the functional requirements of a modern hospital where the patients' convenience and the relationship between the various specializations need to be given due importance. The location of the laboratories, the X-ray units, the operating theatres are all determined by their inter-relationship, with the patients, requirements being paramount. Proper drainage, waste disposal, high standards of hygiene are all important considerations.

I felt that the present hospital had outlived its utility, and even if a lot of money is spent it could not be brought up to the modern standards. Space was also a serious constraint. Being next to the bazaar and right on the main thoroughfare, the noise levels were also intolerable.

I proposed that we built an altogether new superspeciality hospital, and to take care of future requirements, it was suggested by me that the bed strength should not be less than five hundred. My idea was that a well-run hospital with facilities to cater to quite a few of the serious, life threatening ailments could serve the population of the entire northeast from where patients travel to Delhi, Mumbai, etc., to get specialized medical care. Sikkim with its excellent climate and pleasant surroundings could become a sanatorium. I also kept at that time, remote, the possibility of having a medical college in Sikkim, also in mind.

The idea received immediate acceptance from the state

government, and I took up the matter with enthusiasm and earnestness with the Planning Commission, where again it was received with sympathy. In order to strengthen the case, I got the state government to agree to remove the animal husbandry farm at Tadong, and allot this land of around 22 acres for the proposed hospital. This site was chosen with deliberation, as it is at a slightly lower elevation than Gangtok, with slightly drier climate, while commanding a beautiful view of the mountains and the Rumtek monastery.

I engaged 'Hospitalia Consultants' of Delhi, who had a German collaboration, and who had designed the Sher-e-Kashmir Hospital in Srinagar and several others, to prepare a design for a really modern-day hospital, bringing into play the latest advances in this field. All the doctors were involved in this exercise, and I recall several sessions where the doctors argued their cases for this facility or that. Finally, we managed to harmonize their requirements with the design parameters and financial possibilities. The estimated cost, when the exercise was completed in 1989, came to around rupees thirty crore.

Armed with all the arguments, the feasibility study and the finalized design, the matter was taken up with the Planning Commission, who had already accepted, in principle, the need for a modern hospital, in Sikkim. To my great satisfaction, the Planning Commission accepted the proposal in full and included it as part of Sikkim's Five-Year Plan. The phasing of the project and the magnitude of annual financial requirements were also finalized.

Though I had left Sikkim by then, soon enough the foundation stone for this big project by Sikkim's standards was laid by then President of India. R. Venkataraman.

I had originally come to Sikkim for a two year-term in May 1986. The Government of Sikkim wanted me to continue for two more years at least, and, with my parent cadre Assam raising no particular objection, the Centre approved my continuance.

Sikkim was being adjudged as number one state in the whole of India, as regards implementation of Mrs Gandhi's twenty point programme, and the Sikkim government quite generously, if not mistakenly, gave me the credit for achieving this. Sikkim had indeed achieved remarkable progress in almost all the areas of socio economic development. Rural electrification of all villages had been achieved, almost all the villages had been covered by the rural water supply programme, and every child in Sikkim was going to school, there being a primary school within two kilometres of every village. The children received free textbooks, were given uniforms and the schools had reasonably good buildings, furniture and basic equipments. School toilets had been provided in most cases as well as rudimentary sports facilities. Girls' participation was high, and the dropout rate reasonable and declining.

Major strides had been taken, with respect to increasing hydropower generation.

Forest conservation had received particular attention, and a policy involving prohibition of exploitation by private contractors, refusal to permit any wood-based industry, except basically handicrafts and implementation of large scale afforestation programme was accepted by the government. Introduction of LPG and biogas programmes to discourage use of wood as fuel, was taken up. In north Sikkim peoples' need for firewood, given the very cold conditions, had to be however met.

I also took considerable personal interest in repairing the neglect that many of the monasteries had suffered. I saw that the monastery building of Pemayangtse needed immediate attention. I sanctioned marble flooring of the monastery, and strengthening of the roof with steel beams, and all this was done very quickly. I provided required assistance for the complete restoration of the Labrong monastery and took steps to get the landscape done up, water supply and drainage provided.

I also assisted in improving the facilities in the Nyangma training school at Deorali.

Needless to say, the lamas were very pleased with all these. On visits to the monasteries, I was always treated well, the lamas expecting me to drink up all the 'chang' that they so generously ply you with.

While all this progress was based on generous financial assistance from the Central Government, my worry was to see that funds are utilized effectively, that there are no leakages and, very importantly, Sikkim starts generating resources on its own, sooner than later. It was not desirable for the people of Sikkim to develop such a degree of dependency on external assistance, that it robs them of individual initiative, enterprise and a spirit of adventure. Though I preached this creed from every available pulpit, receptivity for such ideas in the government and among the populace was low.

Sikkim enjoys a number of advantages over the other North-

Eastern states. Its accessibility to the rest of India is superior. It is, geographically, just next door to West Bengal. It has no law and order problem and investments are safe, and could be made productive. Labour skills were gradually being built up. Land for industrialization was available and so was water in abundant quantities. Further, Sikkim has enjoyed political stability, a strong government, which has repeatedly declared that it was its intention to make Sikkim a model state. It has been adopting investor friendly postures progressively. Private investment flows can be generated, if the people are encouraged to prepare themselves to be more competitive and shed their phobia with respect to the so-called 'Madhesias' or plainsmen.

In social terms, Sikkim already to my mind represents a model society. The rigidities of caste system are almost wholly absent, the status of women is very high, there is no prejudice or discrimination against women or girl children, divorce is not difficult and there is no stigma attached to it, widow remarriage is not uncommon, girls can choose their partners. Sikkim has never known bride burning or 'sati' and dowry is seldom asked for and in any case not used for ill treatment of the bride. Education of girls has received high priority. Polyandry is still prevalent in a very limited way in North Sikkim and women enjoy great independence, participating in social life as equals. Women are also, generally speaking, more hardworking and play a very active role in preserving Sikkim's very rich cultural heritage.

In November 1989, if I remember correctly, with the completion of five years of the Bhandari government, general elections were called. Though I was part of the Sikkim government, the Election Commission, unfortunately for me, decided to draft me as an election observer, a somewhat thankless task. Without any real powers given to you, you as an observer are supposed to ensure that free and fair poll is conducted, and the law and rules relating to elections are observed by all concerned. No one took you seriously, and all one can do is to report any misconduct to the Election Commission. Your reports are supposed to be treated as confidential.

After the poll is over, and the counting and declaration of results completed the observer is expected to send a detailed confidential report to the Election Commission, covering all aspects of the poll. The election results of 1989 showed that Bhandari had won all the thirty two seats. The opposition had been altogether wiped out, without a single seat in their favour. Though Bhandari was expected to come back to power, there was the belief that his majority may well be reduced and a substantive opposition would emerge in the assembly, a feature which can promote healthier democratic practices.

The results, consequent to which a government could be formed and function, without the usual checks and balances due to the absence of an opposition so vital for a vibrant democracy, were a surprise. In my report to the Election Commission, I *inter alia* discussed the reasons for this surprising performance by the party of Bhandari, namely the Sikkim Sangram Parishad. To a large extent, I argued this was due to the personality of the Chief Minister, his oratorical skills, the performance of his government and the appeal that the CM held for the ordinary voter. However, on the basis of my observations, I also held that the overwhelming victory was due to the quite open way in which substantial sections of government servants worked for the ruling party. I referred to concrete cases, and drew pointed attention to the conduct of a senior IPS officer, whose wife was a candidate of the ruling party. On her behalf and on behalf of her party, he was seen campaigning openly throwing all norms and provisions in the All India Services conduct rules right out of the window.

This report was confidential and meant only for the Election Commission. If any action was to be taken, it was expected that the confidentiality of the report and its authorship will be safeguarded.

But strange or foolish are the ways in which even the highest echelons of governance behave. For I found to my horror that in early 1990, my report was sent to the Bhandari Government for comments and action, in a routine manner, totally ignoring the confidential character of the report and failing to conceal the authorship of the report.

Quite naturally and justifiably the Chief Minister was absolutely livid over the fact that I had dared to submit such a report, when all along he had treated me with such kindness and consideration. He had assessed my performance as outstanding, and had openly paid compliments to me. In his view I was nothing short of a traitor and he held himself eminently justified, in taking this view. There were also elements who encouraged him to take this view, having been somewhat jealous of the confidence reposed by the CM in me.

Herein lies the kind of dilemma that a civil servant faces, so often in his life. I felt that it was incumbent on my part to submit a true and candid account of what had happened, my loyalty being to the Constitution, the laws of the land and to truth. I was not prepared to compromise on the value system I believed in and developed over the years after considerable thought. While I was indeed grateful to Bhandari for all the kindness and consideration shown to me the warmth and affection with which I was treated and the freedom he gave me with respect to the performance of my job, this did not amount to personal loyalty and subservience. Further, as an 'observer' you are answerable to the independent Election Commission of India and I would have failed in my duty if I had not sent a report reflecting the true state of affairs. Such ideas and ideals are, of course, not easily understood, leave alone being accepted by politicians.

I suddenly found that I was *persona non grata* in Sikkim, and it was impossible for me to continue in that state. I sent a detailed letter to the Chief Election Commissioner Peri Shastri, describing to him how the thoughtless action on the part of the Election Commission had landed me in hot waters. I argued how, by this act, the EC had undermined the efficacy and value of the whole 'observer' system. 'Observers' would not submit true accounts if they are not sure of the way their reports are treated. I packed my bags and got out of the state at the earliest possible moment. My very enjoyable, very productive stay in Sikkim ended this on quite a sad note, and all too suddenly.

I however dare say that I did leave a large measure of goodwill in the state, and many were unhappy that I had to leave the state. The Nyangma training school for lamas at Deorali gave me a touching farewell, when all the lamas lined up in a long row and each presenting me with a ceremonial scarf 'the Khada'.

They also presented me with a large 'tankha' with a special prayer for my welfare inscribed at the back. It is possibly because of the goodwill I had left behind and the prayers and good wishes of the lamas that I came back to Sikkim after six years, as Chief Secretary. I landed in Delhi saddened at the way fate had played tricks. Peri Shastri, the CEC whom I met, was very apologetic and wholly sympathetic. He offered to help me in every possible way. Thanks to his efforts and the assistance of the Cabinet Secretary V.C. Pande, with whom I had worked in the Commerce Ministry, who also appreciated the fearless manner in which I had done my duty, and the fact that I had been wronged because of this, I got a posting, in May 1980, in the Cabinet Secretariat.

With the bigwigs: Gulzarilal Nanda and V.V. Giri. New Delhi, 1963

Listening to the "Steely Empress of India". Cachar, Assam, during a visit, 1971

The author as Chief Secretary, Sikkim, with H.H. the Dalai Lama, in the Raj Bhavan, Gangtok, 1997

Right body language. Gangtok, 1997

Seemingly in full command. The author as Chief Secretary, Gangtok, 1997

# 11

# CABINET SECRETARIAT AND THOUGHTS ON INTERNAL SECURITY

The two-year period I spent in the Cabinet Secretariat added a new dimension to my already rich and varied experience. I had the privilege of working with M.K. Narayanan and then with R.P. Joshi for a short period.

Of all the officers I had the opportunity of working with, Narayanan I consider to be easily the most brilliant. He represents that elite band of officers who combine outstanding qualities of the mind with an astonishing capacity for hard work. With a truly photographic memory, almost limitless ability to gather facts and figures, to systematically classify, index and store away information of a bewildering variety, accompanied by an ability for instant recall, he could bring his vast knowledge and analytical skills to bear on any discussion, to elevate the level of the debate to heights, capable of satisfying the most fastidious and demanding of minds. His drafting was absolutely superb. He took great pains in perfecting every document that left his table, which invariably reflected his extraordinary command over the English language, the level of his erudition, the exuberance of his thought and splendour of his diction. The final product, out of his hands, was always a piece of art.

For me, it was a truly rewarding experience. It is a pity, in my view, that the nation has not utilized him more, especially in his area of specialization.

The period I spent in the Cabinet Secretariat allowed me considerable exposure to the problems relating to internal security and external threats to India's security. Some of my thoughts, on these matters, have been reflected in the chapter II on aspects of Governance and in chapters IV and VII on Assam. In this chapter I propose to discuss, in brief, the overall internal security situation in the country, while dealing with the situation in the North-East in detail.

If one surveys the internal security scenario in the country, one cannot escape getting deeply distressed by the ever rising graph of violence in almost every part of the country, accompanied by a decline in the ability and willingness on the part of the state to deal effectively with the growing problems. The institutional mechanisms, created and financed by the government and on whom the expenditure is raising exponentially every year, have seen a severe and sustained erosion in their authority and ability to act because of political interference and discriminatory application of law. The cardinal principles of equality in the eyes of law and equal protection to all citizens, as enshrined in the Constitution of India, have been repeatedly violated. When one set of people, even when they commit the most heinous of crimes, are above law and continue to occupy positions of authority and power, not hesitating to use their power to sabotage the due process of law, how can the state deal with other criminals? Violence and terrorism, which are so widespread in the country, can be directly traced to the institutions of the state, which have lost their ability to act in an impartial and non-discriminatory manner, use double standards in dealing with crime, the perceived partiality of which to a special class of criminals conveys the clear message that criminals do not get punished in this country if they have either money or manage to be part of a special class. The deterioration in the effectiveness of the institutions of governance can also be gauged by the kind of role the judiciary has had to play, willy nilly. The people have had to seek the help of the courts in a number of matters which ordinarily would have been within the province of the executive. From environmental protection to the treatment of noncriminal lunatics, to clearing up of rivers to elimination of bonded labour, the courts have intervened. Because of the fear of punishment judicial orders are complied with, whereas with respect to executive orders, the fear of enforcement has vanished. This may have led to a neglect of and delays in disposing off ordinary, civil and criminal matters, but at least the ordinary citizen has been able to get remedies for his long neglected grievances.

Almost every state of the Union today faces a difficult internal security situation.

Jammu and Kashmir has been on the boil ever since early 1989. The external dimensions of the problem apart, what was basically an articulation of a political demand for greater autonomy, independence or merger with Pakistan, on the basis of the so-called 'principles of partition', has now been converted into a full-scale religious war. Islamic fundamentalism is now the basic driving force of the Kashmiri struggle and is the product of the worldwide phenomenon of the rise of religion as the basis for human conflict. The days when ideology—Fascism vs Democracy, Capitalism vs Communism—and competition for the command over the world's natural resources, were the sources of human conflict seem to be over. As argued by Samuel Huntington forcefully in his *Clash of Civilizations* we see conflicts based on cultural differences, assertion of ethnicity identities, anxiety to preserve separate sub-national identities, and on religion, occurring in several parts of the world. People seem to be increasingly asking who are we, who are with us, and more importantly, who are against us.

The republics of the ex-USSR, bordering Afghanistan, all face threats from religious extremism. Chechenya and Ingushetia have witnessed largescale bloodshed due to conflicts based on religion. In the Balkans, the war between Serbs and the inhabitants of Bosnia Herzegovina, between the Albanians and the Macedonians have both ethnic and religious overtones. The Arab–Israeli conflict has a very strong religious basis. Algeria and Turkey as well as Egypt have been combating Islamic extremists. The Afghan conflict with the Soviets, though, to begin with, was against communism, so liberally and thoughtlessly promoted by the Americans, quickly turned into a religious war. The Americans merrily acquiesed in this process, with inexcusable and amazing shortsightedness, only to create a monster which has now become a serious threat to their own security. Credible evidence is now available as to how the American agencies poured money and weaponry into Afghanistan, through Pakistan, and very gladly but foolishly aided the transformation of the war against communism into a religious conflict. Active participation by Pakistan and Saudi Arabia ensured that while the short-term objective of ejecting the Russians was achieved, a long-term security threat was created for all of Afghanistan's neighbours, with religious extremism as the fundamental driving force. The developments in Afghanistan have had a direct bearing on the deteriorating situation in the Kashmir valley, with greater involvement of religious warriors from outside Kashmir.

Nearer home, Pakistan itself facing the problem of religious extremism with a variety of 'jehadi' outfits increasing their hold over segments of the society. Indeed, the Army itself has been infected by this virus. Other institutions of governance have not remained unaffected. The talibanization of Pakistan is not considered any more an impossibility. A substantial part of the huge flow of weaponry for the Afghan war was diverted to various jehadi outfits in Pakistan itself increasing their lethal potential.

Countries such as the Philippines, with the Moro Islamic Liberation Army, and the Abu Sayyaf group, and Indonesia face serious threats from fundamentalist outfits, who receive generous assistance from the oil-rich countries of the Middle East.

If one considers the history of these recent developments, involving the dramatic rise of Islamic religious extremism, as a source of conflict affecting large swathes of the globe, it would be evident that the demise of the Shah's regime in Iran and it being replaced by the Khomeini order in that country, which totally obliterated the separation of the church from the state, can easily be designated as the starting point, in recent times.

Ever since the middle ages, the world has been witnessing the progressive assertion of non-religious identities as forces, fostering social cohesion, coalescing of people and building of nations. Gone were the days when allegiance to the Pope in Rome and the Holy Roman Empire were more important than language, race or culture. Nations were being built on the basis of unifying factors such as a common language, racial characteristics and cultural practices. Progressively also, religion was relegated to the status of an individual's concern, and the organs of state were getting separated from the institutions of religion. The state was expected to govern the country, working for the welfare of all its citizens, irrespective of which religious persuasion or denomination its citizen groups belonged. No discrimination against any particular religious group was to be permitted. Economics and politics, secularism and democracy became the determining factors.

In the twentieth century these tendencies were strongly reinforced and in country after country separation of religion from politics was effected. Indeed with the rise of communism, the pendulum swung to the other extreme which took active and often brutal steps to altogether obliterate the church. Right up to the nineties, in communist countries, religion was looked down upon, it being regarded as the 'opium of the people'. Though there has indeed been a resurrection of the church in many of the erstwhile communist countries, the principle of separation of the state from the church has been kept well intact. However, the collapse of communism and its replacement by more liberal regimes, the reduction in the effectiveness of the state apparatus, accompanied by a degree of political instability, has opened the doors for the spread of religious fundamentalist ideas, once again founded and supported by the oil rich countries of the Middle East, who see opportunities for expansion of 'Darul Islam'.

To be sure the worldwide trend of separation of the church and the state has received only a few takers in countries where Islam is predominant. Turkey, Algeria, Egypt and some of the Gulf states have made great advances in this area of separating the church from the State, but in many others this principle is held as un-Islamic, and, therefore, to be resisted.

Even in Iran, I recall, having seen during a visit in 1969, when the Shah was in power, that the mullahs were barely visible, confined to their religious institutions, treated with some respect, but allowed to operate within well-defined limits. Teheran, Isfahan, Ghazvin were all vibrant cities with women participating in all walks of life. There were no restrictions on their education or employment and no diktats laying down a dress code. The purdah did not seem to exist. The Shah had ambitions of making Iran a strong regional power, with a modernized society, an advanced economy and strong armed forces. The American influence was strong and visible. One of the charges against the Shah was that he was forcing the pace of change to such an extent that Iran's separate identity was being obliterated, and her traditions were being trampled upon.

All these changes in the way the world was governed, with the separation of the state firmly from the church, were set at nought, and reversed by the Khomeini revolution in Iran, with widespread repercussion in the entire Islamic world. The whole power structure in Iran underwent dramatic changes, with religious leaders assuming temporal power. The clergy in Iran set about transforming the society as per religious diktats, and while in Iran, modernizing influences have received a severe setback, what is of greater concern is the export of this ideology to other parts of the world. The concepts of 'Islamic umma' and 'Darul Islam' and 'Darul harb' have been imparted a new vigour. The organization of Islamic countries focuses attention on unifying Muslims, taking up the causes of Muslim minorities, reinforcing the separate identity of Muslims, and blurring of national distinctions. There is an OIC in this world but no OCC or OBC that is organization of Christian countries or organization of Buddhist countries. Iran's militant ideology, combined with almost limitless financial support from the oil rich Arab countries, have resulted in the growth of a variety of armed outfits, whose objectives range from fighting perceived injustices against Muslims in several parts of the world to establishing an Islamic order all over the world. These outfits target Kashmir, Chechenya, the Philippines and the ex-Soviet Republics for special attention. The USA is regarded as a villain by all these outfits.

The transformation of the Kashmir 'struggle' to a religious war is, to a considerable extent, linked to these developments at the international level.

It is also connected more intimately with developments within Pakistan. Lest it is forgotten, it needs to be highlighted that in 1947, 1965 and in 1971, the Kashmiris offered no cooperation to Pakistan in all its misadventures. In 1972, with the separation of Bangladesh, the whole basis for the two-nation theory, namely religion as the rationale for partition of the Indian subcontinent, had been destroyed. India had consistently argued that India was the home for several religions, that the two-nation theory had no real basis, and that even after partition millions of Muslims have remained in India.

Through the period 1971 to the late 1980s Pakistan could hardly raise the Kashmir issue and it appears that in the Simla parleys, of 1972, Pakistan had accepted conversion of the LOC (Line of Control) into the permanent international border. For close to seventeen years 1972–1989, Pakistan had stopped making even ritualistic noises about Kashmir. This was India's historic chance to settle once and for all whatever remained of the Kashmir question and fully integrate the state with the Indian Union. But this opportunity was missed, and the mishandling of the affairs of the state has provided one more window of opportunity to Pakistan to wrest the initiative and to resurrect a cause, which had been all but lost and forgotten.

India becoming a nuclear power had also discouraged Pakistan from adopting aggressive postures.

While one may point to several unfortunate mistakes in handling the state of Kashmir, including the much-talked-about elections of 1987, leading to heightened alienation and disillusionment of the people. With the democratic process, attention also needs to be focused on the transformation of the Kashmiri society from one that followed the liberal sufi traditions to the one that was made to veer towards the more fundamentalist illiberal and intolerant brand of Islam. Preachers inducted into Kashmir's religious institutions from the schools of UP and Bihar managed to bring about this definitive change in the religious consciousness of the society in the valley through venemous anti-India preachings, promoting the assertion of the separate Islamic identity. 'Kashmiriyat' and the distinct Kashmiri identity were progressively replaced by an aggressive pan Islamic creed.

As is well known, the Kashmiri ethos is an amalgam of different strands of religious and cultural traditions, in particular the sufi practices and the bhakti cult of Hinduism. The interaction of Lalded or Lalla Yogeswari with Mir Syed Ali Handai, a prominent sufi of early fourteenth century is believed to have laid the foundation for inter-religious amity. This was followed by the birth of the unique 'rishi' order founded by Sheik Nuruddin Rishi. He denounced the mullahs for misinterpreting the Quran for their selfish ends. The Shaivaite philosophy had a significant impact in his thinking, as a result of which his followers preferred to call themselves as 'rishis'. The influence of the rishi movement was such that Sultan Zainul Abidin welcomed back the pundits who had left the valley as also built some of the temples destroyed by the bigots. He even prohibited cowslaughter. Hindus, who were forced to abandon their religion, were encouraged to return to their faith. Sanskrit classics were translated into Persian. One of the enduring effects of this creed of tolerance is the fact that Kashmiri Muslims even today follow the customary Hindu Law of the Mitakshara School in succession of properties. Interestingly, many of the mosques and shrines of Muslim saints in Kashmir do not have domes but spires in the style of Buddhist viharas.

No wonder, when, at the time of partition communal frenzy had enveloped large parts of the subcontinent, Gandhiji had spoken about Kashmir as beacon of light and hope. Today, unfortunately, this paradise, imbued with the lofty ideals which has been so much part of its traditions for centuries, is sought to be destroyed by fanatics and terrorists.

These internal developments were taken full advantage by Pakistan which has always held that the whole of Kashmir should be an integral part of Pakistan, and it is the 'unfinished agenda' of the partition. Pakistan had kept a close watch over the developments in Kashmir, and was quick to respond by taking measures to encourage and accelerate the unfortunate developments taking place in the Kashmir valley.

Ever since the humiliating defeat in 1971, and that too at the hands of a woman—the ultimate insult in the eyes of the Islamists—elements in Pakistan had been campaigning for a revenge upon India. These elements have been steadily gaining ground in the army and among various religious bodies. One understands that new recruits to Pakistan army even today are made to swear that they shall revenge the defeat of 1971, Kashmir could easily be the theatre for such a revenge.

The rise of Zia ul-Haq gave a boost to these anti-India sentiments. Zia was one of the shrewdest of leaders Pakistan has ever had, and while projecting an image of a polished, ever polite, diplomatic, charming and balanced statesman, he took full advantage of America's misguided enthusiasm to fight the communists in Afghanistan, not only to ensure continuance of his basically illegitimate regime, which had no mandate from the people of Pakistan, but to build up manifold the strength of Pakistan's armed forces and put the programme for nuclearization of Pakistan on the overdrive. He was able to get fullscale assistance from the Chinese in the development of nuclear weapons, while succeeding in making the Americans look the other way. The skill and finesse with which he managed to keep both the Americans and the Chinese on his side, while making both of them contribute handsomely to the sharp upgradation of Pakistan's offensive potential, deserves admiration. By presenting himself as the star frontline fighter of the dreaded Russian Bear, he was able to get the Americans repeatedly certify that Pakistan did not have a credible nuclear weapons programme, while he happily watched the programme grow into maturity. The Americans acknowledged that he was virtually a dictator with no love for democracy and he was a rogue, but they claimed that he was their rogue and therefore deserved all support. This gave a new confidence to Pakistan to eventually take on India, specially on the Kashmir question.

Zia also islamized not only the Pakistan society, but also the army. Under his benign eye, the seeds for the proliferation of 'madrassas' or religious schools, on a large scale and, for the training of religious warriors, were planted. The Sandhurst trained preserver of British soldierly traditions that the Pakistan army was very much like its counterpart in India, was transformed by new methods of recruitment, and indoctrination, with a definitive role for religious instruction. The induction into the armed forces were from those layers of the society, which had already been islamized. The army was no more the preserve of the elite. The thinking process at all levels was being reoriented. The army was converted into an instrument for waging wars, with a strong religious motivation and orientation. Over the years, the top echelons of the armed forces has come to be dominated by officers, steeped in Islamic ideology.

The implementation of the Shariat law, the promulgation of the hudood ordinance, the proclamation of nizam-e-mustafa, the declaration of Ahmediyas as non-Muslims, meting out punishments in the open, as per Islamic prescriptions, the notorious blasphemy law, all ensured that a fertile field was created for the pre-eminence of extreme religious ideas and leaders. Zia himself was called a 'Mulla in Uniform'.

With such a reorientation and radicalization of the society and the army, it was easy to direct the forces being built up to focus attention on Kashmir. The Afghan episode was winding down, with the triumph of Islamic power. The huge quantum of weaponry and the large body of religious warriors had to find another field to prove their prowess and Kashmir was on offer for ready exploitation. The Afghan war had also spawned a thriving arms industry in all the areas, bordering Afghanistan, and procurement of weapons for the warriors was no problem at all.

The nuclearization of Pakistan is another development which, in my view, greatly increased the boldness of Pakistan to actively and blatantly interfere in India's affairs. Pakistan convinced itself that India cannot and will not retaliate, even in the face of grave provocation, as Pakistan was capable of pressing the nuclear trigger. Its declared policy is use of the nuclear weapon if Pakistan's security is threatened, a phraeseology subject to any interpretation, depending on the circumstances. India, on the other hand, has adopted a 'no first use of nuclear weapons' policy.

Several observers are of the view that Pakistan, which is facing serious internal divisions, has found the Kashmir issue a convenient cementing force, enabling it to continue to portray India as a threat to its integrity and sovereignty. The separatist tendencies articulated by the Mohajirs, the Sindhis and the Baluchis who have been complaining against the dominance of the Punjabis, it appears, pose a real threat to the unity of Pakistan and the country cannot be seen to be compromising on an issue in which it has invested so much, if it is to avoid unleashing of strong centrifugal tendencies leading to the dismemberment of Pakistan. Further, the Kashmir question is possibly the only justification for the huge defence expenditure that Pakistan incurs every year. To portray India as an enemy has many advantages for Pakistan, and there are forces who may not like an outbreak of peace with India.

The unrest is basically confined to the Kashmir valley, though there have been attempts to spread terror into the Jammu region and even into Himachal Pradesh. The Jammu and Kashmir Liberation Front (JKLF), which stood for independence of J&K, has now been replaced by far more militant outfits, supporting merger with Pakistan. This has been an achievement on the part of Pakistan, which does not favour independence for J&K. Over the years, apart from local recruits, foreign mercenaries from Afghanistan, Pakistan and from the Pakistan Occupied Kashmir (POK) have increasingly participated. Pakistan has now full control over the various outfits operating in the valley. It provides training, arms, equipment and finance for sustaining the movement. Pakistan of course, ritualistically denies all this, while continuing a campaign to internationalize the issue and pillory India for alleged violation of human rights.

The mercenaries and recruits, who are trained in the madrassas of Pakistan, have brought an altogether new brand of fanaticism. To die for a religious cause is an assured path to glory, a passage to heaven. The indoctrination is so thorough that suicide attacks by 'Fidayeen' have increased. If in the process, you manage to dispose of a few 'Kafirs', your passage to heaven becomes even smoother.

Some observers regret that attention is almost exclusively focused on views articulated by the separatist groups in the Kashmir valley. No one seems to be interested in the future of the people of Jammu and Ladakh and indeed that of the nearly four lakh Kashmiri Pandits, who have been booted out of their hearths and homes in the valley, only because of their religion, and who are living in pathetic conditions outside their home state.

In sum, we have an extraordinarily difficult situation in Kashmir, and there seems to be no light at the end of the tunnel, even after over ten years of combating insurgency. Both internal and external forces are in full play with Pakistan, unleashing a proxy war, and India's armed forces are under severe pressure.

There are however some silver linings in this quite dark scenario which have emerged very recently. Internationally, Islamic fundamentalism has come to be firstly recognized as a grave security threat. Secondly, there is a congruence of interests in combating this threat among the USA, Russia, Israel, India and even China. Very recently, in a conclave attended by Russia, China and all the ex-Soviet republics bordering Afghanistan, all these nations have signed a declaration vowing to fight the rising Islamic fundamentalism regarded by all the signatories as a common threat. Thirdly, the Americans have definitely downgraded the importance of Pakistan in their security calculations, whereas they have upgraded India. Fourthly, Pakistan is seen as a state which actively aids and abets terrorism, with a large number of religiously oriented training schools, open espousal of jehadi causes, display of arms by a variety of jehadi outfits, open collection of funds and declaration by the military government that jehad is part of its state policy. Pakistan's drift away from democracy has disenchanted several western powers. Fifthly, there are definitive indications of a change in the attitude of the Americans with respect to Kashmir. Bill Clinton's statements during his visit to the subcontinent, that the LOC should not be tampered with, that borders cannot be redrawn with blood, that violence will not be tolerated, and that a lot of developments have taken place since the 1948 UN resolution which impinge on Kashmir, all underline the change in the way the United States has come to view the Kashmir situation. However, the USA still continues to regard Kashmir as one of the most dangerous flashpoints of the world and would like to promote an early peaceful resolution of the problem. By all accounts, the new Bush administration seems to be going forward in the direction charted out by the Clinton administration.

The terrorist attack of September 11 on the World Trade Centre has greatly enhanced the threat posed by international terrorism to the world order. Though it has been repeatedly stressed that it would be wrong to identify terrorism with Islam, the fact remains that the terrorist outfits themselves seem to derive all their inspiration from a religious ideology. Huntington's thesis of clash of civilizations is being validated by the religious extremists themselves. Faced with such a threat, an international consensus is being evolved to combat terrorism of all varieties. India has been drawing the world's attention to the fact that the ideology of international terrorism needs to be viewed as indivisible and there is a deep and intense congruence of interest and methodology among terrorists with linkages with respect to procurement of arms, financial flows and trade in narcotics.

Sixthly, the world over, there seems to be growing realization that there are definite limits beyond which the cause of ethnic and religion-based self-determination and separatism cannot and should not be promoted. The immense damage done in the Balkans by the support extended to ethnic centred divisiveness has been, it appears, registered upon the political conscience of the world leaders. It has also been realized that if all the ethnic-based separatist struggles are to be given, what the leaders of these struggles are demanding, the world may well break up into a thousand pieces, leading to the total breakdown of the UN system and making the world ungovernable.

It is highly significant to note that the international community has now reached a position which regards self-determination and secession as concepts, which cannot be applied to representative democracies. Basically, it is accepted as a legitimate claim by people under colonial domination by foreign rule. Though it is at times regarded as inclusive of the right to freely determine their political status by distinct groups such as minorities by the United Nations, the UN has added a caveat, 'this shall not be construed as authorizing any action which could dismember or impair totally or in part the territorial integrity of sovereign states conducting themselves in compliance with the principles of equal rights and self-determination, and thus having a government representing the whole people without discrimination of any kind'. Scholars have argued that the right of internal self-determination is merely the right of indigenous people to have a representative, democratically elected government and they have an inherent right to secede, only if certain conditions exist. Firstly, they must prove that there is systematic discrimination against them. Secondly, they must prove that they are a distinct self-defined community, inhabiting a compact area, which overwhelmingly supports separatism. Clearly, none of these considerations apply even remotely to Jammu and Kashmir. The Kashmiris have been given privileges not available to ordinary Indians and the state is not inhabited by a homogenous group of people. Thirdly, those demanding separation must prove that avenues of dialogue have been exhausted and all compromise solutions have been rejected. This also does not apply to Kashmir. It would be worth recalling, in this context, the statement of the leader of POK, Sardar Ibrahim Khan, 'From August 13 to October 22, 1947 our state was independent and the result was that we were invaded by Pakistan. Where is the guarantee that we may not be victims of similar aggression in the future? Given the geographical situation of the state, other powers may covet the territory. The state cannot therefore maintain its independence.'

Also from India's strategic perspective, any southward and eastward shift of its frontier with Pakistan can have lethal consequences for the defence of its territory from any potential adversary, and hence to be avoided at all costs. It needs also to be stressed that given the extremely poor record of Pakistan as regards its treatment of minorities, there is the real danger that once Jammu and Kashmir becomes part of Pakistan, as per the designs of Pakistan, there will be no place, whatsoever, for the minority Buddhists or Hindus. From Pakistan occupied Kashmir (POK) the minorities have all been booted out, and they are living as refugees. From the Kashmir valley as well the pundits have been sent out. No amount of guarantees can altogether rule out such a possibility. The people of Jammu and Ladakh have no problem being part of India, and it is only the Muslims of the valley, who want to get out of India, and most of them want independence, and only a small number want to be part of Pakistan. It is therefore a problem between India, and the Muslims of the valley, and if their grievances, most of which artificial or based on religion, can be adequately addressed, then Pakistan can become irrelevant. Of course, one has to deal effectively with Pakistan's ability to export jehadis and terrorism. Theoretically, even if the LOC is accepted as the permanent international border, Pakistan can continue to indulge in cross border terrorism.

In purely economic terms the state of J&K is a huge drain on the nation's resources, with no tangible returns. The Centre has to shell out some Rs 17,000 crore in the next five years to meet the state's non-plan expenditure, as per the award of the last Finance Commission, because the state raises no resources on its own. Large sums are also handed down every year by the Planning Commission to the state, most of which does not result in any accretion to the state's assets because of leakages. Some have therefore argued that India should consider reducing its liabilities, taking recourse to what businessmen call asset stripping, that is let those who want to go, to be allowed to go, and those who want to be with us to remain so.

Lastly, within Pakistan itself, saner voices are being heard that support for the Kashmiri struggle is proving to be far too costly, that the kind of support extended has made the world look down upon Pakistan as an exporter of terrorism, and as a nation that is being controlled increasingly by religious zealots. It is also being argued that Pakistan's economy has suffered because of the fact that these perceptions have virtually stopped all foreign investment, that, in fact, capital and skills are flowing out of Pakistan and the country has earned the unenviable title of a failed state. The economy has recorded a growth of only 2.6 per cent during 2000–01 and has averaged just about 4 per cent during the past decade, barely surpassing the population growth rate. The Pakistani rupee is witnessing a steady decline in its external value, losing around 25 per cent of its value within the past year and the country is experiencing high rates of inflation, while its foreign debt has been increasing and foreign currency reserves have been declining precipitously. The question is being asked whether Pakistan is not paying far too high a price for its Kashmir misadventure. These voices are still very low and have to face those forces which regard the Kashmir issue a binding factor for an otherwise fractured society, and that of the army which may find itself rendered irrelevant if Kashmir ceases to be a flashpoint, and indeed all the jehadi forces also which have made Kashmir the focal point of all their activities.

It is also surprising and indeed extremely strange that Pakistan which has the inglorious record of not respecting the verdict of the people, where elected governments are regularly thrown out by military dictators on one excuse or the other, where democratic freedoms have been suppressed by promulgation of martial law, and whose military rulers had no hesitation in butchering some three million people of East Bengal and sending some nine million souls to India as refugees merely because they exercised their franchise in a manner not to the liking of the West Pakistanis, should project itself as the champion of the rights of the people of Kashmir for self-determination. It is even more strange that this is able to generate a resonance of faith among a section of credulous Kashmiris.

As of now there is no democracy in Pakistan, a democratically elected Prime Minister thrown out of his job and out of the country as well, by the military chief for no particular fault of his except the fact that he committed the cardinal error of seeking to throw the military chief from his own job, whom he himself had appointed and had every right under the Constitution to dismiss. All kinds of undemocratic and unconstitutional things are being done by the ruler, whose legitimacy is in grave doubt including dismissing a duly elected President, and declaring himself the President for a full five year term, while continuing to be the Chief Executive—read Prime Minister—as also the Army Chief. This is nothing but a naked dictatorship in operation, however thick a veneer of respectability it may seek to cloak itself with—a position not very different from that in Germany of August 1934, when the President of Germany, Paul von Hindenburg died. It is not surprising that cynics have pointed out that the only country that has ever been conquered by the Pakistan army is, hold your breath, Pakistan.

There has been a vigorous debate as to whether Pakistan can ever be truly democratic. Suffice it to say that the founder of Pakistan Mohammed Ali Jinnah did not appear to repose great faith in democracy. Dominique Lapierre and Larry Collins in their *Freedom at Midnight* speak of an interesting anecdote which provides a fine insight into the mind of Jinnah. After Pandit Nehru had magnanimously offered the job of the first Governor General of Independent India to Mountbatten, the Viceroy had apparently felt that his usefulness would be greatly enhanced if he had a similar offer from Jinnah as well. Jinnah however had other ideas and he himself wanted to be the GG of Pakistan. Mountbatten protested saying that he had picked the wrong job for, in a British type of democracy which the two dominions were expected to adopt, the GG's functions were basically symbolic and the real power would vest in the Prime Minister elected by the people. This argument did not move Jinnah. 'In Pakistan' he coldly replied, 'I will be the Governor General and the Prime Minister will do exactly what I tell him to do.'

As to the other states, leaving aside the turbulent North-East, criminalization of politics and undermining of the effectiveness of the state apparatus and increasing activities of subversive elements have been major issues for some time now. Even the nation's capital keeps witnessing explosions planted by subversives. States like Maharashtra, Andhra Pradesh, Orissa and Bihar continue to battle with left extremism.

In Maharashtra, the nexus between criminals, the mafia gangs, the smugglers, the builders, the extortion gangs, the movie industry and the connections with the ISI is posing a serious threat.

In Bihar, the state has ceased to exist for all practical purposes, and a variety of armed outfits have been indulging in open warfare. Communalization and criminalization of politics has reached new heights, with Members of Parliament engaging the police in armed battles while resisting attempts to arrest them on charges of the most heinous of crimes. The government protects them, while the police are castigated for their ever-so-feeble attempts to uphold the law of the land. The links of one of the MPs with Kashmiri insurgents, ISI operatives and criminal elements, have been established but no action can be taken as he belongs to the ruling clique in Bihar. The external and internal dimensions of the situation in Bihar has been referred to in some detail in chapter II.

States like Andhra Pradesh and Tamil Nadu have witnessed the rise of outfits with fundamentalist leanings, indulging in attacks on churches, explosions, arson and sabotage. Obtaining supplies of explosives and manufacture of improvized explosive devices does not seem to pose any serious problems.

Tamil Nadu has been exposed to the side effects of the battle for Tamil Eelam by the LTTE, an ethnic conflict, which seems to go on and on, in spite of peace efforts by the Norwegians. Bodies such as TNLA (Tamil National Liberation Army) TNRT (Tamil National Retrieval Troops) have sprung up advocating aid and sympathy for the LTTE as also the concept of greater *eelam* encompassing the state of Tamil Nadu. Tamil Nadu has also witnessed a rise in communal violence.

All over the country, after the destruction of the disputed structure at Ayodhya, the communal divide seems to have sharpened, and aggressive postures are being adopted on even the most trivial of issues. States like Rajasthan, Gujarat, Andhra Pradesh, Karnataka have had to deal with communal riots repeatedly. Such riots seem to be happening with increasing frequency. Bodies like the Students Islamic Movement of India are becoming bolder in making inflammatory statements, taking anti-India postures, and encouraging separatist tendencies. Well-known religious leaders have no hesitation in using Friday prayers to inflame passions and reinforcing and strengthening communal forces. A sense of alienation is being deliberately articulated and fostered. Hindu groups have not been far behind in indulging in inflammatory rhetoric. The Centre has woken up to this kind of threat and has banned a number of outfits whose activities have been considered prejudicial to national security.

From West Bengal has emanated a report, which highlights the proliferation of Islamic schools with a definite fundamentalist orientation. This move is spearheaded by the Barua Rahmani Educational Society which has started a well organized effort to purify education to impart only 'Islamic education' for the children. Within a short time, over one hundred madrassas have sprung up in the districts of Murshidabad, Malda and Birbhum. These schools teach not only religious texts but history which is highly distorted, portraying Aurangazeb as an exemplary ruler, worthy of emulation by the present-day rulers and preaching that the chief source of national income is of all the things the divine act of 'expropriating the property of the vanquished enemy'. The whole alphabet of the Bengali language has been corrupted to incorporate purely sectarian and extremist religious ideas. The destruction of the Somnath temple has been glorified. The Rahmani society has strong Saudi connections and is flushed with Arab funds. Over forty thousand students are being educated in the 109 madrassas of the society, and one can imagine the kind of mindset that this type of education will be inculcating in the young minds at a formative age and the kind of anti-national constituency that is being built up in the districts of West Bengal bordering Bangladesh. The long-term security implications of this kind of activities is yet to be taken note of by the State as well as the Central Government. The state government has not so far, apparently, realized the magnitude of external funding that is involved, nor for that matter, the grave implications of this kind of development.

On the question of flow of foreign funds illegally, to finance terrorist and banned organizations—a related issue with sinister implications for national security—recent reports suggest that the Centre's attempts to curb the flow has been largely ineffective. The

Foreign Contribution (regulation) Act demands registration of organizations, receiving funds from abroad, and prohibits receipt by organizations whose activities are suspect and those that are banned. Enforcement is, however, lax as a result, of which not only those which are engaged in promoting religious extremism but a variety of insurgent outfits including the ULFA and several Kashmiri insurgent outfits continue to get large inflow of funds. Immediate tightening of the enforcement system is called for.

The situation is already receiving the unwelcome attention of the ISI. The nation would have to pay a very high price if these tendencies are not immediately arrested.

Attention needs also to be drawn to growing economic disparity that is taking place among the states of the Union. Broadly speaking, the group of states in the west and south of India are progressing economically and socially, at a substantially higher rate than those in the north and north-east. The states of Punjab, Haryana, Himachal Pradesh, Gujarat, Maharashtra, Andhra Pradesh, Karnataka and Tamil Nadu have been recording consistently higher rates of economic growth, attracting the bulk of private investment, while at the same time succeeding in bringing down their population growth rates. Jammu & Kashmir and the North-East have been plagued by insurgency and this has had a severe impact on their progress. What is of great concern is the poor performance of states like Rajasthan, UP, Bihar, MP and West Bengal. The census of 2001 shows that Bihar has had the highest rate of growth of population in the country, a staggering 2.50 per cent per annum compared to the national average of 1.93 per cent whereas its economic growth is negative. The story is not very dissimilar with respect to the other states in this group.

This growing imbalance in the levels of prosperity is bound to unleash serious sociological, economic and political consequences, and can be the cause of serious civil unrest. Some of the prosperous states have articulated the view that they would not like to continuously subsidize the inefficient states, who pay no attention to either economic growth or population stabilization. They feel that they are being deprived of the resources raised in their own states, which they would like to use for their own advancement, and which, because of the present system of federal taxation and distribution of finances, they are unable to do.

These states, which are showing poor performance on the

economic front, are precisely those where the standards of governance are low and where the law and order situation is unsatisfactory. While public investment is already inadequate and declining, because of financial mismanagement, private investment is wary of entering areas where there is no security. This, in turn, results in increase in the number of unemployed, and consequent dissatisfaction and disillusionment. These states can get caught in the vicious cycle of poor economic performance, combined with high rates of growth of population, leading to dissatisfaction, which in turn generates unrest, which discourages investment, lowering, even further the prospects for economic development. This issue needs the most urgent attention, if the already-difficult security situation in these states is not to become unmanageable.

I will now turn to the volatile situation in the North-East of India. When India attained Independence the then Naga hills district was the only area which witnessed an armed uprising. Today, after fifty years of Independence the entire area is engulfed in unrest, spawning a large number of militant outfits, each demanding independence, and secession from India. A variety of liberation struggles are going on, with the insurgents showing increasing ability to take on the security forces, all equipped with sophisticated weaponry, commanding, apparently, limitless resources and able to recruit their cadres with virtual impunity. Extortion is practised on a wide scale and an atmosphere of fear and insecurity seems to prevail in the entire area.

I propose to discuss the situation statewise, analysing the character and objectives of the insurgency movements and the underlying causes for such widespread unrest.

The Nagas claim for Independence is based on the argument that before the British came and took over their territory, the Naga inhabited areas were never part of India, that in terms of language, culture and other civilizational characteristics, they have nothing in common with India. They claim that, as early as 1929, they had informed the British that they would like to be independent, when and if the British left India. There is also the claim that when the Nagas met Gandhiji he had indicated that he would not force the Nagas to be part of India. In addition to this claim 'for independence', the Naga underground lay claim to large parts of Assam and Manipur as also Arunachal Pradesh. In the case of Assam, the issue regarding Naga claims was adjudicated by a Commission, appointed by the Central Government under K.V.K. Sundaram, and this Commission had rejected the claims of the Nagas.

To achieve the above goals an armed rebellion was unleashed immediately after Independence and has been going on for nearly fifty years. Zapu Phizo, a fiery orator who could speak several of the Naga languages, was able to mobilize the Nagas. Help, at that time, was readily available from China and the initial batches including the NSCN(1)M supreme, Thuingalang Muivah, were all trained in China and provided arms. The Nagas enacted their own version of Mao's famed long March, travelling right up to Kunmin. The Nagas have proved themselves to be tough combatants, and in spite of heavy deployment of troops, the insurgency has not been suppressed so far.

It may be recalled that the Naga National Council under Zapu Phizo declared independence on 14 of August 1947 and organized a plebiscite in Naga areas on 16 of May 1951 claiming that 99.9 per cent voted for independence. This was followed by the establishment of the Naga Federal Government (NFG) under Phizo with its own Parliament 'Tatar hoho' on 22 March as also creation of an armed wing. After considerable bloodshed, a ceasefire was negotiated on 6 September 1964. At the initiative of L.P. Singh, the then Governor of Assam and Nagaland, lengthy negotiations were conducted with the Nagas, resulting in the signing of the Shillong Accord, where the Nagas accepted the Indian Constitution. However, even before the accord was actually signed, the NNC split with Isaac Swu and Muivah opposing the Shillong Accord. By January 1980, the National Socialist Council of Nagaland (NSCN) was formed to carry on the armed struggle for an independent and greater Nagaland—Nagalim, the Naga homeland, which includes large areas of Manipur, Assam, Arunachal Pradesh and even Myanmar. It was in July 1997 that the present ceasefire was initially agreed upon.

The Government of India has been quite sensitive to the feelings and aspirations of the Nagas. A separate state has been created whose territorial extent is exactly the same as was the case under the British. Special safeguards have been provided under article 371 of the Constitution for all the tribes. The state of Nagaland has been granted the status of a special category state, which means plan funds are available almost free and in generous quantities. The land regulations ensure that non-Nagas cannot buy land in Nagaland whereas a Naga can acquire property anywhere. Also the innerline permit system disallows free entry of foreigners into the state.

All this would indicate to a rational observer that the Nagas have been given the right to govern themselves, with respect to all those matters which are of immediate concern to the ordinary citizen. The icing on the cake is that, while contributing practically nothing towards central revenues, Nagas are exempt from paying even income tax—the state gets handsome Central grants with virtually no obligation to repay. The state is also saved of the huge expenditure involved in conducting foreign affairs and defending itself in this hostile world. It is clear that Nagaland cannot stand alone, and would have eventually been taken over by China or Myanmar. Even Bangladesh may cast a covetous eye, given its need for 'lebensraum' for its ever-growing population.

Viewed against this background, it is easy to see how shortsighted the claims of the underground really are. They are also quite hollow.

The claim that the Naga areas became part of India only under the British would imply that the Nagas had no problem being part of India and that too for over one hundred years, when the British were masters, but not when India attained Independence and is prepared to treat the Nagas as equals. The British administered the area with an iron hand as a district of Assam, letting lose punitive expeditions at the slightest provocation. They also converted all the tribes into Christianity destroying, in the process, ancient belief systems and a unique cultural heritage. The governance was a non-participative process, and non-representative in character. All this was apparently acceptable whereas the democratic egalitarian, participative and accommodative order of Independent India is not.

Let it also be stated that the cohesiveness of the 'Naga' society and the emergence of a 'Naga' identity is of very recent origin. No less than seventeen major tribes have been battling with each other in the most ferocious manner, with no mercy or quarter asked for or given, until recently. Each have a different language and cannot even communicate with each other. A corrupt form of Assamese–Nagamese is used as a sort of *lingua franca*. Before Christianity wiped out indigenous beliefs and customs, each of the tribes had their own separate ways of life. Headhunting was common and tribal loyalties were fierce. Even today, identification with one's own tribe is very strong. Intermarriage among the tribes was also uncommon. Hence the so-called 'Naga' identity is an artificial construct, and has been brought about as a device to face a perceived common adversary. Even within the insurgency movement, there are factions based on tribal loyalties. For example, the NSCN (Khaplang) faction has the support of Konyaks, the most populous of the Naga tribes with presence in Arunachal Pradesh, Nagaland and Burma. Khaplang himself is from the Burmese side and is an 'ang' or tribal chief. On the other hand, Muivah is a 'thangkhul' from Manipur. His tribe is hardly represented in today's state of Nagaland. Issac Swu is a 'sema', an influential group in Nagaland.

Further, the argument of becoming part of India only after the British came, and lack of commonality with mainstream culture can be advanced by quite a few ethnic groups in the North-East, and elsewhere. India, is without doubt, a multicultural, multiethnic and multilinguistic country. Except for the fact that the Nagas have been able to take up an armed struggle, which has to be dealt with effectively, through a process of dialogue if possible, and if not, through force of arms, there are no strong grounds to give the Nagas more than what they have already been given.

The problem, however, is that the insurgency has been kept going by a combination of factors. Indeed, it has assumed a self-perpetuating character. Insurgency is by now a lucrative form of employment. You can extort money from anyone by showing the gun and can get various functionaries and contractors to pay up.

Secondly, it is no secret that segments of the movement have developed links with the political class, which gives them a degree of immunity from law enforcement agencies.

Thirdly, given the porous border with Myanmar, and the fact that in that country various rebel groups operate with little interference from the ruling junta, some of whom have ethnic links with the Naga insurgents, ensure that if there is pressure on one side, it is easy to slip over to the other. The thick jungle, poor communication and hilly terrain, all suit the guerilla warriors. The inadequate strength of counter insurgency forces has made it difficult to bring the situation firmly under control.

Fourthly, the nexus between insurgents and those smuggling and trafficking in narcotics, facilitate supply of funds, as also supply of weaponry.

Fifthly, the winding down of the conflicts in Laos, Cambodia and

Vietnam has released a huge horde of second-hand weaponry, and it has been easy for the insurgents to access these sources.

Sixthly, elements in Bangladesh continue to shelter and support insurgency outfits, keeping them beyond the reach of Indian agencies. Transiting through Bangladesh, especially the Chittagong hill tracts, use of the Chittagong port for infiltrating arms and ammunition has often taken place with no interference from Bangladeshi authorities.

Further, within Nagaland, the insurgents continue to have a degree of hold on the population. This is due partly to the threat of use of force to ensure compliance. It is also due to the fact that the democratically elected government has not only failed to satisfy the aspirations of the people, but is seen as a corrupt, inefficient and parasitical organism, at best tolerated and at worst combated against. The ordinary citizen sees the luxurious lifestyles and corrupt practices of the average politician, finding that while this very limited upper crust seems to possess unlimited wealth, his own lot remains where it was. Promises made are broken, and funds meant for development are lost on the way. Corruption has reached unimaginable proportions in states like Nagaland.

When, at times, President's rule is imposed, feeble attempts are made to investigate cases of corruption. These are quickly buried, when the new 'popular' government takes office. I have, personally, seen a case where for a water supply project, whereas a length of galvanized iron pipe can be procured for Rs 650 in Delhi, for around Rs 850 in Guwahati, the price officially charged in the estimate is Rs 12,000. The physical requirement of pipes, for the project, is overestimated manifold, and included in the costs. The beauty of it is that the project is never implemented, no pipes are purchased, no construction ever takes place, but the estimates are approved, the project sanctioned, bills made and money is drawn. Even completion certificates are issued. The looting is at all levels and shared. The common man gets angry and disillusioned when he sees all this going on year after year.

On the contrary, the lifestyle of the insurgent is seen as one of sacrifice, living in the jungles, eating poorly, living the life of a fighter for a cause, his ethical and moral standards seen to be far superior. He seems to suffer the same inadequacies and inequities that the ordinary man in the village seems to suffer. He promises a better, more equitable order, a better life, once the parasitical, alien imposed mechanism is removed.

The signal failure of the constitutionally sanctioned governing system to deliver and redress the people's legitimate grievances, while addressing their legitimate aspirations is, to my mind, a major cause for the continued hold of the insurgents. If all the money that the Centre has poured in had been used for the correct purpose, in an economical and efficient manner, there would have been no unemployment in states like Nagaland, and consequently, the insurgents would find no new recruits. No insurgency can survive for long if it does not have public support.

Further, while the political class has often used insurgency as a convenient excuse for extracting funds from the Centre and compelling the Centre to turn a blind eye to all, the venality that goes on, the steady and massive flow of funds is itself a significant factor in keeping the insurgency alive. The insurgents easily siphon off a good if not major portion of the funds, with the connivance of the powers that be, and through extortion for running their show, pay the cadres and procure arms.

Lastly, let it also be said that the spread of Christianity and the role of the church has been instrumental in reinforcing separatist and secessionist tendencies. The church was apparently safe under the British but it has been propagated that this may not be the case in India.

There has been in operation a 'ceasefire' in Nagaland. While some claim that this has brought relief to the people and improved the chances of a permanent peace, perceptive observers however describe this as 'false peace', as this has given the NSCN (1/M) a tremendous boost, giving it a free hand to operate. It continues to run a parellel administration, engaging in extortion and intimidation. It has helped the NSCN(1/M) to spread its lethal tentacles, not only in the neighbouring Manipur but in Assam, and in the Tirap and Chamingling districts of Arunachal Pradesh. The 4500 strong 'Army' of the NSCN (1/M) is today, arguably, the largest standing group of 'professional revolutionaries'.

The peace has also enabled the NSCN (1/M) to strengthen its fraternal links with other insurgent outfits, streamlining supply of arms and training of cadres. The 'peace initiatives' applauded in some quarters have been quite counterproductive in this case. In the recent talks with Padmanabhaia, Muivah has been demanding extending the ceasefire to states of Manipur, AP and Assam. The purpose clearly is to allow him greater freedom to act and increase the tempo of insurgency in these areas. For reasons that are not clear, the Centre has agreed to this demand, inviting fierce reactions from all the North-East states. The situation in Manipur has spun out of control with widespread protests, loss of lives and property. The imposition of President's rule has brought about a semblance of normalcy. It appears that Muivah's threat to altogether walk out of the peace talks, unless his demand for extending the ceasefire to the states adjoining Nagaland, has probably forced the Centre's hand. However, there are already reports of the underground demanding royalty from the ONGC officials, and expanding their tax collection drives in the areas, brought under the purview of the ceasefire. The extension of the ceasefire to the adjoining states is suspected to be tacit acceptance by the Centre of the demand for greater Nagaland—Nagalim in the language of the insurgents. Fears are being expressed that this may, notwithstanding assurances to the contrary at the highest levels, lead to the total dismemberment of the state of Manipur with unpredictable consequences for the entire region. Because of the stand taken by the North-Eastern states, the Centre has had to revise its decision regarding extension of the ceasefire.

In the case of Assam, it is indeed unfortunate that a state, which had been so well integrated with the civilization of the country, sharing its culture, belief systems, linguistic characteristics, and so much else, whose multi-ethnic population had originated from parts of India, which was contributing handsomely to the wealth of the country, has suddenly given birth to forces which are hostile to all that is Indian, and who have, for nearly twenty years now, done immense damage to the progress of this part of the country. Assam represents the economic fulcrum of the entire North-East, and instability in this state has an impact on all other states, and failure to control the situation has already had worrisome ramifications for the entire North-East.

The United Liberation Front of Assam (ULFA) is easily the largest and most lethal of the many militant outfits operating in Assam. It has managed to retain a good measure of support at the ground level among the Assamese. It has a well-developed armed wing, highly motivated and trained with sophisticated weaponry, and a good support system within and outside Assam. It operates a number of training camps in Bhutan, Bangladesh, Myanmar as well as in

Arunachal Pradesh, Meghalaya and Assam itself.

The ULFA came into being in 1985, and, very symbolically, the initiation rites were performed reportedly among the old ruins of the Ahom capital—Goregaon, near the town of Sibsagar. If one looks at ULFA's declared aims, one finds a mixture of different ideologies, presenting a somewhat confusing picture. There are shades of left extremism, Maoist philosophy, fight against exploitation of Assam by Indian capitalists, xenophobia against all so-called outsiders, and the demand for secession from the Indian Union and independence for Assam. How Assam can be independent when all the surrounding areas are of India, how can it be economically viable, and who exactly are the outsiders, have not been defined and perhaps never been properly considered. What is clear however is that ULFA definitely believes in armed struggle and has prepared itself to take on the might of the Indian state.

Leaving aside this somewhat ill-defined political philosophy, it would be instructive to analyse the reasons for the rise of militancy in Assam in this manner. It is quite surprising that the gentle, very decent people of Assam, with their leisurely lifestyle, with their fondness for dance, music and festivals, should have been driven to take such an extreme measure. After all, the life of an insurgent is no bed of roses, and life expectancy of an insurgent is quite small. Life, generally, is short and brutish and death, sudden and violent. Unless there is extreme provocation, and there is, in their view, no alternative whatsoever, young men will probably not take to arms and cross the rubicon. They may not have assessed the chances of success for their struggle carefully, but the motivation must have been very strong, indeed, to opt for this hard life, an almost indefinite struggle with slim chances of success and a possible shortening of their lifespan.

The ULFA definitely has its origins in the movement against 'foreigners' which started in 1979, under the leadership of the All Assam Students Union (AASU). Though it started as an avowedly non-violent movement, by the late 1980 violence had crept in. Incidents of attack on 'outsiders' were taking place, and the murder of E.S. Parthasarathy, the Commissioner of Upper Assam Division, was a clear signal that the movement was taking a definite turn towards violence.

Efforts to build a counter movement and split the students along communal lines were read by the mainstream Assamese as clear signals that the Central Government was not interested in a settlement of the issue, and was not sympathetic to the cause of the Assamese. While they were fighting for their future, with a 'do or die' struggle, the powers that be were viewed as becoming hostile to their cause, and instead of dealing with the problem, were busy sabotaging the movement.

The installation of the Anwara Taimur Ministry was seen as one more signal of the lack of interest in solving the problem, and as a strengthening of the forces in favour of the soft line towards illegal immigrants.

The forcible conduct of elections in 1983, in spite of a total boycott by the Assamese, the quite brutal manner in which opponents to the elections were treated, was perceived as yet another signal that the Centre, and by extension the Indian state as a whole, was no more willing to tackle the problem and on the contrary had no hesitation in employing brutal methods for suppressing the movement and achieving its political ends. The installation of the Hiteswar Saikia ministry with the support of MLAs who could not claim any mandate by the people of Assam, and who were declared elected, in spite of no participation by the people, in the farce of an election, further angered the Assamese. Hiteswar Saikia, with whatever dubious authority he had, proceeded to denigrate the movement and tried to decimate the leadership. He was shrewd and ruthless and was regarded as an arch enemy of the student movement. He became the target for violent action, and some of his relatives fell victims to the wrath against him.

All these steps were instrumental in convincing a section of the Assamese that peaceful methods had no chance of success and their future was bleak, if they reposed faith in the Indian state to solve their problems. While the foreigners issue was still regarded as the core, all the litany of woes against the Centre, of neglect, of exploitation of Assam's rich natural resources without Assam getting any benefit, while outsiders got jobs in the industries established to exploit Assam's resources, that there was a continuous influx of outsiders, depriving the Assamese of employment opportunities, and taking away their lands, that the composition of the population was being transformed, the Assamese were being reduced to a minority in their own state, were all being articulated with renewed vigour. All these were arguments in favour of declaration of no trust in the Central Government in favour of violence and seccession from India.

The initiative of Rajiv Gandhi in building bridges with the

alienated sections of the Assamese community and, in particular, the student leadership, leading to the signing of the Assam Accord gave a new hope for the prevalence of sanity and return to normalcy in the state. The assumption of power by the AGP—the new political incarnation of the AASU—was seen as new beacon of hope. The elements advocating violence already gathering a following, however, viewed even this with some suspicion, and were looking for quickening of action. The assumption of the AGP government, with some of those who had actually indulged in violence and even in murder as ministers, was seen by these elements as license for carrying out their violent intentions.

It was expected that the signing of the Assam Accord and the installation of the AGP government, largely due to the initiative of Rajiv Gandhi, would be followed up by definitive action to tackle the foreigners issue with some vigour. Unfortunately, instead of this happening the Centre took steps to withdraw whatever promises were contained in these initiatives by enacting the Illegal Migrants (Determination by Tribunals) Act—the IMDT Act. The demerits of this piece of legislation have already been discussed in detail in an earlier chapter (chapter VIII).

To my mind, this enactment is the single most important cause for the rise of ULFA and the spread of militancy in Assam. The coincidence is telling and underlines this view. This enactment was passed in 1985, quite on the heels of the Assam Accord, and the ULFA came into being within a very short while after the enactment in the same year. Tendencies towards violence were already in evidence, but this enactment proved to be the proverbial last straw that broke the camel's back.

It was immediately interpreted as conclusive proof of the real intentions of the Centre, the Parliament of India, and by extension the people of India. The interests of Assam cannot be safeguarded by relying on the Centre, that the Centre was interested only in protecting the illegal immigrants, and not the future of the Assamese, and the democratic process had become a device for increasing the voters, who can be counted upon to support particular parties, were all views articulated with great vehemence. The Assamese felt very strongly that they had again been betrayed by the Centre, as had happened at the time of the Chinese aggression. The speech of Pandit Nehru 'that his heart goes out to the people of Assam' was again and again repeated as a betrayal, an abandonment of the state.

Whatever be the merits of these feelings, there can be no denial that they very greatly helped the cause of all those who had concluded that violence was the only means to achieve their objectives, to protect the interests of the Assamese, and to effectively deal with elements opposed to them. The example of Nagaland was often quoted as to how the Indian state was being made to bend, how even the Indian army was unable to cow down the insurgents. Contacts with the Naga underground had already taken place and the ULFA was welcomed with open arms. The Naga underground was happy that another front was being opened to engage the Indian army.

The ULFA quickly got into gear and used the period of the AGP rule to spread its lethal tentacles in practically all the districts of Assam. The AGP with no experience in statecraft was in no position to tackle any of the problems of Assam. Within AGP there was already dissidence with the CM and the Home Minister pulling in different directions, and several ministers openly flirting with the ULFA. No effective action to tackle the growing menace was taken throughout the period 1986 to 1990, the police stymied and demoralized by the contradictory instructions and confusing signals from the political leadership. The ULFA, using the AGP as a convenient umbrella, established a parallel administration in quite a few districts, establishing check posts, extorting money, harassing businessmen and 'outsiders', ordering about government officers, and spreading terror. The tea gardens became convenient targets for extracting largescale funds. With crores at their disposal, recruitment, training and procurement of weaponry was easy and taken up on a large scale.

At this very period, the Central Government was possibly at its weakest. The Rajiv Gandhi administration showed ununderstandable reluctance to take any effective action. It was facing division within, with the departure of V.P. Singh and Arun Nehru from the scene. Problems in the Punjab were occupying most of its time and attention. The situation in Assam was allowed to drift. Corruption had became a major issue, and the government was preoccupied with combating the challenges which posed a threat to its very existence. Elections were also not far and the V.P. Singh campaign had bitten deeply into the credibility of the administration.

When V.P. Singh became Prime Minister, it was a minority government. Shri Dinesh Goswami of the AGP was a Cabinet

Minister. In spite of the fact that the state of Assam was definitely slipping into anarchy, and there was no safety or security for the ordinary citizen, the constitutional system had broken down in the state, and the AGP government had failed to administer the state in accordance with the Constitution, no action whatsoever was taken, while the situation sharply deteriorated. The V.P. Singh administration would much rather allow all this to happen than annoy its alliance partner. National security, constitutional obligations to protect citizens, combat armed insurrection, all counted for nothing.

This government got embroiled in the Mandal controversy and the Ayodhya issue, further reducing the already low state of its effectiveness. The country has arguably never seen a worse government at the Centre. The nation was in the grip of a crisis of serious proportions. The economy was in doldrums and a balance of payments crisis was looming on the horizon. V.P. Singh had opened a veritable pandora's box of casteist divisions and the social fabric of the nation was being torn apart. All the patient work of the great Hindu reformers and the sacrifices made by Gandhiji and Nehru to build a casteless society in this country, were destroyed in one fell blow by V.P. Singh at the altar of short term electoral gains. By his thoughtless actions, he managed to unleash forces which have immense potential for undermining the unity and integrity of the nation, reinforcing the worst of divisive forces in the society. Caste considerations have now permeated every layer of our society, caste prejudices have penetrated all the layers of the bureaucracy, damaging, in the process the cohesiveness of the instruments of governance and undermining their ability to function as a unified and strong institutional mechanism. Everything in the country is now looked at from the caste angle, and caste has overtaken every other consideration in electoral politics, while caste related cases of violence have multiplied, especially in the North of the country. This has had its own effect on the situation in the North-East.

Fortunately, very soon, the ineffective administration of V.P. Singh folded up and a new government under the leadership of Shri Chandra Shekhar came up. Though shortlived, it dismissed the AGP government and imposed President's rule. This long delay in taking any effective action, had, however, done the damage, for this had enabled the ULFA to build itself up as quite a formidable force, capable of taking on the Indian army. The stage was set for the Indian state to be engaged in another long drawn battle on a eastern front, this time with the ULFA.

The other major armed insurgency in Assam is that of the Bodos. Once again, long delays in taking effective action has made the issue almost intractable. The Bodos, fortunately, only demand a separate state and not independence. The various outfits of the Bodos, which have at times been fighting each other, have managed to challenge the security forces, have links with other insurgent groups of the North-East, and seem to command considerable public support, resources and weaponry. They operate in an area through which vital transport and communication links pass, and by posing a continuous threat and damaging these vital links, the Bodos have managed to increase their lethal potential. Their activities pose a serious danger to the economy of the entire North-Eastern region.

Independent opinion in the area suggest that the Bodo problem is a creation of certain interests to embarrass the nearly formed AGP government. Be that as it may, one cannot altogether ignore the underlying causes for the Bodo unrest. At one time, the Bodos were in almost exclusive occupation of the land area on both sides of the Brahmaputra, which now constitute the Kokrajar, Bongaingaon, Nalbari, Barpeta and parts of Kamrup districts. They were outside the control of the Ahom kings.

In order to protect their interests, as indeed that of other tribes of Assam, regulations were put into place prohibiting transfer of lands from the tribals to the non-tribals. Tribal blocks and tribal belts were constituted, where possession of land by non-tribals was prohibited. They could not acquire title over the land. Further, to take case of their economic development, intensive tribal development blocks were constituted where a package of measures were to be undertaken with funds specifically earmarked for this purpose. Agriculture, irrigation, forestry, animal husbandry, education, health, village and small scale industries were all to receive priority attention.

Now, while all these well-intentioned measures were in place, their implementation was so poor and the machinery responsible so riddled with corruption that the Bodos found that their lands were taken away by non-tribals and the benefits of economic development were unavailable to them. Vast numbers of land hungry immigrants were ready to snap up land that was available, and were prepared to influence the land revenue machinery to achieve their ends. To be sure, the Bodos themselves were not blameless either as they showed amazing willingness to succumb to the temptations offered. Lack of education, poor leadership and greed for ready cash, all played their role. Suddenly, the Bodos realized that in village after village, even within tribal blocks and tribal belts, non-Bodos were becoming pre-eminent.

On the economic front as well, poor implementation and leakages resulted in unsatisfactory results at the ground level. Promises remained unfulfilled, projects remained incomplete and little or no improvement took place in the standards of living, while poverty and unemployment increased. Landlessness and indebtedness were on the rise.

Added to this volatile mixture is the fear of cultural domination by the Assamese. The Assam Sahitya Sabha's insistence on Assamese as the language of instruction, as the language for official use, made the Bodos apprehensive. They had their own language, and were indeed using the Assamese script. The process of cultural assimilation had been going on but, when something was perceived as an imposition, resistance seemed inevitable. The Bodos organized their own Sahitya Sabha, and started demanding the Roman script for their language.

The conversion of a substantial segment of the Bodos into Christianity gave a fillip to the efforts to assert the separate ethnic identity of the Bodo and the demand for the Roman script.

An atmosphere of suspicion and antagonism developed. Sporadic disruption of communication, destruction of public property, selective killing of non-Bodos, extortion, raids on police outfits, establishment of training camps inside Bhutan, have been main features of the Bodo movement.

While the Bodo security force was the main group, other outfits have also emerged, each competing with the other in the game of violence, often killing each other. The All Bodo Students Union has emerged as a force to reckon with.

The demand for a separate state is articulated as an answer to the problems faced by the Bodos. The idea projected is that such a government would better ensure safeguarding the interests of the tribe so that laws meant for the tribals are implemented properly, and the benefits of economic development flow to the Bodos.

The problem with this demand is that in the entire area supposed to be carved out of Assam as the state of Bodoland, the Bodos are nowhere in a majority. In many of the taluks they are no more than twenty per cent, in quite a few ten per cent or less, and in several, they have no presence. How can there be a separate state for Bodos, when the majority in the area are non-Bodos who many not want a separate state. Would this not result in ethnic cleansing of which the Bodos have shown already a distinct propensity to indulge in.

Nevertheless, attempts to tackle the basic grievances of the Bodos have been made with a measure of sincerity and purpose. The Hiteswar Saikia administration, which took office in 1991, initiated a dialogue. The Home Ministry took the matter into its hands and the then Home Secretary Madhav Godbole, with great patience and sagacity, persuaded the Bodos to opt for a regional level, third tier administrative set-up, on the model of the district councils for the hill areas of Assam. Rajesh Pilot, the then Minister of State for Home, stepped in and made the Bodos agree to the formation of a Bodo autonomous council, to be entrusted with the administration of a number of subjects of immediate relevance to the daily lives of the tribal people. Substantial financial assistance for accelerating the development of the area formed part of the package.

I was involved with the later stages of the negotiations and I have the somewhat dubious distinction of signing on behalf of the Government of Assam, the 'Bodo Accord'. On behalf of the Bodos Samsungkhwar Biswathmary signed the accord.

The problem with this accord was that it did not receive the endorsement of all the Bodo insurgent groups. Secondly, the exact boundaries of the council could not be defined, and consequently, claims and counter-claims vitiated the atmosphere.

Though the council took office and was given both administrative and financial support, violence continued, as the disgruntled groups continued their depredations. However, recent efforts by the Home Ministry have been promising, and one may see the end of the problem in the near future. There is already a marked reduction in the level of violence in the Bodo areas. However, the splinter groups can prove troublesome in the future.

Assam also witnessed sporadic violence by a variety of small groups. Efforts to reach a settlement with the Bodos have often been complicated by groups such as the National Democratic Front of Bodoland—which from time to time embarks on ethnic cleansing—

and to maintain which the Government of India smilingly, as it were, sends a good one thousand crores of rupees to Manipur every year. The insurgents get most of the money to run their outfits. An excellent tripartite equation has been worked out, which works solely for the interests of the militants. The people of India are being hence made to finance the insurgency. The Constitutional mechanisms, such as the office of the Comptroller and Auditor General of India, meant for safeguarding the financial interests of the nation and ensure probity in public expenditure have, it appears, given up this area, as lost. The All India Service officers posted to Manipur have basically one major concern, namely 'survive' and at the earliest opportunity leave the state on deputation to New Delhi or anywhere else they can find a slot. I am of the view, therefore, that cartographically Manipur is part of India, but constitutionally only nominally so.

Manipur has also managed to throw up a band of the most venal of politicians. For them principles and politics are mutually exclusive and indeed antagonistic. Horse trading of the worst category and switching of political allegiances for the sole purpose of being in power and keeping their hands on the till, is practised with extreme immorality.

This Manipur model of a set-up of the militants, by the militants and for the militants can easily be replicated in other parts of the North-East and has indeed been adopted at least partly in Nagaland. There is the danger that others may find this model attractive.

Unfortunately, the one weapon that the Centre could have wielded to effectively deal with the situation, namely imposition of President's rule under article 356, has been robbed of its teeth by the Constitutional amendments following the recommendations of the Sarkaria Commission. It was a purely executive decision, yes, sometimes misused, but was nevertheless an effective instrument to bring the states to book for their misdeeds. Now beyond two months, it has to receive Parliament's approval, and as has been seen in recent times, even when there is more than eminent case for the invocation of article 356, because of the interplay of narrow political considerations, it has become impossible for the Centre to intervene effectively and timely. The Opposition, merely because it perceives its task to oppose, and where it happens to support a government even when it is doing nothing but destroying the state and the Constitution has been thoroughly subverted, refuses to endorse the decision of the

Central Government to bring the particular state under central rule. This gives a signal to the state leadership, namely, you are safe to continue your depradations if you manage to get the support of a party or parties capable of exercising its veto power in the Parliament. Strange, unprincipled alliances, therefore, get encouraged. The interest of the nation, the state, the welfare of the people, the threats to security, and nay, even the loyalty to the Constitution, and the laws of the land, which is what our leaders swear to uphold and implement, when they take their oath of office, do not matter in the least, in the calculations of our political parties.

One despairs as to whether sanity will prevail in these circumstances. Informed opinion argue that President's rule must be imposed, not just for six months but for a good two years the entire state apparatus reestablished, the insurgents fought to the finish, the rule of law firmly put in place, and economic issues addressed in full. The flow of funds to the insurgents must be stopped.

Tripura is one more state reeling under insurgency. More than 3000 people have been killed in this state, while around 5000 have lost their lives in Manipur and over 7000 in Assam. The main cause is the sudden and quite belated realization of the original inhabitants of Tribura namely the tribals, that they have been reduced to a minority in their state. The National Liberation Front of Tripura NLFT is now the dominant force having all, but eclipsed the ATTF—the All Tripura Tiger Force. Both are well trained and have access to lethal weapons. They receive support from the ISI and NLFT operates at least a dozen camps inside Bangladesh, while the ATTF has reportedly half this number.

Though generally peaceful, Arunachal Pradesh and Meghalaya have also witnessed degrees of intensity in the activities of insurgents. Arunachal has witnessed the extension of NSCN activities, taking advantage of the so-called ceasefire. Meghalaya is now the haven for a number of insurgent outfits, providing shelter, whenever pressure is exerted on them. It has also its own home-grown outfits, such as the Garo National Liberation Front and Hymwettrept Volunteer Council (HVC) which indulge in extortion, mainly from 'outsiders', target policemen and have managed to spread an atmosphere of fear, even in the state capital Shillong. The Khasi Students Union taking a few lessons from the AASU, exhibits shades of xenophobia, demanding all jobs to be reserved for only tribals, and non-renewal of trade licenses to the Marwaris. The Nepalis, who have been in the hill state for more than half a century, have often been targeted.

While there are no doubt state-specific issues which have resulted in the sprouting of insurgent groups, one must take note of certain central and common causes before discussing whether and what kind of solutions to the problems of the North-East can be evolved.

It is worth noting that the makers of India's Constitution and our founding fathers were very conscious of the fact that the country had suffered from disunity and had been conquered and subjugated because of such lack of unity. Fissiparous tendencies had to be guarded against, and hence the nation opted for a strong Central Government. At the same time, considering the fact that India was a multi-religious, multi-ethnic, multi-cultural country, we provided for participative institutions right up to the grassroot level. In the tribal areas in particular, autonomous district councils were established, with jurisdiction over all those subjects which are of immediate concern to the common man, land, forest agriculture, water management, etc., —special grants were provided under Article 275 of the Constitution for upliftment of tribals. Reservation in Central Government job, almost in perpetuity has been provided to for all STs. Provisions under article 371 ensure protection of customary laws.

Special category status is provided to these states ensuring generous flow of grants. The per capita development expenditure in the North-East is far higher than the national average.

The three-tier system of governance and elections, based on adult franchise, ensure that a villager, even in the remotest corner of the North-East, has a say in the system at the district council level, the panchayat level, at the state level and even at the parliamentary level. Special consideration has been given often to provide adequate representation to the North-East in the Central cabinet and at the highest levels of administration in the Government of India.

Further, our civilization has been an accommodative absorptive and evolutionary process preaching ahimsa, tolerance of other people's belief systems. It does not advocate rigid compliance of a given dogma, does not denigrate the customs and beliefs of others. Lord Krishna in the *Bhagavad Gita* says *'na buddhi bhedam jaanayet'*. Dr Radhakrishnan interprets this to mean 'let him (the enlightened man) not unsettle the minds, not weaken religions devotion of any kind. We must approach the followers of simple faiths—who worship symbols—with reverence, and not needlessly disturb them. This reflects the wide catholicity of the *vedantic* philosophy of our *sanathana dharma*. No wonder, our philosophy has accommodated divinities worshipped by different groups, those of the sky, and the sea, the stream and the grove. In its anxiety, to lose nothing in the march of ages to harmonize every sincere conviction, without renouncing any, it has become an immense synthesis combining within itself varied elements'.

In spite of all this how is it that we have so much anger, animosity, antagonism and conflict in our body politic and lawlessness, and armed insurgency have converted parts of the country into veritable killing fields.

The first and foremost cause to my mind is the continuous and precipitous fall in standards of governance. Weak, unimaginative and shortsighted leaders have systematically devalued and destroyed institutions, instead strengthening those which the British bequeathed us. The grievances of the people have received scant attention, while promises are made but seldom kept. The huge imbalance between the rate of population growth and the performance of the economy has resulted in people's wants getting multiplied, all the time. Socialism, in the form in which it has been applied and practised in India, has encouraged people to expect everything from the government, while robbing them of their initiative. The law enforcement mechanism does not attend to the people's needs, busy as it is serving its masters, who use the machinery to settle scores with their opponents. Discriminatory application of law ensures that a class of criminals escape attention.

It is very difficult for the common man even to get his complaints registered in a police station, leave alone properly investigated and the culprits brought to book. Then the judicial proceedings are so lengthy, expensive and time-consuming that it is a miracle as to how criminals get punished at all. The pendency in our courts is so large that someone has estimated that it will take 325 years to clear the backlog alone and all the while new cases are being filed. It is heartening to note that the Supreme Court has, by taking concerted measures, brought down the pendency very substantially. Apart from the fact that all this results in a loss of respect for the majesty of law, it also encourages people to seek remedies through alternative systems. The insurgents and the naxalities do provide such a system, crude as it is, not observing all the lofty principles of natural justice and rule of law, but effective nevertheless, in attending to the grievances of the people. The same sad situation prevails with the Land Revenue Administration. Exploitation by land owners, non-implementation of ceiling laws, denial of tenancy rights have invariably driven the poor, needy and the downtrodden to take to violence and the naxalites have a special appeal to such people.

When ordinary laws are not enforced, let it be of traffic offences, encroachment upon public property, or petty crimes, and when the common man sees that murderers and those who loot public property go scot free because they have money or influence or belong to a particular category, all respect for law is lost, and the impression gains ground that one need not fear law, that crime pays. It is this kind of perception that leads step-by-step towards whole communities losing faith in the force of law, and formation of groups, who convince themselves that there is nothing to prevent them from taking to guns and challenging the system, supposedly established by law.

One significant manifestation of this weakening of the system is the failure to heed warnings and take timely action. Many of the problems of today could have been easily nipped in the bud, if action had been taken at the very early stages itself, and not allowed to grow into the monsters that they have now become. This generally goes by the description of 'intelligence failure'. To my mind, however, it more a pronounced disinclination to act on intelligence reports due to mainly political considerations. This is surely the case with respect to Kashmir and with respect to Assam. Throughout 1988, and a good part of 1989, Jagmohan, the then Governor of the State of J&K, had transmitted a series of reports describing in detail the deteriorating security scenario in the state, the disaffection that was spreading, the anti-India propaganda that was assuming virulent proportions, the growing support from across the border, etc. His reports were ignored. The drift continued unabated, and by January 1990, the situation was almost beyond retrieval. Kashmir would have been lost, but for the decisive action taken by Governor Jagmohan who returned to Srinagar at the behest of the V.P. Singh government. He deals with this graphically in his book *My Frozen Turbulence.* He had succeeded, it appears, in reversing the downward slide, and the militants, unhappy as they were to find the situation slipping out of their hands, pressurized the weak V.P. Singh government to take him out. The comments from Pakistan only reinforce the view that he had started winning the battle. Had he been allowed to continue, may be the situation would have been different.

In the case of Assam as well, the AGP government deliberately or otherwise took no action to combat the ULFA menace, and New Delhi also kept quiet as the AGP was a member of V.P. Singh coalition government.

While this aspect needs to be highlighted, at the same time the failure of the police machinery to discharge its responsibilities cannot be ignored. If the district police machinery is alert enough and active enough, it is not at all difficult to gather intelligence about the state of mind of the people, the activities of anti-national forces, recruitment and training programmes and efforts to raise resources and gather weapons. The Criminal Procedure Code invests enough powers with the police and the magistracy to take action independently without any need for permission or sanction from anywhere to deal with violations of law. If action is taken at the very first sign of trouble, in accordance with provisions of law, it will not be possible for insurgents to operate, gather recruits and weapons. Unfortunately, the performance on this front has been dismal and getting worse all the while. Places in UP and Bihar have witnessed collection of arms, even in urban centres, right under the very nose of the law enforcing agencies.

The second factor is the kind of progressive reinforcement of divisive tendencies that has taken place.

In the North-East, in particular, there has been a progressive narrowing of loyalties, each person anxious to identify himself with his ethnic group. This has been caused by two significant factors. One is the growing competition for resources—land in particular—and for livelihood and employment, caused by all-round growth in population with no matching expansion and diversification of the economy. This is accompanied by the revolution of rising expectation, with everybody wanting more. This has made the groups view others with suspicion as undesirable competitors and rivals for the limited resources and opportunities. Assertion of one's separate ethnic identity is a means to safeguard one's interests to ensure cohesiveness to collectively meet the challenges from others. Demands for separate statehood and indeed nationhood is considered a means by which a particular ethnic group can ensure its dominance, reduce or indeed eliminate the challenge of other groups. Everyone, therefore, is busy identifying themselves as Bodos, or Lallungs, or Khasis, or Jaintias or Garos. Safety is sought in building up a separate identity and carving out a little piece of real estate from which others can be dealt with from a position of strength, based on attaining a state of majority in that particular area. The other factor, which I have discussed in some detail under chapter II on governance, relates to our present system of electoral politics, which makes aspirants to office appeal for votes on the basis of tribal, caste or community consideration. This reinforces the cry for separate ethnic and cultural identities and separatist tendencies.

These tendencies have been further reinforced by the third factor, namely the poor progress recorded by the states on the economic front. While population has been growing and competition for a piece of the cake intensifies, the cake has not been growing. Public investment, which was the major factor in promoting development, has become increasingly inadequate, in spite of the Centre pouring more and more money into the area. This is because of the decline in the efficiency with which the funds are utilized, diversion of development funds towards non-productive expenditure, failure of investments to generate any returns and leakages. Added to this is the fact that a good part of the funds is taken away by the insurgents. The situation is so bad that the entire budget of the states is inadequate to meet current obligations namely payment of salaries and debt servicing. The Centre deducts the dues from the states while releasing funds and, consequently, some states have not been able to pay even the salaries of government servants. Nothing is left for either maintenance of assets or building of new assets. To be sure, successive administrations have thoughtlessly expanded the bureaucracy with no regard to workload and created an impossible burden on themselves. This was a politically convenient device to relieve themselves of the continuous pressure on the employment front.

As to private investment, except Assam, the other states were never favourite destinations. With the turmoil in Assam, no one is now prepared to invest. Those who remain, like the tea gardens, have had to pay to the insurgents.

Even where the Central Government tries to execute projects, the insurgents interfere to extort funds, forcibly extract contracts for their members, who either do not execute the project or do such a shoddy work that the project gets delayed and its economics goes haywire. Execution of projects becomes a nightmare. The staff posted are under continuous threat. In the case of Nagaland, the underground have successfully prevented the ONGC from carrying out exploration for oil and gas, as they believe that their natural resources should not be allowed to be taken away by the 'outsiders'. The same arguments have been advanced with respect to extraction of the uranium ore reserves in Meghalaya.

The North-East, therefore, is in the firm grip of a vicious circle of no investment leading to failure to create economic opportunities, which in turn breeds ethnic divides and dissatisfaction, leading to insurgency, which again drives out investment. It needs to be noted that Mizoram was also in the grip of an insurgency, but wisdom prevailed and a durable peace accord was concluded. Today, Mizoram is reaping rich peace dividends. Sikkim is another example where peace has attracted investments, created employment and vastly improved living standards.

The fourth factor is the fact that insurgency has assumed a self-perpetuating character, and there are now several strong vested interests who do not want an end to insurgency. I have discussed this adequately while dealing with Nagaland and Manipur.

The fifth factor, namely the role of foreign intelligence agencies particularly the ISI, has by now assumed great importance. Every outfit is fighting for liberation, presumably from India and some call themselves tigers—possibly an effort to model themselves on the lines of Tamil Tigers. In the area, the Royal Bengal Tiger, which once dominated in the entire region, is now a threatened species with some of the groups such as the Bodos themselves contributing to its decline by their depradations in the Manas Tiger Reserve, but so-called human tigers are on the increase.

Chinese assistance was available when the Nagas began their movement but, thereafter, the Chinese appear to have withdrawn from the scene. The Mizos had sought and obtained assistance from Pakistan. There are letters written by Laldenga, the chief of Mizo National Front, to Ayub Khan and positive responses from him. The MNF was given shelter in East Pakistan and arms assistance.

Elements in Bangladesh like the army and BDR now give shelter to almost all the groups of the North-East, allowing them to run training camps, procure arms, raise funds, bank the funds and even run business and own property. Some of the groups like ULFA have become powerful enough to be capable of resisting attempts to deal with them, even if the authorities wish to do so.

The groups have built up quite a strong infrastructure in Bhutan and the Bhutan government has not been able to take action for fear of reprisals.

The most important player in the North-East is, without doubt, the ISI. The ULFA now acts wholly on the dictates of this agency. Elimination of members of the trading community, striking against the security forces, damaging oil installations, killing on a large scale of non-Assamese, BJP and AGP politicians and followers, all point to a deep-seated conspiracy to drive out pro-India interests. The emergence of hitherto unknown units under the umbrella of ULFA such as the Assam Tiger Force, the 'Enigma' and 'Volcano' groups, all well trained and armed, reveal the hand of ISI. It is also suspected that the ISI operatives train cadres in Bhutan, in jungle guerilla and urban warfare. The original ideal of fighting the dreaded 'foreigner' has been forgotten by ULFA and indeed ULFA has been quite soft towards the illegal immigrant issue. On the other hand, there has been a definite intensification of the fight against the Indian state. This change in direction is orchestrated by the ISI.

Those who are familiar with the ruthless manner in which intelligence agencies operate—one has only to read all about Kim Philby—can easily understand as to how once a group seeks assistance it is easy to change its aims and objects to suit the agency's purposes, even if it means downgrading if not eliminating the group's original goals. The groups can be held a hostage, and with threats and intimidation, combined with incentives where necessary, be made to subserve the agency's interests. This is what has happened to ULFA. Some reports indicate that the ISI has been pressurizing the ULFA to indulge in large-scale sabotage of economic assets, which serves the purpose of dealing a heavy blow to the already fragile economy of the area.

Various other groups in the North-East have also developed links with the ISI. The Naga groups, the Manipuris all receive strong logistic support in procurement and transport of arms. Their activities, which weaken the Indian state, eminently suit the ISI's purpose.

More worrying is the spread of ISI influence among the large Muslim population in the western part of Assam, the sensitive Siliguri corridor, and all along the Bengal border, and along the Indo–Nepal border. There is enough evidence of the ISI engaging in subverting the population, spreading disaffection and religious extremism, all calculated to destabilize the area and building up of an anti-India constituency.

One must also refer to the widespread sense of alienation that seems to pervade the North-East. The feeling that the system has failed to deliver, that it has been unable to solve the problems of the people, that very few are better off, that promises are never kept, that there is all-pervasive corruption and inefficiency has bred dissatisfaction all round. Interaction with student groups, who visit some of the more advanced states, reveal that they find that while there is visible progress in these places, these states have remained backward and are probably deteriorating. The usual allegation of 'neglect by the centre' is often articulated. That a great deal of the present situation is the result of the turbulence and instability in the region is not acknowledged. Somehow, our leaders are not able to and seem to be unwilling to explode this myth of 'neglect by the Centre' and tell the people the stark truth. This sense of alienation is no doubt exploited to the full by anti-national forces within and without.

By now also there has developed a brotherhood of insurgents having a common purpose, a common enemy. Each provide the other support, shelter and training. All also show a distinct tendency to take advantage of the legal procedures that the country has, and also exploit the concerns of human rights activists to place the security forces on the defensive. None of them have, it appears, paid any attention as to what exactly will be the shape of things if they do get their independence. Economic viability, ability to defend themselves in this hostile world are matters which they seem to blissfully ignore. Some glibly talk about certain small European nations, ignoring the fact of all that Europe has gone through in the first part of the twentieth century. Europeans have travelled a long way in submerging interests and identities, and have opted for economic integration, a common currency, a common defence system and even a degree of political integration by surrendering their legislative powers to the European Parliament at Strasbourg.

The lessons that need to be drawn from this analysis is clear enough. We need to strengthen the institutional mechanisms, take a hard look at our political system, which seems to divide us rather than unify, and enhance the role of those institutions which strengthen the nation's unity. I have dealt with these issues under chapter II on governance and need not repeat it. In this context, I would like to add that the para-military forces and state police heads have been articulating the view that the withdrawal of the Terrorists and Disruptive Agencies (TADA) Act has placed them at a definite disadvantage. This was an effective instrument in the hands of the police, but, unfortunately, because of the campaign by self-appointed champions of human rights, and certain elements who do not understand or appreciate the seriousness of the threat posed by insurgents and anti-national elements the measure has been removed from the statute book. The Government of India is reportedly drafting a new law which is supposed to take care of the concerns of the human rights activists, but enactment of this measure seems to be far away. What I would also like to emphasize is the urgent need to accelerate the rate of economic growth and drastically bring down the population growth rate. Almost every problem that the nation faces can be ultimately traced to the unbearable burden imposed by the high rates of population growth, and the mismatch between population growth and economic growth. The severe competition for economic opportunities is basically an expression of the growth in numbers. If people are happy with their economic lot, and are gainfully employed, they would not and need not take up guns. We must accelerate the processes already initiated to lessen the dependence of our people on the government and insulate socio-economic development from the inefficiencies of government. Economics and politics should be separated, as far as possible.

The insurgents must be made to realize the futility of their struggles. Extreme positions only invite extreme reactions. There is a great value in working out compromises. Life is indeed full of compromises. Also, no individual is truly independent and no nation can exist in isolation. Every nation has to live within a world system, making adjustments and compromises. Somerset Maugham, in an article on the late Aga Khan, quotes him as saying 'of one fact my years in public life have convinced me; that the value of a compromise is that it can supply a bridge across a difficult period, and later having employed that bridge it is often possible to bring into effect the full measures of reform which originally would have been rejected out of hand'. One wishes all our insurgents will heed this sane advice. Indeed,

I would add that compromise can supply the bridge to cross the deepest and widest of chasms, which divide the conflicting interests and resolve the bitterest of differences. Europe, which was the scene of so much bitterness and conflict, has profited from this principle. No doubt, the vast strides Europe has made as regards economic development and the stabilization of population has eliminated the need to fiercely compete for resources, and the conflict of ideologies has also died down. It may be added that the influence of religion, which was another source of conflict, has also declined, except in stray cases such as in Northern Ireland.

Before I conclude this chapter, I would like to briefly look at the consequences of the distressing deterioration of the internal security situation in the country. The British used to refer to some of the peoples they had colonized as 'lesser breeds without law'. Some have described India as a 'functioning anarchy'; some others as an indigent, violent and ungovernable country." We also rank as one of the most corrupt countries and our cities as some of the most polluted. Some may regard these descriptions as unjustified and extreme, as a reflection of the snobbishness of the West. But it cannot be denied that in some parts of the country anarchy prevails and there are some who are working steadfastly to make India come nearer the descriptions mentioned above. Even though we claim to be a free democracy, our credibility is severely undermined by the prevalent situation. Questions are raised about the true nature of our democracy when, in our Parliament and in our legislatures, committed murderers and criminals occupy seats, become ministers, control the law-enforcing agencies and ensure discriminatory application of law. Foreign investment agencies and credit rating organizations attach considerable importance to these factors, and the quality of institutions of governance, and consequently flow of foreign investment is affected and the cost of borrowing abroad goes up. Political stability, strength of institutions, existence of a well-organized and codified regulatory framework, a level playing field, an efficient judicial system, all count a great deal.

Coalition politics has already done a good deal of damage to the strength and effectiveness of the Central Government. History has shown us that a weak central authority opens the doors for the rise of separatist forces, and is an invitation for external forces. The Indian polity is already badly fractured and the trend seems to be towards further polarization. Parties who have an all-India outlook and following appear to be losing ground. To run a Central Government on the basis of a coalition of regional parties is already quite a nightmare, and if there is further polarization of political forces, the authority of the Central Government may get eroded.

While all this can be termed as political consequences, what is more important is the economic consequences of the progressive worsening of the internal security situation. The nation has had to devote more and more of its resources towards maintenance of law and order, with a multiplication in the number and strength of para-military forces. More and more money has to be spent on equipping them, providing logistic support and on their deployment in insurgency prone areas. Every politician has to be provided protection, static guards, personal security officer, escort parties and commandos. Senior officers in all the sensitive areas have to be protected, and, even in Delhi, security cover has to be extended. All this means more vehicles, more patrol and a continuous drain on the exchequer. The non-plan expenditure has ballooned in all the states affected by insurgency, and so is the case with the Central budget. All this expenditure is basically unproductive as, except for creating some employment, the money does not generate any returns. As a result, the nation's efforts to bring down the fiscal and budgetary deficits have been unsuccessful. Several states have been made bankrupt. Consequently, the resources that could and should have been devoted for development, to build roads, schools, and hospitals, solve the problems of poverty, squalor and urban decay have been reduced. The nation's progress towards prosperity has been slowed down.

In the insurgency affected states, public sector investment has virtually come to a halt. New assets are not being created, while assets created in the past are decaying. Private capital flows, which have never been significant, have completely dried up. With no investment these states are recording very poor rates of economic growth, and more importantly, creating no employment opportunities whatsoever. In the recently-concluded elections in Assam, opinion polls showed that lack of employment opportunities has been highlighted as the number one issue, agitating the voters. Insurgency has, therefore, done enormous damage to the economy of these states by bringing to a grinding halt all investments and wiping out all possibilities for creating new employment opportunities. The ultimate objective of the forces, inimical to India, is to prevent the country from becoming a strong, vibrant economic and military power and, by diverting so much of the nation's resources towards unproductive expenditure and halting the processes of economic advancement in several areas. It would appear that these forces are indeed achieving a measure of success. It would be worth recalling what Somerset Maugham had to say in a perceptive piece he wrote on the importance of moral and ethical values while discussing the causes for the defeat of France at the hands of the German army in the very first year of World War II. While not ignoring factors such as the conflict between the general staff and the Third Republic's Leadership, the sloth and conceit of the French generals, the treachery of the politicians, or the fear of bolshevism of the rich who preferred German rule to communism, and the conflict between the working classes and their employees, Maugham felt strongly 'that these contributory factors were symptoms and effects of a far more fundamental cause, namely the general lack of morality in France of that period. No doubt, there were thousands of French men and women who were honourable, disinterested and patriotic. There were however not enough. Too many politicians were unscrupulous, too many newspapers were venal, too many employers were grasping and tyrannical, too many working people were dishonest, selfish and avaricious. France was defeated from within, well before ever she was defeated from without on the field of battle'. He warns that 'we should be very stupid, if we do not take warning from the fate of France'.

These words of wisdom need to be taken note of by everyone in this country, and can be ignored by us only at our peril. The 'enemy within' is probably more dangerous than the 'enemy without'.

his tasks. If there are suicide bombers, then the situation gets infinitely more complicated. So long as the guerilla enjoys some support and sympathy among the population he can carry on. The task of the security forces is, therefore, very difficult. Accurate operational intelligence and cooperation of the local population become key elements, determining the success of the operations.

Despite all the difficulties, Saikia administration achieved considerable success in reducing the level of violence and tension all around. The fear that had pervaded in state had largely vanished. Saikia himself had become the target of the ULFA and he was provided 'Z' category security with black cats guarding him round the clock. His family, however, suffered considerably as the ULFA had managed to kill his brother and some of his relatives. His health was a question mark, as both his kidneys had failed, and he was living on a kidney donated by his brother. Heavy doses of steroids were administered to him continuously, and his diet was very meagre. He had a pronounced tendency to dose off even while discussions were going on. In spite of all the physical problems he had, due primarily to the great will power he possessed, Saikia could work for nearly sixteen to eighteen hours a day, sleeping for just about six hours. It was not at all unusual for me to get a call from the Chief Minister on something or the other at 12 a.m. in the night or even at 2 a.m.

Hiteswar Saikia had admirable qualities of leadership, and kept a very tight control over his cabinet and the party. While claims that he had brought peace harmony and progress to Assam are justified to a considerable extent, to my mind, if he had concentrated a little more on toning up the administration, strengthening the institutions, bringing about probity and integrity in public dealings, utilization of the resources of the state more economically and effectively and paying attention to the economic progress of the state, his stature would have been greatly enhanced. Unfortunately, on all these matters he cannot be rated high. His shrewdness and ruthlessness were well known, and he used his skills more to retain power, keep his flock together and prepare to win the next election, rather than making an enduring contribution to the state's progress.

He ran the administration with a few cronies, who were prepared to carry out his orders without question and without any regard to principles, rules or regulations. He created the impression that he really did not trust the bureaucracy and paid attention to only those matters which could conceivably yield political dividends even if it meant sacrificing all principles of financial propriety. For example, one fine morning, he created forty thousand posts of primary teachers, apparently to wean away potential supporters of AASU and the AGP, casting an unbearable burden on the cash starved exchequer of the state. The impassioned plea of the Financial Commissioner not to take this step was met by a rude rebuff and a transfer. The state's steady slide towards bankruptcy really started during his tenure. No attention was paid to augmentation of the state's resources.

Saikia was considered an enemy by the AASU, as he did not support the campaign of the 'AASU' against 'illegal infiltrators', while he in turn tried every possible trick to divide the students. He managed to make inroads into the Cotton College, a premier educational institution in Guwahati, by cajoling, persuading and pressurizing the students union. He openly used the Superintendent of Police of Guwahati to get his candidate elected as the General Secretary. It was believed that money and muscle power were openly used.

The Chief Minister was able to make the President, Shankar Dayal Sharma, visit the College and inaugurate a block of buildings. Saikia used the occasion to assert his supremacy over the AASU. The Cotton College had been a stronghold of the AASU for a long time, and it was believed that, prior to this event, it would have been impossible for Chief Minister Saikia to enter the premises of this college.

Saikia had all the authority he needed and a large measure of support from almost all sections of the people and he could have utilized the mandate given to him and the opportunities that were open to do lasting good to the state of Assam and its people. Unfortunately, he was a manipulative and crafty politician, with little or no knowledge of economics. He was not also a successful administrator and being suspicious, concentrated all authority in his hands losing his way in trivialities, trying to do too many things all at a time. He was trying to, also, execute a succession plan, promoting his wife and son as centres of power, who started interfering with the administration and resorting to cultivating some officers who were willing to do their bidding, even with respect to deals which were not above board. His attempts to restart the economy, bring in private investments, etc., were half-hearted and lacked the expertise to achieve definitive results. For example, his efforts to obtain private participation in the power sector, or establish a petrochemicals industry with the help of the Reliance group did not ultimately succeed.

The regime also quickly acquired an unsavoury reputation for being corrupt. For everything, apparently, there was a price to be paid and officers who tried to protest against practices which lacked integrity and which were not in conformity with rules and regulations were quickly rebuffed and transferred. The message was clear—fall in line or get booted out. It is to the credit of the officers that the majority did not succumb to the pressures. Major scandals, however, surfaced frequently—the most serious relating to the Animal Husbandry department, called the LOC (letter of credit) scandal. I had the distinction of heading the one man commission to investigate this scandal. I shall deal with this a little later, but suffice it to say that my report created quite a stir and has been widely commented upon. It earned me the wrath of Hiteswar Saikia who sent me off to the innocuous post of Chairman of the Assam Administrative Tribunal, a slot meant only for parking inconvenient souls, but my report was very favourably received and appreciated by the Comptroller and Auditor General of India, the Central Bureau of Investigation as well as the press for its candid nature and for the courage and integrity I had shown in recording my findings.

Life in Guwahati for everyone had become quite difficult. Though near normalcy conditions prevailed at least on the surface, no risks could be taken. The ramshackle structures, which still served as the Secretariat of Assam, looked now a fortified fortress with armed police all round, metal detectors at various places and security guards at your doorstep. Many senior officers were provided personal security officers (PSO) and armed escort parties to follow them wherever and whenever they travelled. The ministers travelled with even tighter security and the Chief Minister was preceded by a pilot, had security guards in his car, followed by a spare car, two escort parties of black cats, an ambulance and a tail car. Traffic was stopped on all the roads he passed through.

The housing colony was virtually a prison with high perimetre walls, fencing, control of ingress and egress and patrolling by armed guards. The only relieving feature was that someone had the wisdom and, let me stress, courage to provide a floodlit tennis court and a badminton court; courage because this invited uninformed criticism from some quarters, who derided the so-called 'luxury' being provided for the officers.

In spite of all the protection that was provided, many including me had the uncomfortable feeling that those escorting you may not really prove effective if an attack was indeed mounted. They carried outdated weapons and travelled in old, dilapidated vehicles and their training was neglected. All this security, however, greatly increased the nonproductive expenditure of the state, casting an unbearable burden on the cash-starved exchequer and consequently precious resources had to be diverted from the much-needed development and maintenance requirements. The people of Assam, I am afraid, have been rendered an unpardonable disservice by the insurgents in the process.

In the meanwhile, evidence had come to light of the brutal methods employed by the ULFA, who had no compunctions in suppressing dissent and eliminating those who did not fall in line. Absolute and unconditional loyalty was demanded by the 'Leder maximo' of ULFA, Paresh Barua. Mass graves of victims, who had been tortured and killed with inhuman cruelty, had been found in several places.

The ULFA had also now perfected its fund raising methods and had made the big tea companies pay up large amounts of protection money. Even companies like Tata Tea had fallen in line, and a scandal broke out when evidence of large payments surfaced and of providing medicines and treatment facilities to ULFA cadres. This sent shock waves all round. The raising of a 'Tea Garden Protection Force' which was somewhat half-hearted did not really have a serious or lasting impact. Huge funds were apparently collected by the ULFA and slashed away in banks in Bangladesh.

The trading community, mainly the Marwaris, had also become particular targets. Shoot outs, right in the heart of Guwahati's commercial area had taken place and many members of this community had lost their lives in these assaults by what is often colourfully described by the media as 'gunmen'. 'Gunmen' are words which can be truly considered as pregnant with meaning, as it so beautifully covers a variety of outfits, while, at the same time lending a degree of neutrality if not sterility as regards their ideological persuasions, emphasizing the mindlessness of the brutal killings indulged by them. The killings were used primarily as a warning to all those who had not yet fallen in line with ULFA's diktats and were often preceded by ransom notes. It also was part of ULFA's ideology of driving out all those elements who, according to ULFA, were dirty capitalists, intent on exploiting Assam for their nefarious purposes.

In this process, ULFA has succeeded in stopping all flow of private investments. Yes, the tea gardens have remained, but are wary of any fresh investments and are not too keen on expanding cultivation. The Marwaris, who are a tough lot and know how to survive in the most difficult of circumstances, have not run away, either. Without them trade and commerce in the entire North-East will be ruined, but having learnt their lessons, they carry on their normal trading activities, and pay protection money, but profits made are not invested in Assam or in the North-East, but elsewhere. No one in their right mind would put their money down as investment, in these circumstances. The burden of paying protection money is no doubt passed on by the clever traders to the ordinary consumer in terms of higher prices. Ultimately, it is the Assamese who pay the insurgents.

Evidence had also started surfacing of the ISI's increasing hold over the ULFA. A definite change, in direction, had been taking place in ULFA's activities. While the dreaded 'foreigner' was half forgotten, targeting security forces, hitting out at Indian interests and damaging the economy became priorities.

My official responsibilities started with the Department of Municipal Administration (MAD) as it is known in Assam. The municipalities in Assam were in a wretched condition, afflicted by the usual viruses of political intrigue and instability, serious imbalance between revenue and expenditure, abject dependence on government funds which were provided mainly for development, but which were either misused or un-authorizedly used for payment of staff salaries. Civic services were in a very poor shape. The natural endowments of Assam were seriously threatened by such neglect. Rivers were getting polluted, soil was being eroded and natural drainage systems were getting clogged.

The chairmen, who occupied their offices for all-too-brief periods, were frightened of raising additional resources or even collecting what was legitimately due to the municipality, because of the so-called desire to remain 'popular'. Evasion of taxes were rampant, while all chairmen, to please someone or the other, gave jobs to all and sundry, recklessly frittering away resources meant to provide amenities. Payment of all the salaries due was a monthly headache. Frequently the municipal employees went on strike due to nonpayment of their salaries, and when this happened the chairmen merely ran to the government for aid.

I found in Assam, unlike other states, there was no administrative support to the chairmen, such as a cadre of municipal commissioners, who could check the profligacy of the chairmen, bring a degree of expertise and experience in administering civic bodies. I initiated steps to remedy the situation, but the progress made was inadequate. Legislative measures were required and this takes a long time.

The Guwahati city which was administered as a corporation, however, had a commissioner and a dynamic young officer M.G.V.K. Bhanu, who was posted to this office did a splendid job, improving drainage, water supply, waste disposal and building a separate lorry terminal. Since the corporation had been dissolved, I functioned as the Administrator of the corporation. We managed to revise the property tax structure in Guwahati.

More importantly, I took up implementation of the constitutional amendments which were passed by the Parliament in 1992 regulating the processes regarding conduct of elections, financing of local bodies and providing for reservation for women as well as scheduled castes and tribes. Extensive amendments had to be carried out in the Assam Municipal Act so that this Act is brought in line with the constitutional amendments. These amendments to the Act were eventually adopted by the Assam Assembly.

I also drafted a bill to regulate the construction of multistoried buildings and apartment blocks in Assam. Such a regulation did not exist in Assam, and while quite a few multistoried apartments were being built, the rights of the owners and the obligations of the builders were not defined, and in the process, the owners were being exploited. This measure too was eventually adopted by the legislature.

I have mentioned earlier that the Assam secretariat was a mess. Somehow or the other successive governments, after the shift of the capital from Shillong due to the coming into being of the new state of Meghalaya, were unable to decide where exactly the new capital of Assam would be located. Various pulls and pressures were being exerted and at one point Chandrapur—a place not far from Guwahati—was selected and, in fact, Mrs. Gandhi as Prime Minister had laid the foundation stone at this place for taking up construction of the new capital. This was, however, abandoned. Sometime later, Silghat in upper Assam was suggested. The Central Government was prepared to help.

The Hiteswar Saikia government, fortunately, after considering all aspects, took a final decision to make the existing site itself as the permanent capital. At last one could dream of getting rid of all the ramshackle buildings and get a proper secretariat built. I was appointed as Chairman of the Committee constituted to plan the new capital, and synchronize the dismantling of the existing structures and replacing these with the new buildings. With the training in urban planning that I had gone through as a Ford Foundation Fellow in the early years of my service, I got into this task with considerable enthusiasm. I wanted that in designing the capital the cultural heritage of Assam should be duly incorporated, and the layout should harmoniously blend with the surroundings.

I invited a nationwide competition for the design of the capital, and each of the main buildings—the secretariat and the assembly with its hostel—the housing complexes for the ministers, for senior officers, middle level officers and for all the secretariat staff. Provision for a bus terminal, a hospital, a school, a small commercial area, parade ground, were all to be made as also for treated water, sewerage and drainage. Particular attention was to be paid for adequate road space and for parking.

These broad requirements were reflected to the potential bidders. Further, I also laid down the specification for and location of the rooms of the ministers, officers and staff bearing in mind the functional relationship between various departments and among the functionaries within departments. Specification regarding the bungalow for the Chief Minister, the ministers, the Chief Secretary, the senior officers, etc., were also laid down. Given the seismic activity in the area, multistoreyed buildings were to be avoided, except for the Secretariat.

The bidders were asked to submit their plans, as also present models for the various buildings. I organized a full scale display of the proposals and the models, and invited the Chief Minister as also the Speaker of the Assembly to view the models. Their preferences were ascertained and after working out cost estimates, I submitted my report to the cabinet. In all, the work was completed in about six months.

In order to get the required funds, I reflected the cost in the memorandum to be submitted to the Finance Commission, asking for a special grant. When the Finance Commission came to the state, I made a special presentation before them, displaying the plan and layout for the new secretariat and the capital for the state.

The Chief Minister who showed great interest in the new capital initially, and indeed until the visit of the Finance Commission, for reasons unknown to me, soft-pedalled the matter after some time. I believe, however, the AGP government had indeed taken up the project and considerable progress has by now been made.

Urban planning is another area very much neglected in Assam. Though development authorities had been constituted in Guwahati as well as in quite a few towns of Assam, and master plans had been drafted, these authorities were headed by non-officials chosen on the basis of their political allegiance. They permitted deviations from the master plans whenever it pleased them, often for consideration. No effort was made to raise resources or to plan the expansion of towns in an organized manner, providing all the basic facilities, before construction is permitted. Haphazard growth was very much the order of the day. Houses were built leaving no space for roads or drainage or sewerage and with no provisions for water supply or even electricity. These unplanned settlements often blocked natural drains, and during the rainy season water logging and flooding occurred on a large scale.

Where the DCs themselves were chairmen of development authorities, I could exercise my influence, and in places like Jorhat and Tezpur, I got executed projects for planned housing colonies after acquiring the land and providing for all civic amenities. I ensured that the sale of developed land was at a price adequate to meet all the incurred costs.

None of this may sound novel in other parts of India, but in Assam very little of this nature had happened before.

The health and family welfare department was also entrusted to me within a few months of my return to the state. This is a very interesting area of administration and a whole gamut of issues had to be tackled. A very competent officer, Alok Perti, was the Secretary and he had contributed a great deal in streamlining the management of this department. He, however, because of his integrity would not comply with some of his minister's dictates and was therefore eased out. Luckily, he soon got a posting in the Ministry of Health in the Government of India.

There were two directorates in this department, namely, the Directorate of Medical Education, and the Directorate of Health Services. Management of the very large cadre of doctors, manning the various hospitals, and the teaching faculty in the these medical colleges was a huge task.

The medical colleges were in a poor shape, with buildings lacking maintenance and equipment, inadequate as well as old and outdated. One of them, namely, the Dibrugarh Medical College was still housed in barracks built during World War II. The problem, as is the case in many states, is the failure to levy any user charges for all the services being made available and the fact that, with respect to the medical colleges, the fees levied had no relationship with the cost of providing education. It was estimated that while on the average a medical student paid a fee of approximately Rs 2000, the cost per student worked out to be over two lakh rupees per annum. I must say, the quality of doctors was quite high, and in spite of the poor state of equipment and buildings, carried on their duties, with a great deal of dedication and competence. Of course, they were making money from private practice as well.

I was anxious to arrest this decline in standards of service. Utilizing a special dispensation for the North-Eastern states under which a small part of plan funds could be used for maintenance, I managed to obtain sanction for extensive repairs to the buildings and purchase of equipment, to replace the old ones. I persuaded the government to levy user charges for services at the medical colleges, though my proposal to deposit this fund in a separate account, to be used exclusively for the maintenance of assets in the medical colleges, was not accepted. I feared that the moment the augmented revenues get merged with the general revenues, it will be used for other purposes. This is precisely what happened.

Conscious of the high fertility rates, and infant mortality and maternal mortality rates in the state, a proposal to obtain World Bank assistance for a project calculated to bring about tangible improvements on all these fronts had been proposed. Though a couple of years had passed, the project formulation was still barely limping along, stuck at a stage where approval from the Government of India and the World Bank seemed not only far away but quite uncertain. A whole lot of issues had to be sorted out.

I took hold of the report that was to be submitted and found that it had been rather poorly drafted, with several gaps. Ideas had been left vague. It was not worthy of presentation to the world body. I personally reworked the entire project report and brought it up to the required standards. It had a number of novel features, such as, several boat clinics to provide healthcare to the population living in the riverine islands—called char areas in Assam—provision for feeder boats to bring people to the boat clinics, village-level trained health workers—in addition to the auxiliary nurse midwife (ANM) at the primary health subcentres—who were to provide guidance with respect to family welfare, prenatal and post-natal care as well as immunization services, and training centres for family welfare workers. Most importantly, the funding was to be direct to a society formed to administer the programme, so that the World Bank assistance does not get lost in the general revenues of the state and is diverted to other purposes. A project, that had been dragging on for over two years, could now be finalized and very soon I was able to get the required approvals by the Government of India. The World Bank approval was also obtained shortly, and I set up a separate project directorate to implement the programme. This is the first ever project in the North-East to have received World Bank assistance, as earlier, the Government of India had adopted a policy of not allowing international agencies to enter this sensitive region.

When the plague scare took place in Surat and other places of Gujarat, I utilized the opportunity to shake the municipalities out of their lethargy, and frightened the trading community into taking definitive measures to clean up their surroundings. Guwahati's Fancy Bazaar with its innumerable godowns, is home for more rats than humans, and I was able to organize a massive clean up operation with the help of the Deputy Commissioner and the Corporation. We also introduced screening of all passengers coming into Assam by train or bus or air, and detained anyone with even the faintest signs of potential trouble. We managed to avoid, in total, any possibility of importing this dreaded disease.

In the meanwhile, my efforts to combat corruption and inefficiency in the two directorates of the health department were raising the hackles of those affected. These departments, where both integrity and efficiency were in short supply, had officers whose durability was legendary. Irrespective of the government in power, they had the talent to get on the right side of the political bosses, in no time, and acquire absolute immunity as regards any action against them. They were therefore able to carry on their nefarious activities, which included forming of unholy alliances with suppliers, rigging of prices and acceptance of substandard goods. While being outwardly deferential towards you, they clearly knew that you were quite powerless, if you made any attempt to curb their violations of rules or regulations. I was quite aware of their power, but nevertheless took steps to check the more blatant violations especially as regards financial impropriety. I had managed to withdraw quite a few of their decision-making and discretionary powers, and let loose audit parties to check all financial transactions.

Since I was number two in the hierarchy, whenever the Chief Secretary was away, which was quite frequent, I had to discharge the responsibilities of the Chief Secretary. With his fairly heavy involvement with the Tea Industry, H.N. Das the CS, used to travel to Bahamas, to Bhutan, etc., not to mention the frequent flights to Delhi. When the visit of the President, Shankar Dayal Sharma, was to take place, H.N. Das went off to the Bahamas for over a month and the entire task of organizing the visit fell upon me. The President was visiting Assam to give away the Srimantha Shankar Deva National Award for outstanding achievement in scholarship, as also to fulfil a few other engagements. Visits by the President or the Prime Minister are a huge management exercise, involving coordination among a number of central and state agencies, the airforce, the army, etc. Security is a major worry and in the North-East one cannot take any chances, whatsoever. As per the blue book, the Chief Secretary is personally responsible for all aspects of the VVIP's programme, especially the security, and if anything goes wrong your head will be the first to be chopped off. Fortunately, everything during the visit went off with clockwork precision.

Apart from the security aspects, my major worry related to the visit of the President to the famous Kamakhya temple. In this holy centre of great religious significance, the sanctum sanctorum is way below the surface, which can be reached only by climbing down a large number of steps. Given the religious practices in vogue, with the liberal use of oil to light all the lamps, with the deity being surrounded by a small pond and general lack of cleanliness the steps are very slippery. The President suffered from very weak knees and I apprehended that if the steps are not thoroughly cleaned up he could have a fall, with nightmarish consequences. I therefore told the Deputy Commissioner and the temple authorities that no effort, whatsoever, should be spared to scrub each and every step to be spotlessly clean and keep them dry. I am sure the Goddess Kamakhya was on my side as the visit went off without a hitch.

When negotiations with the rebellious Bodos were in their final stages, the CS Das was away and I was called upon to participate in the proceedings and sign the accord on behalf of the State Government in the presence of the late Rajesh Pilot, who was then the Minister of State in the Union Home Ministry and the Assam Chief Minister Hiteswar Saikia. This 'Bodo Accord', which resulted in the creation of the Bodo Autonomous Council, was a definite step forward in resolving this vexed problem. It did not satisfy all sections of the movement who continued to fight for a separate state for the Bodos, with continuing violence. It is only recently that there has been some really tangible progress and it appears that a final resolution of the problem is not very far.

The government, in the meanwhile, entrusted me with the task of preparing the state's memorandum for submission before the newly constituted Finance Commission under the Chairmanship of K.C. Pant. The award of the Finance Commission is eagerly awaited by most states, especially the ones whose finances are in a bad shape and the states try to influence the Commission by every possible means. Basically, however, the exercise is of a technical nature and the strength of your arguments, the cogency with which they are advanced, and the conviction they carry, are of vital importance. I, therefore, took considerable pains to prepare the memorandum carefully paying attention to the veracity of the state's contentions, bringing in all the possible arguments for the special dispensation that Assam was asking for. I included a special section on the proposed new capital for the state, asking for a specific and separate grant for this purpose. I also presented a supplementary memorandum on the state of municipal finances arguing that the state ought to be provided funds for the financial transfers to the local bodies, as envisaged in the Constitutional amendments of 1992 relating to article 243.

Before formally submitting the memoranda, the approval of the State Cabinet had to be obtained and when this matter came up for consideration, a majority of the cabinet members spoke up to say that this is a matter of great importance and should be discussed in a special meeting, with this matter as the sole agenda. They also wanted some time to study all the papers that had been circulated. I was greatly encouraged, not to say flattered, by the keen interest taken by the cabinet ministers and prepared myself to make a detailed presentation, describing the Constitutional provisions regarding the Finance Commission, the significance of each of the terms of reference, the proposals that had been drafted on behalf of the state as well as their logic and the justification for the specific demands, that were to be placed before the Finance Commission. When the special meeting of the Cabinet took place for considering the matter, I was in for a disappointment.

Out of the twenty odd cabinet ministers, only seven actually turned up. No sooner than the commencement of my presentation, the Chief Minister Hiteshwar Saikia got up stating that he knew all about it, and asking me to carry on left the room. I was making a Power Point presentation on a screen and the lights were dimmed. Within the first few minutes half of the six ministers present had dozed off. I carried on manly, hoping that the others, which included the honourable Finance Minister, were paying attention and concluded the presentation in about half an hour. I then paused for questions and a discussion. There were no questions or suggestions or any discussion. The only point that the Finance Minister made was that I should ask for fifty crores more for the new capital.

All my proposals were approved without a word. I was amazed that a matter of such vital importance received such scant attention.

When the Finance Commission visited Assam, I felt that it would be of advantage if I make a fairly lengthy presentation, this I thought will not only create the right impression but will also leave less time for discussions and raising of what may be inconvenient questions, such as the state's failure to augment its resources, its poor record with respect to tax compliance and the burgeoning unproductive non-plan expenditure. After all, I was there to defend the state's interest, and not drawing attention to the less defencible aspects of the state's financial management was fair game. I have no doubt that members of the Commission were not unaware of these matters. I also made a separate presentation on the proposed new capital for Assam, for which I had asked for a special grant. I could see that my efforts were well received and I do believe that the Finance Commission gave a fair deal to Assam, in recognition of the special problems faced by the state. However, the management of the state's finances continued to deteriorate and, in the next five years, things had come to such a pass that salaries are not being paid in time and development activity has come to a halt. Along with the impact of insurgency, this virtual bankruptcy has resulted in the official machinery ceasing to exist in parts of the state, denying the people of even the basic services. Malaria, for example, has been raging with new virulence, causing untold misery and a large number of deaths, primarily because preventive measures have not been taken for sometime, doctors and para-medical staff have stopped functioning due to fear of the militants and buildings of hospitals and public health centres have fallen to pieces, and equipment, beds and furniture have been stolen or destroyed. Militancy has done incalculable damage to the state.

I have mentioned earlier the somewhat unsavoury reputation the ministry had acquired, with allegations well founded, it was believed of widespread corruption. The Chief Minister's own reputation had suffered. His admirers, because of his ability to work hard, had conferred on him the title of 'karma shri'. The mischievous students, who were no admirers of Saikia, countered this by conferring on him the title of 'dhurnithi shri'. The daily situation report of the police, drafted probably by a not too literate or intelligent subordinate and submitted in a routine manner without any superior paying due attention, had reported that the students 'had honoured the Chief Minister by conferring upon him the title' mentioned above, without realizing the true intentions of the students.

What brought this whole matter, of lack of rectitude in public life into bold relief all of a sudden, was a report of the Accountant General that for a couple of years or more drawal of funds from certain budgetary heads operated by the Animal Husbandry department were consistently far far higher than the budget provisions approved by the Legislature. This was an extremely serious matter as it raised suspicions of fraud on a very large scale. The matter was at once brought to the notice of the Chief Minister who agreed that an enquiry should be ordered. C.K. Das, a commissioner level officer, was asked to take up the job. He, possibly, suspected that the fraud was no ordinary matter, and the truth could be highly embarassing. He therefore pleaded that it would not be proper for him to take up the enquiry, as the then

Animal Husbandry Secretary was an officer senior to him. In terms of bureaucratic propriety this was a legitimate enough excuse and the job soon landed on my head.

The decision to get me to enquire into this matter came as a surprise to me, for I had noticed that my popularity rating with the Chief Minister was on a downward slide, given the fact that those who were unhappy over my measures to check corruption in the health department, had been regularly complaining against me to the Chief Minister. I had also stood firm on quite a few matters where I found evidence of attempts to bypass regulations and commit financial impropriety. It is possible that the Chief Minister felt that having given me this responsibility, he could tell everyone that he was getting the matter enquired into by an officer whose credibility was high. He could show that he was sincerely interested in getting to the bottom of the whole matter. I also feel that he knew well enough that whatever came out of the report the ultimate authority to take action rested in his hands. I must say, to his credit, that throughout the period I was engaged in this enquiry, he did not seek to interfere with my work at all. Only once did he check with me the progress that I had achieved, and requested that I submit my report as early as possible. Though I tried to keep my work under wraps, I am sure, he knew in which direction the enquiry was proceeding.

The fraud that came to light during the enquiry was massive, involving siphoning off of some two hundred crores of rupees. I had titled my report as 'Guardians Turned Predators' which I submitted within a period of six months, because I found that every functionary, whose job it was to safeguard the system from fraud, had become a willing participant in the loot, violating every norm, every rule and every canon of financial propriety.

Normally, no funds can be drawn from the Treasury unless there is a proper sanction by a competent authority, the sanction not exceeding the financial powers he was delegated with, and unless there is a budget provision for the expenditure. In addition to this, the Government of Assam had, keeping in mind budgetary constraints, introduced a system of issuing 'letters of credit' (LOCs) to better regulate expenditure. This was considered an additional safeguard.

What, however, was happening was that without any proper sanction or budgetary provisions and even without the LOC huge sums running into crores were being drawn regularly. The directors of

Animal Husbandry were giving sanctions far exceeding their financial powers, without regard to budget limits, and these were being honoured by the Treasury officials. There was collusion at every level. In almost all cases, though the funds were claimed to be for the purpose of a project, there was in fact no project on the ground and no project report had ever been prepared or properly sanctioned. In one case, a sum of twenty-three crores rupees had been drawn for the purpose of building, a compound wall for a small farm covering hardly one square kilometre and when I inspected the farm near the town of Sibsagar no compound wall had ever been built, leave alone a wall whose cost would have amounted to the sum drawn. The entire amount had been fraudulently drawn from the Sibsagar Treasury and fully misappropriated. I had commented in my report that if this huge sum had indeed been utilized, Assam would have had its own version of the 'Great Wall of China'. Everyone from top to bottom had shamelessly collaborated in the massive loot. Many of the Treasury officers, who appeared before me, claimed that they had to pass the bills because of threat from the ULFA. This I could not believe, as none of them had reported this matter to anyone, or sought a transfer, if they were working under such difficult conditions, having to kill their conscience every day.

There was enough documentary evidence to prove that this kind of a loot had started during the last part of the AGP government, albeit on a small scale and vastly expanded during the Saikia government. I indicted, in my report, two ministers of the AGP government, three ministers of the Saikia administration, and over seventy-two officials including three senior IAS officers. There was solid documentary proof as regards their direct involvement, in the fraudulent transactions.

My report had analysed in detail the causes for the state of affairs, and I also made a series of recommendations to remedy the ills of the system. The Chief Minister made a detailed statement on my report in the Assembly, taking credit for having brought out the truth. While outwardly he looked happy with my effort, I knew that my popularity rating had further come down. It appeared that the report had enabled him to improve his image and to claim that he was fighting corruption and was interested in rectitude in public life. In order to reinforce this point, he decided after receiving my report to entrust the whole case to the Central Bureau of Investigation. This was a shrewd move for so long as the CBI was investigating the matter all other actions can be kept in abeyance, and inconvenient questions can also be safely fended off. The CBI takes indeed a long time to bring its enquiries to a successful conclusion and Saikia's political clout in Delhi was st ong enough to ward off any real threat, if at all any such thing emerged. Being in a position to watch the Chief Minister closely, I also had a gut feeling that he knew that his health was declining. He had gone to the USA for a check up, especially as regards the health of his borrowed kidney and the doctors probably did not give him too clean a bill of health. Medical opinion indicates that normally anyone with a borrowed kidney carries on for about twelve to fourteen years, and in Saikia's case this period had been completed. It is therefore possible that he did not much care as to what happened after him.

This judgement of mine is reinforced by the very short-term view that the Chief Minister was taking on a variety of issues. He was in a hurry to get a few of his favourite things done. He was dealing directly with quite a few officers in charge of police stations, by passing the entire police hierarchy, undermining discipline, and destroying long-established practices. Some of these officers, who were happy to be favourites of the Chief Minister, had become a law unto themselves, and were rumoured to be running their own extortion rackets.

The state was sliding towards bankruptcy. The salary bill, which was already bloated, was suddenly increased by a spree of creation of posts such as forty thousand teachers, and by giving a bonus to government employees. No attention was paid to productivity and nothing was done to improve the earnings of the large number of government undertakings. The State Electricity Board slided into a pathetic state due to the inability of the state to invest even on routine maintenance. The generation from all the plants, with an installed capacity of over five hundred mega watts, was a pathetic twenty to twenty-five per cent. The state had to buy power from the North-Eastern Power Corporation (NEEPCO) but could not pay the costs. This company which was generating hydropower could not shut down its plants, and kept supplying in spite of mounting arrears. It finally approached Government of India with its woes who started deducting the dues from the state directly at the source itself, thereby reducing fund flows to the state.

The state treasury had to be shut quite often, while the state had to repeatedly utilize ways and means advances from the RBI, where there were very strict limits. Every month we had to break our heads to meet the basic requirements of running the state. Development activity was coming to a grinding halt. Strangely, when this extremely serious state of affairs was repeatedly brought to the notice of Chief Minister through detailed memoranda, he treated the matter lightly. He would not accept our suggestion that the matter be discussed by the cabinet, and the measures we suggested for austerity in expenditure and for argumentation of revenues be formally accepted at the cabinet level and strictly implemented.

In discussions relating to important matters, including the parlous state of the finances of the state, we got the distinct impression that the CM's mind was quite distracted elsewhere, his attention span very short, and he was not inclined to take any decisions. He was also prone to dose off frequently, leaving us in a quandary.

He was, however, quite busy promoting his wife. She had been conferred a doctorate degree, due possibly to his influence and was given every opportunity to gain prominence. It looked as if he was anxiously preparing for the next elections and intent on ensuring that his war chest was filled to the brim.

Assam is a classic example of progressive destruction of all institutions of governance by successive administrations, with disastrous consequences for the ability of the state to deliver even the most basic services to the people, and for individual, social and national security. This has led to the disillusionment of the people with respect to systems established by law and the Constitution, undermining their faith in democratic processes. Deleterious consequences for the economy, and for the social fabric of the state were also evident, rendering it impossible for the people to look forward to orderly progress and a solution to their problems. With the state machinery failing to protect them, and having presented itself as lacking in integrity, showing little or no concern for the security or welfare of the people, the people of Assam, weighed down by the mounting problems, frustrated and angry, sought protection from whichever insurgent group was prepared to offer them protection, of course for a price. The state was perceived as a parasite, if not a predator, and the governmental machinery existing basically for a limited number of people in its pay, whose entitlements were consuming all the resources that the state could muster, leaving nothing for the welfare of the people. The field was ripe for external agencies, inimical to the nation's security, to exploit the growing dissatisfaction among the people. As of now, the people are caught between the government and the insurgents, both showing no ability to tackle their problems.

'Apres moi le deluge' 'After me the deluge' is what the French King Louis IV is said to have stated when it was pointed out that his extravagance was damaging France. This can quite aptly apply to the mindset of the Chief Minister, who may have for good measure added to the deluge, an earthquake and a tornado.

Lest I be accused of exaggeration, let it be noted that Saikia's record received no appreciation from the people of Assam, and his party was roundly defeated in the elections. Providence did not spare him either for he died just before the actual conduct of elections.

In the meanwhile, I received an invitation for a WHO organized workshop, on the subject of 'New Challenges of Health Care' in Boston USA. The workshop was for three weeks, focusing upon emerging issues such as the demographic transformation—that is the big increase in the percentage of old people in the population—with implications regarding costs of healthcare, HIV and AIDS, etc. It was a fine learning experience, with sessions chaired by world renowned experts. The whole expenses were paid for by the World Health Organization and provided me with a respite from the tensions in the state.

The officers who were unhappy with my efforts to check undesirable practices in the health department had been, it appears, increasing their pressure upon the Chief Minister to stop me from pursuing them. The best way to do this was to throw me out, which the Chief Minister did quite willingly, as by now, my popularity rating with him had taken a nosedive. I found, on my return, that I had been shunted off to the innocuous post of Chairman of the Assam Administrative Tribunal—a job where there was really no work. I had to hold court for just about few days a week, disposing off grievances of government servants who had filed cases on some perceived wrong or the other done to them. I shared the courtroom with the Chairman of the Board of Revenue, whose workload was as light as mine. Such posts were meant to park inconvenient souls, who had refused to fall in line. Everyone knew as to why I had been given the rough end of the stick.

Fortunately, I had in the meanwhile been cleared for a Secretary-level posting in the Government of India and could confidently look forward to getting out of Assam soon. I had to wait for nearly five months wasting my time, as the wheels of government at New Delhi grind finely but slowly. I had all the time I needed to catch up with some general reading and playing tennis.

During this period in Assam, I was able, in a minor way, to make a small contribution to a project whose inspiration came from the great seer, the Mahaswami, Shri Shankaracharya of Kanchi Kamakoti Peetam in South India. The Swamiji, who lived upto a hundred years, was a truly evolved soul, whose almost limitless knowledge of not only spiritual matters, but of worldly affairs, is well known. He could reportedly converse in several Indian and European languages and had a great and abiding interest in the welfare of the common man. He was concerned about the difficulties being experienced in Assam, particularly as regards health and education and wanted that really good facilities be created for providing upto date care for the people. A committee with S.N. Phukan, Judge of the Guwahati High Court (he is now Judge in the Supreme Court), K.P. Barua, who was earlier with the State Bank of India, and a few others was formed. The DGP Subramaniam soon became the main driving force and kept close contact with the Mahaswami. It was decided to establish an eye hospital in collaboration with Dr Badrinath of Chennai, who had a very well established and renowned eye hospital in Chennai, build a school and also a temple which would be an exact replica of the Balaji temple at Tirupathi. Both Lord Venkateshwara and goddess Padmawathi were to be installed and consecrated in the temple. The Kanchi Mahaswami had pointed out that the Kamakhya Temple was regarded as one of the nine holiest sites of the Hindu ethos, and Adi Shankara had visited Kamarupa.

As a member of the committee, I took interest in ensuring that fifty five bighas of land are given by the government for the purpose of building the entire complex. The Chief Minister Hiteswar Saikia was pleased to agree to the grant of this land located along the Guwahati bypass to the airport. Before the full-fledged eye hospital could come up, as an intermediate measure, a smaller version with all modern facilities was set up. Dr Badrinath played a major role in structuring the hospital, training doctors and para medical staff and ensuring that high standards of service are provided.

By the time I left Assam, the land had been handed over, the plans for all the buildings finalized including the temple and construction had actually started. The successor to the Mahaswami, the new pontiff of the Kanchi Peetam, continued to take keen interest and Subramaniam, even after retirement as DGP Assam, has stayed back in Guwahati to complete the work. By now, all the buildings are almost complete and the temple, beautiful against the backdrop of the hills, has been consecrated and is attracting a large number of worshippers.

# 13

# GOVERNMENT OF INDIA—TRIBAL WELFARE

I landed in the Ministry of Social Welfare (now Ministry of Social Justice Empowerment) in charge of a national level multistate apex cooperative body called TRIFED (Tribal Cooperative Marketing and Development Federation of India) Chairman and Managing Director. This organization was responsible for the welfare of Scheduled Tribes, in particular for the production and marketing of their produce. The idea was to free them from the exploitation of middlemen and ensure that the tribals obtain remunerative prices for their products. The majority of the shares were owned by the President of India while the state-level tribal development corporations also participated with some shareholding.

I found this body in a pretty poor shape, with no proper systems in place, no rules and regulations, which would have enabled organized functioning and helped all functionaries to operate as per clearly-laid-down procedures and well-defined limits. Everything seemed to happen in an adhoc fashion, with utter neglect of the basic principles of management and, more importantly, canons of financial propriety. No one seemed to be really concerned as to how effectively the organization was serving the basic purpose for which it was created, namely improvement in the marketing of tribal produce, elimination of the baneful impact of middlemen and general improvement of the economic status of the tribals by increasing their earnings. On the contrary, I found that the organization had entered into quite a few deals which not only could not help the tribals, but were indeed benefiting middlemen, against whom the organization was supposed to fight. Lack of integrity could be suspected in some of these deals.

This was quite an intolerable situation, and I had no intention of allowing this very unsatisfactory situation to continue. I did take about a month to understand fully all that had been going on. I was assisted in this by P.B. Mahishi, an officer of the Karnataka IAS cadre, whose credentials were impeccable and on whose judgement I could rely upon.

I brought this entire situation to the notice of the Minister of Social Welfare Sitaram Kesri and outlined the steps I was planning to take, some of which could be regarded as drastic. I must say, to his full credit, that he told me to go full steam ahead to clean up the Aegean stables and promised his wholehearted and sustained support. I had much feared that my proposals will not be well-received and there will be interference asking to this and not to do that. I was aware of the fact that the caste virus had infected the organization and anything that I did can be misinterpreted with allegations of caste bias. I have no hesitation in saying that this firm support given by the minister was invaluable in allowing me to go ahead and enabling me to achieve very concrete results.

I set about, in right earnest, to draft manuals on administration, on financial management and commercial transactions. I worked on standardizing contracts so that the prevailing practice of entering into contracts with variable terms, quite often benefiting only those on the other side, resulting in huge losses for the organization, could altogether be avoided.

One favourite practice that had prevailed was to enter into contracts based on predetermined prices, without providing for market fluctuations, and often these prices were revised upwards on a plea by the contracting party. No real procedure existed to check as to what was the price paid to the tribal producer, whether the minimum support prices fixed by the state governments were being paid and whether the purchases were all from the tribals. I imposed a total ban on this nefarious practice and laid down that all purchases were to be made only at market prices or at the minimum prices fixed by the government. In order to help the tribals, I prescribed that a premium upto 5 per cent can be paid, depending upon the circumstances, only with the approval of the head office.

It is a sad fact of our national life that even after so many years of our Independence, the lot of the tribals in many areas has shown so little improvement. The tribals of the North-East keep complaining of neglect, but their lot is far superior to the tribals in Orissa or Madhya Pradesh. When I visited some of the areas inhabited by the tribals in the state of Orissa, I was appalled to see the abject poverty, squalor and backwardness of the people who have been, it appears, untouched by any of the schemes of development that is supposed to have been implemented in these areas. In the Koraput, Sambhalpur and Kalahandi districts which I visited, I found that the main, if not the only, source of income available to the tribals is the collection and sale of what is known as minor forest produce, mainly sal seeds, the seeds that fall from sal trees, and mahua, another product of the forest. Of course, there are no facilities for drinking water or health care, or education, leave alone supply of electricity, or roads. There is a minimum purchase price fixed by the government for all these products, and the government has also set up its own Tribal Development Corporation for the purpose of purchasing and marketing tribal products, assuring the tribal of a remunerative price. Strangely, however, the Government of Orissa at the same time has been granting monopoly purchasing rights to a private trader on the quite specious ground that he had established a plant for processing a variety of minor forest produce, thereby negating the very purpose for which the Tribal Development Corporation had been set up. This trader commanded great influence in the Government of Orissa. No one was inclined to check whether he really paid the tribal at least the price fixed by the government. Since he had monopoly rights, the tribal was at his absolute mercy. His agents dominated the various haats—local bazaars—on the periphery of the forest, or near tribal settlements, where the tribal brings his collection of forest produce. Normally the tribal and his whole family collect all that they can during the day, and next morning bring their entire collection by headload to the nearest 'haat'. The agent, whose responsibility it is to buy, makes him wait all the while increasing the anxiety of the tribal, whether at all he can sell what he has brought, and earn some money until he reaches a state of mind where he is prepared to sell his produce at whatever price is on offer, rather than having to carry back all that he and his family had brought all the way after so much toil. The agent then pays the least possible amount and gets away.

Since TRIFED had a mandate to buy tribal forest produce, given the monopoly rights conferred by the Government of Orissa, it had to willy nilly deal with this private trader and had entered into a financing arrangement for largescale purchases, to be eventually processed in his plant. The price payable to him was fixed in advance, and was well above the minimum price fixed by the government, in the comforting belief that it was, in the process, getting the tribal a truly remunerative deal. No one checked the actual prices paid to the tribal while the trader was merrily certifying that he was indeed paying to the tribal the price fixed in the contract, minus a commission for his services. He had managed to get his bread buttered on all sides with generous flow of funds, fixed prices for him, immunizing him from any market fluctuations and no check as to what prices were paid to the tribal. In fact, he was being given periodic increases in prices, whenever he asked for it, without any check to find out if the increases were justified or not.

I found this entire arrangement the exact antithesis of all that we were supposed to do, to ensure that the tribal gets a fair price and that he does not get exploited by the middlemen. I, therefore, took up the matter vigorously with the Government of Orissa, arguing that the monopoly rights given to the private trader should be withdrawn and the entire business entrusted to the Tribal Development Corporation of Orissa, if we are to bring about any improvement in the miserable living conditions of the tribals. I visited Bhubaneswar, the state capital, met the Chief Secretary and officials in charge of the forest and tribal development departments, and presented my arguments forcefully. But such was the power and influence that this private trader wielded in the corridors of the secretariat that all the officials I spoke to listened to me politely, gave broad smiles, pregnant with meaning, but did nothing and promised nothing. They gave me the impression that they had no power to change or influence policies in this regard, formulated as they were at the political level. I was amazed that the plight of the tribals counted for so little, while tall claims were all along being made of the special attention that tribal welfare was receiving at the hands of successive governments, and indeed votes were gathered on the basis of such claims. I had brought this matter to the notice of the PMO, and thanks to the interest taken by the Secretary to the PM, Yogender, the PM Narasimha Rao addressed a letter to the Orissa CM urging him to do away with the monopoly granted to the private party, but even this had no effect.

I was shocked to see that copies of all my letters to the Orissa

Government couched in strong language describing the exploitation of the tribals by the private trader and the supreme unconcern that he showed towards their welfare and not paying them even the minimum price laid down by the government were made available to him. He, I am sure, knew very well that all the song and dance I was making would be of no avail.

TRIFED had unfortunately fallen deeply into the clutches of this private trader, by not only entering into arrangements for the purchase of products for which he had been given monopoly rights, but even for products where he had no such rights. There was absolutely no need to have done this, and he taking full advantage of the uncalled-for generosity of TRIFED, purchased substandard goods, charged prices out of tune with the market, kept asking for higher prices, all gladly agreed to by TRIFED. It was obvious that the intention behind all these actions was not the welfare of tribals, and perhaps not even honourable.

I had to spend a whole lot of my time trying to recover the crores of rupees that had been advanced to this mighty individual.

There were other deals equally bad and equally unrelated to the welfare of the tribals, and I ended up referring these to the Central Bureau of Investigation (CBI) for taking up criminal cases under the prevention of corruption act.

In my efforts to deal with specific cases, where lack of integrity was apparent, I initiated proceedings and dismissed two senior officers, compulsorily retired a number of others, suspended quite a few and started action against them. One of them, a Kuki tribal from Manipur, had created an impression that he could do anything and no one could touch him as he was a tribal. He tried every means that he could exploit, approached various ministers and MPs to stall the proceedings against him. I was warned that the actions that I was taking would land me in deep trouble, but every time I met the Minister Sitaram Kesri, he raised no objections to the actions I had taken. To be sure, I had to take all and every precaution to make it absolutely certain that there were more than adequate grounds for me to take action, that there was unimpeachable documentary evidence to prove the cases, that all procedural requirements were flawlessly and meticulously observed, that the principles of natural justice were given due weightage, no one can detect any bias whatsoever, and the punishment imposed was in proportion to the proven charges.

I also took great pains to see that in each and every transaction concluded during my own tenure, all the canons of financial propriety were observed most punctiliously, and tribal welfare was kept as the major objective.

The steps I had taken were not only unprecedented, but had hurt quite a few who had got used to deriving undue benefit from the system. Naturally, there were quite a few hostile reactions. Complaints to the National Commission for Schedule Castes and Tribes were sent, and cases filed in the Andhra Pradesh High Court, making all kinds of wild allegations of caste bias and what have you. I had to send detailed replies to all these, taking great care to refute every one of the allegations, as a consequence of which none of these bodies could interfere with any of the steps taken by me.

I wanted that the organization should adopt sound management practices, and apart from the manuals and instructions, computerized the entire financial and commercial wings of the head office, as also some of the more important branches. I introduced a training programme for all the executives inviting management specialists.

I am not sure how much long-term effect all this has had. TRIFED's basic problem has been and continues to be its abject dependence on the state governments and the state-level cooperative organizations for achieving its objectives. Apart from the kind of lack of interest that I have referred to in the case of Orissa, the state-level organizations come to TRIFED only when they are in trouble, to sell poor quality products, which they themselves are unable to sell in spite of repeated efforts, and at prices out of tune with the market prices. If TRIFED helps them by buying such products, at the prices asked for, there is no chance of selling these without making heavy losses. TRIFED has helped in finding export markets for a few tribal products and these have been quite profitable, which is really an exception.

TRIFED has also been entering into back-to-back arrangements with private parties to make largescale purchases of agricultural produce such as soyabean from tribal areas, particularly in Rajasthan and Madhya Pradesh. This arrangement had the merit of boosting the demand for commodities such as soyabean and mustard, stabilizing prices, ensuring remunerative prices to tribal farmers and also generating a return for the organization. The parties were encouraged to come to TRIFED, as this offered them the possibility of obtaining credit outside the banking system. I systematized this part of business by introducing transparent procedures, open advertisement, standardizing the contract, and building in checks to ensure that the purchases were made from tribals only.

I was also concerned that TRIFED had done so little for the North-East where there is indeed a large population of tribals. I strengthened the branch office at Guwahati, obtained the services of a dynamic officer Absar Hazarika from the Assam government, and attempted to expand the purchasing programme, as also revive a plant built by TRIFED for producing citronella oil which had been shut down due to poor management and inadequate efforts to market the final produce, namely citronella oil. I cannot claim great success with respect to these efforts.

TRIFED is one of those organizations created, if I may say, with a certain amount of misguided enthusiasm, and misplaced optimism, based on the belief that creation of one more bureaucratic organization is another magic wand which can remove the woes of the tribals and function as an answer to the problems faced by the tribals. A Chinese proverb says that 'if a man is hungry do not give him a fish to eat, but teach him how to fish'. The deep wisdom of this proverb would indicate that to improve the lot of the tribal, his ability to stand on his own feet should be improved by education, training, building of new skills, creation of employment opportunities, reducing, his dependence upon one or two traditional vocations and diversification of the tribal economy. Provision of basic infrastructure, roads, electricity, water supply and educational and health facilities are vital. In other words, an integrated and coordinated strategy is required. This no doubt exists on paper, but if it is implemented, for which both political will and administrative efficiency is required, one can see a better tomorrow for the tribal. TRIFED can be far more effective and its activities far more beneficial, if it is incorporated as an important element in this coordinated effort.

# 14

# SIKKIM AGAIN

Early in 1996, the Chief Minister of Sikkim Pawan Chamling had enquired as to whether I would be prepared to come to Sikkim as Chief Secretary. S. Varadan of the Gujarat cadre, who was the then Chief Secretary was scheduled to retire and Sikkim was looking for a suitable candidate. I believe, the reputation and good will that I had earned during my last tenure in Sikkim as Development Commissioner, had influenced the Chief Minister. It is also possible that the circumstances in which I had to leave Sikkim in 1990, which I have described at the end of chapter X, due to my having fallen out of favour with the then Chief Minister Nar Bahadur Bhandari, had something to do with this move to get me back to Sikkim and may be also the blessings of the lamas' of the Deorali Nyangma training school, which I had received at the time of my departure. It was also perhaps a case of a sort of poetic justice. Bhandari was now out of power and Chamling had played a very important role in the defeat of Bhandari at the hustings.

Bhandari, who had won the 1989 November elections to the Sikkim Assembly, with his party getting all the thirty-two seats, had reportedly become increasingly unpopular because of his autocratic ways, and complaints of suppression of democratic freedoms had surfaced. Dissidence within the Sikkim Sangram Parishad had grown and Chamling had unfurled the banner of revolt. He campaigned that darkness had descended upon Sikkim, that Sikkim was nothing less than a dictatorship, and the people of Sikkim were being enslaved by denial of their rights. He reportedly carried a candle to the Assembly, claiming that the darkness that had descended upon Sikkim needs to be dispelled by lighting the candle of freedom by everyone, and he was taking the first step in this direction. This highly emotive and symbolic protest created quite a ripple all round and evoked a strong resonance in the hearts and minds of the people.

Sikkim had also experienced, in a mild way, the impact of the 'Mandal effect' which had brought forward the whole issue of positive steps for the upliftment of the backward classes. The scheduled castes and scheduled tribes had benefited by the policy of positive discrimination in their favour and the acceptance of the 'Mandal Commission' report by the V.P. Singh government sought to extend this policy to the other backward classes. This has had its impact on the politics of the whole country, and Sikkim could not be immune from its effects. Bhandari belonged to the upper crust of the society, belonging as he did to the Chetri Bahun group, whereas Chamling, presented himself as the champion of the other backward classes, which greatly increased his electoral appeal.

Chamling, throughout his political career, has stood for and campaigned for the welfare and advancement of the poor and more disadvantaged segments of the community. He had, invariably, been elected from his constituency at Namchi with possibly the biggest margins by any legislator in Sikkim and definitely among the current crop of legislators. He enjoyed unquestioned popularity and loyalty of his voters, and when he took up a cause, he invariably received widespread support. His revolt against Bhandari, therefore, was a very serious challenge and its gravity escalated with each passing day. Bhandari's handling of the agitation by the Sikkim police also added to his woes.

More than anything else, to my mind, Bhandari's approach to the issue regarding application of the Indian Income Tax Act to Sikkim, proved to be a decisive blow against his leadership. Sikkim had its own income tax law, which had been allowed to continue to be in force for years after the merger. This was a simple law, applicable to all income earners, at a more-or-less flat rate, with few, if any, exemptions. It was enacted, possibly, well before the principles of progressive taxation of individual incomes had been accepted, as a sound canon of taxation, and had been adopted by almost all countries. Under article 371(F) of the Constitution of India, Sikkim's old laws, i.e., laws in force at the time of the 'merger' were permitted to continue in force. The President had, however, been vested with the authority

as Development Commissioner and I was happy to get an opportunity to continue this *'affaire de coeur'*.

Sikkim is one of those peaceful and tranquil places that one very seldom finds mention in the newspapers, where violence and bloodshed get so much more attention. A man from deep South once asked if Sikkim was not the place from where all the Sikhs came. I can't blame him. Sikkim figures most of the time in the news bulletins only when the weather report comes into focus, as it rains so much in Sikkim, or when landslides occur. Of course, Baichung Bhutia, the great footballer and India's captain; Danny Denzongpa, the Hindi film actor, the Dansberg beer that comes from the brewery he has established, and watches manufactured by the Sikkim Time Corporation (SITCO) which are now found in most of the big cities, have all made Sikkim better known than ever before.

Sikkim has often been described as the last 'Shangrila'. As is well known this refers to a magic 'paradise' on earth conceived and described in James Hilton's 'Lost Horizon' (1933) where everyone is happy, living in an idyllic utopia, free from the pressures and cares of everyday worldly existence. Buddhist lamas are supposed also to live in this place. If there is any place in this country which comes 'very near this paradise' it has to be Sikkim.

I have discussed several interesting features of Sikkim's very rich and colourful past. I would like to add here that though shrouded by the thick mists of legend and mystery, the original inhabitants of Sikkim, the Lepchas, reportedly came into contact with the ancestors of the Bhutias, somewhere around the fifteenth century. 'The strangers rode on huge pigs and carried long sticks that made a noise like thunder' was the awed reaction of the Lepchas to the entry of Bhutias, who were basically of Tibetan origin, as they came on horseback and carried guns. Their leader Kheye Bhumsa was a nobleman from Eastern Tibet, and was famed for his superhuman strength. Childless and yearning for a son, Kheye Bhumsa met the Lepcha priest Thekong Tek at a place called Kabi Long Chok about twenty kilometres from Gangtok, on the highway to North Sikkim and sought his blessings. In the course of time, he had three sons with whom he returned to Sikkim. The grateful Kheye Bhumsa swore a brotherhood pact with Thekong Tek at the abovementioned Kabi Longchok. To this day, this pact is celebrated in Sikkim. This story symbolically stamps a sort of seal of approval of the alliances between the traditional Lepcha–Bhutia ruling elite. It is believed that Phutsog Namgyal, the first Chogyal of Sikkim who was consecrated at Yoksum, in 1642 by Llatsun Chhempo and two other high lamas, is a descendant of Kheye Bhumsa.

I have earlier mentioned about the importance of monasteries in Sikkim, their grandeur, and their architectural features. Among the monasteries, Pemayangtse occupies the pride of place, all other Nyangma monasteries being subordinate to it. Pemayangtse means 'the most perfect, sublime lotus'. Commanding a breathtaking view of Kanchanjunga, it remains even today an incomparable repository of religious art. The 108 monks of this monastery represent the leading Bhutia families of Sikkim. The Kagyat dance was choreographed by the third Chogyal of Sikkim Chador Namgyal who had built the Pemayangtse monastery. This and other dances in honour of the Kanchenjunga are performed in the palace chapel at Gangtok, by the monks of Pemayangtse.

Tashiding is another famous monastery. Legend has it that Guru Padmasambhava Guru Rimpoche once shot an arrow vowing to meditate wherever the arrow fell. The spot was marked by a small shrine. The present beautiful monastery was built by the sister of Chador Namgyal, Pedi Wangmo, who had intrigued to murder her own brother and sent him to exile in Tibet. It is considered one of the holiest of shrines in all of Sikkim and is famous for the Bumchu festival. According to sacred lore, Gandak Chhempo, one of the high lamas who had consecrated the first Maharaja of Sikkim, blessed a jar of water on completing the chanting of the sacred mantra *'Om mani padme hum'* five billion times. This consecrated the water and endowed it with miraculous properties. The water inside the ancient jar, although three hundred years old, has neither evaporated nor lost its freshness. During the Bumchu festival this water is used for divination. It is poured into twenty-one cups of equal size. A prophecy about the fortunes of Sikkim in the year to come is made depending on whether the water poured out is less than, equal to or more than these twenty-one cups. So great is the faith in this divination ceremony that apart from the large crowd from all over Sikkim, senior IAS officers of Sikkim would invariably go for this festival, watch the proceedings with bated breath and come back and tell me with great solemnity, the results of the year's ceremony.

The 'chorten' at Tashiding called Thongwa Rangol, which preserves the relics of Manjushri, another revered Bodhisattva, is considered to be most sacred, whose mere sight, it is strongly believed, dissolves all sins. The devout circumambulate the chorten, keeping it always on their right. The walls are decorated with slabs of stone inscribed with the mantra *'Om mani padme hum'*

I have visited Tashiding as also the chorten and I can consider myself cleansed of all sins, one of the more tangible and enduring benefits of being posted to Sikkim. Incidentally, the mantra, *Om mani padme hum*—the great mantra of six syllables—O Jewel of the Lotus - is addressed to the Bodhisattva Avalokiteshwara. Found on prayer flags, inscribed on stones, and on prayer wheels, embossed on temple walls, it is said to be the essence of happiness, prosperity and knowledge as also the means of deliverance. His Holiness, the Dalai Lama, is the fourteenth reincarnation of Bodhisattva Avalokiteshwara.

The climb to the Tashiding monastery is really steep and arduous and I found that devotees and those who carry supplies on their backs to the monastery have a hard time, stopping to catch their breath every few yards. I thought that a proper pathway with steps could easily be built and persuaded the rural development department to get this done. Soon enough a good cemented pathway came up. I may have earned quite a bit of merit in the process.

Chador Namgyal, whose sister had built the Tashiding monastery, was one of the most interesting figures in Sikkim's history. His name means the 'All Victorious Thunderbolt Bearer', and was a pious Buddhist, but throughout his life had to contend with the murderous intrigues of his sister, Pedi Wangmo. Her conspiracies led to the invasion of Sikkim by the Bhutanese and in 1700 the hapless Chador had to take refuge in Tibet. It was eight years before the Tibetans could persuade the Bhutanese to vacate Sikkim. Chador spent his exile in monasteries and returned a scholar. He is credited with writing a book on monastic discipline, devising the Lepcha script, choreographing the famous warrior Kagyat dance, in honour of Kanchenjunga, and commissioning the building of the Pemayangtse monastery.

Pedi Wangmo, however, had not given up, and with the aid of the palace physician had the monarch slain as he was taking a bath in the thermal spring at Ralong. Later, in expiation, she ordered the construction of the Tashiding monastery. She was however not spared and was killed in the manner reserved for highborn persons, a ceremonial scarf the *'Khadha'* was stuffed down her throat.

All nature is sacred in Sikkim, and lakes and water bodies

particularly so. The lake at Khechoperi in West Sikkim is considered the most holy and devotees come from far and near as pilgrims to pay their obeisance to the lake. It is believed that below the surface of the lake, on a clear day, the footprint of Guru Padmasambhava, the patron saint of Sikkim, can be seen.

Guru Padmasambhava, as mentioned earlier, had brought Tibetan Buddhism into Sikkim. It was the state religion under the Chogyals, and remains to this day a powerful force in shaping thought and action in the state. Buddhism of Sikkim is of the Vajrayana school, itself an offshoot of Mahayana school, whose main exponents were the great Indian masters, Nagarjuna and Shantha Rakshitha. While retaining all the essential teachings of Gautama Buddha, it incorporates a great deal of tantric traditions.

Today Buddhism is attracting more attention in the West than ever before. This is primarily because Buddhism appeals to the most rational of minds. It is not derived from any revealed dogma, laying down a system of beliefs to be obeyed without questioning. It is entirely logical and based exclusively on actual worldy experience 'Vyavahara'. According to Buddha, everything has to be investigated under the luminosity of logic and reason. If anything does not withstand such scrutiny, it is to be rejected. All sentient beings are born in suffering —*dhukkha*— and all suffering has a cause. The Buddha was unique amongst all of humanity's spiritual guides, in that he neither blamed nor credited a Supreme Being who arbitrarily plays with us. As Einstein was to say in our own times, 'God does not play dice'.

The true causes of suffering are the three poisons of attachment, anger and ignorance. Everything that happens is because of a cause-and-effect relationship. The solution to suffering is therefore to seek the causes, and eliminate these so that their effects are nullified. There is no compulsion in Buddha's teachings, and dissent and arguments are welcome.

Of course, one may say that a great deal of this teaching is similar to what one finds in the *Bhagavad Gita,* where at the end of the 'Gita Upadesha', i.e., the entire discourse, the Lord clearly tells Arjuna, his pupil, that he has taught him what he considers to be right, and it is for Arjuna to think over it and accept it if it appeals to his sense of reason. The concepts advanced by the Lord are very similar to the teachings of the Buddha.

The other distinctive feature of Mahayana Buddhism is the belief in reincarnation, and more especially the Bodhisattvas, who are those divinities who, because of the great merit earned by them, are destined to attain the status of Buddha. But such is their deep compassion that they postpone their attainment of nirvana until they have enabled the humblest of worshippers to the highest state and therefore keep taking birth. Chief of the Bodhisatvas is Avalokiteshwara-'The Lord who looks down', an embodiment of love and compassion. His Holiness the Dalai Lama is the fourteenth reincarnation of Bodhisattva Avalokiteshwara. Another Bodhisattva Manjushri destroys error and falsehood, and is considered an embodiment of spiritual perfection.

High lamas, who get reincarnated, are revered as rimpoches invariably again become lamas and reside in monasteries.

The Bodhisattvas are all installed for worship in monasteries, along with Goddess Tara, or saviour—dolma in Tibetan—and mahakala the destroyer of evil, the spiritual equivalent of Lord Shiva.

I have referred to all this because I found in Sikkim, almost every day, some foreigner or the other knocking on my door, asking for extension of the permit, which enabled him or her to stay in Sikkim, and invariably it was for the purpose of studying Buddhism under the guidance of one monk or another. The majority were women, and from Europe or the United States. A few came from Japan and one or two from Mongolia or Taiwan. Out of curiosity, I used to ask them as to why they were leaving the comfort of their homes and desired to live in the comparatively austere conditions in a monastery, and observing the strict discipline involved in monastic life. The above represents a brief summary of what they told me and what I had learnt about the religious life in Sikkim. All of them had either embraced Buddhism or were intending to do so. I also found many lamas acquiring fluency in English and even German and French and travelling quite frequently abroad. In France, there are already quite a number of monasteries and one of them, at Bordeaux, is an exact replica of the Rumtek monastery. In the United States as well, there are a large number who have embraced Buddhism. Whenever his Holiness the Dalai Lama visits countries outside India and gives discourses, he is always received with great respect and his preachings seem to evoke a tremendous response—spiritual vibrations—from his audiences.

The job of a Chief Secretary is an extraordinarily interesting one and since the procedures at the state level are less cumbersome and time consuming once you command the confidence of the political leadership, and in particular the Chief Minister, you can take any number of initiatives and see them all the way to actual fruition. There is a great deal of satisfaction that one can achieve and, in a place like Sikkim, earn the gratitude of the people.

As Secretary to the Cabinet, you function as the principal adviser to the political executive and the Chief Minister and it is your responsibility to ensure that all matters which require to be submitted for approval to the Cabinet are brought up in the proper form, after due consultation and coordination with all the concerned departments, clearly bringing out in very specific terms what exactly is the decision or direction or approval that needs to be given by the Cabinet. I found that proper guidelines as to the manner in which the Cabinet memoranda are to be formulated did not exist and I remedied the situation.

Inter departmental coordination is another area where the Chief Secretary plays a crucial role. A lot of delays take place because of squabbles between departments and one plays the role of a mediator, and a moderator in the settlement of disputes and, in the process, speeding up decision-making, all the while ensuring that legal requirements are fulfilled and the canons of financial propriety are fully observed.

Relations with the Governor, matters relating to coordination with the legislature and its various committees, meticulous observance of constitutional requirements, personnel management, all matters concerning the various ministries of the Government of India, are all matters which occupy a great deal of your attention. Since the Chief Secretary is invariably the Home Secretary as well, all political matters, law and order, relations with the judiciary and management of the police also falls within the ambit of his functions.

Of course, any matter of any importance can be taken up by the Chief Secretary, to whom the entire bureaucracy is answerable, and there are really no limits to the initiatives that can be taken, if one had the time and the inclination to do so. Indeed, you are expected to bring to bear your knowledge, experience and skills upon all matters concerning the state. The important thing however is to command the confidence of the political executive and, in particular, that of the Chief Minister.

The Chief Minister, Chamling, was a delightful person to work with, and it was clear from the beginning that he had reposed great confidence in me and wanted that I should get things done. Many of the officers had worked with me during my earlier stint in Sikkim, and they, it appears, welcomed the opportunity to work with me again.

Apart from streamlining the working of the governmental machinery, I wanted that Sikkim should be enabled to take a big leap forward, on the path of economic and social development, an objective very much in tune with the thinking of the Chief Minister. I found that the young, directly recruited IAS and IPS officers, who had come to the state to be of outstanding quality, possessing excellent academic qualifications—B Tech's from IITs, MBAs from the elite management institutions—and what have you. They displayed great commitment to their jobs, and with a high degree of integrity, commanded the confidence of the political executive. Generally speaking, the bureaucracy was responsive, if the right leadership is provided.

The hospital project, that I had initiated when I was Development Commissioner, had made some progress, but the building was yet to be completed, though more than five years had gone by since the laying of the foundation by the then President R. Venkataraman. Sikkim had, in the meanwhile, taken a bold new initiative of drafting the services of Manipal Pai Education Group, who had established an enviable record in running educational institutions in the state of Karnataka, to run the hospital, and start a set of institutions for higher education namely an engineering college, a medical college, a management institute, etc. This was a unique collaboration between the state government and private enterprise. After due consultation with Government of India, Sikkim had passed an act creating a university, called the Sikkim Manipal University of Health, Education and Technological Sciences, under which the management was entrusted to the Manipal group. Apart from bearing the building cost—which had come to Sikkim as part of plan funds all other investment was to be made by the Manipal Education Foundation, as also bear the cost of running the hospital, the University and the colleges. Of course, since no charity was involved, the investments and the running costs were to be met from the fees to be levied on the students. Freedom to levy appropriate fees was part of the arrangement, subject, of course, to any regulation that may govern the matter.

I found that the project needed a big push and while I set a deadline for the completion of the building, set in motion the processes involved in starting the university, the engineering college and the medical college. I did not realize at that time that I had quite a battle on my hands, as at each stage, I encountered stubborn and mindless opposition. While the construction process was being speeded up, I issued the necessary notification for the implementation of the Act, and date for the coming into being of the University. Dr Ramdas Pai was the Pro Chancellor of the University while the Governor of Sikkim was the Chancellor, and I was requested to become the Vice Chancellor in addition to my duties as Chief Secretary. The Governor and the CM persuaded me to accept this which I did on condition that I shall draw no remuneration, whatever, for this additional responsibility. Necessary applications for recognition by the All India Council for Technical Education, for the Engineering College and to the Government of India in the Ministry of Health seeking permission to start a Medical College as required under the Medical Council of India Act and Regulations, were filed. The AICTE were quite fast and after an inspection of the facilities created gave their approval. We would however go ahead and open the hospital—for which no one's permission was required—and inaugurate the University and the Engineering College. By May/June 1997 all this could be completed.

We kept pressing the Health Ministry to expedite clearance for starting the Medical College. This ministry started questioning the validity of the act, as it envisaged creation of a hybrid animal—a government–private enterprise collaboration—which they were not familiar with. They, in the usual bureaucratic style, referred the matter to the Ministry of Human Resource Development. This ministry had its own question to ask, but initial reactions were favourable. However, when the matter was submitted to the Minister for Education, S.R. Bommai, he set himself dead against the proposal. He had, it was rumoured, a few bones to pick with the Pai Foundation of Manipal. Whatever the reason, he took the stand that the act creating the university was invalid and wanted that the matter be referred to the Ministry of Law. The Chief Minister of Sikkim and I met S.R. Bommai and placed all the arguments in favour of allowing us to go ahead and establish the medical college. But Bommai would not budge. I met the Law Secretary and explained to him the whole matter. Precious time was getting lost, and I made the CM address the Prime Minister on this matter. The Deve Gowda ministry, of which Bommai was a member, did not last long and when I.K. Gujral took over as Prime Minister we thought we could achieve some definite progress. Still the issues raised by Bommai had to be answered adequately, and I took up the matter with the PMO, persuading the Secretary to the PM to take a meeting to sort out the issue. The CM had taken up the matter with the new PM and he, in turn, asked the Home Minister to take a meeting to get the matter resolved. This meeting took place only in November 1997 and I made a detailed presentation before the Union Home Minister Inderjit Gupta.

Bommai had doubted the constitutional and legal validity of the Sikkim Act on the ground that the Act should have been reserved for the assent of the President, as it was with respect to a subject included in the concurrent list of the Constitution's schedule VII and that it was a mixed bag with no precedents involving, as it did, a collaborative arrangement between a government and a private entity. The Education Ministry was, it appears, in the process of drafting a central legislation, which would adequately address matters such as private participation in higher education, and it was suggested that Sikkim should wait till such a legislation is enacted and then bring its venture within the framework of such a legislation. For the time being, however, the Centre recognized only two types of universities, either a purely government entity or a purely private set up, and hence was not inclined to permit the Sikkim Act to be implemented.

In my presentation, I refuted each and every one of these arguments. I stated that the law had been enacted by the Sikkim Assembly in exercise of the soverign authority vested in it by the Constitution, that it related to a subject included in the concurrent list and hence fell within its legislative competence, that it had been assented to by the Governor of Sikkim who had the powers to do so vested in him by the Constitution, that there was no compulsion to refer the matter for the President's assent, that there was no repugnance between the Sikkim Act and any Central Act, and therefore there can be no constitutional or legal obstacle to the implementation of the Act. I pointed out that the Governor, who gave his assent, was no less than a former Union Law Minister, Shiv Shankar, who definitely knew what he was doing and had given his consent only after considering all aspects. I also advanced all the economic and social reasons as to why Sikkim should have a superspeciality hospital, as to why a hospital cannot by itself be economically viable and needs to be supported by a Medical College and as to why Sikkim deserves institutions of higher learning which did not exist at that moment. From the Home Ministry's point of view, I also pointed out that as a North-Eastern state, for whose all round development the Centre was committed, Sikkim deserved special consideration.

The Home Minister, who was quite old, listened carefully to my presentation, though occassionally nodding off. The Law Minister Ramakant Khalap seemed to agree with my arguments. The Education Secretary merely repeated the issues raised by his Minister while the Health Secretary did not have much to say. In fact, the Law Minister interjected by saying that enacting a central legislation may take a long time and it was unnecessary to make Sikkim wait for this. He stated that Sikkim was undertaking a unique and interesting experiment and should be encouraged.

It was however the action minded, practical and no-nonsense Home Secretary Padmanabhiah, who took the lead to arrive at a clear decision and administered the 'coup de grace' by stating in effect that my arguments had clearly brought out that there was constitutionally or legally nothing objectionable to the implementation of the Sikkim Act and the Home Ministry was ready to issue an *'Obiter Dicta'* in this regard. G.K. Pillai the very able and clear headed Joint Secretary chipped in, supporting my stand, stating that there were any number of State Acts, relating to subjects included in the concurrent list which have never been referred to the Government of India for the assent of the President, and whose validity has never been questioned by anyone anywhere. The Home Minister nodded his agreement and the Health Secretary agreed to process the application submitted for establishing a Medical College in Sikkim.

I had won the day, and was glad that there was now a fairly bright light at the end of the tunnel. The battle however was far from over, as the Ministry of Health started indulging in some nitpicking of its own, by wanting compliance of the Medical Council of India's stipulations to the last letter. Two issues proved troublesome, one, which stipulated that the applicant must own twenty-five acres of land upon which the hospital and medical college are to be built, and the second that the applicant should own and operate a hospital with at least three-hundred-and-fifty beds, with attendant facilities.

As to the first we had just about twenty-three acres, and my arguments that it was impossible to get a compact plot of twenty-five acres in one place in a state like Sikkim, with a very steep hilly terrain, was not accepted. Twenty-five acres and not one inch less was the stand. After wasting quite a bit of time the Ministry agreed to inclusion of an adjacent pilot of about three acres, which the Government of Sikkim transferred to the University, to make up the full quota of twenty-five acres.

The second proviso required that the hospital's ownership, which was still 'dejure' with the Government of Sikkim, had to be transferred to the University, through a legally valid instrument. The possession had long ago been transferred and it was being completed, equipped and run as part of the University. At this stage there was suddenly a good deal of hesitation in the government. Elements who were unhappy that a new hospital was coming up which might damage their private practice, and some misguided and professional mischief mongers had started a whispering campaign, arguing that the university will be run on commercial lines, and profits will be taken away from Sikkim and giving away the hospital to the University would amount to a sell out. They had also filed a case in the Sikkim High Court levelling all kinds of allegations. However, fortunately, the Chief Minister was not unduly swayed by these arguments. Some elements within the bureaucracy had also quite foolishly worked against the proposal.

Fortunately, these negative influences did not prevail and a formal lease deed, in perpetuity, was executed providing for payment of an annual lease fee to be paid by university to the Government.

The Health Ministry agreed, thereafter, without much loss of time for sending a team of specialists from the Medical Council of India to inspect and submit a report, certifying that adequate facilities had been created for starting a medical college.

In the meanwhile, the engineering college had been started and functioning very well, using part of the hospital building temporarily. I worked on acquiring the land for a permanent campus near Rangpo. This is a beautiful area surrounded by hills and located near a river. Plans for the new building were drawn up and as of now the buildings have been completed and the college is functioning from the new premises. From the national highway to Gangtok those buildings present a truly panoramic view.

Bommai, however, for reasons not clear, had the recognition for the engineering college accorded by AICTE, withdrawn, on the untenable and baseless ground that classes had not been started as per the permission given earlier. This created a piquant situation and consequently a lot of nervousness among the students. I kept knocking at various doors in the Government of India and at the AICTE and writing innumerable letters but nothing worked. I had planned to take recourse to legal action but fortunately when the new NDA Government took over in New Delhi and when we presented our case to the new HRD Minister Murali Manohar Joshi, things moved fast and recognition was restored in no time.

The MCI team which came for inspection of the facilities for the proposed medical college created new difficulties. They were reportedly corrupt and were only interested in benefits which they were not entitled to. The matter had again to be agitated before the Ministry of Health.

The hospital was in the meanwhile fully equipped and manned and the people of Sikkim were now receiving excellent healthcare of the highest standards. After considerable delay and after crossing quite a lot of unnecessary hurdles the medical college has at last come into being. The dream that I had, when I was Development Commissioner, was at last being realized.

I had been of the view that Sikkim's enormous hydropower generation potential should be tapped. I regarded this as equivalent to the oil resources of the middle east. It had been estimated that over three thousand megawatts can be generated, and while the initial costs may be high, the running costs were low and what is more hydro power is eminently eco-friendly. I found that Sikkim had been dabbling with the idea of private sector involvement and had in fact invited international tenders for one of the projects on the Teesta river. No decision had however been taken. The whole issue of private sector power production was being debated at various levels, and a host of issues remain to be sorted out. I found a few individuals with uncertain credentials canvassing one deal or the other submitting various terms. On the other hand, studies conducted by the Central Water Commission and the Central Electricity Authority had clearly established the feasibility and viability of no less than five projects on the Teesta river. The biggest and economically most attractive was in the upper region, in North Sikkim, near the Dzongu area, a preserve of the Lepchas, capable of producing some one-thousand three-hundred megawatts during the peak season, but this had created a lot of misgivings in the minds of the Lepchas who thought that implementation of such a big project in the area would result in the influx of a very large number of people from outside the area, and this may pose a serious challenge to their traditional culture, upsetting the population balance. There could also be irreparable damage to the ecology. Many experts, however, claimed that these fears were groundless, as the manpower for the construction of project will be limited and can be taken back on completion. On the other hand, the local people, particularly those who were educated, will find new employment opportunities, not only for running the project, but also by starting industries utilizing the abundant power. These arguments did not, however, convince the local people.

There were, however, no such objections to a proposal for a project near Singtam, capable of producing some five-hundred and thirty megawatts. I studied the proposal and suggested to the Chief Minister that instead of wasting time and effort in trying to get private capital, we could ask the National Hydro Power Corporation (NHPC) to take up the project. They had earlier indicated their willingness to do so, and the Union Ministry of Energy was prepared to extend their support. NHPC was already engaged in implementing a 60MW project on the river Rangit in West Sikkim and can easily redeploy the personnel from that project. NHPC was prepared to invest the entire three thousand crore rupees involved. I pointed out to the CM that handing over the project will be viewed by everyone as a clean deal and no one will raise any unnecessary issues. He agreed at once and the Chairman of the NHPC soon visited Sikkim with his team and signed an agreement. The project involved displacement of not more than about a hundred families, and was considered eco-friendly, as a good part of the project was designed to be underground. It took a few months to get all the clearances, especially with respect to the project's impact on the environment, but as of now implementation of the project is in full swing.

The other major initiative that I took related to urban planning. I could see that Gangtok was already suffering from all the major ailments afflicting most urban settlements in the country. Except for a small area around the ridge, the palace, near the secretariat, the Raj Bhavan and along Bhanupath, the rest of the town had grown in an unplanned manner, with highrise buildings perched precariously on the steep hillsides. Narrow roads, too many automobiles, poor drainage, sewerage and sanitation facilities were problems that could not be easily tackled. Several areas were congested and civic services could not cope with the rapid growth. The area being seismically unstable and very vulnerable, it was folly to have built so many highrise buildings. There was no scope for expanding the town which had basically spread along the national highway—a sort of ribbon development.

The solution was to create a new town which could be organically linked to Gangtok. A proposal of this nature had been formulated for building a township across the valley at a place called Ranka, which could be accessed by a road and can be linked by a ropeway. The Rail India Technical and Engineering Services (RITES) had started work on preparing a detailed plan for the new township. I was concerned about the financing and management of the project and injected the idea that the project should be basically self-financing and should be run by a business oriented structure. HUDCO was willing to participate by financing the project, and I felt that the developed land should be sold at prices which would recover all the costs of development and building of the infrastructure.

To partially take care of Gangtok's own transportation problems, apart from introducing a one-way regime during peak hours, I conceived a ropeway project, linking Deorali to the main secretariat, which apart from alleviating the transport situation could also serve as a tourist attraction. RITES again prepared the project report and after some unnecessary delays caused by court cases, the project has been taken up for implementation.

I had taken interest in creating a zoological park near Ganeshtok, well above Gangtok, when I was Development Commissioner, and this project had been taken up with earnestness by the Forest Department and a really fine nature reserve had been created.

I tried to bring in a new work culture in the secretariat by my example of getting to the office around nine in the morning—the commencement time was ten a.m.—ensuring that no file remained with me for more than a day, introducing an evaluation and monitoring system, holding regular communication meetings with all the officers, computerization of land records, and of certain functions in the finance department, improving management of the fairly large number of public undertakings, and strengthening the

extension of the Act.

Some thoughtless, self-styled intellectuals with chauvinistic inclinations, without understanding the rationale behind this decision, and the concrete benefits that would flow therefrom, started expressing serious reservations, and articles were written in the local papers. Without much logic, it was claimed that extension of the Act would result in an erosion of the present system under which only those who were registered as Sikkim subjects were eligible for employment in the Government of Sikkim. It needs to be stressed that this dispensation related only to Sikkim government jobs and had nothing to do with Central Government jobs, which was the focus of attention under the Central Act envisaging compulsory notification of vacancies. Suddenly, the whole issue became emotional, as in Sikkim, the privilege of possessing a Sikkim subject's certificate is endowed with an extraordinarily emotive content and a feeling has been generated over time that it is a precious heritage which needs to be conserved at all costs, and any move even remotely suspected to interfere or reduce the importance of this exclusive privilege is to be stiffly resisted. When deep emotions are stirred, reason has no place, and the opposition suddenly found that an issue was at last available for them to agitate, whip up the emotions of the people and if possible disable the government and ensure that the Panchayat elections are not held.

The Chief Minister realized that this issue could be made to quickly escalate into an explosive situation, and that the opposition was working hard at igniting the people's feelings through false mischievous and malicious propaganda. He, therefore, decided that the request that we had made to the Government of India to enforce the Act in question should be withdrawn. A move which could have resulted in very substantial benefits to the people was thus thwarted by mindless opposition. The Central Government had no difficulty in agreeing to our request for non-enforcement.

But the opposition continued to pillory the government, asking as to why the request was made in the first instance, and that there was no assurance that the Central Government would not, on its own, impose the Act. Having caught hold of an issue which had such a fine potential for mischief, the opposition was not going to let go of this wonderful opportunity to embarrass the government and turn the people against the government. They had possibly assessed that the case against the government filed in the High Court with respect to the Panchayat elections was not going their way.

While this was going on, with the government trying to defuse the situation, three or four young men wanted to meet me when I was in the office. My staff officer mentioned that they were interested in understanding the issues relating to establishment of the employment exchanges in the state, a proposal which had been firmly shelved, but which was still being used by the opposition to stir up trouble. I thought I should welcome the opportunity to explain to these young men the government's position and when they were ushered in to my chamber, I did not suspect that they were really mischievous elements acting on behalf of the opposition, seeking only more material to cause embarrassment to the government. When I answered their questions relating to the employment situation and reiterated the government's position they seemed satisfied and just as the discussion was about to end, one of them, seemingly innocently asked me a question on the Sikkim subject's certificate. I mentioned that apart from other benefits, persons, who have such a certificate automatically become Indian citizens. I had not said a word about the abolition or withdrawal of this certificate, as I was only too aware as to how important this matter is in the Sikkimese mind.

Bent on mischief as they were, and acting at the behest of the opposition, these people who met me, got published in a local paper a couple of days later a story stating that I had told them that the 'Sikkim subject certificate should be completely removed'. This false and concocted story, which was possibly engineered by the opposition, was immediately made the second focal point for the ongoing agitation. Bhandari was very much in the forefront of the agitation, and it is possible that he did not like my return to the state as Chief Secretary, having been sent out by him, and it was also rumoured that the opposition had taken note of the excellent relationship between me and the Chief Minister, as a consequence of which several initiatives were being successfully brought to fruition. Though I issued an immediate and strong contradiction, no one was in a mood to find out the truth, and overnight this issue became a rallying point and was used for all it was worth to inflame passions.

The opposition called for a bandh, and I, understanding the sinister implications of the move, took all possible measures to see that the bandh did not succeed. The opposition wanted to close the schools, get the students involved and draw the government servants into the agitation. Already some elements among the government servants were critical of the government without understanding the correct situation. On the first day, the opposition did not succeed in enforcing the bandh. That afternoon the High Court pronounced its verdict filed by the opposition in its effort to stop the Panchayat elections, dismissing the petition. This was a decisive factor in making the opposition launch a full-fledged agitation. They now formed an opposition alliance and demanded the resignation of the Government for the so-called failure to safeguard the interests of the Sikkimese. Since I had been accused of a great folly—false though the accusation was—my ouster was also demanded. The Chief Minister had gone to West Sikkim, and I contacted him requesting him to return to the state capital at once.

The situation was now taking an ugly turn, with students deserting their classes. Bhandari and others addressed meetings and inflammatory rhetoric was employed. The agitation was fortunately confined to Gangtok. With limited force, it was difficult to ban meetings and enforce prohibitory orders and I also did not want anyone to level accusations of denial of democratic rights. I sat in the control room and monitored the unfolding situation. The opposition perceived that they were gaining strength and creating a response from the public and hence became more vociferous in demanding the resignation of the government. It is possible that the opposition was trying to wean away some of the MLAs in an effort to reduce the strength of the Chief Minister's party. By the evening the situation was getting worse, and I found the CM quite perturbed, if not demoralized. I told him that the opposition was getting its message across to the people loud and clear, whereas the government or the ruling party had remained silent. The people were believing the version of the opposition, which was false and mischievous. He reacted somewhat vaguely that he was planning to address a meeting three or four days later. I immediately suggested that this may be too late, and persuaded him to speak on the radio to all the people of Sikkim that evening itself, and address a meeting next day positively. He agreed to this and did the needful.

His speaking on the radio (there was as yet no television in Gangtok) and the address next day had only a limited impact as there was not enough time for his party cadres to mobilize the people, and the opposition, which had by then gathered some following, had placed a fairly good number of its supporters to heckle the CM. The police had a very difficult time keeping the supporters of the two sides from clashing.

Moments after the CM's departure, the opposition leaders including Bhandari managed to occupy the stage and let lose a tirade against the government. Bhandari was at his acerbic best and used all his oratorial skills to create the maximum possible impact. The opposition possibly sensed that the tide was turning in their favour, and were now demanding that the government should be dismissed by the Governor. The government servants had now gone on strike, and the next day the opposition took out a fairly large procession which, while passing near offices of the power department, threw brick bats and caused some damage to the building. They were bent upon marching to the main Tashiling Secretariat and it was only the determined action of the Superintendent of Police, Gangtok, Negi and the Commandant of the Sikkim armed police Akshay Sachdeva, both young IPS officers, who threatened to open fire if the mob moved an inch forward towards the Secretariat, that prevented the mob from invading the Secretariat. If they had indeed come to the Secretariat, judging by the ugly mood of the mob, mayhem would have followed. I was almost alone in the Secretariat with only my personal staff, as all others had deserted their posts, and was in considerable danger at least for a short while.

The Chief Minister later in the day tried to speak to a gathering of government servants, but they were in no mood to listen to reason.

That evening the cabinet members who assembled in the CM's residence 'Mintogang' looked almost shell-shocked. The CM had been summoned by the Governor. Though a decision had been taken that the CM will address a public meeting the next day for which the party cadres had been asked to mobilize and bring people from all over Sikkim, the DGP P.C. Sharma and I noticed considerable hesitation and uncertainty as to whether the effort will succeed. The CM was also probably aware of the opposition's efforts to get hold of some of his MLAs.

He asked us to accompany him to meet the Governor, Choudhary Randhir Singh, a Harayanvi Jat, an old Congressman, and who was member of the Rajya Sabha for long years.

Normally, the Governor was a jovial man, but this evening his mood was distinctly sombre. The opposition leaders had just departed having demanded that he dismiss the Chief Minister, and having threatened that they will not allow the Chief Minister to hold his meeting next day in the main stadium of Gangtok, the Paljor Namgyal Stadium, and if he attempted to do so, there would be violence and bloodshed. They planned to hold their own meeting at that very venue. The Governor somehow displayed a strange attitude, vaguely supportive of the opposition's stand. Instead of roundly condemning the threat to use violence, he was trying to persuade the Chief Minister to hold his meeting in another venue. This, to my mind, was a suggestion to retreat, in the face of violence.

The CM, being a mild man, was trying to politely state that he had to hold the meeting to correct the false, mischievous and malicious propaganda that was being carried on. I spoke up arguing that it would be quite improper to accept a situation where the Chief Minister of the state is prevented from addressing his people in a venue he has chosen, as this would amount to abrogation of authority. A government constituted by law cannot bow before a threat of violence. We would take all measures to prevent violence and it was our duty, as government servants, to enable the Chief Minister to address the meeting without any let or hindrance. This invited the wrath of the Governor and he reprimanded me by saying that I was a hardliner who always took uncompromising stands. I kept silent thereafter, and while the DGP Sharma with a few well-chosen words supported my stand, the Governor concluded the meeting in a huff stating that he had done his duty and now if there was violence, it was no more his responsibility, but ours.

The CM looked quite unhappy, when we drove back to his residence, where most ministers were waiting. The question whether they should go ahead with the meeting in the face of the threat by the opposition was being debated, while rumours were coming in indicating that the opposition would prevent the CM's partymen from bringing the people to Gangtok. While some ministers were not sure of their ground, Garjaman Gurung, the then Minister for agriculture, spoke quite firmly that the meeting must be held and largescale mobilization must be made to bring as many people as possible to hear to the CM. When asked for our views, both the DGP and I responded that we will take every possible measure to ensure smooth flow of traffic to Gangtok and prevent any unruly elements from entering the stadium and disturbing the CM's meeting.

Unknown to me and possibly even the Chief Minister, a drama was being enacted that night on the side lines, with the opposition drafting the Congress party's support to form an alternative government in Sikkim. The then Congress President Sitaram Kesri had been sounded as also Oscar Fernandes, one of the General Secretaries. They were veterans in 'real politik' and had the sense to consult Shiv Shankar, a respected Congress leader and a former Governor of Sikkim, with whom the CM had maintained excellent relations. Shiv Shankar, who knew the real situation in Sikkim and the credentials of the opposition leaders, scotched the whole move in no time. It is possible that the Congress leaders had spoken to the Governor and tried to influence him, and this was perhaps one reason for the kind of attitude he displayed during the meeting with the Chief Minister. Our clear assurance that we will ensure that there is no violence and that there is no obstruction of traffic to the state capital and to the venue of the CM's meeting was perhaps, a deciding factor, when the CM finally took the decision that he will go ahead with the meeting and there shall be no change in the venue.

Someone had in the meanwhile rang up my house and had issued a threat that my house will be attacked with bombs. This had unnerved my servants, though my wife was quite calm. The DGP took note of this and posted an extra picket around the house, and arranged for patrolling especially on the road that ran just above my house from where it was easy to hurl an explosive.

True to our word, we got to the control room, and the DGP took personal care to make all the arrangement, for ensuring smooth flow of traffic and smooth conduct of the meeting of the CM. Heavy police presence was noticeable next morning and the DC and SP were asked to personally take charge of ensuring that there was no disturbance. I was keeping a nervous watch over the situation and by nine a.m., a fairly sizeable crowd of the CM's supporters had gathered in the stadium and more were arriving every minute. The ruling party's flag could be visible now in large number. The opposition tried to take out a procession towards the stadium, but they were not allowed to proceed and when they turned violent, they were disbursed by using some force. By eleven it was clear that the stadium will be more than full.

I rang up the Governor and stated that I had ensured that there will be no violence and had been able to ensure that the CM was able to address his people. The Governor's tone was altogether different now and he was quite effusive in complimenting me.

Soon thereafter I met the CM in 'Mintogang' and he looked far more relaxed. I mentioned to him the political moves that had taken place during the night, about which I had been informed by the Resident Commissioner in New Delhi. The RC had spoken to me somewhat nervously, as he had heard rumours that I had suffered a heart attack and was hospitalized. Some had even speculated that I had left the state, mistaking the departure of the Chief Justice, who had retired, to be my exit. The Chief Minister did not seem to know all the details of what had happened and was relieved that the serious threat seemed to be emerging on the political front had been smothered. He was also happy that his meeting would be well attended and he would now be able to effectively silence the opposition. I mentioned to him that immediately after his meeting, I planned to impose a total ban for about a week or so on all meetings and processions. He agreed with this as he did not want the opposition to start their agitation all over again. I rang up the Governor again and apprised him of the latest situation and he sounded happy and indeed complimented me on my better judgement.

I proceeded to the control room and convened a meeting to discuss further steps. We knew we had substantially overcome the situation and I, after ascertaining the views of all those present, instructed the DC and SP to impose a ban on all further meetings and processions. I wanted that, in order to ensure that this ban is effectively enforced, an augmentation of force at our disposal. I rang up the Union Home Secretary, Padmanabhiah, and requested him for the return of the CRP battalion that had been kept in Sikkim, for use by the Sikkim administration but which had been taken away to meet the urgent needs in Assam. As an alternative I asked for three or four companies of the Rapid Action Force (RAF), which I promised to return after a few days. He wondered as to why there was so much nervousness when the government had a clear majority in the Assembly. I did not want to go into such questions, but pressed him to accept my request for force. He agreed to do what he could. I spoke also to the Joint Secretary (Police) MHA Arya and Joint Secretary, North East G.K. Pillai, both fine, positive and dynamic officers. They came back to me within an hour and said that they can arrange to airlift two companies of Rapid Action Force from Jamshedpur that very evening to the nearest airport Bagdogra, if I agreed to bear the cost. I agreed at once and arranged for the transportation of the force from the airport that night. By five a.m. next morning, the RAF were deployed, sending shivers down the spine of trouble makers, with their fearsome looking uniforms and batons. Both the DGP and I agreed that the RAF should be used more as a show of force, and actual crowd control should still be taken care of by the Sikkim Armed Police, unless there was an extreme situation. Bhandari had already alleged that the Chief Secretary was guilty of bringing 'outside' forces to be used against his local people.

The show of force and enforcement of the prohibitory orders had the desired effect and Gangtok quietened down almost wholly. The opposition however attempted to take out a procession which was stopped by the Sikkim Armed Police under the leadership of its dynamic commandant Akshay Sachdeva, and disbursed by lathi charge. The leaders of the agitation including Bhandari were in the procession and they beat a very hasty retreat. The SAP, who had been taunted by the opposition for over three days, were happy to have a chance to have a go at these agitators, and some in the front line had quite a few broken bones. The leaders, who had taken care to be well behind the others, managed to escape without any damage except bruised egos.

With this, normalcy was restored. I persuaded the CM to call a meeting of all the government officers and again explain to them as to how they had been thoroughly misled and appeal to them to get back to work. I quickly restarted the election process which had been halted because of the agitation, and we were in the event able to conduct the Panchayat elections without any further trouble. Needless to say that the results were a significant victory for the CM, greatly strengthening his support at all levels.

It was unfortunate that a determined effort was made, using a non-issue, to destabilize the government in this sensitive and strategic state, but fortunately the ultimate outcome was strengthening the position of the ruling party than the other way about, thanks to timely and effective action taken.

About this time, a proposal to install an impressive statue of Guru Padmasambhava in a place near Namchi had been conceived and had received the enthusiastic approval of the Chief Minister. His Holiness the Dalai Lama was to be invited to lay the foundation stone for this statue.

His Holiness is, as per protocol, treated as a visiting head of state, and this involves meticulous planning of every aspect of the visit. There is a fairly big settlement of Tibetan refugees in Sikkim, who had fled Tibet and had been looked after with great care by the Chogyal. His sister Princess P.T. Yapshi—also known as Princess Coc Coola—had played a very important role in organizing relief to the desperate refugees who had come with nothing and who bore all the markings of the persecution they had been subjected to. For these refugees the visit of their God King was an event of momentous importance. For the Sikkimese too, who revered the Dalai Lama, the visit assumed tremendous significance. I visited the area where the statue of Guru Padmasambhava was to come up, a walk up the steep hill for over two hours and finalized all the arrangements. On the way down, being quite tired, somewhat weary and unwary I stepped on a slippery moss covered stone and had a great toss, but luckily did not break any bones. I was disoriented for a minute or so but soon recovered.

To meet His Holiness is a spiritual and elevating experience, without compare. I consider myself extremely fortunate that I was enabled by providence, I should say, to interact with such an evolved and perfect being, who exuded an aura of divinity combining this with extraordinary humility. The *Bhagavad Gita* refers to such a being as '*Paramatma samahitaha*' or coequal to the supreme being. I have already mentioned that the Dalai Lama is a Bodhisattva—a reincarnation of Avalokiteshwara—the Buddha of peace, love and compassion.

His Holiness has a wonderful sense of humour. During an 'at home' hosted by the Chief Minister at 'Mintogang', His Holiness finding that I was from the south of India, stated that the Mahayana Buddhism owed a great deal to Indian masters—Nagarjuna and Shantharakshitha—and added that in Tibet they were known as people who had lived in the 'land of the coconuts' meaning the south of India. The Governor, a Harayanvi Jat, who had only half understood what his Holiness was saying, asked me as to where Nagarjuna was from. Before I could reply, His Holiness with a child-like and mischievous laughter told the Governor that Nagarjuna was not from Haryana.

While in his meetings and discourses, His Holiness prefers to speak in Tibetan, translated where necessary into English by his secretary. For a meeting to speak to the elite of Gangtok, he was requested to speak in English so that everyone can understand him. Though his command over the English language is indeed very good, and he communicates very well in this language with world leaders, His Holiness likes to joke about his inadequacies with respect to this language. He keeps his secretary handy to translate where necessary a sentence or two which, he finds it more convenient to get across in Tibetan. Midway of his speech, he had difficulty pronouncing the word 'globalization' and asked his secretary to correctly pronounce the word. He could not manage it either and made a pretty mess of it. His Holiness burst out laughing saying 'see I cannot pronounce it, he cannot pronounce it, what a difficult word this is'. His innocent laughter basically at himself brought down this house and truly endeared him to the audience.

I was given the unique privilege of welcoming His Holiness on behalf of the Sikkim government. To create the right effect I wore the distinctly unique Sikkimese traditional attire the 'Kho' with a red sash around my waist, and presented, His Holiness the ceremonial scarf the *'Khadha'* which he returned to me, by placing it on my shoulders. I considered myself blessed by His Holiness.

In my speech referring to the fact that His Holiness is an avatara of Avalokiteshwara, I said 'Avatara means descent. The purpose of the avatara is to inaugurate a new world, a new dharma. The avatara by his teaching and example shows how a human being can raise himself to the status of—even equivalence to the supreme—*'Paramatma samahitaha'*. The avatara phenomenon represents not so much the contraction of divine majesty into the limitation of the human form but more to the possibility of the elevation of the human being to an exalted status.' Stating that the avatara helps us all to attain a higher spiritual plane, I quoted the Buddha who had while referring to the avatara process said 'know vasettha that from time to time a Tathagata is born into this world, a fully enlightened one, blessed and worthy abounding in wisdom, and goodness, happy with the knowledge of the world, unsurpassed as a guide to erring mortals, a teacher of Gods and men, a blessed Buddha. He proclaims the truth both in its letter and it its spirit, lovely in its origin, lovely in its progress and lovely in its consummation. A higher life doth he make known in all its purity and in all its perfectness'.

I mentioned that we have the good fortune of welcoming such a Tathagata.

I referred to the commitment of His Holiness to ahimsa, to peace and compassion and his advocacy of creating a zone of peace, demilitarization and disarmament. I compared His Holiness to Mahatma Gandhi about whom Rabindranath Tagore stated 'Here was living truth at last and not merely quotation from books. When love and truth came to the door of India that door was opened wide. At Gandhi's call India blossomed forth to new greatness, just as once before in earlier times when the Buddha proclaimed the truth of fellow feeling and compassion among all living creatures'.

I concluded that these words very aptly apply to His Holiness and his mission in this world.

Needless to say that my speech was very well received. The full text of this speech is placed as an annexure to this book.

In a meeting with the Chief Minister, His Holiness had referred to certain problems faced by the Tibetan refugees in Sikkim. The CM asked me to meet His Holiness and see what can be done. So apart from the formal calling on which I had already done, when His Holiness was gracious enough to present me with a ceremonial scarf, the *khadha,* a specially long white *khadha,* I now had a second opportunity to be in his presence. His Holiness referred to the problem of the refugees still living in temporary shelters, without proper water supply or electricity, whereas Government of India had built for them proper dwellings with all the facilities. I knew about this problems, for some local malcontents due to some vague fears, were protesting against the refugees moving into these dwellings, as they wanted them to go away from Sikkim. If I could get the CM's approval, in no time this issue can be sorted out.

The second was a proposal that His Holiness wanted to pursue, namely to set up a plant for manufacturing Tibetan medicines in Sikkim. Sikkim was already home for a very wide variety of medicinal plants—apart from some five hundred odd varieties of orchids—and if one knew what kind of machinery is to be installed a plant can be set up. I felt that I could persuade the government to provide the land and buildings. His Holiness agreed that he would send his experts to plan the buildings and advice on the machinery, once the Government of Sikkim agreed to the proposal in principle. I promised to respond very shortly, on both the matters. The first issue was easy to solve, and when I explained the matter to the CM he readily agreed that the Tibetan refugees should be allowed at once to move into the dwellings built by the Government of India. With respect to the second as well, he gave his agreement in principle, indicating that we could invite experts from Dharmasala for setting up a plant for manufacturing Tibetan medicines. Tibetan medicine was already quite popular in Sikkim and is gaining growing acceptance the world over. I wrote immediately to His Holiness indicating that both his wishes have been honoured and we would be happy to go ahead with the project for Tibetan medicines. I may have committed a breach of protocol in addressing directly a Head of State but His Holiness, gracious as he was, did not seem to mind and not only sent me a letter of thanks, but when one of my colleagues in the Sikkim government, Mrs Renchen Dolma Rechoung met His Holiness in Dharmasala, His Holiness was kind enough to send me a religious painting—a *thankha*—with a prayer inscribed and a message of 'good wishes to the Rao family' written in His Holiness's own handwriting with his signature. I was really touched by this noble act. This 'thankha' is, no doubt, one of my treasured possessions.

Very soon, His Holiness' emissaries came to Sikkim and they were able to settle on a piece of land for the factory and areas where medicinal plants can be grown on an extensive scale. They were instrumental in preparing a project report. The Sikkim government agreed to the implementation of the project.

The Cabinet Secretary, T.S.R. Subramaniam, visited Sikkim for just a weekend. I was keen to enable him to understand the strategic importance of Sikkim and took him to the Chinese Tibetan border at Nathula. This place on the border is only about fifty kilometres from Gangtok, well within range of Chinese heavy guns and goes through some glorious natural scenery. The road hugs somewhat perilously, the mountain slopes and is at times disrupted by landslides during the rainy season and blocked by snowfall in winter. A lovely lake—Tsongu lake—set like a blue diamond amidst the mountains is on the way. Across Nathula is the Chumbi valley and one can see the peak of Chumalhari, deep inside the valley a breathtakingly beautiful site in winter in particular. The Chumbi valley was part of Sikkim and in fact used to be the abode of the Maharajahs whose Tibetan wives were more at home in the drier climate in the valley. It was the British who made the Maharajas shift to Gangtok.

It needs to be mentioned that Sikkim occupies an extremely important position from the nation's strategic point of view, and has not been formally recognized as part of India by the Chinese. They continue to show Sikkim as an independent kingdom along the northern borders of India. When the issue is raised even at the highest levels, the Chinese have a standard reply namely they accept the de facto status but are as yet to give de jure recognition. The Chumbi valley which was part of Sikkim for centuries, was reportedly given as a gift to one of the Tibetan wives, and Krishna Menon had pressed the Chinese to return this to Sikkim.

While discussing these matters with the Cabinet Secretary, I mentioned to him the fact that the Government of India was yet to settle the claims of the Chogyal's successors, even though nearly twenty-five years had gone by since the merger. I had taken considerable interest in the matter and had found that queries raised by the Home Ministry, as regards the claims, had not been answered properly due to negligence or otherwise. I ensured that all the queries were adequately answered. The Princess of Patiala, a lawyer and a lady with an imposing presence, was representing the Chogyal, and she was helpful in enabling us to answer the queries. I felt that if the Chogyals claims are settled in a proper and satisfactory manner with a touch of generosity, this can greatly help in persuading the Chogyals, successor to execute the instrument of accession. This may not have been, strictly speaking, necessary but in any case non-settlement of the claims for such a long time did not reflect well on the Government of India. The Chinese can also be silenced effectively.

Mr. Subramaniam intervened at once in the matter and the Home Ministry held a couple of meetings to discuss all the issues involved. I pointed out that the Government of India was gracious and generous in settling the privy purses of the Rajas and Maharajas of the princely states, after the country's Independence—in a few cases compensation was paid for horses, carriages and even concubines—and the same attitude should be displayed with respect to the claims of the successors of the Maharaja of Sikkim. My views were accepted and this long- pending issue was brought significantly forward towards a final settlement.

The other issue that concerned the Cabinet Secretary related to the Rumtek monastery where a serious controversy had developed with respect to the issue of succession to the sixteenth Gyalwa Karmapa who had died in 1981. The Karmapa lineage is considered even more ancient than that of His Holiness the Dalai Lama, the present Dalai

Lama being only the fourteenth reincarnation of Bodhisattva Avalokiteshwara, whereas the Karmapas had completed sixteen reincarnations. This issue had certain implications in the sphere of international relations.

The sixteenth Karmapa was a highly respected figure, credited with miraculous powers. Many swear of having personally witnessed the miracles, and it appears when his body was brought to Rumtek—he had died in the USA—before the cremation the heart had come out. The sixteenth Karmapa had a large international following and had many institutions set up in western countries. The Rumtek monastery, the Dharmachakra had plenty of resources, with contributions flowing in from abroad. It is easily one of the richest of religious institutions.

After the death of the sixteenth Karmapa, till his reincarnation is identified and formally installed in the Dharmachakra, the affairs are to be managed by a trust and the four regents, who were primarily to deal with religious matters. Of the four regents, Tai Situ Rimpoche, Samar Rimpoche, Jamgon Khongtrul Rimpoche and Tsurpu Glyatsep Rimpoche, the third mentioned Rimpoche had died in an accident reportedly on his way to Dharmasala. The circumstances of his death were viewed with some suspicion in certain quarters. The responsibility of locating and identifying the successor now fell on the shoulders of the three regents.

It may be mentioned that the premier centre of the Karma Kagyu sect is in Tibet—namely the Tsurpu monastery and the sixteenth Karmapa had to flee from this monastery due to persecution by the Chinese after the takeover of Tibet by communist China.

In 1992 Tai Situ Rimpoche claimed to have discovered the letter left behind by the sixteenth Karmapa, containing instructions regarding the identification of his reincarnation. The identification process is a lengthy and detailed exercise, with well laid-down procedures that are expected to be observed scrupulously. Apart from the indications given by the deceased lama, the child identified is put through several stringent tests before the final seal of approval is given.

The letter, claimed to have been discovered by Tai Situ Rimpoche, was studied by the regents and possibly others and several doubts were raised such as the authenticity of the handwriting, the age of the letter and whether the letter was in fact written prior to the demise of the sixteenth Karmapa, the language and grammar employed, etc. Since these could not be properly resolved a final decision was postponed for about seven months. The doubts were expressed mainly by Samar Rimpoche who, being related to the sixteenth Karmapa, was considered very proximate to the high lama.

However, without waiting for the final resolution of the doubts regarding the letter—a forensic test had also been suggested—Tai Situ Rimpoche it appears in some haste travelled to Tibet and soon enough zeroed in on a child Ugyen Thinley Dorje in village Bakor in the Kham province of Tibet whom he recognized as the seventeenth Karmapa and declared him to be so. What was strange was that this reincarnation was recognized with great alacrity by the People's Republic of China (PRC), a communist government, which officially denounces all religions, has been engaged in surpressing religious practices denying religious freedoms, and had been brutal in its efforts to obliterate Tibetan Buddhism. The destruction of Buddhist temples, the ill treatment meted out to Tibetan lamas, and the heavy hand with which followers of His Holiness the Dalai Lama are dealt with, have all been widely publicized. The communists had not conferred such a recognition before, though they had captured the Panchen Lama. How and why did the godless communists confer their blessings on the reincarnation identified by Tai Situ Rimpoche? What influence Tai Situ was able to bring to bear on the Chinese to get such a favourable response? Were the Chinese planning to cultivate the seventeenth Karmapa as their protege, as they had done in the case of the Panchen Lama, and use him as one more instrument for reducing the influence of His Holiness the Dalai Lama, while increasing their hold upon the religious consciousness of the Tibetans? Is it an act on the part of the PRC to demonstrate to the world that they have a decisive say in the religious and temporal affairs of Tibet? Are they preparing themselves for a post Dalai Lama situation? All these were troubling questions, which required clear answers. The newly discovered reincarnation was, it appears, brought to Lhasa and then to the Tsurpu monastery with some ceremony under official patronage of the Chinese government. This conundrum, wrapped in an enigma, has kept the strategic thinkers guessing, who feel quite uncomfortable about the long-term strategic implications for India, keeping in mind the fact that the Rumtek Dharmachakra in Sikkim had become the centre for the Karma Kagyu lineage. The Karma Kagyu sect has, over the years, acquired a substantial following within and without the country. The black hat, the most sacred symbol of the Karmapas is kept in Rumtek.

His Holiness the Dalai Lama had given, in the meanwhile, his approval for the recognition of the reincarnation and with this the issue should have been considered as finally settled. The vast majority of Buddhists in Sikkim and elsewhere regarded this as the final seal of approval and felt that no further proof is required.

Samar Rimpoche and his followers however not only refused to recognize the reincarnation, and went about looking for—in their opinion—the correct reincarnation and indeed identified another child Thaye Thinley Dorji who they proclaimed as the right and proper seventeenth Karmapa. The Tai Situ followers and Samar followers within the Rumtek monastery had clashes and in order to maintain law and order the state government had to intervene. The followers of Samar Rimpoche who were in a minority were thrown out of the monastery. In the process of restoring order the state government officials handed over the keys of the monastery to the Tai Situ group, and more importantly the keys of the room where the all-important and priceless black hat regarded as the Kagyu crown, said to have been woven from the hair of a thousand celestial maidens and valued at some $ 30 million is treasured along with other precious objects of veneration. Legally it would have been more appropriate to entrust the monastery to the duly constituted trust and not to one of the warring groups.

The Samar group has been threatening to take recourse to legal action while the reincarnation recognized by them has been installed in Kalimpong, not far from Gangtok.

The sudden escape of the Karmapa recognized by the Chinese and blessed by His Holiness the Dalai Lama from Tibet and his arrival in Dharmasala has raised some more perplexing questions. How did he escape when he must have been under the watchful eyes of the Chinese? How did he travel such a long distance in bitter cold without being apprehended by the Chinese? How did he manage to escape the vigil on the tightly patrolled border? Did the Chinese themselves engineer his escape? These questions are yet to be satisfactorily answered. However, if it is established without fear of contradiction, that the incarnate Karmapa has indeed escaped, because he could not accept the tyranny of the Chinese and he wanted freedom to carry on his religious pursuits, then strategic observers may be able to breathe more easily:

The activities of Tai Situ Rimpoche has, to a great extent, complicated the situation. His credentials are suspect in the eyes of the Government of India, and for a considerable period he had been declared a *persona non grata* and had been banned from entering India. He has also been under investigation by the Central Bureau of Investigation for certain deals which are suspected to be not above board. Due to pressure from some quarters, and much against the advice of Central Government agencies, and indeed their protests, Tai Situ has been allowed to reenter the country, and soon after his arrival the Tibetan Karmapa made his dramatic escape. One wonders if there is any connection between the two events.

As of now the controversy remains unresolved, but in Sikkim demands for bringing the Tibetan Karmapa to Rumtek have been articulated and are getting stronger. The Chief Minister of Sikkim has also met the Karmapa. In the meanwhile, a third claimant Dawa Tsangpo Dorjee, a Sikkimese monk, has emerged who has been claiming that he is the true reincarnation and had laid his claim as early as 1991. He has also claimed that his candidature had been accepted by the deceased regent Jamgaon Khongtrul Rimpoche. He has been stating that the other two claimants are only interested in the enormous wealth of Rumtek, whereas his is a genuine claim.

Sikkim is prone to natural calamities, particularly landslides, due to the fact that the mountain ranges are geologically young, and the fact that the rains are very heavy during the summer. In Gangtok, because of uncontrolled construction activity, natural drains have been blocked and this worsens the situation greatly. After a disaster in the summer of 1997, I managed to persuade the government to ban all further allotment of sites and construction activity in Gangtok. A scheme for improving drainage was taken up. More importantly, I raised a disaster relief group equipped and trained to deal with emergencies of various types, especially landslides. I got the experts from the civil defence school in Nagpur to prepare a comprehensive plan for immediate action whenever a disaster strikes, train the selected personnel and conduct periodic drills.

As with my last tenure, I made a very large circle of friends in Sikkim. All of them are very important to me, but my relationship with the Densappa family is something special. So also is the friendship with Princess P.T. Yapshi, also known as Princess Coo Coola, and her daughter Princess Sedounla and her brother Prince Jigme.

Jigdal Densappa was Additional Chief Secretary of Sikkim and had just retired. A fine gentleman to the core, with cultivated and refined manners, civilized in all that he does, he truly, to my mind, is an embodiment of the very essence of Sikkimese culture and civilization. He belongs to the class of nobles and the title Densappa signifies the fact that one of the ancestors had acted as the regent of Sikkim during a brief absence of the Maharajah. The family is known as the Burmiok Kajis and Jigdal's brother who in a reincarnate lama is known as the Burmiok Rimpoche. The family are Borphungpas of ancient lineage. Jigdal Densappa's father was Chief Secretary of Sikkim during the Chogyals time and was also adviser to the Government of Bhutan. He was one of the most respected figures in Sikkim. I have had the pleasure of meeting him in his village home in Burmiok and in his old age he had become even more religious than he was earlier. He wore only the traditional Sikkimese dress the 'Kho' and had his hair plaited in the very traditional style. He is credited as having laid the foundations for an excellent educational system in Sikkim. A lot of teachers were brought in from all parts of India.

Jigdal himself had played an important role at the time of the merger and is a signatory of the merger document. His stately home with a fine view of Kanchenjunga is run on very British lines and lavish is the entertainment that one receives at his residence. He is very religious, at the same time, attaches great importance to the preservation of Sikkim's unique culture and traditions. He is a trustee of the Rumtek monastery. He, with his exalted value system, has refused to accept any office after retirement showing an extraordinary degree of self-abnegation and works voluntarily as a good samaritan looking after the sick and needy from his Burmiok and in the field of education. I have no end of admiration for this fine human being, who has managed to remain a bachelor, thought he cuts such a dashing and handsome figure, always dressed impeccably, retaining a charm which can enchant anyone.

Princess Sedounla had become a friend even when I was Development Commissioner. A very distinguished looking lady, with refined tastes and delightful manners, she was a well known interior decorator. Her mother, Princess P.T. Yapshi, is the sister of the late Chogyal and used to be the official hostess at the palace hobnobbing with Presidents and Prime Ministers. She was considered one of the most beautiful women of Sikkim and conducted herself always with regal dignity. I had quickly sorted out a land compensation case, involving acquisition of land belonging to her by the army and she was extremely gracious in expressing her gratitude to me and put me down as one of her friends, which to me was an honour. She had participated intimately in the turbulent part of Sikkim's past and has her regrets. She has very interesting stories about the VIPs she used to deal with, and about Hope Cook, the American Maharani of Sikkim. She no doubt found Pandit Nehru a charmer and as she put it he was 'quite a flirt in his own way'. T.N. Kaul of the ICS, who was in the Ministry of External Affairs dealing with Sikkim, had, it appears, all the time in the world to dance with her, even in his office, having disposed of the business at hand in double quick time. I tried to encourage her quite a few times to write her memoirs, which are bound to be highly interesting and though she kept promising, I wonder if she will really do it. She has wonderful collection of photographs with a host of VIPs.

Her title P.T. Yapshi apparently signifies that she belongs to a family in which His Holiness the Dalai Lama has taken birth. The Princess during her younger days used to travel on horseback to Lhasa via Nathula, a really arduous journey of some seventeen days, through difficult territory, with some stoppages on the way.

Her memories, mostly pleasant and some not so pleasant, keep her occupied most of the time with occasional travels to Calcutta and Bhutan. Otherwise she seems to live in splendid isolation, remaining a fine representation of Sikkim's colourful past.

I also had occasion to meet the present Prince Wangchuk Namgyal, whose noble and very regal bearing greatly impressed me. A very cultivated, civilized and erudite young man, he has now taken to religious training in a big way, restoring to retreats at frequent intervals. He is still a bachelor and has often to ward off interested females and has so far been successful. He was gracious enough to give me and my wife a fine lunch in the palace, the only other guest on that occasion being the quite formidable Princess of Patiala, his legal advisor.

I maintained excellent relations with the army formation stationed in Sikkim. The General Officer Commanding P.S. Bindra was a fine officer with a very military bearing and a very professional outlook and was deeply interested in military history, a subject with which I myself had more than a nodding acquaintance. He and his wife Ujjwala Bindra became very good friends of my wife and I.

During the Chinese aggression, and after, the army had taken over large tracts of land particularly in North Sikkim. Quite a lot of the tracts had been permanently acquired but there were still a lot of areas which had been merely requisitioned, the erstwhile owners getting a pittance as yearly rent. A lot of the area had not been utilized, and I felt that the army could release substantial areas which the owners will be only too happy to get back, given the fact that with the growth of population, the value of land even in remote areas had gone up. General Bindra was very helpful in this, and a detailed review was conducted to determine what areas are really essential for the requirements of the forces, and which can be safely released. This step greatly helped the local population. He was very helpful in streamlining procedures for entry of local civilians for grazing purposes and for travelling from one village to another remote village in the areas controlled by the army. The army could also be counted upon to effectively assist the administration at the time of natural calamities as indeed it did in April 1997.

In Sikkim, all nature is sacred and lakes and mountains particularly so. The Guru Dongmar lake almost on the Tibetan border is one of the holiest, being very near the origin of the Teesta. This great river actually has its origin at a place nearby called Cholamu. The local people travelled long distances to worship at the lake. There were really no structures as local beliefs were against any structure. The lake is believed to have been visited and blessed by the patron saint of Sikkim Guru Padmasambhava—Guru Rimpoche. Somehow, a belief was created in recent times associating this lake with Guru Nanak and the army took the initiative of building a Gurudwara on the banks of the lake. They should have consulted the state government before erecting the structure and soon enough local sentiments flared up. I did not want that the matter should escalate into a controversy. Local belief systems and sentiments need to be honoured and there should be no conflict between the army and the civilians.

I wanted that this structure should be dismantled. At the same time, the Forest and Environment Department had been drawing my attention to the killing of wild animals, particularly yaks and the rare blue sheep, due to their stepping on mines, getting entangled in barbed wires, and an odd case of shooting by trigger happy officers or men.

The damage that was being done to the ecology and environment by the road-building activities in the area, with largescale soil destabilization and destruction of precious forests was also a matter of concern. Army camps in the area were also hosts of feral dogs and these dogs tend to infect the wild animals.

I decided to visit the area to get to know first-hand all about the area and the problems that had cropped up. The GOC, who had been notified about my trip, felt he should accompany me. In fact, he drove me most of the way, in his comfortable station wagon. Though the road is good, passing through Chungthang and Lachen it gets very steep as one has to climb to heights of nearly eighteen thousand feet before getting into the environs of the Tibetan plateau. The landscape is breathtakingly beautiful, starting with mountains covered by thick alpine forests, then on to heights where the vegetation gets sparser and sparser, until one reaches altitudes where there is only snow. As one reaches the peaks and starts the slight descent into the plateau, the landscape is suddenly transformed into a dry arid desert, with no trees, little or no moisture and only some snow here and there. Heavy bone-chilling winds keep blowing all the way, especially near the Tibetan plateau and it is very difficult to stand in the open for more than ten or fifteen minutes. And this was in the month of March, a comparatively warmer period. Conditions would be far far worse in deep winter. Formations are stationed all over the place and the troops spend quite a while in these isolated deserts under extreme conditions and also manage to keep themselves fighting fit, a truly awesome and admirable feat. Such is the price the nation has to pay for her freedom. If these conditions are harsh one can understand what would be the problems at Siachen, where the circumstances are infinitely more difficult.

To see the Himalayas from the other side of the mountain range is a truly memorable experience. When we reached the Guru Dongma lake area, I found the Gurudwara built by the army very much there, and there was quite a bit of destabilization of the soil. The structure itself was not large but while this by itself was considered objectionable, what was even more so were the writings claiming all kinds of things including visit by Guru Nanak, etc. The army agreed to get all these writings removed and ultimately dismantle the structure leaving, if at all, a token presence. Steps were also to be taken to eliminate feral dogs, fence the areas mined, so that animals do not get killed or, what is worse, get injured or maimed resulting in great agony and painful slow death, and fences so constructed as to avoid entanglement of the animals.

North Sikkim, easily the most beautiful of all the districts of Sikkim, is now being opened up gradually for tourists. It contains some of the finest of Sikkim's natural assets with its own unique flora and fauna. Home to the large variety of orchids (some five hundred and forty), medicinal plants, fine alpine forests, some trees taking as much as one hundred years to reach full maturity, it contains a whole reserve for rhododendrous . When they bloom in summer time the colourful picture they present is incomparable.

The Lachung valley and the Yumthang valley beyond are to my mind comparable to the Tyrol of Austria with snowclad mountains on both sides, with trees covered with powdery snow and a gentle river flowing down. Dancing rivulets flow into the river at various points. In deep winter the area gets covered by snow and the water freezes in the night, sometimes for days together.

I had advocated a policy of cautious and controlled expansion of tourism, as I was anxious that Gangtok should not go the Darjeeling or Simla way and the fragile eco-system in the area should not suffer because of over-exploitation of the potential. Also, it was necessary to create proper infrastructural facilities before allowing tourists to come in. The Tata Consultancy Services were commissioned to prepare a twenty-year perspective plan. Trekking-river rafting, adventure tourism all have great scope in Sikkim.

The end of the Gujral government in New Delhi required conduct of one more election to the Parliament's lower house. Basically, an exercise in management and optimum utilization of resources, I envisaged no serious problem. The main responsibility for the conduct of elections is that of the Chief Electoral Officer and the Returning Officers in the district. At a time when his role was crucial, the CEO Shrestha disappeared without informing me or taking proper permission on the excuse that his wife had fallen ill.

Already the Director General of Police P.C. Sharma had been transferred to New Delhi as Special Director in the Central Bureau of Investigation, and, given the lengthy procedures involved, no replacement had been provided. I had to take serious note of the misconduct of the CEO, and with the approval of the Election Commission placed him under suspension and initiated departmental proceedings. Without a DGP and the CEO, I had to take personal change of the conduct of elections. Fortunately, in Sikkim, there are really no serious problems in the conduct of elections, unlike Assam where every step is fraught with difficulties, and except for minor incidents involving law and order, the elections went off without a hitch. The ruling party's candidate won with a sizeable majority.

I have earlier referred to the importance attached to the 'old laws' of Sikkim proclaimed from time to time by the Chogyals, and the safeguards provided by the Constitution, preserving the validity of these laws, while discussing the question of application of the Indian Income Tax Act to Sikkim, as also the land laws which prohibit transfer of land to non-Sikkimese.

The old laws as well as customs and practices, most of which are no more in vogue, have some extraordinarily interesting features. Those dealing with the conduct of war remind one of the code laid down by the great law-giver Chanakya in his *'Arthashasthra'*. It is believed that these laws were founded on statements spoken by Raja Me-long-dong who lived in India before the time of the Buddha (914 BC). They were written down by Kunga Gyaltsen who was born in 1182, and is of Tibetan descent. The laws are believed to have been rewritten in 1653 by Dezi Sangya Gyatso, a viceroy of Tibet and were adopted in Sikkim.

The laws relating to war lay down that before waging war the strength of the enemy should be carefully ascertained and whether it will be ultimately profitable or not. Care should be taken to see if the dispute cannot be settled by diplomacy before going to war. Messengers should be well received, and a messenger of peace should never be killed. If two or more enemies combine against you every effort should be made to separate them. Before launching operations, the layout of the enemy territory should be thoroughly examined. The wounded should be properly cared for, and while crossing rivers order should be maintained and those behind should not push forward. No one can doubt the wisdom of all these dictums. It is also laid down that those who have given up their arms either on surrender or otherwise should not be killed, and anyone doing so is to be derided as a coward.

One of the laws relates to the conduct of government servants who are enjoined upon to leave off their own work and devote themselves entirely to government work and to obey orders. As to the law of evidence, the person giving false evidence is to be fined. Laws relating to punishment for grave offences such as murder, for small offences, rioting, using arms, thieving, destroying property, disobeying village headman, giving bad advice, had all been codified. What is important to note in all this is the fact that the principles of natural justice was given great importance. Capital punishment was to be given only in extreme cases, and most offences were punishable with fines.

The laws also covered certain aspects of personal relationships. For example, if a husband wishes to be separated from the wife he has to pay compensation of a minimum of 18 zhos, the amount increasing depending on the length of their association. On the other hand, if the wife wants to leave the husband she has to pay 12 zhos and a suit of clothes. Payment of fines were also laid down for adultery. Interestingly, should a man and a woman cohabit during a journey there is no fine.

Old customs, though no longer in vogue, also make interesting reading. If the eldest brother takes a wife she is common to all the brothers. If the second brother takes a wife she has to serve the brothers younger to him. The eldest brother is not allowed to cohabit with the wives of his younger brothers. If a girl conceives before marriage and afterwards marries the father of the child the child is considered legitimate but the man is fined a bull or its equivalent which goes to her relatives. A woman is not dishonoured if she has a child before marriage. The marriage ties were not very strong and a marriage could be dissolved at any time by either the man or the woman. All very egalitarian incorporating advanced concepts of gender equality, I have no doubt.

I would like to conclude this chapter by saying I had been treated by the Chief Minister and all his colleagues with great courtesy and uniform kindness and consideration throughout my tenure as the State's Chief Secretary. The Governor Choudhry Randhir Singh was invariably courteous and appreciative of my work. I received unstinted cooperation and assistance from all my colleagues.

It is a period which I look back with great satisfaction, happiness and considerable pride, for having done my duty without having to compromise on any of the principles or the value system which had become part of me over the years.

# 15

# SUMMING UP

When I started writing this book some five months back I was quite uncertain as to whether I will complete what I had, perhaps somewhat foolishly, ventured into, but with the completion of each chapter my confidence level increased and it appeared that I could easily go through the whole exercise. The shape of the book also evolved gradually as I did not start with a preconceived contour for the entire work. It has been, without doubt for me, an exciting journey down memory lane, reliving the past, all the experiences varied and extensive, all the trials and tribulations and indeed the triumphs, the ups and downs, the pleasures and sorrows and the achievements and disappointments. No doubt, it has been a very bumpy ride, and, at times, I did get disheartened but at no stage was my life without considerable excitement, the unexpected turning up with unfailing regularity. Writing the book also compelled me to become computer literate.

As I enter that stage in life, which is called vanaprastha, I have no doubt that providence has been kind to me, that I have been lucky in getting opportunities one after another to help the common man, take some action or the other which is of assistance to the people at large and be a public servant in the true sense of the term. I have tried to observe the dictum in the *Bhagavad Gita: 'karmanye vaadhikaraste, ma phaleshu kadachana, ma karma phala hetur bhur, ma te samgostva akarmani'*, (to action alone hast thou a right and never at all to its fruits; let not the fruits of action be thy motive; neither let there be in thee any attachment to inaction). It is not always possible nor is it easy to live by this dictum whose value and wisdom is no doubt infinite, for on occasion I have indeed gone through the pangs of disappointment when my work did not receive due recognition, and indeed when my honest and dedicated performance resulted in my receiving the rough end of the stick. This is possibly the experience of many, both in public service and elsewhere. But these have never deterred me from continuing to perform my duties as efficiently and honestly as possible. The true reward has been to me the esteem that I earned from all those who worked with me and who have given to me their respect, love and affection most generously.

It is possible that I have not done as well as some others with respect to career advancement, especially as regards post-retirement 'goodies', but I believe to obtain these 'goodies' one has to have a particular bent of mind, which I do not think I possess and perhaps it also calls for compromises which many may not be willing to enter into. A clean conscience is to my mind very valuable and is not to be bartered away for anything.

The burden of my song, throughout this book, has been the urgent need for greatly strengthening the institutions of governance, for non-discriminatory application of laws, speedy redressal of people's grievances, acceleration of economic growth, stabilization of population and reinstatement of merit and achievement as governing criteria in all walks of life. My lament and apprehension is that the security of this country in the face of the many internal and external threats, is being seriously undermined by the inability and unwillingness, of the powers that be, to take concerted measures to address all these concerns. I have bemoaned the fact that our governing systems and mechanisms for dispensation of justice have become like cobwebs strong enough only to confine the weak, but too weak to take on the strong, and we have not been effective enough in controlling the rate of growth of population. Rabindranath Tagore had lamented that India had become 'the eternal ragpicker at other people's dustbins'. This lament is over sixty years old and unfortunately holds good even today, and unless we attend to the needs I have repeatedly stressed I wonder if this lament can become invalid soon.

One issue which has troubled me throughout my career, is the pronounced propensity of the human being to become violent at the slightest of provocations even in a country like ours, which has given the world the message of *ahimsa,* which has produced the Buddha, Gandhi, Mahavira and a host of others who preached tolerance, and which fought and obtained its Independence through a struggle based upon the principles of satya and ahimsa—truth and nonviolence. We witness, so often, the proclivity to get violent, to fly at each other's throat and to commit depredation on a large scale. The human being is a bundle of contradictions; men who are gentle and kind who would be shocked and indignant if a dog is hurt, who would fly to the protection of a crying child or a maltreated woman, get suddenly transformed and persistently indulge in doing wrong and violence to millions of humans including women and children, in the comforting belief that by doing so we are doing our duty to our family, or city or the state or to our religion. Having seen and controlled riots, communal and otherwise, and violence of a variety of forms, has made me wonder as to why there persists even today such a pronounced propensity to get violent, by ordinary decent human beings who stand to lose so much by becoming violent and whose daily struggle to keep body and soul together gets no better by such violence. Is there something in our genes which periodically makes us get so violent?

Man is the only animal in this world who kills, for purposes other than food. All other animals attack only in self defence including protecting one's territory or when they are hungry. The normal tendency of an animal is to back away, avoid a confrontation and attack only if it perceives that there is no other avenue of escape. On the other hand, man kills defenceless animals with sophisticated weapons from a safe distance often hiding himself, and calls it a sport. While fortunately this 'sport' has received almost universal condemnation, and has declined sharply, and there has been a recognition of animal rights, innocent animals continue to be trapped and killed for trade and for greed. And man kills and maims other humans for a variety of reasons, which have nothing to do with hunger.

Man's cruelty to man has seen a pattern of escalation, which is unbelievable and particularly in the first half of the twentieth century, the scale and intensity of devastation has been truly horrendous. The European civilization, which prides itself of so much progress in the field of science and technology, is at the same time guilty of using a great deal of this progress for the sole purpose of killing human beings and destroying their assets more effectively, on a larger and larger scale and more inhumanely leaving long time and enduring scars on the body and on the individual's psyche.

While the cutthroat competition for the world's natural

resources, colonization of the world, the over-anxiety to preserve the perceived security, sovereignty and territorial integrity of nation states, to protect so-called separate identities, ethnic, linguistic, etc., have all played important roles in provoking human beings to wage war on each other with ever increasing lethality, I am afraid, organized religion has also played a significant role and possibly will continue to do so in the belligerency of humans. Indeed, the abovementioned factors have all become less and less important as large swathes of the world achieve higher and higher standards of living and population in these areas has either stabilized or is declining. Also, precisely, in these very areas of the world, religion has declined in its ability to influence thought and action and has become the private concern of the individual, with the church and the state firmly separated from each other. Western Europe is a prime example of this phenomenon, as today peace and prosperity reign in an area, which has seen centuries of hatred and conflict and such horrendous destruction of lives and property. To be sure the competition among humans has not disappeared, nor is it less intense, but humanity has devised more subtle ways of competing, of enforcing a nation's will on another, of perhaps more humanely cutting the other fellow's throat, if this, possible, using knowledge as the cutting edge, keeping the threat to use force in the background. At the same time, humanity has not failed to evolve more effective institutional mechanisms to resolve conflicts, protect the more disadvantaged and vulnerable and punish the intransigent without destroying them, differentiating the welfare of the people from the misbehaviour, irresponsible as it often is, of their governments. The chances of humanity banishing war as an instrument for enforcing the will of nations seem to be brighter today than ever before. The fact that wars may result in total destruction of both the belligerents has no doubt helped.

In spite of all this, religion as a source of conflict seems to be more enduring and when religion gets mixed up with politics, resolution of conflicts becomes infinitely more complex and difficult. The thought, irreverent one may say, has often troubled me as to whether organized religion has done more harm than good to humanity? Is it the fault of the world's religions or is it the fault of the religious teachers, who, in the perceived interest of their religion, do not hesitate to provoke aggression? Or is it the fault of the practitioners of religions, the followers, who seem to use or misuse religion for

of His Holiness, a Tathagatha whose whole life is an eloquent testimony of that great quest for the truth of life and existence and the mysteries of mind and matter and indeed issues well beyond these. The *Rig Veda* calls such seers 'Masters of "Truth-Light" who made the Truth good by the Truth'.

The quest for truth is also the quest for the Ultimate Reality for the Supreme Being and it calls for inner discipline of an extraordinary degree, and realization comes through intensive knowledge and experience—*Svaanubuthi.* Inner discipline leads one to transcendental wisdom, where one gets to know and feel the ultimate, where one senses Supreme peace, Supreme bliss and Supreme knowledge. The *Kathopanishad* calls this discipline as hard as walking on the razor's edge. It may demand sacrifices of the highest order as Mahatma Gandhi said in 1925 and I quote from his '*Experiments With Truth*'. 'I worship God as truth only. I have not found him but I am seeking after him. I am prepared to sacrifice the things dearest to me in pursuit of this quest. Even if the sacrifice demanded be my very life, I hope I may be prepared to give it.'

The Buddha also calls the task of seeing the truth face to face as more difficult than to shoot and penetrate with the tip of a hair split a hundred times a piece of hair similarly split. His Holiness has expressed that many of the world's problems and conflicts arise because we have lost sight of the basic humanness that binds us all together as a human family. He drew attention to the basic wish of everyone to live in peace but he highlighted that even when we have achieved one type of freedom, widely celebrated, these seem to give rise to fresh economic difficulties and unleash long buried ethnic and religious tensions containing the seeds for a new cycle of conflicts. His Holiness advocated creation of a zone of peace with particular reference to Tibet, suggesting that the whole area should be demilitarized and there must be prohibition on the manufacture and stock-piling of weapons. His Holiness was deeply impressed by the situation in Costa Rica where he saw how a country could develop successfully without an army to become a stable democracy committed to peace and the protection of natural environment with the added advantage of being able to use funds, that would have otherwise been used for stock-piling of arms, to education, health and economic and social development. His Holiness is a lifelong advocate of *ahimsa* or non-violence which is a powerful idea that was refined, adopted and implemented by Mahatma Gandhi.

We have the honour today to welcome such a personality, an *avatara purusha,* who like the Buddha himself, and Gandhi, is engaged in wiping out every tear from every eye through love and non-violence and setting a shining example by the kind of discipline and example that he has set for all of us to emulate. While describing Mahatma Gandhi, Rabindranath Tagore said 'He stopped at the thresholds of the huts of the thousands of the dispossessed, dressed like one of their own. He spoke to them in their own language. Here was living truth at last, and not only quotation from books . . . . . When love came to the door of India, that door was opened wide. At Gandhi's call India blossomed forth to new greatness, just as once before in earlier times, when Buddha proclaimed the truth of fellow-feeling and compassion among all living creatures.'

This same description can be aptly applied to His Holiness whom we have the honour to welcome in our midst and whose holy presence has inspired the people of Sikkim and whose presence has blessed this land. We bow to His Holiness with reverence and seek his blessings.

May His presence elevate our thinking to a higher plane, may he lead us to a higher path, away from the crass materialism that has invaded our lives, cleansing our souls from the evils that so permeate modern present-day's societies and make us all better human beings.

# INDEX